AF588349

Towards a New History of Work

Towards a New History of Work

Edited by

Sabyasachi Bhattacharya

in association with

and

Published by
Tulika Books
35 A/1 (ground floor), Shahpur Jat, New Delhi 110 049, India

First published in India in 2014

ISBN: 978-93-82381-35-8

Printed at Chaman Enterprises, Delhi 110 002

Contents

Acknowledgements

This collection of essays may be said to be the work of an editorial collective. But for the joint effort of Rana Pratap Behal and Prabhu P. Mohapatra as well as our colleagues on the Association of Indian Labour Historians (AILH) Executive Committee, Indu Agnihotri, Chitra Joshi, Madhavan Palat, Dilip Simeon and Shashi Bhushan Upadhyay, this book would not have seen the light of day. We owe a debt of gratitude to the authors of the papers in this volume for their cooperation and prompt response to editorial queries, and requests for revision or abridgement. Our thanks also go to those who funded the conference where the papers collected in this volume were initially presented: V.V. Giri National Labour Institute, Indian Council of Social Science Research and Indian Council of Historical Research. It is a pleasure to recall the cooperation we have consistently received from Mr Yajurvedi as well as his successor Mr P.P. Mitra, Directors General of the V.V. Giri National Labour Institute (VVGNLI). This, and the volume which will follow, form a part of the series of works on labour history which figure in the list of titles published by Tulika Books, New Delhi. We would like to express our appreciation of the enthusiastic support we received from Ms Indira Chandrasekhar and Ms Maya John of Tulika Books. Needless to say, the editor alone is responsible for the errors and shortcomings which remain uncorrected.

SABYASACHI BHATTACHARYA

Foreword

I am pleased to present the selected research papers which were deliberated at the IXth International Conference on Labour History jointly organized by the V.V. Giri National Labour Institute (VVGNLI) and Association of Indian Labour Historians (AILH) in March 2012. This conference was organized under the aegis of the Integrated Labour History Research Programme, a larger collaborative research initiative of VVGNLI and AILH.

The research papers in this volume address very important issues in labour history. To begin with, these essays make a departure from the general run of labour studies in looking at the long-term history of labour, sometimes going back to pre-modern India. Moreover, some of the authors of the papers in this collection also raise an important question: is it enough to examine what is conventionally called 'labour history' to explore a more extensive terrain of 'the history of work'? Let us bear in mind the following facts. In our times it is difficult to call many workers in the information technology industry, the industry using the most modern technologies, as 'labourers' in the accepted sense of the term. Then again, we have in the countries often designated as developing economies, a huge number of the economically active population who are self-employed but not 'labourers' in the same sense as those employed in the formal sector of industry, i.e. the classic 'industrial worker'. This is the consequence of the expansion of the so-called informal sector. Further, when we look beyond the immediate present to historical experience of the long-term kind, we recognize work being performed, i.e. value addition being made, without the engagement of the worker as a 'labourer'. For these and many other reasons, it seems worthwhile to consider the category 'work' as a comprehensive category that is as worthy of attention as what we conventionally call 'labour'.

The issues and the debates we witness around these categories in the essays in this volume appear to be very significant in the context of the present conditions of labour and the employment scenario in India. It is of great value to us to gain a new perspective, both from the long-term historical vision of the authors as well as the comparative, cross-cultural and international scope of the studies presented in this volume.

P.P. MITRA
Director General
V.V. Giri National Labour Institute

Towards a New History of Work

Introduction

Sabyasachi Bhattacharya

In 2012 the Association of Indian Labour Historians, in collaboration with the National Labour Institute in New Delhi, organized a conference on the theme 'Work and Non-Work: Histories in the Long Term'. It has fallen to my lot to edit the present volume, and to say a few words to introduce the themes as well as the papers presented at the conference and collected in this volume. I might add that this collection of essays is the first of two volumes which have been planned for publication, and I would like to thank, on behalf of the organizers of that conference, all the participants at the conference and the authors in the present volume.

Why did the conference organizers and participants propose to look beyond 'labour history' to look at 'the history of work'? Let us begin from the contemporary context. At this moment of history we are in the midst of a huge change which compels our attention to turn to the notion of 'work' as distinct from that of 'labour'. This change appears to us in the form of a technological transformation that affects not just our view of history but our life itself. Every moment that we use the computer, the internet, the cyber networks, we experience this transformation. That brings home to us, more than the theoretical ramifications of the information revolution which has gained academic attention, the fragility of the conventional boundary between 'labour' and 'work'. Why does that boundary look fragile or porous now, and why do we need to look beyond the notion of 'labour' to the wider notion of 'work'?

To answer that question, let us address the present context of the information regime. A variety of concepts have been used to grasp the structural aspects of the new information regime. One of the earliest attempts was that of Manuel Castells, who put forward the concept of 'informational society' to understand 'a specific form of social organization in which information generation, processing, and transmission become the fundamental sources of productivity and power, because of the new technological conditions' (Castells 1996: 21). Dan Schiller (1999) has talked about 'digital capitalism', and long ago Alvin Toffler (1980) had anticipated some of these efforts. We shall use the term information capitalism for the same purpose, to capture the central characteristics of the emerging system. However, this larger question is not immediately part of our agenda because our focus will be on the impact on work. That aspect of the new information regime has not yet been studied thoroughly. Among others in the past decade, Nathan M. Ensmenger (2003) has perspicaciously commented on it.

> Despite their obvious importance to the history of information technology, computer programmers represent a perplexing problem for the historian. . . . Neither labourers nor professionals, they defy occupational categorization. . . . The ranks of the elite programmers included both high-school dropout and PhD physicists. Defined by their mastery of the highest of high technology, they were often derided for their adherence to artisanal practices. (Ensmenger 2003: 161)

It is interesting that to the extent there developed social networks and formal organization among the technical workers in the area of information technology – traditional-type trade unionization never worked in this community – the occupational community modelled themselves on the artisanal guild. Examples are Systems Administrators' Guild founded in 1975, Silicon Valley Web Guild from 1996, HTML Writers' Guild founded in 1994, Graphic Artists' Guild from 1995, etc. (Benner 2003). Benner cites a statement made by the founder-president of the HTML Writers' Guild:

> The name 'guild' was chosen in order to look back at the older, medieval-type guilds. What we liked from that model was the notion of sharing knowledge – that building web design was something of a craft – not purely artistic or purely technical. . . . For many people it is not just a technical exercise, but a creative outlet. (Benner 2003: 186)

Benner's comments suggest a comparison between the medieval guild and contemporary guilds in Silicon Valley. The major point that emerges is the self-perception among the practitioners in the industry, which converges on their role as artisans in a guild. A space for creativity, individuation, freedom to work at home and serving a virtual market were part of this perception.

Many others have also observed that the information technology revolution has created a space of relative freedom for some of the workers. This is the result of the relocation and dispersal of work, often to the home of the workers. In fact, this situates such information technology workers in a position analogous to that of the late medieval or early modern European artisans – an interesting recursive pattern in labour history. In the early stage of industrialization, recently termed as the stage of proto-industrialization, the place where work was performed was more often than not the artisan's home, the rhythm of work was decided by the artisan (not by a supervisor or employer as in the factory), and the tools were owned by the artisan (unlike the factory context). With the advance of industrialization, the increasing use of heavy machinery and capital-intensive techniques, and non-human or non-animal power (steam power to begin with, and then electricity) the balance turned against dispersed artisanal production and in favour of concentration of the workforce in the factory. That is well known. Today, the information technology and the infrastructure of many service industries, and the practice of out-sourcing allow, I suggest, a revival of the artisanal mode of production under information capitalism. Once again, a good deal of work can be done in the worker's home, flexibility enables the worker to determine his/her own rhythm of work, and the basic tools are owned by the worker; once again, out-sourcing and sub-contracting by business corporations today puts them in an intermediary entrepreneurial role, like that of the pre-industrial European 'putting-out' merchant. This change has had, and probably will increasingly have, an impact on the nature of work (for example, a greater degree of individuation and freedom in labour process) and its perception by the worker (for example, his dissociation or isolation from fellow-workers is a major consequence).

A change in the nature of work, not only in the information industry but elsewhere as well, was the theme of some academic studies as early as the 1980s. The path-breaking work was perhaps that of the colloquium on 'New Forms of Work and Activity' held by the European Foundation for the Improvement of Living and Working Conditions in Brussels in 1986, and the resultant volume edited by Ralf Dahrendorf, E. Kohler and Francoise Piotet (1986), and another conference organized in 1983 by the World Futures Society in Washington DC (Howard F. Didsbury 1983). While the short-term prognostications and prescriptions of such conferences appear from today's point of view rather dated, the recurring theme they underline is a continuing concern, i.e. the need to examine the impact of information technology on work.

It will be obvious to the reader of these pages that we have used the example of the impact of the new information regime on work in order to instantiate a wider trend towards rethinking the notion of 'work', and to look beyond the notion of 'labour'. Let us briefly sum up the reasons for such rethinking. First, when we consider the vast numbers of the self-employed who produce goods and services without being in someone's employment, it seems that the term 'worker' possibly accommodates them better than the term 'labourer'. In the less developed countries where capitalist relations do not exhaustively define all production relations, we have a large proportion of the economically active population belonging to this category. Secondly, the same proposition holds for the workers of the pre-capitalist era, the artisans and others who remained self-employed even if they were tied to a dependency network with putting-out merchants and the like. The term 'labourer' appears to be inappropriate, as some authors in the present volume have argued, to people of that class in the pre-modern period in India or elsewhere. Thirdly, consider categories such as the priests in temples, the clerics in the church, scholars as distinct from scribes, or for that matter the artists – all essential denizens of old civilizations. They undoubtedly performed 'work', but is the term 'labour' equally appropriate? Perhaps it is unnecessary to multiply examples. To sum it up, it may be argued that 'work' is a more inclusive category that comprehends activities which need to be taken into account though they lie beyond the limits denoted by the term 'labour'.

Long before the contemporary discussion we have touched upon above, a thinker who anticipated the endeavour to distinguish 'labour' from 'work' was Hannah Arendt. As early as 1958 in her work on 'the human condition', the text of her lectures at the University of Chicago in 1956, she made some seminal observations on that subject. Our attempt to introduce the theme of 'work' will remain incomplete unless we take into account her ideas, however briefly. Arendt expounded her well-known thesis of the *vita activa* being the sum-total of three fundamental human activities: labour, work and action. Interesting as it is, her philosophical exposition in general is for the present not as much relevant as some of her observations on labour and work. Drawing upon an immense fund of scholarship, especially in the classical languages, she observes that the distinction between labour and work is rarely recognized in scholarly literature. And yet 'every European language, ancient and modern, contains two etymologically unrelated words for what we have come to think of as the same activity', i.e. labour and work (Arendt [1958] 1998: 80).

Despite the inability of most scholars to see the distinction between labour and work, Arendt argued that this evidence of language is of decisive importance: 'It is language, and the fundamental human experiences underlying it, rather than theory, that teaches us' that labour and work are different things (ibid.: 94). The basic difference, she goes on to say, was the one recognized by Locke, the difference between '*labour* of our body and the *work* of our hands' (ibid.: 79). Earlier the Greeks recognized that difference between the activity of craftsmen and that of the slave. Arendt, on similar lines, differentiates between labour which ensures the survival of the individual and the species, and on the other hand, work or the activity of *homo faber*, ranging from the tool-using artisan to the creators of the satellite launched into space.

In Arendt's view what labour produces is for immediate consumption, things or services which do not last, while work produces things of relatively permanent value which defy time. There may be questions about that but for the present the important point she makes is quite another. She situates the notions of labour and work in a historical narrative of western thought she constructs. The Greeks as a rule, she says, did not hold in high regard work of artisans and the like, and their dis-esteem for labour was greater.

> The opinion that labour and work were despised in antiquity because only slaves were engaged in them is a prejudice of modern historians. The ancients reasoned the other way around and felt it necessary to possess slaves because of the slavish nature of all occupations that served the needs for the maintenance of life. (Ibid.: 83)

The disregard for both labour and work, as defined by Arendt, in antiquity is contrasted by her with the high evaluation of labour in modern Europe. The modern age saw

> the glorification of labour as the source of all values. . . . The sudden, spectacular rise of labour from the lowest, most despised position to the highest rank, as the most esteemed of all human activities, began when Locke discovered that labour is the source of all property. It followed its course when Adam Smith asserted that labour was the source of all wealth and found its climax in Marx's 'system of labour' where labour became the source of all productivity and the expression of the very humanity of man. (Ibid.: 85, 101)

Although Hannah Arendt rejects this evaluation of labour, because according to her it is to the detriment of our understanding of the distinction between labour and work, her insightful analysis of the high evaluation of labour since Locke, Smith and Marx helps us understand the central position occupied by the notion of 'labour' in the modern era. We may not, in developing a new approach to the history of work, assume the Arendtian position but her observations serve to illustrate the interesting questions that approach raises.

Finally, a caveat may be useful. Perhaps caution is to be exercised against pushing the argument too far in focusing upon a history of work to the detriment of research in labour history. In contra-distinguishing work from labour, one must not forget the fact of permeability between the two. Once again we may instantiate that from contemporary experience in the domain of information technology. While information is capital, along with certain material inputs which also constitute capital, information is also, theoretically speaking, the *disembodied product of labour*, largely mental labour. Therefore it is important to examine the work processes and relationships which produce this output, information as disembodied labour under information capitalism. These processes and relationships often suggest that the early stage of artisan-type engagement of creative minds in information technology – what you might like to call work and not labour – soon gives way to the stage of factory-like mass production techniques in software, a regime of labour inhabited by 'body-shoppers', out-sourced cheap service providers, 'cyber labour' of the lower stratum, etc. (vide the research on 'cyber *coolies* in the business processing offices' in India, Ramesh Babu 2004). It is interesting to recall what has been recently chronicled: as early as the 1940s, John von Neumann and Herman Goldstine 'differentiated between high level conceptual activities involved in *planning an algorithm* and the tedious but straightforward work of *coding it into machine readable form*. . . . Whereas the planners were typically scientists and engineers . . . The coders were low-status' (Ensmenger 2003). According to Ensmenger, the system planners and programmers, developers of creative innovations and 'work-arounds' to make up for the shortcomings of the early machines, initially enjoyed 'a certain degree of immunity from managerial imperatives. . . . The perceived lack of managerial control over the programming process provoked tension within the corporate structure.' According to him, the hierarchy between corporate managers and the software engineers of various categories (basically, how to tame the artisan) and the hierarchy within the latter category is the major theme of the organizational transformation of information technology production.

Arguably, this hierarchization of work in information technology, noticed by a witness no less than John von Neumann, leads inexorably to the re-emergence of labour of a different kind in the industry, and it instantiates how 'work' shades off into 'labour', the permeability between the two and the broad range of work/labour in *teletravail*, telework or *telearbeit* (Dahrendorf 1986; Downey 2003). Is it possible that the new information technology may create an elusive notion of freedom from managerial control, an unreal idea of being at liberty to form one's own agenda as an artisan, indeed an illusion that technology is a neutral thing that creates opportunities for the worker to break out of being labour on call? It is interesting to recall that two seminal thinkers of the last century, M.K. Gandhi (1909) and Martin Heidegger (1954), underlined the illusion created by technology.

> Everywhere we remain unfree and chained to technology, whether we passionately affirm or deny it. But we are delivered over to it in the worst possible way when we regard it something *neutral*; for this conception of it, to which today we particularly like to pay homage, makes us utterly blind to the essence of technology. (Heidegger 1954)

We cannot pursue here this idea further, but this too is an issue we need to think about when we consider technology-induced differentiation between work and labour.

There are many other issues which need rigorous re-thinking in the agenda of constructing a 'history of work'. In considering how the nature of 'work' is being transformed, the term 'work' needs to be defined because in common parlance it means many things. If value addition to a marketed product or service is the criterion, a *pro tem* working definition accepted since Adam Smith, there are problems to sort out. For instance, there may be work which is socially useful but *not* marketed, for example, the home-maker's or housewife's work, a vital question from the gender history point of view. And what is the value addition made by the military officers and soldiers whose chief object seems to be destruction of value created in another domain? And again, who defines what is 'work' and what is 'leisure'? It is evident that what is work to one man is 'leisure activity' to another. For example, to the golf players I know of, it is a leisure-time activity, and I gather it is 'work' for the professional golf player. Issues like this need to be addressed in the agenda of the 'history of work'. Further, given the permeability between 'work' and 'labour', arguably, 'labour history' continues to be relevant to our concerns. That is amply demonstrated by the essays in the following pages, while some essays are indeed infused with the evolving notion of history of work.

The essays collected in the present volume have been arranged thematically into four sections in order to highlight some issues in focus at the conference, and also to allow a cross-national perspective to develop. The authors were requested to revise the papers they presented at the conference in 2012. I would like to thank them for complying with that request. In a few instances there was a delay in obtaining the revised version and that partly accounts for the fact that it took about one year to send the final text to the press.

The first group of essays addresses the long run of history, extending to the late medieval and early modern period. We have here essays by Jan Lucassen of the Institute of Social History at Amsterdam, on monetization in relation to proletarianization in India from the thirteenth to the nineteenth country; Suraiya Faroqhi of Istanbul Bilgis University, on data in Ottoman records on the working population from the sixteenth to the nineteenth century; and Vijaya Ramaswamy of Jawaharlal Nehru University, New Delhi, on taxation of artisans and non-agricultural workers in south India, from the twelfth to sixteenth century. All these essays have a strong methodological interest, focusing on the potentials and problems of utilizing currency, archival records and inscriptions as sources.

An innovative concept of 'deep monetization' is deployed by Lucassen to analyse the data on coinage with a view to using data on the circulation of small-value coins as an index of the degree of monetization. That analysis allows him to draw some tentative inferences with regard to changes in labour relations, entitlements in the rural sector and occupational shifts in urban areas during proto-industrialization in South Asia. The essay throws a shaft of light on the long-term trends affecting workers from the thirteenth century onwards, and also provides a comprehensive survey of the relevant literature.

It will be interesting to see if future work on the subject will attempt to quantify the depth of monetization, for example in terms of the ratio of monetary to non-monetary transactions, or frequency distribution of low-value coins located in the known sites of wage workers' employment.

The essay by Faroqhi surveys the records generated by the Ottoman bureaucracy which have been preserved in Istanbul and records maintained by the *qadis* or judges elsewhere in the empire till about 1840. Ranging from the tax records regarding the peasantry in the fifteenth to sixteenth centuries, through the seventeenth-century records of military assignments, to the official registers maintained till the 1840s, there exist a vast range of sources. Faroqhi points out the limitations of the data, for example in respect of the rural economy, or the absence of women in the records. But she also points to the potentials of data from these sources on the development of urban crafts, monetization, the nature of the Sultanic 'command economy', as well as wider questions relating to the Ottoman polity which survived the onslaughts of Napoleon and the Russian Tsars and the European powers ranged against the Ottoman Empire in defence of Greek rebels. In this day and age when West Asian studies are dominated by questionable notions about the 'clash of civilizations', this essay opens up a new perspective.

Vijaya Ramaswamy in her essay chose the extremely difficult task of tracking labouring communities, especially those in artisanal work, in the maze of medieval inscriptional records of taxes imposed on them. She also uses earlier canonical texts like the *Gautama Dharma Sutra*. Apart from the complexities of tax terminology, there are problems in the systemization of epigraphic categorization of *shilpi*s, due to regional and temporal variations. Despite these problems the essay puts together a great deal of data collected from sources dispersed in different sites and archaeological reports, to situate the various artisanal communities in relation to the state and the tax collection system.

The second group of essays comprises those on work communities and the development of their identity. Karuna D.W. Miriam and Santosh K. Rai, both of Delhi University, write about the weavers' communities in nineteenth-century south India and in colonial United Provinces (now Uttar Pradesh), while Attila Aytekin and H.T. Sengul of the Middle East Technical University write about the state and working-class identity in Zonguldak coal basin in the Ottoman Empire. While these essays address the same type of questions, there are interesting differences as well. The essays on India are based on rich archival data of the colonial period, while the essay on the coal miners in Turkey is unusual in its extensive use of oral data. Caste, or its equivalent in the non-Hindu population, as one would expect, figures prominently in the Indian essays, while the state seems to be the '*locus* of consciousness' for the Turkish coal miners and their '*habitus* is structured' by the dominant presence of the state. Further, 'classness' is certainly more pronounced in the Turkish case as presented here, and identity appears to form primarily in terms of class, not any alternative sense of community.

Karuna's essay points to the weakness of a stereotype in colonial and post-colonial writings on south Indian textile industry – the attribution of 'a disproportionate prominence to a handful of castes recognized as weaving castes'. Her archival data suggest the participation of a much wider range of castes including the so-called untouchable in textile work in the late eighteenth and nineteenth centuries. She draws important inferences from the narrative of the gradual exclusion of the untouchable castes from the industry in course of the nineteenth century, particularly in terms of its impact on their life and the perception of their status. Aytekin and Sengul broadly survey the development of the coal mines at the Zonguldak coal basin in several phases; the landmarks being the opening of the mines by the Sultan (1848), the infusion of French capital (1896), the new regime that began with the foundation of the Republic (1923), the nationalization of the mines (1939), the beginning of decline (from 1980 approximately), and massive unrest and strikes (1990–91). Though the role of the state has been changing on the whole, 'the *habitus* formed around the mines, the working-class *habitus*, has been structured by the presence of a state-controlled local economy'. Hence the authors emphasize that the state was 'a very important locus of consciousness' for the workers.

Santosh Kumar Rai's study focuses on the inter-relationship between the family, neighbourhood and the community among the weavers' community in the eastern part of what was known as the United Provinces (present-day Uttar Pradesh) from the 1870s to the end of British rule. Methodologically, an important point he makes is that he feels the need to look at the process of continual reconstitution of the community, rather than look at it as a given thing with fixed characteristics. Secondly, his study of the household as the locus of production suggests that while the weavers were far from being economically autonomous, home-based production allowed a certain degree of autonomy to the artisans in terms of 'notions of work, time, space and leisure for the weavers amidst their own cultural context'. Thirdly, he shows that 'a shared hierarchical understanding' of intra-family and capital–labour relationship infused the perception of asymmetries of 'social power' in the artisans' world.

The third group of essays looks at two of the oldest occupations in history, that of soldiers and sailors. We have here the scope to look at history of the longer range. Moreover, in older times in societies where self-employment or servitude was common, employment of mercenary soldiers or sailors by the oldest business corporations, the East Indian Companies, or by the state in Asia or Europe, provide interesting case studies of wage-labour employment. A third interesting feature of much employment was that often these employees were multi-ethnic in composition. Alessandro Stanziani, of the Ecole des Hautes Etudes en Sciences Sociales and Wissenschafts Kolleg zu Berlin, offers an examination of the current stereotypes about the mercenaries and peasants in empire-building in his wide-angled picture of a vast space which is now called Eurasia. Matthias von Rossum of the Virje Institute at Amsterdam offers an empirically rich study of Asian maritime labour, followed by an essay on Indian soldiers in the English East India Company by Sabyasachi Dasgupta of Visva Bharati University, West Bengal.

A military revolution enabling the west to sweep all before it and gain global hegemony was the foremost among the 'Killer Apps of Western Power', to use Niall Ferguson's phrase. Unlike Ferguson's (2011) popular and sometimes garbled history-in-a-capsule, Alessandro Stanziani offers a complicated answer to a similar question: what accounted for the military might of Muscovy and Qing China, and what enabled them to recruit military labour? He considers the links between economic growth and warfare, between military recruitment and the labour market (including labour made available by non-market factors like serfdom and slavery), and the links between political structures like the despotic state and the colonized frontier territories and military expansion. His survey of the historiography of that vast subject is strengthened by a critical comparative method which digs deep into Russian history – and there are suggestive comparisons made with Qing and Mughal history. Basically his argument seems to be that Muscovite military might was not just an outcome of despotic power and the institution of serfdom. It was a result of the adroit deployment of 'peasants–soldiers–*colons*' – a substitute for a permanent army. It was a sign of 'backwardness' in West European eyes, but it worked. Qing military expansion also depended heavily upon colonization of the northern frontier by Han peasants and Manchu warriors; however, unlike Russia, Chinese expansion was accompanied by a more pronounced dependence on trade networks to feed the army. At the back of these strategies were factors which Stanziani brings into his analysis: the environmental specificities of the catchment areas of military recruitment and of the frontier territories, the strength of manpower and surplus availability, and the relationship between the central power and the frontier magnates. 'Recruitment of military labour' appears to be an inadequate description of the complex ways in which men-in-arms were deployed by the late medieval and early modern imperial powers. Given the complex interaction of factors, when we talk of the military policies of these powers, a question that needs to be asked is: who made it all come together – where did agency rest?

A young maritime historian, Matthias von Rossum, has packed his essay with a great deal of data from the Dutch East India Company and other contemporary sources, on the volume of shipping in Asian and intra-Asian trade, estimated demand for sailors for such shipping, the ethnic composition of crews and ratio of Asian sailors to the total number of sailors, labour productivity per tonnage, wages paid, etc., for the period 1690–1790, and in some data for series from 1600. This in itself is a considerable achievement from the point of view of maritime history. From the point of view of labour history, the following are important. First, the recruitment of Asian soldiers occurred initially in India and later it shifted to Southeast Asia. Typically, sailors were from Malabar, Surat and Bengal in India; from China; and from Malaya, Acheh, Solor, Timor, Laos, Macao, etc. The recruitment was truly international. Secondly, there is on record a fully developed system of wage work and the Asian sailors' wages were not below par (approximately equal to wages paid to European sailors). It was only in the nineteenth century that Asian sailors began to be degraded as *lascars* on lower wages. Thirdly, the estimates of labour productivity per tonnage class of Dutch East India Company ships with mixed crews, including Asian workers, compared favourably with the productivity of ships with crews of European nationalities. On the whole, the essay by von Rossum contributes substantially to the history of Asian maritime labour in the seventeenth and eighteenth centuries.

Unlike the essays of Stanziani and von Rossum, Dasgupta's study is limited to a narrow band of time, i.e. the middle decades of the nineteenth century. However, the essay poses an interesting question: what was the self-perception of the soldiers employed by the English East India Company – did they perceive themselves as personnel in 'military labour', or did they not? Dasgupta's contention is that the Bengal *sepoy* (soldier) abhorred the representation of the *sepoy* as anything other than a 'fighting man'. In his perception he was far from being a person providing labour. In fact, such a soldier would sedulously avoid any assignment, like digging a trench, which would be expected of a labourer in the farm. That kind of work would diminish the status of a 'proud fighting man' to that of a labourer and therefore to be eschewed at any cost. At the same time, he considered employment in the service of the English East India Company as a soldier as highly desirable for it opened up avenues to status advancement in rural society.

Historians are generally quite content with their own constructs but it is worthwhile to ask, how was 'work' or 'labour' perceived by those who actually performed it? In the fourth group of essays we have essays which elaborate on that perception of work, the complexities of self-perception and the socially ascribed status of workers in different domains. Nitin Varma reports from Berlin on his research on the workers' notions about working in the plantation industry in eastern India; Claudio H.M. Batalha of UNICAMP, Brazil, writes about the perception of work among working classes in Brazil in the late nineteenth and early twentieth centuries; and Marcelo Badaro Mattos of Universidade Federal Fluminense writes about changing perceptions in the historiography of the working class.

There are two parallel narratives about labour in the tea plantations of Assam in colonial India. In the catchment area for labour recruitment there was a widespread notion that unscrupulous deception was the means used by the recruiting agents to entice the poor, that entry into contract to work there was tantamount to bondage, that plantation work was a regime of oppression, and that escape from the plantation and return to the village (home) was well-nigh impossible. On the other hand, British capital and the management controlling those plantations represented them as veritable gardens where the pleasant work of plucking tea-buds awaited women (such pictures adorned advertisements of the industry), rice ration was assured to each immigrant family, employment for a specified number of years was assured, and the plantation labourer had the right to return home after expiry of contract. Nitin Varma produces overwhelmingly strong evidence that the representation of workers' life by the plantation owners was a pack of lies. That, however, was perhaps the easier task for the author. His main objective is to explore popular mentality in respect of plantation labour in Assam, and this is one of the finest explorations in Indian labour history.

To get at the cast of mind in the catchment area for plantation labour recruitment, Varma has used a variety of sources: recorded rumours current in that area; folk-songs which refer to plantation labour; the evidence embedded in language in the terms and notions regarding plantation work; occasional and rare instances of popular opinion being recorded by missionaries, civil servants, journalists and the likes. He also uses, of course, depositions made by workers before committees of enquiry, including one of 1894 in which the collected data was so damaging to plantation interests that it was kept confidential. The proponents of the planters' interests also talked of popular mentality, but they saw in it nothing but baseless prejudice born of ignorance. Varma shows that the anxieties and resentments that one sees in the sources mentioned above were not baseless. In some instances, no doubt, local cultural specificities came into play – for instance, there was a preference for 'circular' migration over permanent migration, there was a resistance to the idea of a contract which appeared to the worker as a kind of bondage, or again, there was a strong distaste for food being served regardless of caste on the steamboats on the way to plantations. But we must recall that despite all that 1.18 million persons migrated to Assam between 1871 and 1901, the majority of them as plantation labour. The basic factors behind the 'unpopularity' of Assam tea plantations were perfectly rational – not to be dismissed as ignorance or cultural dissonance between a primitive people and industrial capitalism. It was rational to be wary of a contract that bound workers to an unknown employer and existence, as well as rational to resist the illegal regime of discipline maintained by tea planters, the increasing intensification of labour, the collusive malpractices of the '*sahib–babu–sardar*' combine to deprive labourers of their dues, and the incarcerated life in the compound or garden under panopticonesque surveillance.

The only other essay in this volume addressing the important issue of mentalities is Claudio Batalha's work on Brazilian workers' perception of workers as a class. Here things are a little complicated due to the interface between three different but intersecting discourses: (a) the discourse of rights of slaves and privileges of free men in the early days when abolition of slavery slowly progressed; (b) the contraposition of the privileges of white men versus rights of black people who figured prominently among artisans; and (c) the discourse of class, positing the working class against the traditional privileges of the organized craftsmen. Batalha's narrative of the interaction between these discourses, mainly through his documentation of various craftsmen's and workers' associations, yields a clear picture of the intricate complexity of and divergence between various perceptions of work and workers. There are interesting parallels between that history and developments elsewhere. The self-perception and organized activities of the craftsmen remind one of the powerful stratum of 'labour aristocracy' elsewhere, like the Association of Engineers in England. The discourse of race is not without parallels in the discourse of caste in India. The concerns reflected in discussions of slavery and the problematic status of slaves or even ex-slaves in Brazil call to mind the analogous discourse in many countries where the 'Masters and Servants' laws regulated production relations. And the reluctance of craftsmen of high rank to perform the duty of lowly labourers by carrying implements of trade is still to be seen in India; in fact, it has even been institutionalized in some advanced economies through regulations made by trade unions minutely specifying jobs of different categories of employees. Thus Batalha, in his study of Brazilian workers and their mentality, has touched upon a set of issues which may be said to be universal.

This volume appropriately ends with a survey of labour historiography. Marcelo Badaró Mattos in his essay looks at labour historians' perception of workers in a comparative perspective. Perhaps it can be stated without fear of contradiction that the general trend of researching labour history in the latter half of the twentieth century was to concentrate attention on the workforce in the organized industries, and within that domain, on the institutional history of trade unions. This was largely due to the availability of sources, and in part due to the theoretical focus on that section of the working class which was supposed to be the head and front of the working-class movement. Only in course of the recent decades have we seen endeavours to expand researchers' vision beyond trade union organizations and leaders to the workers' movements, beyond such movements to the quotidian history of working-class lives, and beyond the organized sector to the informal sector where we see the labouring poor in the less developed countries. Marcello

Mattos examines these historiographic trends and identifies the major trend as 'enlargement' of the historians' perception of the working class. The essay provides a critical review of historical writings since the 1980s in Brazil and India in relation to global thought trends on the subject. Implicitly the essay also outlines an agenda of labour history, which merits our attention.

Within the limits of this volume it was possible to include only twelve essays, and it has been planned that a second collection of papers presented at the same conference will follow. It has often been said in recent times that academic interest in labour history has declined drastically. Be that as it may, the International Conferences on Labour History organized by the Association of Indian Labour Historians and the National Labour Institute in New Delhi continue to attract labour historians from different parts of the world, and there are important issues which have been raised in the essays in the following pages. If this collection generates interest and encourages further research, the aim of this volume will have been served.

References

Arendt, Hannah ([1958] 1998), *The Human Condition*, first edition 1958, reprint, Chicago: Chicago University Press.

Benner, Chris (2003), 'Computers in the Wild: Guilds and Next-Generation Unionism in the Information Revolution', *International Review of Social History*, Supplement 11, Vol. 48: 181–204.

Castells, Manuel (1996), *The Rise of the Network Society*, Vol. I of 'The Information Age: Economy, Society and Culture' series, New York: Blackwell.

Dahrendorf, Ralf, E. Kohler and Francoise Piotet (eds.) (1986), *New Forms of Work and Activity (European Foundation for the Improvement of Living and Working Conditions)*, Luxemburg/Dublin: EC.

Didsbury, Howard J. (ed.) (1983), *The World of Work: Careers and the Future*, Bethesda, MD: World Future Society.

Downey, Greg (2003), 'The Place of Labour in the History of Information-Technology Revolution', *International Review of Social History*, Vol. 48, Supplement 11: 225–61.

Ensmenger, Nathan M. (2003), 'Letting the Computer Boys Take Over: Technology and the Politics of Organizational Transformation', *International Review of Social History*, Vol. 48, Supplement 11: 153–80.

Gandhi, M.K. ([1909] 1939), *Home Rule for India or Hind Swaraj*, first edition, Durban, 1909, reprint, Bombay: Navjivan Publishing House.

Heidegger, Martin ([1954] 1977), 'The Question Concerning Technology', first edition, *Vortrage*, Pfuligen: Neske, 1954, translated by William Lovitt, in *The Question Concerning Technology and Other Essays*, New York: Garland Publishing.

Ramesh, Babu P. (2004), 'Cyber Coolies in BPO: Insecurities and Vulnerabilities of Non-Standard Work', *Economic and Political Weekly*, Vol. 39 (5), 3 January: 492–97.

Schiller, Dan (1999), *Digital Capitalism: Networking the Global System*, Cambridge, Mass.: MIT Press.

Toffler, Alvin (1980), *The Third Wave*, New York: Bantam Books.

The Long View

Work in Early Modern Times

Deep Monetization, Commercialization and Proletarianization

Possible Links, India 1200–1900

Jan Lucassen

This essay introduces the concept of 'deep monetization' – measured by the circulation of small-value coins – into the study of long-term labour history. This is exemplified by a case study of the Indian subcontinent between 1200 and 1900. The results are highly preliminary. Most of the space is devoted to the technique of data collection and the analysis of relative shifts in patterns of coin circulation. Several periods of increasing and decreasing levels of deep monetization become visible. In the last section of the essay, an attempt is made to link these patterns to possible shifts in labour relations. Apart from occupational shifts related to urbanization and the advent of proto-industries (and later colonialism), the changing nature of entitlements in the rural society is taken into account.

Introduction

Economic and social historians traditionally attribute much value to monetization. They see this process – measured by the degree to which interpersonal exchange is expressed in money value or to which currency plays a role in this exchange – as a crucial step in economic development. And, for that matter, in social relations as well. This may be true in general; it certainly applies to India. Take, for instance, the famous Indian scholar and politician B.R. Ambedkar (1891–1956). From his time as a student at Columbia University when he showed interest in economic issues (his MA thesis in 1915 was on 'Ancient Indian Commerce'), he held that the shift 'from kind economy to cash economy' was caused in the first place by 'the British system of revenue and finance'.[1] Without denying the impact of British colonial rule on Indian economic development, most professional historians interested in monetization have rather concentrated on earlier periods.

Those of the so-called Aligarh school of history, in particular Irfan Habib (from the 1960s), Aziza Hasan (in the 1960s/1970s), Shireen Moosvi (from the 1980s) and Najaf Haider (from the 1990s), have developed the theme of the monetization of the Mughal Empire by basing it mainly on sources written in Persian. Other Indian historians have studied the same topic primarily on the basis of western sources, like Om Prakash, Sanjay Subrahmanyam and Sanjay Garg (who have looked at Dutch, Portuguese and English sources, respectively). Subrahmanyam's influential edited volume, *Money and the Market in India 1100–1700* (1994), especially stands out. More recently, the economic historian Amiya Kumar Bagchi and Krishna Mohan Shrimali have made important contributions to this debate. In this respect the Canadian scholar John S. Deyell and his British colleague Frank Perlin certainly have to be also mentioned, among others.[2] Deyell published a number of seminal studies since the 1970s, in which he proposed and developed several methods to quantify Indian coin production. His data analysis focuses both on the period preceding the Delhi Sultanate and on the early Mughal period. Frank Perlin, a prolific British author, has been active in this field rather briefly, i.e. while teaching at the Erasmus University in Rotterdam between 1980–95. Concentrating on eighteenth- and nineteenth-century written sources on Maharashtra and northern India, he focused on coin circulation of small denominations issued by minor mints, and their implications for economic and social history.

The work of these authors has found wide acceptance, but some of it has also triggered critical discussions, methodologically as well as historically. This has been the fate of, for example, Moosvi's attempt to establish the amount of stock of silver coins *c.* 1600,[3] and equally so Deyell's reconstruction of the period 750 to 1250, mainly on the analysis of coin hoards.[4] Perlin's conclusions about monetization and subsequently India's integration into a colonial empire which involved deindustrialization and relative demonetization (blatantly differing from Ambedkar in this respect!) have also been questioned severely. Shailendra Bhandare remarks that Perlin is not a numismatist, while Sanjay Garg comments that relative demonetization of India till the mid-nineteenth century 'can at best be a temporary and localized phenomenon'.[5]

The current historiography distinguishes five 'cycles of monetization', as Najaf Haider calls upswings in the use of coins:[6] the early Delhi Sultanate, the early Mughal Empire, the late Mughal Empire and especially its successor states, and, finally, the full-grown colonial state from, say, the second quarter of the nineteenth century onwards. Attempts to estimate absolute levels of monetization are extremely rare, and neither have the different sub-periods been linked directly. Nevertheless most authors seem to think that each cycle represents a higher level than the previous one.[7]

Whether one agrees with specific scholars or not, basing themselves on the work of many numismatists not mentioned here, they have shown how important, feasible and promising the history of monetization of the Indian subcontinent can be. It goes 'beyond basic numismatic calendaring', although

Sanjay Subrahmanyam (from whom I borrow this phrasing) in 1994 stated that the real monetary history of India before 1500 still remains to be written. He is convinced that for the time being there is a great need for precise regional studies, and I could not agree more.[8]

The direction of this essay is however different. Instead of restricting ourselves in time and space, I think we might make some immediate progress by distinguishing clearly between different social functions of currencies.[9] After all, not all coins were used by all people. By concentrating on the functions of specific currencies (high-, medium- and small-valued), we may not only advance in the field of monetary history, but also – more importantly – in understanding the implications of monetization for other historical developments, *including the history of work and of labour*. To begin with, we have to leave the general concept of monetization for the more specific concept of '*deep monetization*'. Most of the paper will be devoted to the application of this concept to India between 1200 and 1900, and methodological questions will have to dominate at this preliminary stage of research. Finally, however, I will reach the ultimate goal of this whole exercise where I will reflect on the implications of deep monetization for long-term labour history.

Monetization, Deep Monetization and Indian Historiography

Virtually all classical histories of monetization begin by explaining the introduction of coins around the middle of the first millennium BCE, more or less simultaneously, in the Eastern Mediterranean, in India and China, by an increasing need for currencies in inter-regional and international trade.[10] In this narrative, coins and trade are inseparable. However, this may at best be only a partial explanation as well-developed international trade is much older and for millennia could do without currency. Besides, it was continued for another two millennia in other parts of the world (the Americas and Sub-Saharan Africa). We therefore should be careful in exclusively linking trade with monetization. Instead, we should look for other exchange functions of currencies. Wage payments, for example, may be equally important or even more important for the explanation of the introduction of coins or of variations in its use over time. In contrast to most authors who restrict themselves to the role of money for a smooth exchange of goods (including trade), we have to include also the exchange of services (including work, both free and unfree).

Apart from the distinction between functions, we should try to link these with the outer appearances of currencies. Materials (mainly metals until one century ago, before the advent of small fractions of paper money) and weight matter should be considered most because they primarily determine the intrinsic value of means of exchange. In the case of fiduciary money, the outer appearance matters even more as the public can no longer derive value from weight and purity. In short, not all types of coins are equally useful for each type of exchange. Gold and heavy silver coins are mainly used for savings and trade settlements, medium-sized silver coins for the payment of taxes[11] and rent (and under certain circumstances also wages), whereas small silver but particularly copper coins (often erroneously called 'small change') are used in daily payments (including wages). Medium-sized coins fit best in systems of weekly or bi-weekly payments; smaller coins if wages are paid daily. Besides, small change is necessary in order to enable food and other market purchases by workers of all kinds. The production and circulation of small coins therefore may be related to the occurrence of wage payments.

Recently, some scholars have introduced the concept of 'deep monetization'. For Bhandare it 'involve[s] the use of coined money in the lowest stratum of a transaction system based on the introduction of cheap, low–denomination coinage', which he also calls '"microcosmic" money economies'. Koenraad Verboven does not give as much a formal definition, but makes two important additional remarks. First, that: 'In deeply monetized societies social actors are tacitly and explicitly taught that specific social settings (for instance market exchanges) require money for exchanges and transactions to occur and that we can and should accept "money" in exchange for goods and services.' Second, 'that "deep monetization" does not imply full monetization. . . . No pre-industrial economy ever came near to being fully monetized. Gift exchange, command economics and redistribution remained important structural principles that governed the flow of resources.' Without using the term, much earlier, Robert Wicks combined some of these elements by quoting Robert Renfrew – 'the existence of any low-denomination coinage, used within the jurisdiction of the issuing authority, is an indication of market exchange' – and by adding this comment: 'The presence of multiple denominations, especially in base-metal coin series, opens the door to wider usage, allowing for the possibility that the coinage was utilized in marketed transactions.' To summarize, this image of 'deep' denotes *the permeation of the usage of coins deep into society until reaching the large mass of the working population.*[12]

The proliferation of small-value coins points to increasing numbers of small-value transactions by an increasing part of the population, and might entail a shift from personal to impersonal obligations. Such shifts may be necessitated either by occupational specialization or by changing value systems in inter-personal relations. An example of the first is the shift at village or regional level from self-supporting households to occupationally specialized households where farmers, millers, bakers, shoemakers, soldiers, etc., have to exchange goods and services. The second may be exemplified by already specialized local or regional societies that no longer prefer to express their mutual dependency in terms of moral obligations, but rather in terms of credit and debt, expressed in money.

Processes of occupational specialization and monetization of this kind may occur simultaneously, but monetization may also develop long after occupational specialization takes off. Another variant – often simultaneous with occupational specialization – is the emergence of social inequality, where certain groups in society manage to impose tributary obligations on most others. Such tributary relations may or may not be monetized. The former is exemplified by monetary tax systems; the latter by the imposition of servitude, slavery or other forms of unfree labour (for a summary, see Figure 1).

It should be stressed here that we need a very broad approach to the way impersonal exchange of goods and services may be organized. Essential is the expression of mutual obligations in a standardized, impersonal way. There are three big variants. First, in goods (the concept of 'barter' covers this only partially where one good is exchanged against another), like fixed grain payments for labour – documented already for Mesopotamia and Egypt before Alexander the Great.[13] Second, in metallic (or paper or metallic) currency – in the available literature best studied of all. Third, currency in non-metallic (and non-paper) forms, for which cowrie shells, bitter almonds and beads are well-known examples, but for which, in principle, any tangible and manually easily portable substance may serve. Many more distinctions of barter and currency are relevant and available, but they have to rest here.

It may be clear that monetization, and especially deep monetization, is directly linked to general historical debates, more particularly to those on economic development and economic growth, and on labour history. For those parts of the world where numismatic evidence is abundant, but written sources on monetization and occupational structures, for whatever reasons, are less abundant, there is already a certain tradition in numismatic and monetary

FIGURE 1 ***Human Exchange Relations and Monetization***

	Payments in kind	*Monetized payments*
Exchange of goods as a consequence of occupational specialization	Communal (*jajmani*-like) mutual obligations	Selling and buying own produce at commodity markets (and subquent spending of earnings in markets)
Exchange of services	Communal and personal mutual obligations	Wage payments in coins (and subsequent spending of earnings in markets)
Imposition of obligations or duties	Tax payments in kind; unfree labour	Tax payments in coins

history to use data on coin production as proxies for economic development at large. This also applies to India.

For many reasons, India seems to be also an extremely fine laboratory for the study of deep monetization. Frank Perlin has already made a convincing plea for the importance of the production and circulation of the lower denominations. Many written sources corroborate the impact of small currency on the life of the population in general. Let me quote one about the scarcity of copper coins in Bihar in 1795:[14] '[T]his species of coin is the principal currency amongst the manufacturing and labouring class of people in this quarter, hence a deficiency of this currency in circulation, whether real or artificial, the evil will fall principally on the lower classes of people.'

This essay necessarily will have to develop first the necessary tools for the reconstruction of major trends in deep monetization. Although this concept as such is not restricted to specific parts of the world or specific periods, the focus in this essay is on India, 1200–1900. It also attempts to trigger a discussion on possible implications for the economic and social history of the subcontinent. The choice for this case is not only given by the rich historiography available on monetization and the recent publication of excellent catalogues which may serve as a solid basis of analysis. In the framework of global history in which increasingly continents and subcontinents are compared, India is always mentioned as an important case, but so far case studies lag far behind those on China and Europe.[15] As said, the relative lack of written sources for labour history before the colonial period might be an extra reason to look for alternatives as proposed here. The development of a long-term labour history of the Indian subcontinent may be enhanced by the study of long-term trends in deep monetization, more precisely of its relation with the processes of commercialization, commodification of labour and proletarianization.

Available Data and Methodology: India 1200–1900

Whereas direct quantitative information on total circulation are lacking as a rule before the advance of modern economics in the second half of the nineteenth century, historians studying earlier periods have to rely on data about the composition of coin hoards or coin production. Frequency analysis of coin hoards is widely used in numismatics.[16] It tells us about historical preferences in hoarding coins (a proxy for but not identical to circulation patterns), and shifts in these patterns *through* time as the youngest coin in a hoard is mostly taken as a date *post quem* for the hiding. Apart from finding such shifts (a most important result as such!), hoard analysis is less suitable to reconstruct production figures over long periods of time. The most important reason for the limitations of this method is the lacking availability of information on most hoards that are turned to the surface, as most findings are not recorded as such and these coins reach the collector's market or disappear as scrap in the melting-pot. Therefore, those which come under the eye of specialists and receive able cataloguing can be seen only occasionally as representative of the content of all hoards. Besides, hoarding of small currencies is rather the exception because those who have to hide coins have an understandable predilection for gold or larger silver, which per weight represents more value. Thus these minor denominations as a rule are found as stray finds, therefore escaping systematic numismatic analysis. Most importantly, the coin hoard method, because of differences in hiding practices (more or less, war and social turmoil in different periods) and in representativeness over time, is less suitable for the goal set in this essay.

John Deyell's major contribution on Mughal coin circulation offers a quick introduction to the available reconstruction methods for long-term production trends, including the study of coin hoards.[17] This is also the basis of his later book on the period 750–1200.

One method he mentions there but does not use himself, is the cataloguing of coin types per ruler, i.e. defining a coin type by ruler, mint and year.[18] Instead he adopts – in his own words – a less accurate approach, which is shown for copper coins in Table 1.[19] He starts out by adding up 'the total specimens of copper coins for each reign preserved in five [most important British and Indian] museums' (column A in table). Next, he provides the

TABLE 1 ***Deyell's reconstruction of the general availability of copper coin types in museums as 'a useful index of the relative annual copper coin production during each reign' of the most important Mughals, 1556–1759***

	Total no. of specimens in 5 museums	*No. of mints*	*Average years per mint*	*Specimens in 5 museums per mint year*	
	A	B	C	*D = A/BC*	*D2 (excl. Elichpur)*
Akbar, 1556–1605	1304	59	40	0.552	0.552
Jahangir, 1605–1627	85	12	23	0.308	0.308
Shahjahan, 1628–1658	80	15	30	0.178	0.178
Aurangzeb, 1658–1707	145	26	40	0.139	0.130
Shah Alam I, 1707–1712	35	12	5	0.583	0.218
Farrukhshihar, 1713–1719	6	12	6	0.083	0.091
Muhammad Shah, 1719–1748	52	12	29	0.149	0.060
Ahmad Shah, 1748–1754	18	3	6	1.000	0.500
Alamgir II, 1754–1759	37	8	5	0.925	0.714

Source: Deyell 1987b: 161.

number of mints in production per reign (B, according to Singhal 1953) and 'the average number of years the mints were in the possession of the Mughals for each reign' (C).[20] The relation between these three figures (D = A/BC) 'indicates a general decline in empire-wide annual copper production' from 1556 to 1748, which confirms broadly Irfan Habib's observations.[21] This trend shows even more clearly by leaving out one single mint (Elichpur in Berar), which in later reigns became the single most active copper mint. In a way, Machhlipattan near Madras performed a similar local function (see Table 1).

A third method used by Deyell is the frequency analysis of coins from hoards. Two hoards, consisting of copper *dams* only (1,774 and 1,002 pieces respectively), turning out to be truly random samples, may be therefore taken as representative of the copper circulation in the Delhi *suba* in the years 1602–04. Such large hoards of copper coins are unfortunately rarely available for scholarly analysis in comparison with hoards of silver and even gold coins (see Tables 2 and 3).

In the last two tables I have smuggled in a fourth method which Deyell mentions, but applies only occasionally and unsystematically, which is the determination of the rarity of coins.[22] I have taken the opportunity to compare Deyell's results for frequency of circulation with actual collectors' market prices of old coins (as expressed in modern numismatic catalogue

TABLE 2 ***Deyell's reconstruction of the availability of copper dams from 10 most important mints in two coin hoards for the period*** AH ***963–992 (1554/55–1583/84) as compared with catalogue prices***

Rank	*Mint*	*Suba*	*Approximate tally of coins issued*	*Per cent of 445*	*Market price in quality fine*	
					KM	*US$*
1	Narnol	Agra	445	100.0		
2	Ajmir	Ajmer	63	14.2		
3	Delhi	Delhi	47	10.6		
4	Fathpur	Agra	43	9.7		
5	Agra	Agra	42	9.4		
6	Urdu	None	37	8.3		
7	Dogaon	Awadh	35	7.9	28.19	7.00
8	Bairata	Agra	22	4.9	30.10	18.00
9	Alwar		18	4.0		
10	Lahore	Lahore	16	3.6		

Source: Deyell 1987a: 56 (approximate tally of coins issued = the tally of type coins found for each mint, multiplied by the percentage of the number of minting years to the total number of minting years); Bruce 2008: 946–47 (only available for AH years 1010–13, instead of 963–92).

TABLE 3 ***Deyell's reconstruction of the availability of copper dams from 10 most important mints in 2 coin hoards for the period Ilahi year 30 (AH 993/994 = CE 1585/1586) to year 50 (AH 1013/1014 = CE 1605/1606) as compared with catalogue prices***

Rank	*Mint*	*Suba*	*Approximate tally of coins issued*	*Per cent of 200*	*Market price in quality fine*	
					KM	*US$*
1	Narnol	Agra	200	100.0	32.21	9.00
2	Urdu	none	172	86.0	32.29	7.00
3	Bairata	Agra	113	56.5	32.50	7.00
4	Chitor	Ajmer	71	35.5		
5	Gobindpur		69	34.5	35.12	7.00
6	Ajmer	Ajmer	58	29.0		
7	Delhi	Delhi	45	22.5	32.90	7.00
8	Dogaon	Awadh	45	22.5		
9	Ujjain	Malwa	36	18.0	32.28	9.00
10	Allahabad	Allahabad	33	16.5		

Source: Deyell 1987a: 57; Bruce 2008: 946–47 (only Ilahi years 45–50, thus leaving out 30–44).

prices, and as available for 1600 CE onwards). This little experiment, covering only the last years of Akbar's reign, shows a high correlation between the relative frequency of *dams* in these two hoards and the frequency of similar pieces actually offered in the collectors' market, where prices between US$ 7–9 for (later) Akbar *dams* may be interpreted confidently as the indication 'very common (cc)' in other catalogues (see below). It also may serve as a preliminary introduction to the method applied in this essay that is explained below.

This in fact is a fifth method, the reconstruction of production figures and production capacity of mint houses in order to combine these with rarity indicators of coin types struck there. This is especially important because the same classical hammer-and-anvil method was used during the whole period studied here, with the exception of the big colonial mints of Calcutta, Bombay and Madras that came after 1835. This manual die-striking technique in India goes back to the fourth century BC and was identical to the one practised in the Mediterranean.[23] The lower matrix was embedded in an anvil, the upper was in the form of a hand-held punch which was hit by a hammer man. Upper matrixes were worn much quicker than the lower ones. From a letter written in 1804 by the British Collector of Allahabad, we know that for the striking of silver coins, twenty-two upper and eight lower matrixes were needed – so nearly three times more upper than lower ones.

A sixth and last method, which so far is underdeveloped for copper coins but widely discussed for silver coins, traces the availability of metals for coinage. In this case copper mines and copper at imports into the subcontinent.[24]

On the basis of the foregoing historiographic and methodological overview, I will adopt the following approach to study deep monetization trends in the Indian subcontinent.

(a) The unit of analysis is the entire subcontinent because in such a large geographical unit (like elsewhere in the pre-modern world), monetary circulation of coins was not confined precisely to the polities where they had been produced. This even goes for small coins, although less so than for higher-value coins.[25] On the other hand, exchange of coins between the Indian subcontinent and surrounding territories (with the possible exception of Afghanistan) was limited until the nineteenth century, when colonial Indian coins started to circulate in East Africa, the Gulf and Malaya. In my database I distinguish between southern, north-western, north-central and north-eastern India.

(b) The time-frame has been taken as long as feasible, which means the period 1200–1900. This is determined by the availability of good and coherent catalogues, which is the case since a few years. An excellent starting point is the catalogue published by Goron and Goenka in 2001, of all known coin types of the Delhi Sultanate and similar Muslim states. Before 1200, not only is cataloguing less well developed, but, more importantly, the dating of coins is much more uncertain. Mainly before the advent of the Muslim states, Indian coins rarely bear years in one of the prevailing eras and often even no reigns. Their dating is consequently too imprecise to allow for an attribution to quarter-centuries in which they have been produced.[26] This after all is the shortest meaningful period possible, and therefore it constitutes my temporal unit of analysis (so, all in all, I distinguish twenty-eight quarter-centuries). After 1900, another complication arises: the circulation of small-denominated paper money with a much shorter life-time than coins.

(c) Units of analysis are coin types, for which Deyell provides a useful definition: 'Essentially, numismatics is the science of classification of coins, and the unit of study is the coin-type, a differentiable category of coin possessing a unique appearance, metrology, metallic composition and message content.'[27] Numismatists cataloguing coins of a certain period may sometimes differ about the value to be attributed to the variable 'message content', but all seem to agree that different texts are decisive. Although some would classify a different date or even a month (as practised in the Mughals' Ilahi chronology) as a type, others do not consider differences in years as sufficient for typology purposes.[28] The latter method has been applied for this paper.

(d) In order to catch deep monetization, I will restrict myself to small coins, here defined as all copper and billon coins, as well as silver coins weighing less than 5 grams. This excludes half-rupee pieces and higher values from the sixteenth century, as well as similar coins in a more remote past. Heavier silver coins represented too much value for the common man, and, as a consequence, were never received by the majority of the population or only a few times in their life.[29]

(e) A listing of the small-value coin types of India in 1200–1900 provides only a first glimpse of deep monetization patterns. The next step, a reconstruction of their numbers in circulation, obviously provides more insights. Only from 1835 is this possible for all issues of the British colonial mints (and even much later for the still surviving 'native' mints). Previously, such figures are available only for a handful of coin types. These will be used of course (see Table 6 below), but for the great majority an indirect method has to be found. In order to estimate coin production (and thus coin circulation) before 1835, we have to extrapolate from the data of the few types for which we have data, to the rest. The key proposal on how to do this, which is not used on a grand scale so far as I know, is to determine the rarity of coin types in the collectors' market as reflected in coin catalogues, and to use it as a proxy for coin production.[30] For the catalogues to be used, this presupposes of course a certain uniformity in typology and indications of rarity, expressed either in symbols or in market prices. This is true for the six most important catalogues used for this essay. If we accept that there is overall a more or less fixed relation between actual rarity in the collectors' market and numbers struck in the past (as suggested in Tables 2 and 3 above), these catalogues provide us with a relative yardstick for measuring coin production intensity. Two sorts of information are available for different coin types (or even for separate years) in the major catalogues. First, qualitative indications of rarity, which are widely accepted among numismatists and coin collectors. These run from '*cc*' for *very common*, '*c*' for *common*, 's' for *scarce*, to '*r*' for *rare* and '*rr*', '*rrr*' and '*rrrr*' for higher degrees of rarity. Second, indications of market prices, differentiated by degree of preservation. In this essay I will use only indications for the preservation quality 'fine' (i.e. showing 'fairly heavy wear over all of the coin' but still showing all important details), valuated in US$ at the time of publication of the catalogue (in this case, editions varying between 2002 and 2008).

(f) The penultimate step is the reduction of these two systems of rarity indication to one for the entire period. This has been possible because for some hundred coins, mainly dating from the seventeenth century, both indicators are available.[31] Fortunately, they show a high degree of consistency, which makes it possible to convert price classes into the symbolic rarity indicators, and consequently to apply one set of rarity indicators to the entire data base (see Table 4).[32]

(g) The last step is the application of weights to the rarity indicators 'cc', 'c' and 's' in order to present the results in one graph (see section under 'Relative Overall Trends: Acceleration and Stabilization Periods 1200–1900' and Figure 2, below).[33]

A database containing all types of answers to the specifications just discussed, and containing thousands of different types for the periods *c.* 1200–1750 and 1850–1900, is the basis for the preliminary conclusions in this paper. A few words on the catalogues used may be useful.[34] For the greater part of India between 1200 and 1550/1700, an excellent catalogue by Stan Goron and J.P. Goenka is available for the Sultanate of Delhi, its successors the Suris, and its Muslim competitors and successors like the Sultans of Bengal, Madura, Gujarat, Malwa and Kashmir. From 1600, world catalogues, although by far not as reliable as Goron/Goenka, may serve our purpose for the moment. The period in between the reigns of the first three Mughals is covered by an excellent catalogue for Babur and one for Akbar, but the intermediate reign of Humayun has not yet received equal numismatic attention and is certainly under-represented in my database so far.[35] Also the coinage in the south deserves more attention than I could devote to it now.[36] Apart from these weaknesses to which a few dozen more missing types could be added,[37] my main problem lies in the century between 1750 and 1850, which for that reason is still missing in my database. As a consequence of the

TABLE 4 *Congruency between two systems to indicate rarity of Indian coins in different catalogues*

Indicated by symbols		*Indicated by market prices (in US$) for the grading 'fine'*
Very common	cc	0–10
Common	c	11–15
Scarce	s	16–25
Rare	r	26–35
Very rare	rr	36 and more
Extremely rare	rrr	
Only one or a few specimens documented	rrrr	

weakening of the Mughal Empire and the success of the colonial powers, first and foremost the British who prevailed in the second half of the eighteenth century, minting activities proliferated all over the country. On the one hand, this shows how important the demand for metal means of exchange was, irrespective of whether centralized polities could meet it or not. On the other hand, numismatic evidence of exactly which types have been made where and when is still very weak. Although the big world catalogues pretend that all information is available, detailed studies of the coppers in early nineteenth century demonstrate how wide the gap is between the prevailing catalogues and what we wish to know.[38] I hope to contribute to narrowing this gap a little bit in the near future.

Another gap, which will never be filled by any cataloguing however perfect, is quantifiable information on the circulation of non-metallic currency, especially *cowries* in north-eastern India about which a lot has been written already, and bitter almonds,[39] as well as on remuneration in kind (mostly grain) of labour and other services (see below). Consequently, the data presented restricts itself to metallic small currency, but of course the circulation of non-metallic currencies and practices of payments in kind have to be weighed in any final discussion about proportions between payments and non-paid services (whether forced or not) on the other.

Historical Framing of the Numismatic Listings

Before jumping to the analysis of the database, we are reminded by Wicks that: 'While the physical characteristics of a coin series, as well as its geographical distribution, can provide valuable clues to its function, the precise role of that coinage must be confirmed by a study of literary sources.'[40] Over the last years I have had the opportunity to do exactly this by combining historical sources on wage payments, and the production and circulation of a number of copper coins in early-nineteenth-century northern India, on the one hand, with numismatic evidence, on the other. Occasionally, it is also possible to find more production figures of certain hand-struck coin types. Combined with information on their geographical distribution (from hoards and stray finds), this is a starting point for understanding their function. This basis is still too narrow to convert directly rarity indicators for all other types into production figures, but it is not to be excluded that a larger set of data will make such a procedure possible in the near future. This will also open the way to construct one common picture for pre- and post-1835 patterns. In the following sub-sections, two different types of evidence will be produced. To begin with, some state-wide cross-sections between 1300 and 1600, followed by production figures of a few dozen manually produced coin types as far as known to me, for the seventeenth, eighteenth and nineteenth centuries. Only at the end of the nineteenth century we touch firmer ground with the first national estimates of coin circulation, based on actual production figures.

'National' Cross-Sections, 1300–1600

At the beginning of the fourteenth, sixteenth and the seventeenth centuries, four widely diverging reports on state expenditure, state treasury at moments of 'regime change' and on taxation provide a first proxy for circulation patterns and maybe even figures. Although full of uncertainties and providing coverage at the expense of depth, they are all we have for the earliest centuries covered is this essay. Enough reasons to present them here briefly.

State expenditure and coin circulation: the Delhi Sultanates, c. 1300

The earliest period for which at least some indications for coin circulation are available is the reign of Alauddin Muhammad, Delhi Sultan 1296–1316. He is known for spending 10 million *tankas* cash per year on his 20,000 Turkish Mamluks (500 *tankas* per person) and 210 million *tankas* on his 900,000 cavalrymen (234 *tankas* per person).[41] Even if we do not accept fully the veracity of the excessively high numbers of cavalrymen under arms as such, these are impressive sums of money. Most likely the coins needed had been produced recently by this same Sultan.[42] Billon '6 gani' coins (25 per cent silver) weighing 3.5 grams were stamped during eleven years (AH 701–05 and 711–16). Besides, there were the equally heavy '2 gani' coins (containing *c.* 15 per cent silver), coined during seventeen years (AH 696–711 and 716). The mint house is not given, but supposedly it was Delhi where most gold and silver coins of this Sultan were also struck under the famous mint master Thakkura Pheru. Both billon coin types are classified as 'very common', and therefore must have been produced in large numbers. Supposing that the Delhi mint mainly worked for the needs of the treasury, which in its turn had the army as its main expenditure, this mint house must have been able to coin per annum at least 1 million billon coins at the start of the fourteenth century.

State treasury and coin circulation in the Mughal Empire, c. 1526

After the battle of Panipat (1526) where Babur and his son Humayun defeated the Delhi Sultan Ibrahim Lodi, the acquired accumulated treasures of the Lodis amounted to 70 lakh (7 million) pieces, donated by the father to his son. This treasure must have been Lodi currency, more particularly '*Sikandaris*' or black *tankas*.[43] As the billon *tanka* of 80 *ratis* weighed about 9 grams, the gift was bulky, weighing 63,000 kilograms of specie.

We may compare these figures to the taxes Babur could levy from the newly conquered territories, amounting to 520 million *tankas*. Only in Tirhut (northern Bengal, famous for its silver issues) the sum consisted of 255,000 silver *tankas* and 2,750,000 black *tankas*, but in all other provinces

TABLE 5 ***Production of billon 80 ratitankas, Delhi, 1451–1526***

Type (Goron and Goenka 2001)	*Rarity*	*Years struck (AH)*	*Number of years struck*	*Coin name*
D 690	cc	856–866,		
872–892	33	Bahluli		
D 705	cc	894–909	16	Sikandari
D 706	cc	900–922	23	Sikandari
Total			72	

of the erstwhile Delhi Sultanate, revenues were expressed in *tankas* without qualification.

If this information is correct and if we may suppose that, (a) this sum corresponds with the total circulation, and (b) that this equals the total production of black *tankas* since Sikandar Shah Lodi (1488–1517), we are dealing here with an average annual production of at least 10 million pieces per year. Even if we extend the period back to the middle of the century, when Bahlul Shah Lodi (1451–89) started his extensive coinage of 80 *ratitankas* – extensive because these billon (16 per cent silver) '*Bahlolis*' now are classified by collectors as very common – the Delhi minting capacity is impressive. Covering in total three-quarters of a century, we reach an annual production of nearly 7 million pieces on average (see Table 5). Besides, billon and copper fractions were struck as well, all of which are still common or very common.

In sum, we may conclude that the mint house of Delhi in the period 1451–1517 (when, apart from some *tankas* and their fractions, hardly other types were coined) had the enormous capacity of maybe 7–10 million pieces per year.

Taxation and coin circulation in the Bengal Sultanate, c. 1550

According to the *Ain-i-Akbari*, the revenue of all Bengal (excluding Orissa) in the late sixteenth century was 472,726,681 copper *dams* (or 11,818,167 silver rupees or 12,831,152 silver *tankas*). Deyell compares this with his estimates of the great re-coinage in Bengal of 1493 (3.15 million *tankas*) and 1538 (2.68 million rupees), as well as with his estimates of average annual *tanka* production based on die-count analysis for the period 1493–1576.[44] Combining his annual production estimates with an average loss in circulation of 2.5 per cent, he suggests a stable coin circulation of 30 million *tankas* between 1494 and 1519, a rise to about 37 million by 1538 and 30 million rupees in 1575. If the order of magnitude of all these estimates is acceptable, the two great re-coinages mentioned must have affected 10 per cent of the circulating coins. It would follow also that *c.* 1550, annual coin production might have been one-thirteenth of annual revenue receipts, and that total circulation was sufficient to meet about three years of revenue demand (if fully realized) in the same coins.

Tax sum and coin circulation in the Mughal Empire, c. 1600

Having tried to establish a relation between Babur's tax sum and coin circulation/coin production, we may do the same for the Mughal Empire in *c.* 1600, when the total tax sum in the vastly expanded empire had risen to 3,630,000,000 *dams*.[45] In making the same assumptions *ut supra*, that this sum corresponds with the total circulation, and this equals the total production of *dams* so far (i.e. since the production of the *Suripaisas* from 1543 onwards), we are dealing here with an average annual production of at least 60 million pieces per year, or – taking the ten most important mint houses – 6 million pieces on average per mint. Remarkably, this achievement is nearly the same as that of Babur's time, albeit that *dams* were much bigger than erstwhile *tankas* and therefore less easily produced, and, most importantly, that at the same time an impressive silver production had taken place.

Production Figures and Production Capacity of Traditional Mints, c. 1500–1870

Let us now move to more solid grounds where less assumptions have to be made, and investigate production and production capacities of traditional mints, relying on manual striking. For two dozen of them sufficient numbers have been published, unfortunately some only for silver. Most and best figures are available for the early colonial period of the British occupation when working mint houses in newly conquered territories fell into their lap, and which as a rule they tended to continue, at least for a number of years. Thanks to Paul Stevens' still ongoing work, ample information on these 'transitory mints' has become available recently, and can be added now to data provided mainly two decades ago by Frank Perlin (see Table 6).[46]

We may conclude that the main mint houses of north and central India, employing hundreds of workers, were well capable of striking up to 5 million coppers a year. If manufactured for years in a row, this implies the existence in dozens of millions of one and the same type of currency, like it happened in the times of the Suris and Akbar. Smaller mints, as the examples of Broach, Surat, Saugor (until 1823), Bankot, Chhachrauli, Jagadhri, Chandore, Indore and Alwar show, may have produced under similar circumstances several hundred thousand or even several million pieces of one type. After partial mechanization, outputs of 5 million and more coppers per year became within reach.

Output figures for silver coins are overall slightly higher. Although struck by the same hammer-and-anvil technique, their fabrication, on the one

TABLE 6 ***Maximum or average capacity realized (millions of pieces per year) in manual coin production***

Mint	*Period (maximum production year in brackets)*	*Number of silver pieces*		*Number of copper pieces*	
		Annual average	*Annual maximum*	*Annual average*	*Annual maximum*
Surat	1634–72 (1647)	4.125	7.5 (10)	3.75	
Rajmahal	1676	2.5		–	–
Murshidabad	1722		12.16	–	–
Benares	1748–76			3	5
Ahmedabad	1750		(3.09–) 6.17	–	–
Calcutta	1758–75	(6.2)	c. 10	–	–
Pune and Chakand	1793–1805	0.1–1.75			
Srinagar (Bundelkhand)	1794–1819	0.4–1.8			
Chandore	c. 1800		5		
Delhi	c. 1800–30		1–1.25		4
Amber/Jaipur	1802–03	(1.25) –5			
Farrukhabad	1802–05	3–3.4			
Surat	1802–13	0.07		1.15–1.28	
Broach	1803–29	0.9	1.84	0.75	0.96
Saugor	1806–23	0.4–1.08	1.7		
	1827–35*	2.15		5	
Bombay	1808–18			2.5–3	
Banares	1815–20*			7	
Ahmedabad	1817–18		2.62		
Bankot	1820–21			3–4.8	
Indore	–1823		2–2.75		
Chhachrauli/Jagadhri 0.1–0.15	1830				
Chandore	1832	0.18		1.7	
Alwar	1856–68			0.19	0.29
Indore	1875		3.0		

Note: * with improved machinery (but not yet steam)[47]
Source: See Appendix.

hand, took more time because less weight tolerance was accepted for the more expensive silver (roughly twenty times more than copper); on the other hand, minters earned higher piece wages by coining silver than copper coins, and had good reasons to speed up its production as far as possible.

All coins in this table that have been compared to the available catalogues – in line with earlier conclusions of this essay – turn out to be still very common in the market and valued accordingly.

Relative Overall Trends: Acceleration and Stabilization Periods, 1200–1900

It is time now to come up with the results of the exercise so far: the weighted number of types struck, 1200–1750, and up to now available in my database. As Figure 2 shows, a clear pattern of ups and downs arises.

To begin with, the periods showing clearly an increase of production:

(i) A first acceleration took place in the period 1275–1325/1375, followed by a low

(ii) A second acceleration in the period 1425/1450–1525, followed by an even more impressive acceleration period;[48]

(iii) A subsequent third and major acceleration from 1525 until at least 1600.[49]

It is too early to reflect extensively on these results, but a few historiographical observations on the three acceleration periods may be in place. The

Figure 2 *Weighted number of types, 1200–1750*

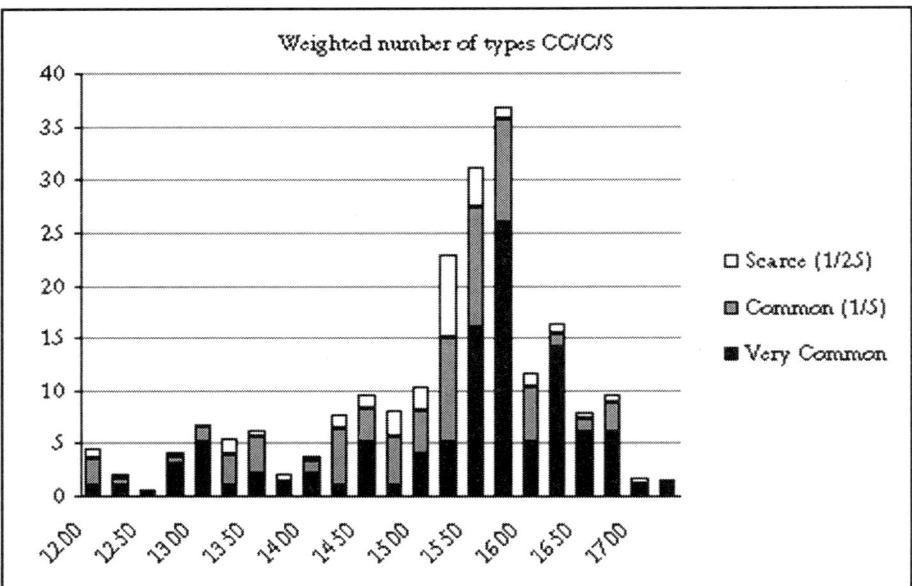

first acceleration period started with Balban on the Delhi throne (1266–87), and was continued under the Khaljis (1290–1320) and the first Tughluqs. In these years, production per mint may not have changed substantially, but rather, the number of mints was expanded from five mint towns under Iltutmish (1210–35) to twenty-one different ones under the late Khaljis and the first Tughluqs.[50]

The second acceleration period did not so much start in the Delhi Sultanate (where only during the Lodi era from 1451 onwards did coin production pick up), but in other Sultanates like those of the Bahmani Sultans of the Deccan, the Sultans of Jaunpur, of Gujarat, of Malwa and of Kashmir.

The third and most impressive production growth started under the short-lived Suri dynasty in Delhi (1538–54) and the first Mughals, to find its apogee during the long reign of Akbar (1556–1605). At the same time, some of the Sultanates (like Gujarat, for example) maintained a rather impressive production. Among the princes who had a lasting impact on coin production in India, Sher Shah Suri (1538–45) was maybe the most important one. His innovations in this field were the abolition of the coinage of billon, which he replaced by an extensive series of copper coins (mainly *dams* of *c*. 20 grams, initially called *paisas*) and silver ones (rupees of *c*. 11 grams, originally called *tankas*), as well as the establishment of nearly forty provincial mints. Twenty of these also struck copper coins.[51] One can easily see that Akbar continued and extended the system introduced by his Suri predecessor.

When we look at the regional patterns in the period of top production, 1525–1600, we see a remarkable shift from the north-west (meaning in this case especially Gujarat and Kashmir) to the central regions of the north.

The regional division also betrays the insignificant small-coin production of the north-east (predominantly Bihar and Bengal). This is probably due to the large share of the non-metallic *cowries* in that part of the subcontinent, documented extensively from the sixth up until the nineteenth century.[52] The relatively small share of the south may partially be due to under-registration because – as said before – some catalogues for southern issues still have to be processed. However, this certainly will not change the overall picture substantially.

What the figures collected so far do not yet show are two more upswing periods.[53] A fourth period is very likely to be situated in the second half of the eighteenth century, when the failing production of the shrinking Mughal state and the demise of the vestiges of the last Sultanates was more than supplemented by the proliferation of medium and small mints all over India. Perlin has very suggestively proposed this development without, however, strong quantitative arguments. According to him, this was the local and regional answer to a growing demand related to the spread of new sectors

FIGURES 3–5 *Weighted coin production numbers per region, 1525–49, 1550–74 and 1575–99*

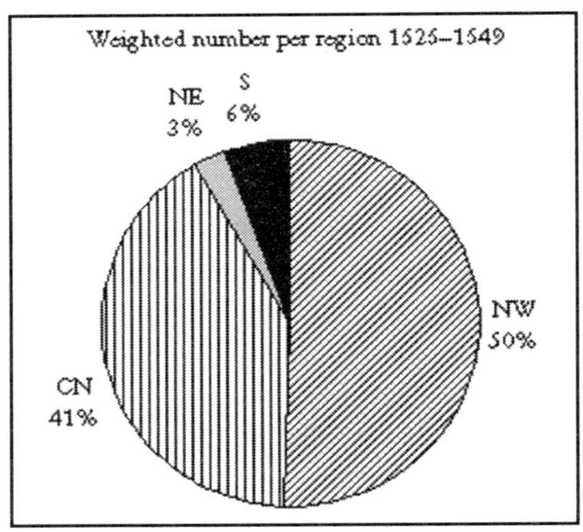

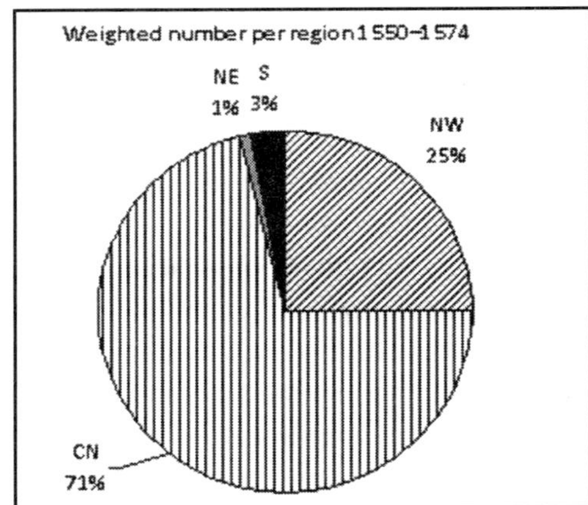

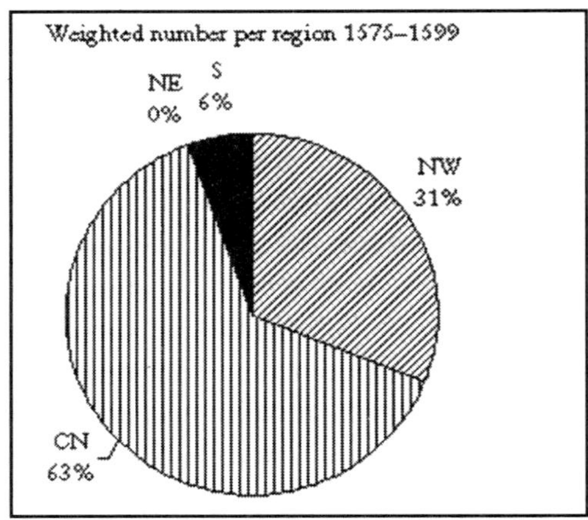

Key: S = southern India; NW = north-western India; CN = central northern India; NE = north-eastern India.

depending on wage labour (e.g., poppy and indigo production).[54] A fifth phase started, as has been already demonstrated, with the advent of mechanized production in the 1830s.

The results presented here for *deep monetization* to a considerable extent fall in sync with partial conclusions available in the literature for *monetization at large*.[55] In particular, Akbar's prolific coin production has been emphasized already for a long time.[56] The data presented here are especially more precise on the surge in the heyday of the Delhi Sultanate, and especially on the sometimes neglected importance of the Suri prelude to Akbar.

Both the dating and the dating of the lows, however, deserve much more attention. In order to describe these less spectacular periods, we first have to pay attention to the technical problem of keeping a certain circulation at the same level. Due to wear and loss in circulation, numismatists apply 'as a rule of the thumb [that] a particular coinage issue would diminish to half its original issue in twenty years, to one quarter in forty years, and to one eighth in sixty years [or] the stock of coinage in circulation suffered a diminution of two and a half per cent annually unless replenished'.[57] As my analysis rests on twenty-five-year periods, this rule implies that in order to maintain the same level of circulation, production in a particular twenty-five-year period should stay at least at 62.5 per cent of the level of the previous period (and this last level should be maintained forever, so to say).

Taking this rule into account, it is now possible to distinguish three periods of diminished coin circulation:

(i) The relatively short period from 1225/1250 until 1275
(ii) The less clearly distinguishable period from 1325/1375 until 1400/1450 (the possible lull, 1475/1500, is not convincing enough to be discussed here)
(iii) The long period from 1600 until at least 1750 (the preliminary end of my database), only interrupted by a short recovery, 1625–50.

Like before in the presentation of the upswing periods, some brief historiographical comments may be made.

The decrease around the middle of the thirteenth century has not been extensively reviewed so far in the literature, in which all attention has been drawn by the discussion on the nature of 'Indian feudalism'. The ideas of R.S. Sharma on this phenomenon have been challenged eloquently by John Deyell in his classic *Living without Silver* (1990), but far from convincingly according to Subrahmanyam and later Shrimali.[58]

The low-swing period of the late fourteenth and part of the fifteenth century has drawn the attention of several scholars, but firm conclusions are still wanting. Haider suggests a silver famine as its cause and possibly something like 'second serfdom' as its outcome.[59]

Also, the low coin circulation figures for the seventeenth and especially for the early eighteenth century have been remarked by a number of historians and numismatists, but both causes and consequences remain in the dark.[60] One of the reasons may be the attention drawn by the massive inflows of the American silver since 1590, mainly via Europe, which immediately were converted into silver rupees with a high and stable purity. So, in this case, monetization and deep monetization trends clearly diverge. This growing gap between rupee circulation and small, mainly copper coin circulation was accompanied in the first half of the seventeenth century by a weight reduction of the copper *dam* by one-third. Concomitantly prices rose and possibly, therefore, money wages as well.[61]

From Relative Overall Trends to Absolute Production Figures and Circulation Per Capita

As the title of this essay shows, I am not so much interested in monetization for its own sake – however exciting a topic which combines material and archival sources – but in its effects on society or, vice versa, as a reflection of societal change (particularly in terms of change in labour relations). Unavoidably, we then have to envisage a most difficult question: to what extent do the changing trends in deep monetization and demonetization affect the lives of 'ordinary people'? A most difficult question, because it asks for a conversion of overall national trends into trends per capita. This means that population data are needed, but precisely here lies a major problem as historians tend to disagree substantially. Besides, until the reign of Akbar no reliable demographic estimates whatsoever are available as far as I know, certainly not independently from numismatic evidence which itself often is taken as one of the indicators of economic development.

The first available written source for demographic history, the *Ain-i-Akbari*, contains many statistical or semi-statistical clues for the late sixteenth century. Interpretations of these data, however, have not so far led to unanimity among historians. Moosvi's estimate of roughly 150 million inhabitants of India certainly is the most influential, but there are serious challengers who argue for a mere 90 million.[62] As compared to the 197 million around 1800 on which there is widespread consensus, this anyhow means an increase between 1600 and 1800. If we are allowed to attribute a wider validity to population developments in Bengal (the best studied part of India in this respect), an important part of this growth must have taken place in the eighteenth century.[63] In the nineteenth century India's population increased from 197 million in 1800 to 237 million in 1850, and to 285 million in 1900.[64]

What do these most wanting demographic basics tell us about deep monetization per capita? Unfortunately there are no demographic data before the beginning of the sixteenth century because of lack of any data. However, even without population figures for 1500, we may safely conclude that the steep rise of deep monetization between 1500 and 1600 (some 200 per cent) cannot be explained by demographic growth alone, although it most likely will have taken place.[65] I suggest therefore that deep monetization per capita in the sixteenth century must have increased as well. By the same line of argument, the ensuing strong decrease of deep monetization of 1600–1750 also must have meant a decrease per capita, taking into account the net population growth between 1600 and 1800, even if we would locate it mostly in the latter part of the eighteenth century. As I have not been able to establish deep monetization levels for the period 1750–1850 (although assuming growth as argued above), it is impossible to state whether this also means increased circulation per capita, given simultaneous population growth as demonstrated for Bengal.

In August 1829, the construction of the new mint in Calcutta was completed with a capacity enough 'to supply two-thirds of the coin required for the circulation of India'.[66] The rest had to come from the mints of Bombay and Madras. Between 1831 and 1835 the Calcutta mint, although not yet powered by steam (that only happened in late 1835), threw no less than 87 million new coppers into circulation (both *pies* and half-*annas*).[67] This means more than 15 million pieces per annum on average.[68] Once fully mechanized and empowered by steam, these figures rose in the last decades of the nineteenth century, in certain years, from 100 to 200 million. Given a population rise between 1825 and 1900 of some 30 per cent, this is an impressive (ten times) increase of production, even if we allow for the fact that the Calcutta mint in the 1830s only had to cater to the Presidency with at most 15 per cent of India's population,[69] as against – as we just saw – 66 per cent afterwards. According to this very rough yardstick, deep monetization may have doubled or more[70] in the second half of the nineteenth century, which is in accordance with Ambedkar's notion as given in the introduction to this essay.

These coin production figures for India (mainly from the mints of

TABLE 7 ***Circulation of small coins per capita in India, c. 1880***

	Total circulation expressed in rupees	*Circulation per capita*	
		Expressed in rupees	*Expressed in most common denominations (either silver 2-anna pieces, or copper quarter-anna pieces)*
Small silver	92,600,000	0.366	3 (or one 2-*anna* and one quarter-rupee)
Copper	48,100,000	0.190	12
Total	140,700,000	0.556	

Source: Lucassen 2007: 367.

Calcutta, Bombay and Madras, but occasionally also from private mint houses in Birmingham) can now be linked to authoritative circulation estimates and, thanks to official censuses taken, to estimates per capita (see Table 7).

Now it is also possible to present this in concrete terms of the demand for coins to pay out wages by way of a hypothetical model (see Table 8). Nothing more, nothing less; but important, I think, to visualize possible links between labour relations and coin circulation.

This hypothetical model is based on the following assumptions: (a) that about the same time 10 per cent of the total population was remunerated in wages;[71] (b) this percentage of people were paid on an average one rupee per week; (c) these wages were paid out weekly; (d) in small coins (an equal mix of silver 2-*anna* pieces and copper quarter-*anna* pieces); and (e) that all these coins made the full circle within one month and without taking into account losses (*ut supra*). If these assumptions are acceptable and if this tenth part of the population needed half of the circulating small coins, whereas the other part of the working population which had to sell its produce in the market (much less frequently, so more likely in one, half and quarter-rupee coins) would need the other half as change and in order to pay their creditors, the results of this model would be consistent with the circulation figures given by contemporaneous financial experts.

The first virtue of the model is that the change of one parameter necessitates that of another one. For example, suppose that only three-quarters of

TABLE 8 *Hypothetical model of the demand of small coins for paying wages in India c. 1880*

Labour relations	*Per cent*	*Weekly payments of one rupee per person*	*Pieces*	*Rs*	*Monthly circulation per capita Rs*
Adults, working mainly for wages	10	Half in silver 2-*annas*	8	0.5	0.125
Adults remunerated otherwise (mainly peasants and craftsmen)	40	Half in copper 1/4-*annas*	32	0.5	0.125
Not able to work (mainly children)	50	Demand for small change to pay creditors weekly[72]			
Total population	100	Copper 1/8 and 1/12 *annas*	4	0.07	0.016
			44	1.07	
		Total demand for wage workers			0.266

the wages at the time were paid out in coins and the other quarter in kind (grain or rice), it might necessitate increase in the demand of the non-waged part of the population, the frequency of wage payments,[73] the velocity for these small coins (more than one month), etc.

It also offers a first opportunity for historical comparisons with Akbar's time.[74] Najaf Haider, basing himself on Irfan Habib, estimates the share of the primary sector in the national income (Rs 542 million rupees at 11.42 grams of fine silver) at 66 per cent, comprising 85 per cent of the population. One-quarter of these depended on wage labour. Besides, the secondary sector (11 per cent of gross national product) and the tertiary sector (23 per cent of gross national product), comprising together 15 per cent of the population, mostly consisted of independent craftsmen, but also wage dependants (he mentions building construction, mining, *karkhanas*, the military and the civil service).[75] Together, no less than one-quarter of the households may have depended for their income on wages, which – like three centuries later – represented about 10 per cent of the total population.

It is tempting but still too early, I think, to make direct comparisons between the importance of wage payments at the end of the sixteenth and the end of the nineteenth centuries on the basis of the circulation figures of Figure 2 and Table 7 (of course, taking into account different wage levels expressed in coins and different coins produced), before more is known on remuneration modalities in India during the last centuries. To this theme, the final section of this essay is devoted.

Intensity Shifts of Deep Monetization in India, 1200–1900 and Labour History: Suggestions for Discussion

In the earliest Indian texts, contemporaneous to the spread of coins in the subcontinent, wage as a means of earning one's living is mentioned. According to Manu, seven forms of acquisition of wealth are consistent with *dharma*, including employment in labour. Gautama specifies for which societal classes this applies. Whereas the Brahman receives gifts and the Kshatriya lives from conquest, the Vaishya's modes of earning income are primarily agriculture, trading, tending cattle and moneylending, but also wages. For the Shudra, only wages in exchange for the performance of service are available.[76]

If these are the basic rules of the game, with the advent of Islam a new element was introduced, as suggested by Hussain in his exemplary book on politico–economic development and monetization in medieval Bengal.[77] He points to a strong relation between increased coin circulation on the one hand, and the spread of Islam, urbanization and state formation on the other. As urbanization implies increasing specialization into non-agricultural occupations, deep monetization patterns may in the first place be influenced by occupational shifts. The second factor has to be found in changing interdependency patterns and remuneration systems, in particular in the countryside, where in the period envisaged, by far the majority of the population lived. As Hussain points out rightly, urbanization went hand in hand with Muslim state formation, both in the Sultanates and during the Suris, and under Akbar. Wicks dubs this process 'monetary imposition'.[78] From the late eighteenth century, colonialism provided the impetus for a new round of urbanization.[79]

Urbanization, state formation and the concomitant occupational urbanization (including the military) certainly may explain the surge in per capita monetization during the sixteenth century, but for the demonetization trends in the period *c.* 1600–1750 and the recovery afterwards, important explanations certainly also have to be sought for in the countryside – mostly in the agricultural sector, but we should not forget rural industries. The blossoming textile industries in south India, but also in Bengal and other regions, implied a sometimes partial shift away from agriculture.[80] In the south this went hand in glove with the rather sudden increase of the production of small *kasu* ('cash') coins in the second half of the eighteenth century.[81] The enlargement of my database with a great number of very common small south Indian cash coins, produced mainly after 1750 (although often not dated and even anonymous) by mints like Gingee, Thanjavur, Pudukottai, Madurai, Sivaganga, Tirunelveli, Trichy and Arcot, will expectedly make this clear.

Two shifts in agriculture and their social implications have to be discussed here: shifts in entitlements from reciprocity to remuneration, and, where remuneration occurs, shifts from payments in kind to payments in coins. The most simple, but also persistent model of the Indian countryside is an endless landscape of fields and villages – leaving aside the so-called 'tribal areas'. In these villages, families of craftsmen and specialists in different occupations, confined within castes, were entitled to a part of the local harvest, as were, conversely, peasants to the products of village specialists. This reciprocal type of labour relations, avoiding remuneration and payments, and in no need of markets, supposedly was the basic Indian social formation, and its entitlement system is commonly known as '*jajmani*'.[82]

A few years ago, the Japanese anthropologist Akio Tanabe came up with a more developed model, encompassing many more families within one entitlement unit and thus opening a window to monetization questions. He bases himself on the eighteenth-century Khurda in Orissa, but suggests that it has a wider validity for the principalities and kingdoms 'in the hilly tracts in east and central India', and compares it with similar formations (the '*nadu*') in south India.[84] In pre-colonial Khurda (1776–77), the basic and highly integrated social unit of entitlements was no longer the village, but rather a fortress and (ideally) twelve surrounding villages. This inter-village 'micro-regional' unit was linked to other similar units, together forming a kingdom in which also the king and the units mutually were entitled to goods and services (one of the main functions of the king was ritual sacrifice, which made it a 'sacrificial community').

Interestingly for us, the 1776–77 documents analysed at length by Tanabe demonstrate 'the introduction of new administrative technologies such as accounting in *cowrie* currency, which reinforced the trend to monetization already under way as a result of the growth of a market economy that connected the locality to wider networks of economic exchanges'.[84] Remarkably, the same documents containing a complete monetized account or value assessment of all entitlements (the value of land, goods and services), contain only very few entries of actual payments in *cowries*. The actual payment of shares to the entitlement-holders was given mostly in the form of land (86.47 per cent of the total distributed resources) or of goods and services (12.17 per cent), whereas the actual usage of *cowries* as medium of transaction accounted for only 1.35 per cent of the total distribution of the resource in the system of entitlements.[85] That is only one part of the story, however, as *cowries* were used extensively in local weekly markets – but so far there is not enough data to ascertain to what extent market exchanges were important for the overall economic activities of the villagers.[86]

The study of the extent of markets certainly may provide an indirect clue to changing labour relations, if only for the simple reason that where people bought and paid with coins, they must have earned the coins somewhere else. The emergence and demise of markets, their nature, and the availability of *shroffs* (or *sarafs*) at markets[87] for exchanging silver and copper coins and *cowries*, should all be on the agenda of labour historians. More direct information on the occurrence of wage labour in agriculture and elsewhere, and the extent to which wages were paid in cash or kind may be found in the works of early colonial observers like Francis Buchanan for Mysore and Bengal, and William Henry Sykes for the Deccan. But for the problems posed here for a much longer period, they can only be a starting point, although a very valuable one.[88]

By way of conclusion I want to go back to what is possibly the most fundamental discussion, that of the *implications of the shifts between systems of reciprocal labour and labour markets and relations*. Robert Wicks makes the following statement:

> Although the main purpose of a monetary system is to facilitate the exchange of goods and services and the discharge of fiscal and other obligations, *the presence of money does more than simply reduce transaction costs*. With the advent of money, economic relationships become abstracted and less personal, motivated by values independent of such factors as kinship ties, the status of individuals involved in the transactions, and personal obligation. With the advent of money also cash payments tend to replace

> seasonal labour obligations, further weakening traditional means of maintaining power and influence. While it could be argued that these tendencies are the cause rather than the result of the adoption of money, they nonetheless signal that critical changes are taking place within the society.[89]

On several occasions Wicks quotes Polanyi. Without doing injustice to earlier authors like Georg Simmel, it is no exaggeration to state that most other scholars in the field refer to the basic remarks on money use made by Karl Polanyi in the 1940s–60s.[90] In a strong statement which, if true, would refute the whole argument of this essay beforehand, he writes:

> Let us make our meaning more precise, No society could, naturally, live for any length of time unless it possessed an economy of some sort; but previously to our time [the twentieth century] no economy has ever existed that, even in principle, was controlled by markets. . . . Though the institution of the market was fairly common since the later Stone Age, its role was no more than incidental to economic life. . . . Division of labour, a phenomenon as old as society, springs from differences inherent in the facts of sex, geography and individual endowment; and the alleged propensity of man to barter, truck, and exchange is almost entirely apocryphal.[91]

In a more nuanced way, he explains:

> Indeed, all archaic kingdoms made use of metal currencies for the payment of taxes and salaries, but relied for the rest on payments in kind from granaries and warehouses of every description, from which they distributed the most varied goods for goods and consumption mainly to the nonproducing part of the population, that is, to the officials, the military, and the leisure class. This was the system practised in ancient China, the empire of the Incas, in the kingdoms of India, and also in Babylonia.

In these, supposedly more homogenous societies, but also in more stratified societies, what he calls 'feudal' redistribution is the key next to production for one's own use, called 'householding'.

> We find, as a rule, the processes of redistribution forming part of the prevailing political regime, whether it be that of tribe, city state, despotism or feudalism of cattle or land. The production and distribution of goods is organized in the main through collection, storage and redistribution, the pattern being focused on the chief, the temple, the despot or the lord. Since the relations of the leading group to the led are different according to the foundation on which political power rests, the principle of redistribution will involve individual motives as different as the voluntary sharing of the game by hunters and the dread of punishment which urges the fellaheen to deliver his taxes in kind.[92]

I have quoted Polanyi here at length neither because he is such an influential inspiration for scholars till today, nor to ridicule his statements made nearly seventy years ago, but to show – notwithstanding his exceptional conceptual clarity – how imprecise his historical representation is, or, more generally, how he scarcely allowed for historical developments between the Neolithic and the Industrial Revolution. For him, even the Greco–Roman world, in spite of its highly developed trade, formed no watershed. No wonder that for Polanyi, markets before the Industrial Revolution were primarily 'meeting places for long-distance trade'.[93] Even the advent of mercantilism and the putting out system did not change human relations:

> Whether the cheap machinery was owned by the worker or by the merchant made some difference in the social position of the parties and almost certainly made a difference in the earnings of the worker, who was better off as long as he owned his tools; but it did not force the merchant to become an industrial capitalist, or to restrict himself to lending his money to such persons as were.[94]

But the study of reciprocal relations need not be *a*historical, as the Khurda case has demonstrated already. This historicizing tendency can also be found in what might be called a sub-section of reciprocity studies, those dealing with gift-giving in the tradition of the French scholar Marcel Mauss, and, like Polanyi's theories, leaning heavily on ethnographic evidence.[95] Just to give one example, Gadi Algazi has analysed feudal relations in rural southern Germany at the end of the Middle Ages and indicated that what looks like reciprocal obligations of lord (protection) and serfs (maintenance of the lord) was in fact the outcome of conflict: 'Reciprocity would turn from a fundamental norm to a disputable construct located within shifting fields of power.'[96] If this is true for the pre-modern gift in Europe, it equally might apply to work and labour in India.

Reciprocity is certainly a constituting part of the history of the Indian subcontinent in the period under scrutiny (1200–1900), but that does not imply that we are faced here with immutable structures, making any attempt to write the labour history of India before colonialism uninteresting and therefore a waste of time.[97] Deep monetization patterns and especially shifts in these patterns cry for answers which take labour relations seriously into account. Apart from urbanization, state formation, militarization and the emergence of rural industries (all fascinating topics for labour historians in their own right), changing labour relations in the countryside have to be considered seriously as well.

Appendix: The Structure of the Database

To illustrate how the database is built (for the period 1200–1750 and 1830–1900, with some gaps for the south), I present here in tabulated form the results for the first quarter-century, 1200–24 (all-India).

	Copper						*Billon*	*Silver <5 grams*	*T*
	Adli L	*Adli* H	*½ Paika* L	*½ Paika* H	*Paika* L	*Paika* H	*Jital*		
Average weight in grams	0.6–0.8	0.9–1.6	1.3–1.7	1.8–2.5	2.7–3.6	3.8–4.5	3.0–3.6		
Types cc							1		1 (1*)
Types c						1	12		13 (3*)
Types s			3	1	2		16		22 (1*)
Types r	1	2	4	2	7	1	4		21 (0*)
Types rr							2	1	3 (0*)
Types rrr	1						1	1	2 (0*)
Types rrrr									0
Total number of types	2	2	7	3	9	2	36	2	63 (5*)

Notes: H = heavy, L = light
*Weighted numbers (without decimals), see Figure 2 above.
Source: Goron and Goenka 2001.

Acknowledgements: An earlier version of this paper was presented on 15 February 2012 at the Workshop 'Money as Social Circuit: Anonymous Currency and Named Credit', organized by Akinobu Kuroda at the Institute of Advanced Studies on Asia, University of Tokyo. I thank the participants for their valuable comments.

Notes

1 B.R. Ambedkar, *History of Indian Currency and Banking*, Bombay: Thacker and Company, 1947: 27, as quoted in Garg (2008): 203–04. Cf., e.g., Subrahmanyam (1994a): 2, 8, for a different view.

2 For important works of these historians see the Bibliography. I refrain here from mentioning specialized numismatic publications.

3 Perlin (1987): 343–44; Perlin (1993): 238–39. Cf. Moosvi (1987a): 88 where, not without humour, she characterizes her own attempt as one 'that I once bravely undertook'; for a critique of Moosvi, see Subrahmanyam (1994b): 213, 218.

4 Shrimali (2002).

5 Bhandare (2008): 37; Garg (2008): 206–08, reacting to Perlin (1983): 27, 31.

6 Haider (2007): 300–02.

7 It may be superfluous to say that this has no implications as such for the development of national income or of real wages; cf. Scheidel (2010).

8 Subrahmanyam (1994a): 41, 43 (quotation), 56. This is not to deny at all the importance of numismatics, as is shown, for example, by the widespread use made by historians of Singhal (1953).

9 Cf. Wicks (1992): 6, borrowing from Joe Cribb: 'money is a convention established

in relation to payments which dictates that particular objects with agreed measures of value are recognized as the regular means of discharging the obligation to pay', which implies pre-existing socially determined 'forms of transactions'.

[10] The following after Lucassen (2007a).

[11] Recently a good example has been provided for Bengal. See Dyell (2010): 83–86.

[12] Bhandare (2008): 37 (without reference); Verboven (2009): 91–93, 105, 119; Wicks (1992): 16. From private correspondence, I learnt that Verboven 'invented' the term for a paper delivered in June 2008, independently from Bhandare. Bhandare was inspired by Perlin's work more in general, not by a specific passage. When using the term for the first time in 2008, both authors were not aware of each other. So far, I do not know of its usage before 2008.

[13] Lucassen (2007a). Cf. Wicks (1992); Verboven (2009); Scheidel (2011).

[14] Garg (2008): 106, quoting the Assay Master of Patna Mint, 17 February 1795.

[15] Parthasarathi (2011). See also Ellis (2005).

[16] Deyell (1987b); Deyell (1990); Deyell (2010); Perlin (1993): 240–41 for critical remarks; Wicks (1992): 15–16.

[17] Deyell (1987b). For coin types for which enough specimens are available for research, die-count analysis is also an option; see Deyell (2010).

[18] Hasan (1969). For a critique, see Subrahmanyam (1994b): 204 and Deyell (1976).

[19] Deyell (1987b): 162: 'Alternatively the mint years figure may be calculated by adding together the mints issuing copper coins in each year of the reign, as listed in the seven museum catalogues above, discarding duplication between catalogues. The former [the method he actually applies, discussed in my text] is a good approximation of the latter, and less tedious to perform, so I use it here. The results from both methods should be similar, certainly as to the trend; but the latter method will give more accuracy.'

[20] Ibid.: 'which figure is not necessarily congruent with the number of regnal years in a reign: for example, during periods of expansion of the Mughal frontier during the reigns of Akbar and Aurangzeb, the southern mint towns were often occupied for only a fraction of the whole reign, and they reduce the total years of mint possession for those reigns, commensurately'.

[21] Habib (1987).

[22] Deyell (1994): 113, 135; Deyell (2010): 67.

[23] The following after Garg (2007): 354–56. Also see Deyell (2010). Already before the introduction of steam engines, several mechanical improvements had been introduced, which cannot be discussed here in detail. See Stevens (2008a) for Bombay, 1818–22.

[24] Haider (2002): 60; Prakash (2007): 348; Lingen and Lucassen (2007); Shimada (2006).

[25] See Lingen and Lucassen (2007).

[26] Consequently, a successful extension of this approach to earlier centuries would rather have to use hundred-year periods.

[27] Deyell (1990): 13.

[28] Deyell (1976) himself has shown what the impact can be of neglecting different typology systems for historical analysis, in discussing Hasan (1969).

[29] Lucassen (2007b). It also has the additional advantage that problems of re-striking of coins related to spatial differential price levels of precious metals, as sometimes occurred with silver rupees (and so not primarily emerging from demand for circulation purposes), practically can be ruled out – as can Gresham's law.

[30] For earlier attempts to apply this method to specific coin types, see Lingen and Lucassen (2007) and (2012).

[31] Goron and Goenka (2001); Rahman (2005) – he does not distinguish between 'cc' and 'c'; Liddle (2005) – he does not distinguish between 'c' and 'cc'. In this case I

have attributed 'cc' to all types with four or more different issuing years. Valentine (1914) – only 6 *falus* of Humayun, all valuated by me as 'cc'. These are compared to prices in Bruce (2008), and Krause and Mishler (2002). For the period 1600–24, this is possible for 72 rarity valuations out of 125 types in total; for 1625–49, for 32 out of 103 types in total; for 1650–74 for only 4 out of 45; and for 1675–99 for only 5 out of 78 in total.

[32] Differentiation according to fourteen weight-classes and even to metals (copper and silver) has yielded no significant results. That is why one conversion table suffices. For the analysis, I will concentrate on the coins within the 'cc'/'c'/'s' brackets.

[33] This has been done rather arbitrarily on the basis of impressions from section 3 of this essay, 'Historical Framing of the Numismatic Listings'. As an experiment different weights have been tried out, but they do not influence the overall trends.

[34] See Goron and Goenka (2001) and Bruce (2008) for the seventeenth century; Krause/Mishler (2002) for the eighteenth century; and Bruce (2004) for the nineteenth century.

[35] Rahman (2005) for Babur, and Liddle (2005) for Akbar, partially overlapping with Bruce (2008). For now I have only been able to use Valentine (1914) for Humayun (1530–40) .

[36] The two excellent catalogues for south India by Michael Mitchiner, published in 1998, use a different typology system from the others consulted by me, and therefore I still have to adapt Mitchiner's system to make it compatible with the rest of my database. I expect that especially the coppers of the later Pallavas (thirteenth century), the later Pandyas (fourteenth century) and of late Vijayanagar may have an impact on my data for the south, but not overall.

[37] For example, the (very ill-dated) medieval Kangra *jitals*.

[38] For example, Lingen and Lucassen (2007) and (2012).

[39] For example, Perlin (1993): 270–72; Deyell (2010); Jan Hogendorn and Marion Johnson, *The Shell Money and the Slave Trade* (Cambridge, 1986).

[40] Wicks (1992): 16. See also Lingen and Lucassen (2007); Lingen and Lucassen (2012); Lucassen (2007b). Also, the admirable series of articles by Paul Stevens.

[41] Deyell (1990): 221, 225, 253–63. Deyell writes: 'sums in the tens of millions and hundreds of millions silver tankas' (ibid.: 221), thereby suggesting that the foot soldiers received other types of coins than the cavalrymen. Also the remarkable difference in remuneration of horse and foot soldiers (500 vs. 234, where exactly the opposite relation might be expected) suggests that different coin types were involved. On the basis of Goron and Goenka (2001): 38–39, I think that the foot soldiers were paid out in billon 'six *gani*' coins against the horse soldiers in silver *tankas*. The latter coins of this reign, struck by the mint of Delhi during all years AH 695–715 are classified as 'very common' and 'common' for the mints of Dar-al-Islam and Deogir. As 1 silver *tanka* equalled the value of 60 billon coins of 6 *gani*, the salary of a horseman would be twenty-eight times as high as that of a foot-soldier. This seems a big difference, but given the maintenance of the horse and grooms, this is not impossible.

[42] Deyell (1990): 262, fn. 11. In 1389 / AH 718: 'at the present time the current coins are those of King Alauddin'.

[43] Rahman (2005): 29–33, quoting H.N. Wright, *The Sultans of Delhi, Their Coinage and Metallurgy* (Delhi, 1936): 257–62, and Edward Thomas, *The Chronicles of the Pathan Kings of Delhi* (Delhi, 1871), who states 20 *Sikandaris* per rupee and 8 *Sikandaris* per *shahruki*.

[44] Deyell (2010); 97–98.

[45] Blake (1987): 133. For a discussion, see Datta (2000), and Ellis (2005): 19 (net tax receipts or *jama* reached at best two-thirds of the sums imposed).

[46] In a more elaborate working paper in progress, I have given more details. The references are included in the Bibliography of this essay.
[47] For mechanization in Benares, see Garg (2008): 127.
[48] This conclusion will be reinforced probably by including Vijayanagar in the database in the future.
[49] This conclusion will be certainly reinforced by including Humayun more completely in the database in the future.
[50] Goron and Goenka (2001): 12–13.
[51] Ibid.: 89–92; Deyell (1987a); Singhal (1953).
[52] Deyell (2010): 73–75.
[53] But which are confirmed by my preliminary results for his period; preliminary because of the very proliferation of often smaller mints. The period 1750–1850 provides some data collection problems which I have not yet fully overcome. I hope to finish this final stage in the near future.
[54] Perlin (1987); Perlin, (1994b). For an overview of the discussion regarding the 'revisionists', see Subrahmanyam (1994a). For later arguments, see Datta (2000); Robb (2007): 124–50; Mukherjee (2011).
[55] Haider (2007): 300–02.
[56] See, e.g., Richards (ed.) (1987); Subrahmanyam (1994a): 52; Subrahmanyam (1994b); Haider (2002): 60; Haider (2007): esp. 200 and 302 ff.
[57] Deyell (2010): 97.
[58] Deyell (1990); Subrahmanyam (1994a): 11–19; Shrimali (2002); Haider (2007): 314.
[59] Haider (2002); Haider (2007): 301.
[60] See Subrahmanyam (1994a).
[61] Haider (2007): 310–11; Prakash (2007): 341–43.
[62] Moosvi (1987b): 399–405; Thapar (2002): 54. For much lower estimates, see Ellis (2005): 19–20, basing himself on Ashok V. Desay and Sanjay Subrahmanyam.
[63] Among others, Datta (2000). This is a well-documented revision of Dyson (1989): 9, based on Visaria and Visaria 1984, who state that between 1760 and 1820 growth was zero, possibly negative.
[64] Morris (1974); Dyson (1989).
[65] Remember that population growth in the nineteenth century was about 40 per cent and that only in the twentieth century it surpassed the 200 per cent threshold.
[66] Garg (2008): 262.
[67] Ibid.: 196. Cf. Perlin (1993): 253–54 (after Pinsep, *Useful Tables* 38: 308,000 coins per seven-hour day); Bruce (2004): 723. As the total value in 1831–35 was Rs 1,238,508, we may suppose that the far majority of this production must have consisted of half-*annas*. Catalogue prices show how extremely common these coins are – as we might have expected.
[68] Cf. Garg (2008): 197. In 1835 the Calcutta mint master tried to assess the implications of plans to replace all circulating copper coins, in particular *trisulpaisas*, by completely new and now fully mechanically manufactured new coin types. This operation would entail a loss of Rs 571,340. Because the loss for defacing Rs 10,000 worth of old and depreciated coins received at the rate of 64 pice per rupee was estimated at over Rs 6,277, we may estimate the total circulation at that moment at 58 million pieces. For silver I have not found circulation data for the first quarter of the century, but for gold it is estimated at Rs 24.5 million in 1796 (ibid.: 208), or over one rupee per inhabitant of Bengal – a figure which is not too meaningful as the big majority of the Bengalis would never touch a gold coin in their whole lifetime. For coin circulation in Bengal in *c.* 1800, also see Gupta (1984): 240–45; Robb (2007): 129.

[69] Mukherjee (2011): 165.

[70] Velocity not only increased by more coins available, but from the late nineteenth century also with the advent of the railways. See Gupta (1984): 244–45. I suppose that the impact on the 1880 reconstruction (Table 7) still was limited enough not to disturb directly comparisons with previous periods.

[71] Roy, in IISH-Collab Global Labour Relations.

[72] In the period 1880–84, 29.8 million copper 1/12 *anna* pieces were coined and 205 million 1/4 *annas*, or about seven times more (no 1/8 *anna* pieces were coined in those years).

[73] Cf. Prakash (2007): 325. The frequency of wage payments (daily, weekly, monthly) co-determines the size/value of the smaller coins in demand for this purpose (only). As wage workers enjoyed not much credit, most of them needed to be paid weekly or even daily. See Lingen and Lucassen (2007 and 2012).

[74] In this essay I will abstain from a comparison with the situation in 1918, as offered by Prakash (2007); 344. For an interesting reconstruction of labour relations in Mysore in *c.* 1800, see Sivaramkrishna (2009): 721.

[75] Haider (2007): 293–94, 315; cf. Ellis (2005). Haider does not take into account slaves separately. On the other hand, they too could be remunerated in cash. See Fukuzawa (1991): 116–30.

[76] Derrett (1957): esp. 69–70, 76, 87, 90–92. Cf. Lucassen (2007a).

[77] Hussain (2003); cf. Deyell (2010).

[78] Wicks (1992): 10 (and chapter 3).

[79] There is much need of a good and encompassing overview of urbanization figures for India before 1850/1900. Those in world overviews (like Chandler and Fox, *Urbanization, 800–1800*) and even in overviews of India (Habib 1982: 166 and Visaria and Visaria 1984: 466) certainly are not sufficient and should be supplemented with more recent ones. For Bengal, see Mukherjee (2011): 166.

[80] Parthasarathi (2001 and 2011); Riello and Roy (2009).

[81] Primarily based on the listings in Mitchiner (1998): 196–245, combined with Krause and Mishler (2002); as far as these coins can be dated earlier, they might raise my results for the pre-1750 years. Textile workers in Bengal will have been paid mostly in *cowries* until late in the eighteenth century.

[82] The literature on this topic is endless. For a classic presentation see Neale (1957), referring to Henry Sumner Maine's *Ancient Law* (1906), but for a comprehensive discussion see Tanabe (2005).

[83] Ibid.: 250–51.

[84] Ibid.: 357.

[85] Ibid.: 366 (Table 1).

[86] Personal communication from Akio Tanabe, whom I would like to thank here cordially.

[87] I am actually collecting information on taxes paid by the *shroffs* (*sarrafs*) in the major markets of Bengal for their exclusive right to exchange copper coins (the '*pycemahal*'), which might provide some more information. See also Mukherjee (2011).

[88] Sivaramkrishna (2009); Sykes (1838; original reports 1826 and 1829). Also see Mayer (2006). For the interpretation of such sources fundamental considerations are to be found in Verboven (2009).

[89] Wicks (1992): 7 (my emphasis). These critical changes also may involve monetary debt and credit relations and consequently power relations. Debt bondage is a case in point in Indian labour history. Cf. also Verboven (2009): 112, 116–18; Graeber (2011) provides a gloomy picture of debt relations.

[90] Poggi (1993), based on Georg Simmel, *Philosophie des Geldes* (1922); Polanyi

(1944): esp. chapters 4 to 6; Polanyi, Arensberg and Pearson (1957); Neale (1957); Dalton (1971).

[91] Polanyi (1944): 43–44. He blames the 'fallacy' of attributing too much value to markets first to Adam Smith, followed by many others. His main authorities are Richard Thurnwald and Bronislaw Malinowski (cf. Wagner-Hasel 2003: 148–49), but also Firth and Weber.

[92] Polanyi (1944): 51–52 (mainly after Thurnwald).

[93] Ibid.: 59, after Max Weber.

[94] Ibid.: 74.

[95] Algazi, Groebner and Jussen (2003) – gifts have to be distinguished from other forms of interaction like market exchange, compulsory tribute and barter); cf. also see Wicks (1992): 14.

[96] Algazi, in Algazi, Groebner and Jussen (eds.) (2003): 127.

[97] Also see Washbrook (2010).

Bibliography

Algazi, Gadi, Valentin Groebner and Bernhard Jussen (eds.) (2003), *Negotiating the Gift: Pre-Modern Figurations of Exchange*, Göttingen: Vandenhoeck and Ruprecht.

Allen, Robert C. (2009), *The British Industrial Revolution in Global Perspective,* Cambridge: Cambridge University Press.

Allen, Robert C., Jean Paul Bassino, Debin Ma, Christine Moll-Murata and Jan Luiten van Zanden, 'Wages, Prices, and Living Standards in China, 1738–1925: In Comparison with Europe, Japan, and India', Working Paper 316, Department of Economics, Oxford University, Oxford.

Bagchi, Amiya Kumar (ed.) (2002), *Money and Credit in Indian History: From Early Medieval Times* New Delhi: Tulika Books.

——— (2002), 'Introduction: Money, Banking and Finance in India since Early Medieval Times', in Bagchi (ed.), *Money and Credit in Indian History*: ix–xli.

Bayly, Chris (1988), *Rulers and Townsmen and Bazaars: North Indian Society in the Age of British Expansion, 1770–1870*, Cambridge: Cambridge University Press.

Bhandare, Shailendra (2008), 'Jamgaon, Harda and Khachrod: Three New Mints under Sindhias of Gwalior', *Journal of the Oriental Numismatic Society,* 197: 32–37.

Blake, Stephen (1987), 'The Structure of Monetary Exchange in India', in Richards (ed.), *The Imperial Monetary System of Mughal India.*

Bruce, Colin R. (ed.) (2004), *Standard Catalogue of World Coins 1801–1900,* Iola, Wi: KP Books.

——— (2008), *Standard Catalogue of World Coins 1601–1700*, Iola, Wi: KP Books.

Dalton, George (ed.) (1971), *Primitive, Archaic and Modern Economies: Essays of Karl Polanyi,* Boston: Beacon Press.

Datta, Rajat (2000), *Society, Economy and the Market. Commercialization in Rural Bengal, c. 1760–1800*, New Delhi: Manohar.

Derrett, J. Duncan M. (1957), 'The Right to Earn in Ancient India: A Conflict between Expediency and Authority', *Journal of the Economic and Social History of the Orient*, 1, Part 1: 66–97.

Deyell, John S. (1976), 'Numismatic Methodology in the Estimation of Mughal Currency Output', *Indian Economic and Social History Review,* Vol. 13, No. 3: 393–401.

——— (1987a), 'The Development of Akbar's Currency System and Monetary Integration of the Conquered Kingdoms', in Richards (ed.), *The Imperial Monetary System of Mughal India*: 13–67.

——— (1987b), 'Long Term Production Trends for Copper Coins in the Mughal Empire', in Richards (ed.), *The Imperial Monetary System of Mughal India*: 160–64.

——— (1990), *Living without Silver: The Monetary History of Early Medieval North India* New Delhi: Oxford University Press.

——— (1994), 'The China Connection: Problems of Silver Supply in Medieval Bengal', in Subrahmanyam (ed.), *Money and the Market in India 1100–1700*: 186–218.

——— (2010), 'Cowries and Coins: The Dual Monetary System of the Bengal Sultanate', *Indian Economic and Social History Review*, Vol. 47, No. 1: 63–106.

Digby, Simon (1982), 'The Currency System', in Tapan Raychaudhari and Irfan Habib (eds.), *The Cambridge Economic History of India, c. 1200 – c. 1970*, Vol. I, New Delhi: Orient Longman.

Dyson, Tim (ed.) (1989), *India's Historical Demography*, London: Curzon Press.

Ellis, Frank W. (2005), 'In What Way, and to What *Degree*, Did the Mughal State Inhibit Smithian Growth In India in the Seventeenth Century?', London School of Economics Working Paper No. 14/05, May.

Fukuzawa, Hiroshi (1991), *The Medieval Deccan: Peasants, Social Systems and States, Sixteenth to Eighteenth Centuries*, New Delhi: Oxford University Press.

Garg, Sanjay (2007), 'Dies and Minting Scenes from India', in Lucia Travaini and Alessia Bolis (eds.), *Conii e scene di coniazione*, Rome: Quasar: 353–70.

——— (2008), 'History of the Currency Legislations of the East India Company, 1772–1835', unpublished Ph.D. thesis, Jawaharlal Nehrau University, New Delhi.

Goron, Stan and J.P. Goenka (2001), *The Coins of the Indian Sultanates, Covering the Area of Present–Day India, Pakistan and Bangladesh*, New Delhi: Munshiram Manoharlal.

Gaeber, David (2011), *Debt: The First 5,000 Years*, New York: Melville House.

Grover, B.R. (1994), 'An Integrated Pattern of Commercial life in the Rural Society of North India during the Seventeenth and Eighteenth Centuries', in Subrahmanyam (ed.), *Money and the Market in India 1100–1700*: 219–55.

Gupta, Ranjan Kumar (1984), *The Economic Life of a Bengal District: Birbhum 1770–1857*, Burdwan: University of Burdwan.

Habib, Irfan (1982), 'Population', in Tapan Raychaudhari and Irfan Habib (eds.), *The Cambridge Economic History of India, c. 1200 – c. 1970*, Vol. I, New Delhi: Orient Longman: 163–71.

——— (1994), 'The Price Regulations of 'Ala'uddinKhalji: A Defence of Zia' Barani', in Subrahmanyam (ed.), *Money and the Market in India 1100–1700*: 85–111.

Haider, Najaf (1996), 'Precious Metal Flows and Currency Circulation in the Mughal Empire', *Journal of Economic and Social History of the Orient*, 39: 298–364.

——— (2002), 'The Monetary Basis of Credit and Banking Instruments in the Mughal Empire', in Bagchi (ed.), *Money and Credit in Indian History*: 58–83.

——— (2007), 'Structure and Movement of Wages in the Mughal Empire', in Lucassen (ed.), *Wages and Currency*: 293–321.

Hall, Kenneth R. (1994), 'Price–Making and Market Hierarchy in Early Medieval South India', in Subrahmanyam (ed.), *Money and the Market in India 1100–1700*: 57–84.

Hasan, Aziza (1994), 'The Silver Output of the Mughal Empire and Prices in India during the Sixteenth and Seventeenth Centuries', in Subrahmanyam (ed.), *Money and the Market in India 1100–1700*: 156–218.

Hussain, Syed Ejaz (2003), *The Bengal Sultanate: Politics, Economy and Coins (AD 1205–1576)*, New Delhi: Manohar.

Krause, Chester L. and Clifford Mishler (2002), *Standard Catalogue of World Coins 1701–1800*, Iola, Wi: KP Books.

Liddle, Andrew (2005), *Coinage of Akbar: The Connoisseur's Choice*, Gurgaon: Kapoori Devi Charitable Trust.

Lingen, Jan and Jan Lucassen (2007), 'The "Mansuri" or "Munsooree paisa" and Its Use: Combining Numismatic and Social History of India, *c.* 1830–1900', *Numisatic Digest*, Vol. 31: 187–220.

Lingen, Jan and Jan Lucassen (2012), 'Copper Circulation in Northern India in 1830', *Numisatic Digest*, Vol. 34–35: 148–83.

Lucassen, Jan (2007a), 'Introduction: Wages and Currency, 500 BCE – 2000 CE', in Lucassen (ed.), *Wages and Currency*: 9–58.
Lucassen, Jan (2007b), 'The Logistics of Wage Payments: Changing Patterns in Northern India in the 1840s', in Lucassen (ed.), *Wages and Currency*: 349–90.
Lucassen, Jan (ed.) (2007), *Wages and Currency: Global Comparisons from Antiquity to the Twentieth Century*, Bern: Peter Lang.
Mayer, Peter (2006), 'Trends of Real Income in Tiruchirapalli and the Upper Kaveri Delta, 1819–1980: A footnote in honour of Dharma Kumar', *Indian Economic and Social History Review*, Vol. 43, No. 3: 349–64.
Mitchiner, Michael (1998a), *The Coinage and History of Southern India. Part One: Karnataka–Andhra*, London: Hawkins.
——— (1998b), *The Coinage and History of Southern India. Part Two: Tamil Nadu and Kerala*, London: Hawkins.
Moosvi, Shireen (1987a), 'The Silver Influx, Money Supply, Prices and Revenue Extraction in Mughal India', *Journal of the Economic and Social History of the Orient*, Vol. 20: 47–94.
——— (1987b), *The Economy of the Mughal Empire c. 1595: A Statistical Study*, New Delhi: Oxford University Press.
Morris, Morris David (1974), 'The Population of All–India, 1800–1851', *Indian Economic and Social History Review*, Vol. 11, Nos. 2–3: 309–13.
Mukherjee, Tilottama (2011), 'Markets in Eighteenth-Century Bengal Economy', *Indian Economic and Social History Review*, Vol. 48, No. 2: 143–76.
Neale, Walter C. (1957a), 'Reciprocity and Redistribution in the Indian Village: Sequel to Some Notable Discussions', in Polanyi, Arensberg and Pearson (eds.), *Trade and Market in the Early Empires: Economies in History and Theory*: 218–36.
——— (1957b), 'The Market in Theory and History', in Polanyi, Arensberg and Pearson (eds.), *Trade and Market in the Early Empires: Economies in History and Theory*: 357–72.
Perlin, Frank (1987), 'Money-use in Late Pre-Colonial India and the International Trade in Currency Media', in Richards (ed.), *The Imperial Monetary System of Mughal India*: 232–373.
——— (1993), *'The Invisible City': Monetary , Administrative and Popular Infrastructures in Asia and Europe, 1500–1900*, Aldershot: Ashgate.
——— (1994a), *Unbroken Landscape: Commodity, Category, Sign and Identity, Their Production as Myth and Knowledge from 1500*, Aldershot: Variorum.
——— (1994b), 'Changes in Production and Circulation of Money in Seventeenth and Eighteenth Century India: An Essay on Monetization Before Colonial Occupation', in Subrahmanyam (ed.), *Money and the Market in India 1100–1700*: 276–308.
Poggi, Gianfranco (1993), *Money and the Modern Mind: Georg Simmel'sPhilosopy of Money*, Berkeley: University of California Press.
Polanyi, Karl (1944), *The Great Transformation*, New York and Toronto: Farrar and Rinehart.
Polanyi, Karl, Conrad M. Arensberg and Harry W. Pearson (eds.) (1957), *Trade and Market in the Early Empires: Economies in History and Theory*, Glencoe Ill.: The Free Press.
Parthasarathi, Prasannan (2001), *The Transition to a Colonial Economy: Weavers, Merchants and Kings in South India, 1720–1800*, Cambridge: Cambridge University Press.
——— (2011), *Why Europe Grew Rich and Asia Did Not: Global Economic Divergence, 1600–1850*, Cambridge: Cambridge University Press.
Prakash, Om (1976), 'Bullion for Goods: International Trade and the Economy of Early Eighteenth Century Bengal', *Indian Economic and Social History Review*, Vol. 13, No. 2: 159–87.
Prakash, Om (2007), 'Long Distance Trade, Coinage and Wages in India, 1600–1960', in Lucassen (ed.), *Wages and Currency*: 323–48.
Rahman, Amanur (2005), *Zahir–uddin Muhammad Babur: A Numismatic Study*, Karachi: Amanur Rahman.

Richards, John F. (1994), The Economic History of the Lodi Period', in Subrahmanyam (ed.), *Money and the Market in India 1100–1700*: 137–55.

Richards, John F. (ed.) (1987), *The Imperial Monetary System of Mughal India*, New Delhi: Oxford University Press.

Riello, Georgio and Prasannan Parthasarathi (eds.) (2009), *How India Clothed the World of South Asian Textiles, 1500–1850*, Leiden and Boston: Brill.

Robb, Peter (2007), *Empire, Identity and India: Peasants, Political Economy and Law*, New Delhi: Oxford University Press.

Scheidel, Walter (2010), 'Real Wages in Early Economies: Evidence for Living Standards from 1800 BCE to 1300 CE', *Journal of the Economic and Social History of the Orient*, Vol. 53: 425–62.

Shrimali, Krishna Mohan (2002), 'Money, Market and Indian Feudalism: AD 600–1200', in Bagchi (ed.), *Money and Credit in Indian History*: 1–39.

Shimada, Ryuto (2006), *The Intra-Asian Trade in Japanese Copper by the Dutch East India Company during the Eighteenth Century*, Leiden and Boston: Brill.

Singh, M.P. (1985), *Town, Market, Mint and Port in the Mughal Empire 1556–1707: An Administrative–cum–Economic Study*, New Delhi: Adam.

Singhal, C.R. (1953), *Mint–Towns of the Mughal Emperors of India*, Bombay: Numismatic Society of India.

Sivaramkrishna, Sashi (2009), 'Ascertaining Living Standards in Erstwhile Mysore, Southern India, from Francis Buchanan's *Journey* of 1800–01: An Empirical Contribution to the Great Divergence Debate', *Journal of Economic and Social History of the Orient*, Vol. 52: 695–733.

Stevens, Paul (2004a), 'The Coins of the Bombay Presidency: The Bankot Mint', *Oriental Numismatic Society Newsletter*, 179: 28–32.

——— (2004b), 'The Coins of the Bombay Presidency: The Transitional Mints of the Deccan', *Oriental Numismatic Society Newsletter*, 181: 24–30.

——— (2005), 'The Coins of the Bombay Presidency: The Mints of the Northern Districts', *Oriental Numismatic Society Newsletter*, 182: 25–32.

——— (2006), 'The Coins of the Ceded and Conquered Provinces of the Bengal Presidency', *Journal of the Oriental Numismatic Society*, 188: 18–23.

——— (2007), 'The Coins of the Ceded and Conquered Provinces of the Bengal Presidency – The Farrukhabad mint', *Journal of the Oriental Numismatic Society*, 190: 37–43.

——— (2008a), 'Dr Stewart's Copper Patterns for Bombay 1820–1821', *Journal of the Oriental Numismatic Society*, 195: 31–35.

——— (2008b), 'The Early Years of the Calcutta Mint, 1757 to 1765', *Journal of the Oriental Numismatic Society*, 197: 37–47.

——— (2009), 'The Coins of the Ceded and Conquered Provinces of the Bengal Presidency – Saugor (later Sagar) and Related Mints', *Journal of the Oriental Numismatic Society* 199: 29–36.

Subrahmanyam, Sanjay (1994b), 'Precious Metal Flows and Prices in Western and Southern Asia, 1500–1750: Some Comparative and Conjunctural Aspects', in Subrahmanyam (ed.), *Money and the Market in India 1100–1700*: 186–218.

Subrahmanyam, Sanjay (1994a), 'Introduction', in Subrahmanyam (ed.), *Money and the Market in India 1100–1700*: 1–56.

Subrahmanyam, Sanjay (ed.) (1994), *Money and the Market in India 1100–1700*, New Delhi: Oxford University Press.

Sykes, William Henry (1838), 'Special Report on the Statistics of the Four Collectorates of the Dukhun, under the British Government', in *Report of the Seventh Meeting of the British Association for the Advancement of Science; Held at Liverpool in September 1837*, Vol. 6, London: Murray: 217–336.

Tanabe, Akio (2005), 'The System of Entitlements in Eighteenth-Century Khurda, Orissa:

Reconsidering "Caste" and "Community" in Late Pre-Colonial India', *South Asia: Journal of South Asian Studies*, N.S. 28, No. 3: 345–85.

Thapar, Romila (2002), *The Penguin History of Early India: From the Origins to AD 1300*, London: Penguin.

Valentine, W.H. ([1914] 1971), *The Copper Coins of India*, London: Spink.

Visaria, L. and P. Visaria (1984), 'Population (1757–1947)', in *The Cambridge Economic History of India, c. 1757 – c. 1970*, Volume 2, *Cambridge:* Cambridge University Press: 463–532.

Verboven, Koenraad (2009), 'Currency, billion and accounts: Monetary Modes in the Roman world', *Revue Belge de Numismatique et de Sigillographie*, 140: 91–124.

Wagner–Hasel, Beate (2003), 'Egoistic Exchange and Altruistic Gift', in Algazi, Groebner and Jussen (eds.), *Negotiating the Gift*: 141–71.

Washbrook, David (2010), 'Merchants, Markets and Commerce in Early Modern South India', *Journal of the Economic and Social History of the Orient*, 53: 266–89.

Wicks, Robert S. (1992), *Money, Markets, and Trade in Early Southeast Asia: The Development of Indigenous Monetary Systems to AD* 1400, Ithaca, NY: Cornell University.

Ottoman Working People as Reflected in Ottoman Official Sources

Suraiya Faroqhi

The Ottoman Empire was a bureaucratic polity, and its officials have produced an enormous number of records.[1] Fortunately many of these documents survive in the archives of the central administration in Istanbul or else in those maintained by Islamic judges (*qadis*) over the length and breadth of the empire. Originally these latter records were kept in the places where the judges had once officiated, and today they are usually to be found in the national archives of the countries now established on the former Ottoman territories.[2] After 1840 or thereabouts, the reports of French, English and other consuls are often a useful complement, at least where the condition of artisan industries is concerned. But for our purposes these 'outsider' records are not very helpful, as we will focus here on the early modern period which, according to a convention widely accepted among Ottomanist historians, ends at the same time, namely in the 1840s.

But in spite of the riches available in the Ottoman archives, and which, due to an intensive effort in cataloguing and document-publishing, increases almost every month, I still think – and presumably by the end of this essay, my readers will agree – that when it comes to working people, the limits of our information are painfully obvious.

Peasants in Fifteenth- and Sixteenth-Century Tax Registers

I begin with the countryside, where of course the vast majority of the population lived and worked. Already, in the fifteenth century, the administration began to produce registers in which officials intended to record all tax-payers (*tahrîr* or *tapu-tahrîr*); and in some cases the non-tax-paying servitors of the Sultan were partially included as well. This practice continued into the last quarter of the sixteenth century; the ideal – though not always the reality – was to repeat these counts every thirty years. Enumerators went from one village to the next, and grouped their results by district (*kaza*), sub-province and province (*sancak*, *eyalet*). In addition to the names and patronyms of the tax-payers, the list at the end of every village contained an array of mostly agricultural taxes, partly to be paid in kind and partly in money. Agricultural taxes consisted mostly of tithes, but usually the peasants paid more than one-tenth, up to one-fifth if they were unlucky.[3]

Through this practice the accounting bureaus (*defterhane*, headed by the *defterdar*) intended to keep track of people and revenues usable as military tax-grants (*timar, zeamet*); to the latter were assigned monetary values, and without such records it would have been impossible to know which revenues could be included, for instance, in a grant amounting to 3,000 or 5,000 silver coins (*akçe*).[4] This arrangement also shows that the Ottoman system of military tax-grants, from its very beginning, was firmly predicated upon the circulation of money even in remote corners of the countryside; it could not have worked in a 'natural economy'.

If records survive for the entire period during which *tahrîr*s were compiled, they show population growth/decline. Thus these registers allow historians to document that the increase which occurred in the western Mediterranean world during the sixteenth century came to pass in the latter's eastern section as well. Throughout the region, the losses of the Black Death and its aftermath were thus compensated.

When scholars first began to study *tahrîr* registers, they were quite enthusiastic – and in our present-day perspective, excessively enthusiastic – about the value of the registers as sources for questions posed by twentieth-century historians.[5] For a while, Ottomanists liked to think that they were dealing with the 'census records' of the fifteenth or sixteenth century; but while censuses are only indirectly connected to taxation, early modern Ottoman enumerations were an aid to taxation in the strict sense of the term. Accordingly, they give no indication of household size, as only tax-payers – in other words, adult males – were of interest to the recorders.

Moreover, for the historian trying to find out something about the peasant economy, one of the major pitfalls is the fact that all taxes were recorded for the village collectively, while farms were family- and not village- or clan-based enterprises.[6] We thus cannot say anything about equality or inequality among peasant families. We also do not know who was related to whom, as in the absence of surnames we can only discern – if fleetingly – that Hasan was the son of Mehmed, or vice versa. Yet family structures are crucial, as presumably cousins or nephews cooperated at least in certain matters, even if they were not always friendly in everyday life.

Another source of problems is the fact that for the most part, women are completely absent; as a result, relations mediated through mothers or sisters cannot be retrieved. Yet women could inherit, receiving private properties such as houses or vegetable plots from their natal families or their husbands if the latter predeceased them.[7] Only widows running the farms left by their dead husbands for the benefit of minor sons have left traces in the registers, and that too only in certain Balkan provinces. Even in the 'family trees' that certain dervish sheiks composed, covering a milieu in which sons quite often succeeded their fathers, males descended from males and – if we believe the compilers – did not need any mothers.

Moreover, if villagers made extra income from rural crafts such as spinning or weaving, the *tahrîr* registers, which cover non-agricultural dues but marginally, make no mention of the fact. Yet, as Huri İslamoğlu, the foremost connoisseur of this question has indicated, it is likely that rural crafts and the cultivation of specialty crops became widespread especially after the population increased substantially during the 1500s.[8] For in many places, the growth in agricultural production was not enough to support a larger number of peasants, especially in the drought-ridden years of the late sixteenth century.[9] Moreover, as previously noted, sixteenth-century villagers needed to defray certain dues in money: if they were not Muslims – and this applied to a large section especially of the Balkan population – they had to pay the head-tax known as *cizye*; and, in addition, all peasants of whatever religion paid the so-called plough taxes (*resm-i çift*) which may have started out as labour dues and were always collected in current coin.[10] To earn the requisite money, peasants must have sold part of their produce in the nearest town market, an institution with which they were familiar in any case, as the tax-takers had the right to demand that 'their' peasants carry the grain collected as dues to a place where it could be sold.

As apparent from this discussion, present-day Ottomanists have become somewhat disillusioned with the *tahrîr*s, although admittedly for the late 1400s and throughout the 1500s, these are our principal 'window' on rural society. As a result, only a few fundamentally important *tahrîr* studies have appeared during the last twenty years, and most of the secondary literature cited here dates to the period between 1940 and 1990.

There is yet another reason for this relative disillusionment: in addition to the limitations of the registers due to their purpose as a basis for taxation, they present problems due to what we may call 'the human factor'. In some places the enumerators found that the population had fled, and they could only copy the figures from a previous register. Occasionally they recorded this uncomfortable fact but often they did not, and only a careful comparison of several registers will show which figures are spurious. As for the harvest data that underlay the computation of the tithes, the enumerators had to trust the information given by peasants and locally based tax-takers, which might or might not be realistic.[11] Last but not least, in parts of Anatolia peasants shared the land, not always amicably, with nomads and semi-nomads, who were notoriously difficult to track down and record. In the late 1500s, the administration sometimes registered what had formerly been non-sedentary people as 'regular' villagers that were easier to control and tax. Sometimes population growth did indeed oblige nomads and semi-nomads to settle down; but in other cases these 'new peasant districts' may have been no more than a convenient administrative fiction. Moreover, in Anatolia lifestyles intermediate between villages and nomad tents were quite common, so that sometimes officials may have had genuine difficulty categorizing the people they were supposed to describe.

After 1600

After tax-farming replaced military tax assignments as the dominant form of revenue collection, from the late sixteenth century onward, the great workload and expense involved in preparing the *tahrîr*s must have been considered unnecessary; and in the seventeenth century Ottoman bureaucrats compiled such registers only in exceptional cases, usually after new conquests such as Crete or, very fleetingly, Podolia.[12] There are other tax registers from the 1600s (*avarız defterleri*) that historians have mined for population data, but they present so many technical problems that it seems best to omit them from this short summary.[13]

The eighteenth century, wedged in between the high point of Ottoman power in the 1500s and the emergence of a modern-style state in the later 1800s, is still the great unknown when it comes to Ottoman rural history. Not that sources are lacking: from the mid-1700s onward, we possess the so-called *Vilâyet Ahkâm Defterleri* / Registers of [Sultanic] Commands [sent to] the provinces, which among many other matters, also contain documents relevant to peasant affairs.[14] For the most part these cases probably were initiated either by tax-takers or else by wealthier villagers who had the money to take their cases all the way to the central administration. Moreover, given the distances involved, it is hardly surprising that the surroundings of Istanbul are far better covered than other regions.

A study of a mostly rural district in the Istanbul area during the 1740s to 1760s has resulted in some unexpected conclusions: first of all, while the holders of *timar*s (*sipahi*s) and other tax-grants had by this time lost much of their military role, they were still very active in tax collection, at least where the vicinity of the capital was concerned.[15] The administration facilitated the *sipahis*' tenacious hold on power – quite independently of their utility as soldiers – by considering that the tax registers of the sixteenth century, supplemented by a few edicts of seventeenth-century Sultans, formed the model *ne varietur* for conditions in the countryside. This policy must have made it difficult for peasants who wanted to profit from the Istanbul market to develop their holdings. Even so such attempts were not altogether lacking, and included the cultivation of cherries and even artichokes for a well-to-do clientele.

In the 1840s, at the very end of the period to be discussed here, Ottoman officialdom, in an effort to place tax collection on a more secure footing, initiated a series known as the *temettuat defterleri*. These registers are much more interesting to the social historian than their sixteenth-century predecessors, as they contain information on all properties from which people might make a livelihood, whether agricultural or non-agricultural. Unfortunately, not every province possesses these registers – they are conspicuously absent from Syria and Egypt, which were at the time in the hands of Mehmed/Muhammad Ali and therefore not really accessible to the Ottoman financial administration. Scholars pursuing detailed work on these registers also have found that the records were sometimes 'negotiable'. In parts of western Anatolia, for instance, at one point it became clear that local notables were not prepared to pay taxes on the basis of their properties as recently registered in the *temettuat defterleri*. Consequently, the authorities had a new record compiled in which the basic data had been altered so as to be more 'acceptable' to the potential tax-payers.[16] We are, of course, free to assume that the poorer peasants were quite often the victims of such arrangements.

Due to the difficulties outlined here, rural economies have not been at the top of the Ottomanist scholarly agenda for the last twenty years or so. A few brilliant and very recent exceptions however must be cited: we have already encountered the work of Sam White on Ottoman climate history, which obviously is of first-rate importance for the rural historian.[17] In addition, there is the work of Nicolas Michel and Alan Mikhail on the Egyptian countryside of the Ottoman period; their studies are all the more remarkable as there are very few *tahrîr*s concerning this province and those that do exist are extremely difficult to interpret.[18]

Where non-scholarly motivations for this relative lack of interest are concerned, it bears remembering that the recent economic growth in Turkey has been fuelled by trade and manufacturing more than by agriculture; and environmental history is having a hard time establishing its credentials. This set of present-day experiences must have contributed toward limiting scholarly concern for Ottoman peasants and rural life.

Urban Working People under Stringent Government Controls

By contrast, studies of craftspeople are currently flourishing.[19] In part this interest, which emerged only in the 1990s after a lengthy period of neglect, may be due to the fact that artisans can be viewed – and have been viewed – as small-scale capitalists. This perspective is attractive in the present-day Turkish environment characterized by capitalist expansion, although the guilds dominating the early modern Ottoman craft world attempted to ensure a modest livelihood for every member and thus opposed trends that might have ultimately led toward proto-capitalist enterprise. Attempts of individual craftsmen to enlarge the scope of their businesses thus often resulted in complaints, whose documentation forms a principal source for the historian of urban working people and which will concern us later on. At the same time these complaints demonstrate that in spite of what guild ideology might enjoy, artisans with entrepreneurial ambitions were not entirely lacking.

Throughout, the Ottoman administration did not encourage its subjects to enrich themselves: the tax-paying population sometimes featured in official parlance as the *reaya fukarası* or 'poor subjects'. In the eyes of officialdom, low prices and therefore a very modest remuneration of the producers were desirable, because they cheapened warfare and also the major Sultanic construction projects that often demanded logistics quite comparable to those necessitated by campaigns.[20] The Sultans' government tried to wage war and achieve other aims of the elite 'on the cheap', by decreeing the prices of – in principle – all goods sold in the market. These administratively determined prices were known as *narh*, and their listings took up a page or two in the register of the local *qadi* or else, as in the case of Istanbul, might occupy an entire record book (*narh defteri*).[21] In practice, regulation was most comprehensive in the capital, while in provincial towns usually only some of the basic foodstuffs and occasionally raw materials were so regulated. Certainly, even by administratively determining the prices of a few key goods it was possible to control the local market, particularly if the economy of the town in question was not very complex. But, presumably, artisans did have somewhat more space for manoeuvre if the administration had not prescribed every detail.

The prices and fees that artisans officially could demand allowed for a profit of 10 per cent, or of 20 per cent if the task to be undertaken was especially difficult. However, there are reasons for doubting that craftspeople always abided by the rules. After all, survival was at stake: these men had to pay taxes, the head tax/*cizye* if they were non-Muslims and market dues no matter what their religion might be.[22] Often the guild administrators, to say nothing of provincial governors and their retinues, collected additional dues. Moreover, in Istanbul, where fires were a constant danger and fire insurance was unknown, many people might lose their houses and goods at least once in their lifetime, and given the climate of the Balkans and Anatolia, housing and at least elementary heating arrangements were indispensable for surviving the winter. It is therefore quite possible that the *narh* was applied with great stringency when the Sultan's palace and the imperial elite were the purchasers, while artisans had more leeway when selling to ordinary customers.[23]

Artisan Conflicts

Artisans and their guilds are known to us principally because of their disputes. Also because, sometimes, the estate inventories (*tereke*) of craftsmen found their way into the registers of the Islamic judges.[24] While records of Christian and Jewish artisans can be found in the documents of their community courts as well, the Islamic court records survive in far greater numbers. In addition, it was not rare for non-Muslims to take their cases to the Islamic courts, perhaps because they felt that the decisions of these judges who after all enjoyed the Sultans' backing would be easier to enforce.

Due to entries in the *qadi* registers, we have some idea of the disputes that might arise when artisan guilds found themselves in a relationship where one guild used the product of another as a raw material. Tailors relied on the workmanship of the *gaytancıs*, family-operated enterprises manufacturing the decorative braid which typically ornamented kaftans, while shoemakers and saddlers depended upon tanners for leather, and were out of work if the latter sold their products elsewhere. Artisans producing similar items had to agree which group was to manufacture which type of shoe, cloak or pot. Where the high-end market was at issue, this division of labour probably had to be renegotiated whenever new goods became fashionable. Other disputes that ended up in the *qadi* registers concerned standards of workmanship, or at least the complainants claimed that they were out to get rid of competitors with insufficient training (*ham-dest*) who caused trouble to customers by low-quality work.[25] In some cases this may indeed have been the real issue; but there is reason to suspect that sometimes established masters were simply out to prevent younger competitors from setting up workshops. After all, studies of the inheritance inventories found in certain Ottoman *qadi* registers have shown that even the average well-to-do household – to say nothing of the poor – contained relatively few items.[26] Artisans thus had every reason to worry about insufficient demand.

Moreover, for the sixteenth and seventeenth centuries, we occasionally find Sultanic edicts concerning artisan problems that could not be solved locally and that the complainants had submitted to the central administration. In these cases what survives is not the original complaint but the Sultan's response, or, to be exact, that of the officials empowered to use his name. However, as the Ottoman bureaucracy normally summarized the petitions received as introductions to their responses, we often know the gist of the complaint even though the exact words used by the petitioners remain obscure. These edicts never survive in the original but rather in the shape of somewhat abridged register copies (*Mühimme Defterleri* / Registers of Important Affairs) prepared just before the final version was written and expedited. About ten of these chancery registers, for the most part dating to the 1500s, are available in print; and these publications contain indexes that allow us to track down the documents relevant to artisans without too much trouble.[27] However, the vast majority of the surviving chancery registers has not been published, and these original volumes have no indexes of any kind. We can only imagine that apprentice scribes spent long hours leafing through these tomes whenever their superiors needed to refer to a particular edict.

Thus only a very nasty thesis advisor would encourage his/her graduate students to look for edicts referring to craftspeople in the *Mühimme Defterleri*. It is more economical during scarce research time to jot down whatever is germane to artisans when researching a different topic – for which these registers do provide a significant number of documents. But from the mid-seventeenth century onward, a specialized variety of register came into being that focused on the responses to complaints of low-level administrators, and sometimes even of ordinary subjects (*Sikâyet Defterleri* / Registers of Complaints).[28] These registers, being more 'down-to-earth', contain many more edicts relevant to the artisan world, but like the *Mühimme Defterleri*, they list these texts in a very roughly chronological order, and without any reference to the fact that one complaint may have come from Belgrade/Serbia and the following one from Cairo/Egypt.

This relative lack of systematization did not apparently cause many bureaucratic headaches before the mid-1700s. But in the middle of the eighteenth century, the central government apparently attempted to compensate for the retreat of direct administration in favour of local magnates and notables by increasing the volume of correspondence with its subjects. This flood of paper could not possibly have been handled by the previous manner of record-keeping, and so the copies of edicts going out to provinces, large and small, now entered registers dedicated to a single province (*Vilâyet Ahkâm Defterleri* / Registers of [Sultanic] Commands [sent to] the provinces), of the type which we have briefly encountered when dealing with peasant affairs. Once again, the large number of documents in these registers does not exactly facilitate the task of the researcher looking for texts relevant to crafts. But if the province in question contains a major city, the chances of finding such documents are quite good. Particularly the *Vilâyet Ahkâm* registers concerning Istanbul are rich, for in the later 1700s the Sultan's government seems to have been quite frantic about its perceived loss of control and ready to intervene in minute details of artisan life that we today would think the province of low-level officials in the city administration.

Interestingly, artisans, at least in Istanbul, responded by asking not for less but rather for more intensive regulation, and as in the eighteenth century a growing number of craftsmen had come to work in large commercial/industrial complexes known as *hans/khans*, mutual surveillance was greatly facilitated. While in the early 1600s quite a few artisans had been able to circumvent the rulings of their guilds and thus enlarge their enterprises, by the late 1700s this kind of 'muddling through' must have become all but impossible.[29] I am not sure why Istanbul artisans had become so enamoured of state control: possibly the increasing sale of positions as guild headmen to soldiers/officials willing to give up their salaries to the treasury had made many guildsmen rather sceptical about the possibility of achieving a solution of their problems on a guild level.[30]

In Conclusion

The concerned subject is so vast that a short paper such as this one can only scratch the surface. But even so, a few conclusions are possible. First of all, we are dealing with an economy in which the use of money and markets was widespread, and in which cities reached an impressive size, even though most of them would have looked small when compared to their Chinese or Indian counterparts.

Secondly, the Ottoman government sponsored a 'command economy' meant to further Sultanic projects, with war as the first priority. However, especially before the mid-1700s, this command economy was not so ubiquitous as to stifle all initiative on the part of the 'poor subjects': whatever the administration might say, peasants migrated to towns or changed their fields into vineyards and vegetable patches, and so responded to urban market demand. At the same time, artisans created wealth from often elegantly designed textiles, copperware or faience for the use of the elite, even though they and their families often lived in great poverty. Apparently, artisans found it easier to make a moderately prosperous living in places which the central government had trouble reaching, particularly the great city of Cairo with its long tradition of top-level artisan production.

Within the Ottoman polity there was a tension or contradiction that I feel needs to be addressed more seriously than has been the case to date: on the one hand, as was true of many other early modern polities, the *raison d'être* of the empire was warfare. When the soldiers had no prospect of booty with which to supplement their more than meagre pay, they were likely to rebel, and rebellions could cost the Sultan his throne and the viziers their lives. Politically speaking, it therefore made sense to send these potentially dangerous men to the front, and here the demands of elite figures and ordinary soldiers converged.[31] On the other hand – once again similarly to other early modern polities – the 'economic productivity of the subjects' did not suffice for the expenses which warfare imposed upon them. When, in the second half of the eighteenth century, these wars became so costly that artisans and merchants were ruined, the result was an economic depression in which the empire narrowly missed going down. Moreover, the Ottoman Empire, which survived the onslaughts of Napoleon, the Russian Tsars, the rebels in Greece that set up a separate state under the protectorate of Western European powers (1821), the Wahhabi uprising and Muhammad Ali, was a polity that differed profoundly from that which we have discussed here. But that is a different story to be tackled some other time.

Last but not least, vast sectors of the productive lives of peasants and artisans remain a closed book. We do not know how family relations operated in towns and villages, or what the contribution of peasant and artisan wives may have been to the household economy. We do not even know anything about the yearly incomes of Istanbul artisans not employed in the construction sector.[32] Nor can we tell what proportion of urban migrants ultimately found places in urban guilds, and how many remained marginal for the rest of their often very short lives. To some of these questions we may ultimately find limited and provisional answers. But on the whole, we float in a veritable sea of ignorance.

Notes

[1] For detailed information, the homepage of the Başbakanlık Arşivi-Osmanlı Arşivi in Istanbul is the appropriate source. For general information, see the collective work, *Başbakanlık Osmanlı Arşivi Rehberi* (2000).

[2] For those *sicil*s today in Turkey, compare Akgündüz *et al.* (eds.) (1988–89).

[3] This discussion owes a great deal to Singer (1990); Lowry (1992).

[4] Scribes compiled special so-called abridged (*icmâl*) registers to make the assignment of *timar*s easier. Those dating to the 1520s and 1530s have mostly been published. See, for example, Sarınay *et al.* (eds.) (2001).

[5] See, for example, the pioneering study of Barkan (1940–41a and 1940–41b). On the population increase of the 1500s, see Barkan (1951).

[6] While in some villages, especially in the neighbourhood of Istanbul, there were a few slaves employed on farms, on the whole slave labour in the countyside was rare. Villages that lived mainly by manufacturing were also seldom found. I will therefore use the terms 'peasants' and 'villagers' interchangeably.

[7] In the 1970s and 1980s, the problematic we may call 'women and property' was in the forefront of Ottoman women's/gender history. The pionering study was Jennings (1973). Also see Faroqhi (1992). Today, the emphasis is more on violence towards women and women defending their interests in court.

[8] Inan (1994). The author has written a lengthy new introduction to the recent reprint of the Turkish version of the classic work, *Osmanlı İmparatorluğunda Devlet ve Köylü* (2011).

[9] Kuniholm (1990); White (2011).

[10] Inalcık (1959).

[11] Singer (1994). She recounts some telling examples of peasants who made fun of the recording officials and refused to give them usable answers.

[12] Kołodziejczyk (1994); Gülsoy (2004).

[13] Demirci (2009).

[14] For a published selection, see Kal'a *et al.* (eds.) (1997–98). Especially important are the volumes titled *Tarım Tarihi* (A History of Agriculture) and *Esnaf Tarihi* (A History of Artisans).

[15] Faroqhi (forthcoming).

[16] Kaya (2008).

[17] White (2011).

[18] Among this author's many articles, see Michel (2005); Mikhail (2011).

[19] Faroqhi (2009).

[20] Çizakça (2013).

[21] Kütükoğlu (ed.) (1983).

[22] The poll tax paid by non-Muslims at times may have constituted up to 40 pe cent of the funds available to the central administration. See Darling (2006): esp. 125.

[23] This suggestion comes from Kafadar (1986).

[24] Faroqhi (2003).
[25] For an older article but that remains a classic, see Inalcik (1969).
[26] This point has been well made by Grehan (2007).
[27] For an example, compare with Binark *et al.* (eds.) (1993).
[28] Only one example is available in print: Majer (ed.) (1984), Vol. 1; Vol. 2 never appeared.
[29] On the relative flexibility of guilds in the seventeenth century, see Gerber (1988); Yi (2004); Hanna (2011). On the constraints of the eighteenth century, see Genç (1994).
[30] Genç (1994); Faroqhi (2007).
[31] See the janissary song translated by Zarinebaf (2010): 183–86.
[32] On the construction sector, see Özmucur and Pamuk (2002).

References

Akgündüz, Ahmet *et al.* (eds.) (1988–89), *Şeriye Sicilleri* (Registers of the Islamic Courts), 2 vols., Istanbul: Türk Dünyası Araştırmaları Vakfı.

Barkan, Ömer Lütfi (1940–41a), 'Türkiye'de İmparatorluk devirlerinin büyük nüfus ve arazi tahrirleri ve Hakana mahsus istatistik defterleri' (The great population and land censuses of imperial Turkey and the statistical registers to be accessed by the ruler only), *İstanbul Üniversitesi İktisat Fakültesi Mecmuası*, I, 1: 20–59.

——— (1940–41b), 'Türkiye'de İmparatorluk devirlerinin büyük nüfus ve arazi tahrirleri ve Hakana mahsus istatistik defterleri' (The great population and land censuses of imperial Turkey and the statistical registers to be accessed by the ruler only), *İstanbul Üniversitesi İktisat Fakültesi Mecmuası*, II, 2: 214–47.

——— (1951), 'Tarihi Demografi Araştırmaları ve Osmanlı Tarihi' (Research in historical demography and Ottoman history), *Türkiyat Mecmuası*, X: 1–26.

Başbakanlık Osmanlı Arşivi Rehberi (A guide to the Archives of the Prime Minister, Ottoman [section]) (2000), Istanbul: T.C. Başbakanlık Arşivleri Genel Müdürlüğü, second edition.

Binark, İsmet *et al.* (eds.) (1993), *3 Numaralı Mühimme Defteri (966–968 / 1558–1560)* (Chancery register No. 3), Ankara: Başbakanlık Arşivleri Genel Müdürlüğü.

Çizakça, Murat (2013), 'The Ottoman Government and Economic Life: Taxation, Public Finance and Trade Controls', in Suraiya Faroqhi and Kate Fleet (eds.), *The Cambridge History of Turkey*, Vol. 2, Cambridge: Cambridge University Press: 241–75.

Darling, Linda (2006), 'Public Finances: The Role of the Ottoman Center', in Suraiya Faroqhi (ed.), *The Cambridge History of Turkey: The Later Ottoman Empire,* Vol. 3, Cambridge: Cambridge University Press: 118–34.

Demirci, Süleyman (2009), *The Functioning of Ottoman Avâriz Taxation: An Aspect of the Relationship between Centre and Periphery: A Case Study of the Province of Karaman, 1621–1700*, Istanbul: The Isis Press.

Faroqhi, Suraiya (1992), 'Two Women of Substance', in Christa Fragner and Klaus Schwarz (eds.), *Festgabe an Josef Matuz, Osmanistik, Turkologie, Diplomatik*, Berlin: Klaus Schwarz Verlag: 37–56.

——— (2003), 'How to Live and Die Rich in Eighteenth-Century Bursa: The Fortune of Hacı Ibrahim, Tanner', in Jean-Paul Pascual (ed.), *Pauvreté et richesse dans le monde musulman et méditerranéen* (Poverty and wealth in the Muslim Mediterranean world), Paris: Maisonneuve and Larose: 99–118.

——— (2007), 'Purchasing Guild-and Craft-based Offices in the Ottoman Central Lands', *Turcica*, Vol. 39: 123–46.

——— (2009), *Artisans of Empire: Crafts and Craftspeople under the Ottomans*, London: I.B. Tauris.

——— (forthcoming), 'A Study of Rural Conflicts: Gegbuze/Gebze (District of Üsküdar) in the mid-1700s'.

Genç, Mehmet (1994), 'Ottoman Industry in the Eighteenth Century: General Framework, Characteristics and Main Trends', in Donald Quataert (ed.), *Manufacturing in the Ottoman Empire and Turkey 1500–1950*, Albany: SUNY Press: 59–86.

Gerber, Haim (1988), *Economy and Society in an Ottoman City: Bursa, 1600–1700*, Jerusalem: The Hebrew University.

Grehan, James (2007), *Everyday Life and Consumer Culture in Eighteenth-Century Damascus*, Seattle, London: University of Washington Press, 2007.

Gülsoy, Ersin (2004), *Girit'in Fethi ve Osmanlı İdaresinin Kurulması (1645–1670)* (The conquest of Crete and the establishment of Ottoman administration), Istanbul: Tatav.

Hanna, Nelly (2011), *Artisan Entrepreneurs in Cairo and Early Modern Capitalism (1600–1800)*, Syracuse, NY: Syracuse University Press.

Inalcık, Halil (1959), 'Osmanlılarda Raiyyet Rusûmu' (Among the Ottomans: Taxes paid by the subject [population]), *Belleten*, Vol. XXIII: 575–610.

——— (1969), 'Capital Formation in the Ottoman Empire', *The Journal of Economic History*, Vol. XXIX (1): 97–140.

Inan, Huri İslamoğlu (1994), *State and Peasant in the Ottoman Empire: Agrarian Power Relations and Regional Economic Development in Ottoman Anatolia during the Sixteenth Century*, Leiden: E.J. Brill.

Jennings, Ronald C. (1973), 'Women in Early Seventeenth-Century Ottoman Judicial Records – The Sharia Court of Anatolian Kayseri', *Journal of the Economic and Social History of the Orient*, Vol. XVIII, 1: 53–114.

Kafadar, Cemal (1986), 'When Coins Turned into Drops of Dew and Bankers Became Robbers of Shadows: The Boundaries of Ottoman Economic Imagination at the End of the Sixteenth Century', unpublished Ph.D. thesis, McGill University, Montréal, Canada.

Kal'a, Ahmet *et al.* (eds.) (1997–98), *İstanbul Külliyatı I, İstanbul Ahkâm Defterleri* (A collection of Istanbul [sources]: the registers of orders sent by the sultan), 10 vols., Istanbul: İstanbul Büyükşehir Belediyesi.

Kaya, Alp Yücel (2008), 'In the Hinterland of İzmir: Mid-Nineteenth Century Traders Facing a New Type of Fiscal Practice', in Suraiya Faroqhi and Gilles Veinstein (eds.), *Merchants in the Ottoman Empire*, Leuven: Peeters: 261–80.

Kołodziejczyk, Dariusz (1994), '*Defter-I Mufassal-I Eyalet-I Kamaniçe*', *The Ottoman Survey Register of Podolia (CA. 1681)*, 2 vols., Cambridge MA: Ukrainian Research Institute of Harvard University.

Kuniholm, Peter I. (1990), 'Archaeological Evidence and Non-Evidence for Climatic Change', *Philosophical Transactions of the Royal Society*, A330: 645–55.

Kütükoğlu, Mübahat (ed.) (1983), *Osmanlılarda Narh Müessesesi ve 1640 Tarihli Narh Defteri* (Administratively decreed prices among the Ottomans and the register of [such] prices dated 1640), Istanbul: Enderun Kitabevi.

Lowry, Heath (1992), 'The Ottoman *Tahrir Defterleri* as a Source for Social and Economic History: Pitfalls and Limitations', in *Studies in Defterology, Ottoman Society in the Fifteenth and Sixteenth Centuries*, Istanbul: The Isis Press: 3–18.

Majer, Hans Georg (ed.) (1984), *Das osmanische Registerbuch der Beschwerden (Şikayet Defteri) vom Jahre 1675: Faksimile, Register* (The Ottoman register of complaints from the year 1675), Vol. I, Vienna.

Michel, Nicolas (2005), 'Les Services communaux' dans les campagnes égyptiennes au début de l'époque ottomane' ('Community services' in the Egyptian countryside at the beginning of the Ottoman period), in Muhammed Afifi, Rashida Chih, Brigitte Marino, Nicolas Michel and Işık Tamdoğan (eds.), *Sociétés rurales ottomanes* (Ottoman Rural Societies), Cairo: Institut Français d'Archéologie Orientale: 19–46.

Mikhail, Alan (2011), *Nature and Empire in Ottoman Egypt: An Environmental History*, Cambridge: Cambridge University Press.

Osmanlı İmparatorluğunda Devlet ve Köylü (State and peasant in the Ottoman Empire), (2011), Istanbul: İletişim, reprint.

Özmucur, Süleyman and Şevket Pamuk (2002), 'Real Wages and Standards of Living in the Ottoman Empire, 1489–1914', *The Journal of Economic History*, Vol. 62 (2): 293–321.

Sarınay, Yusuf *et al.* (eds.) (2001), *370 Numaralı Muhâsebe-i Vilâyet-i Rûm-ili Defteri (937/1530)* (The account book of the Province of Rûm-ili, or the Ottoman Balkans), 2 vols., Ankara: Başbakanlık Arşivleri Genel Müdürlüğü.

Singer, Amy (1990), '*Tapu Tahrir Defterleri* and *Kadı Sicilleri*: A Happy Marriage of Sources', *Târîh*, I: 95–125.

——— (1994), *Palestinian Peasants and Ottoman Officials: Rural Administration around Sixteenth-Century Jerusalem*, Cambridge: Cambridge University Press.

White, Sam (2011), *The Climate of Rebellion in the Early Modern Ottoman Empire*, Cambridge: Cambridge University Press.

Yi, Eunjeong (2004), *Guild Dynamics in Seventeenth-Century Istanbul, Fluidity and Leverage*, Leiden: E. J. Brill.

Zarinebaf, Fariba (2010), *Crime and Punishment in Istanbul 1700*–1800, Los Angeles, Berkeley: University of California Press: 183–86.

Taxing Professions in Medieval South India

Vijaya Ramaswamy

31. *Shilpino maasi maasyekaikam karma kuryuhu.*
Each artisan shall monthly do one day's work for the king.

32. *Etena aatmopajeevino vyakyatah.*
Similarly for those who live by their bodies (jugglers, dancers, acrobats, etc.) apart from the ones who labour/work with their hands for their living.

– *Gautama Dharma Sutra*, with the commentary *Mitakshara* written by Haradatta[1]

Vast numbers of workers who constituted an integral and seminal part of early Indian economies find their presence recorded in historical documents in inverse proportion to their contribution. The working groups that do find mention in the ancient texts are generally those covered by the term '*vishti*' or forced labour. It is, however, possible to salvage the presence of the working class from the plethora of inscriptions which we have beginning from the early medieval period, roughly from the seventh century AD, to the late medieval or 'pre-modern' period which, technically, could be as late as the eighteenth century.

The present essay intends to track the presence of the working/labouring communities in early south India through the prism of inscriptional evidence on taxes imposed on professions, especially artisanal professions. In identifying the trope for such a study, I have chosen to adopt the standards prescribed in the *Gautama Dharma Sutra,* one of the earliest Sanskrit texts to discuss the canonical position on taxation. This text, written anywhere between the third and sixth century BC,[2] has a major medieval commentary by Haradatta who lived in the twelfth century AD. Haradatta's interpretation of the *Gautama Dharma Sutra* No. 32, which states, '*etena aatmopa jeevino vyakyatah*', explains it in the context of the previous one, namely, '*shilpino maasi maasyekaikam karma kuryuhu*', meaning 'each artisan shall monthly do one day's work for the king'. According to Haradatta, '*aatmopajeevi*' would therefore mean the taxes payable by those who support themselves by their personal or manual labour. The commentator adds that these could include jugglers, dancers and others who live by their bodies, apart from those who work for their living. The next *sutra* brings within the ambit of taxation, small-time transporters. To quote *sutra* No. 33:

> *Nauchakreevantashcha*
> And [the tax] payable by those who make their living from boat and carts. (That is, boatmen and cartiers should similarly give one day's labour to the king in the form of tax.)

In all these cases, beginning from the term '*shilpi*', tax was levied in terms of one day's labour rendered to the state on a monthly basis. This study will analyse the tax structure by juxtaposing the positions on taxation taken by normative texts like the *Manusmriti* and *Yajnavalkya Smriti* against the social reality reflected in medieval inscriptions.

This, then, is the trope within which this essay will study the theme of 'taxing professions'. The pun on 'taxing' is a deliberate one since it draws attention to the fact that all the above-mentioned professions, which include all artisanal work (*shilpi* is here used as a generic term for craftsmen), involved intense physical labour. The epigraphical data on 'taxing professions' is not a systematic one either in terms of continuities in space and time, or in terms of the hermeneutics of tax terminologies. Despite its disparate nature, the surprise is that evidence of this kind exists. Therefore, despite the tentative nature of such an exercise, it is being attempted here since I believe it is extremely seminal to understand working-class history.

Foregrounding Medieval Taxation: Terms and Conditions of Taxation in Sanskrit Canonical Texts

In early India, the income of the state came from different sources – taxes, especially land revenue; tributes; tolls; customs and other forms of public receipts including voluntary cess or contributions; and last but not least, wealth obtained from invasions and loot. Canonical positions on land revenue, however seminal to a larger debate on fiscal resources, are not central to this essay and will therefore only find a brief mention here. The last source, namely plunder, which was mistakenly perceived by Stein and other historians to be the only avenue for the wealth of the state, will also not be discussed here, except perfunctorily. Nor will the idea of tribute forming an important source of state revenues be discussed, except to point out that this may perhaps have been the foundation of a fiscal system in Indian antiquity.

The *Mahabharata* has a passage relating to Prithu, the son of Vena and the 'first' king, after whom the earth is named 'Prithvi'. It states: 'The earth in her own divine shape came to him with riches and precious jewels.'[3] Clearly, this was intended as tribute to a sovereign authority – the king. I propose in this article to look at the conceptual foundations of both the two remaining categories, consisting of taxes and public receipts. One of the earliest texts to discuss the principle of taxation is *Gautama Dharma Sutra*.[4] P.V. Kane places this text between the third and sixth century BC. The text uses multiple terms like '*kara*', '*shulka*' and '*balidhanam*' to indicate tax.

Land revenue is regarded as the most important fiscal resource of the state. According to the *Gautama Dharma Sutra* (*prashna* 2, *adhyaya* 1, *sutra* 24), land was divided into three categories, and while the most fertile was taxed at one-sixth of the yield, average land was taxed at one-eighth and below-average land at one-tenth of the total yield. The rates given in the *Manu Samhita* are almost the same, except for the yield from inferior soil which was taxed at one-twelfth rather than one-tenth. The *Acharadhyaya* of *Yajnavalkya Smriti*, stating the king's share as one-sixth of the total usufruct, also says that this is towards his exertions in protecting his subjects (*Yajnavalkya Smriti*: 335). The *Mahabharata* epic also adheres to the one-sixth figure (*Santi Parva*, LXXI: 10), but clearly states: 'Milk the cow but do not hurt the udder.'[5] Elsewhere the epic states: 'Just as the calf can bear burdens strengthened by the milk . . . so the people when they are prosperous.'[6]

Both the *Gautama Dharma Sutra* and *Manu Samhita* state that the tax on '*pashu hiranyayoho*' (cattle and gold) should be taxed at one-fiftieth, which is just 2 per cent (*Gautama Dharma Sutra*, 2, 1, *sutra* 25). The combination of cattle and gold (which also implies other precious metals like silver) is interesting since both cattle wealth and wealth in the form of gold or coins served as indicators of affluence in early days. In fact, cattle were first used as a standard of exchange in commercial exchanges before monetization of the economy. The medieval commentator Haradatta says: 'If one gets a profit of 50 *nishka*, he should annually give one *nishka* to the state.'[7]

Petty merchants/shopkeepers, termed '*vanik*', had to pay one-twentieth of their profits on sale of commodities. Here the commentator clarifies that this was what was called '*shulka*'. The last professional group that had to make cash payment as tax was a motley group of petty traders, most probably itinerant, since they are mentioned as being different from the shopkeepers. This group comprised vegetable and fruit vendors, sellers of liquor and meat, flower sellers and sellers of medicinal herbs, sellers of fodder and firewood (*Gautama Dharma Sutram*, 2, 1, *sutra* 26).[8]

The canonical injunction on taxes on trade and traders in Gautama's *Sutra* can be contrasted with the *Manu Samhita* and the *Rajadharmanushasana Parva* of the *Mahabharata,* which are the only other texts that have something to add on this matter.

According to the *Rajadharmanushasana Parva* (87): 'It is the duty of the king to fix rules [rates] of taxation on the traders, having considered their sale and purchase, increase [profit] and [expenses on] the way, food and clothing' (vide Ganguly 1926: 132). According to the *Manu Samhita* (vii, *sutra* 127):

> The king should take taxes from the merchants on their article after proper enquiry as to the prices of sale and purchase of communities, the distance over which they are brought, the expenses on the way for carriage and for safe-guarding them from thieves and robbers and calculation of profit on total expenses. (Vide Ganguly 1926: 132)

The canonical injunction regarding professionals, like craftsmen and artisans, carpenters, masons and sculptors, clearly indicates that these groups should not be made to pay taxes in cash but instead give a day's labour as tax to the state every month. *Sutra* 31 of Gautama states: '*Shilpino maasi maasyaikam karma kuryuhu*' (*Gautama Dharma Sutra*, 2, 1, *sutra* 31). The next *sutra* (ibid., *sutra* 32) states that those who make their living by exerting their bodies, '*ethena aatmopajeevino vyakyatah*', should also contribute one day's labour. Haradatta clarifies that this group meant people like woodcutters, dancers and others. Another canonical text that has some references to taxation, *Shukraniti*, states that physical labour given as tax should not be monthly but fortnightly (Ganguli 1926, Pt. II: 141). Similar are the tax rules for boatmen and drivers of wooden carts – '*nau-chakreevantashcha*' (*Gautama Dharma Sutra*, 2, 1, *sutra* 33). Gautama also stipulates that the state should in turn take care of their food and other needs for the day – '*Bhaktam tebyo dadyat*' (ibid., *sutra* 34).

From the nature of the canonical tax laws, one can see that while landowners and merchants were placed higher in the socio-economic scale, next to the Brahmins and Kshatriyas, the Sudra artisanal castes engaged in professions like smithy, carpentry and masonry occupied a very low status on the social ladder. In fact the *Gautama Dharma Sutra* states that they should accept and use the clothes, slippers, umbrella and mats given to them by the upper castes. It further enjoins that they should accept the left-over food of upper castes. Gautama concludes this section by stating '*shilpa vrittishcha*', meaning that masons, etc., should do their work observing these rules (ibid., *sutras* 60–62).

While the *Gautama Dharma Sutra* seems to be silent on the issue of '*sunkam*', which can be broadly said to define tolls, customs and other regulations relating to trade movement, the evidence for these primarily comes from the political treatise, *Arthashastra*, dated roughly to between the fourth and third century BC, which states: 'Imports harmful to the state and luxuries are to be discouraged by taxation' (*Arthashastra*, II, 21).

Contextualizing Taxation in Medieval South India

It is important, albeit briefly, to foreground the broad debate on taxation in the context of Asiatic societies since intellectual stereotypes have come in for re-examination in the recent North versus South debates.[9] In tune with the 'Orientalist' perception, the absence of a taxation policy was touted as the hallmark of Oriental, in fact Asiatic states. Edward Said, in defining Orientalism, stated that the Orient was a 'system of ideological fictions' whose purpose was, and is, to legitimize western cultural and political superiority.[10] Stephen Batchelor writes: 'As the colonizing powers came to identify themselves with order, reason and power, so the colonized East became perceived as chaotic, irrational and weak.'[11]

It is in keeping with such a view of the Orient that it was argued that in societies based on rapaciousness and plunder, there could have been no systematic procedure for good governance which includes a regular tax structure. It has been believed in the context of medieval south India that no taxation system existed, and that the early medieval states such as the Pallava and Chola dynasties sustained their polities through predatory raids and periodic tributes extracted from subordinate chieftains (Stein 1980).[12] In fact, George W. Spencer (1976) coined the phrase 'plunder politics' to describe the fiscal base of medieval peninsular polities like the Chola state. It is necessary to point out here that plunder as a source of revenue was accepted by the canonical scriptures and is borne out by inscriptional evidence which refer to making of silver and gold images for the temple from plundered metal. The *Yajnavalkya Smriti* and its commentary, the *Mitakshara*, state: 'There exists no higher duty for kings than this that what they have won in battle, they should give that wealth to Brahmanas' (*Mitakshara*, *sutra* CCCXXXIII).[13] The *Mitakshara* seems to endorse this point of view. However, the fact of plunder politics being a historical reality in south India does not mean the absence of a regular source of revenue for the state through an organized system of taxation.

The plethora of studies on the south Indian economy that are based on medieval inscriptional evidence points to a very different economic reality in the peninsular region. The ubiquitous presence of taxes and tax officials both in the countryside (especially in the context of land revenue) and in the towns (pertaining largely to tax on commerce and crafts) clearly points to a complex grid of taxation and tax enforcement agencies. A compendium of tax terms was put together by the Indo–Japanese team of Karashima and Sitaraman (1972), followed by a three-volume compendium of *The Concordance of Names in the Chola Inscriptions* (Karashima, Subbarayalu and Matsui 1978) which provides an impressive range of tax officials.

To conclude this brief discussion on the fiscal structure of Asiatic states, not only do we have overwhelming evidence for a tax structure in medieval state formations in south India, we also have a plethora of inscriptions dealing with caste/community protests against heavy taxation both in Chola and Vijayanagara times. I would like to cite a verse from the '*Acharadhyay*' of the *Yajnavalkya Smriti*, authored by Vijnanesvara, a twelfth-century commentator on the *Smriti*. *Sutra* No. 336 reads: '*Chatuh taskara durvrattah, mahasaahasikaadibihi, Peedyamano prjaha, rakshet Kayasthaihi visheshathaha*' – it is the king's duty to protect his subjects from 'cheats and thieves as well as Kayastha'.

Since the last category 'Kayasthaihi' refers to accountants or book-keepers, their inclusion in the company of cheats and thieves is noteworthy. The *sutra* seems to suggest that book-keepers tended to be fraudulent in their methods of account-keeping. Since the professional caste of Kayastha, or accountants and book-keepers, enters into inscriptions and other literary texts only in the early medieval period around the ninth century AD, this reference may have its origin in the twelfth-century commentary, *Mitakshara* of Vijnanesvara.[14] Finally, Yajnavalkya states that in a situation where the king over-taxes his subjects and fails to protect them from exploitation, if the people revolt, half the burden of guilt lies with the king for he has collected these taxes. The precise Sanskritic passage is:

> *Arakshamanah kurvanti yat kinchit kilvisham prajah*
> *Tasmat cha nrpateh ardham yasmat grahnati asau karaan.*[15]

Here I have interpreted *kilvisham* to mean revolt, although the word literally means committing an offence. In the context of the above *sutra* this interpretation seems justified. Canonical evidence therefore not only testifies to a multilayered tax structure, but also recognizes the possibility of revolt against an unfair regime including an excessive tax burden.

In the context of voluntary cesses, it must be pointed out that these were invariably collected by craft as well as merchant communities towards temple charities such as celebration of festivals, involving public feeding among other features such as cultural and ritual performances. This was called '*manganmai*'. Injunctions regarding these would logically not come under the ambit of canonical injunctions on taxation. Although it lies outside the ambit of state revenues, figures involving '*maganmai*' form a significant part of the inscriptional material on professional and commercial levies, and will therefore be looked at in this essay.

Professional Taxes in Early India

Inscriptions refer to tax payment in monetary terms as *kasayam* and *kasukadamai*. The term '*kasu*' means money,[16] and the terms '*ayam*' and '*kadamai*' both refer to 'taxes'. Land revenue, especially on wet lands, was paid in cash. The administrative text *Parasara Madhaviyam* of the fifteenth century, stated to have been written by Madhavacharya, the minister of the Vijayanagara king, says that the calculation of the tax should be based on the size of the landholding, seed quantity sown, average profit and current value of the grain.[17] This canonical precept is confirmed by common fiscal practice reflected in the inscriptions.[18] According to colonial records, the conversion of tax from kind to cash was in terms of 30 seers of grain, which would equal a tax payment of one rupee.[19]

Canonical evidence, as has been shown, seems to suggest the absence of taxes on professions in early south India, while inscriptional evidence clearly points to the contrary. While the poorer artisans, like leather workers and more specifically cobblers, may have paid the state dues through their labour, there are tax terms to show that more affluent craftsmen, like weavers, goldsmiths and oilmongers, paid their taxes in cash. Those professional communities who paid their taxes in cash were known as *kasayakkudi*.[20]

Taxes on artisans, craftsmen and crafts were of two, sometimes three kinds. The tax could either be on the professionals themselves, or on their professional capital or assets. For example, the tax on dancing girls, called *devaradiyar* or *soole*, would either be on their person, i.e. '*sooledere*',[21] or on their professional capital, in this case their mirror! This tax was known as '*kannadidere*'.[22] Similarly, weavers would pay either a professional tax such as '*kaikkola-kadamai*' or pay a loom tax, usually called '*tari irai*' or '*tari kadamai*', which would again vary according to the nature of the textile being produced on that loom, i.e. whether it is cotton or silk.

The third kind of professional tax that one encounters in the inscriptions is on the raw material of the professional. For example, inscriptions refer to a tax on iron ore.[23] There was, further, a separate tax on iron-mining.[24]

The Buchireddipalem copperplate inscriptions of the Pallava king Simhavarman II[25] gives a long list of taxes collected from the village Vidhuvattagrama (now Viduvalur in Kovur taluk of Nellore district in Andhra Pradesh). Simhavarman II was one of the early Pallavas and can be chronologically placed in the sixth century AD. The taxes listed are as follows: from peasant cultivators (*nahalamukhadharaka*), from water-diviners or those who show where wells may be dug (*kupa darshaka*), weavers (*tantuvaya*), all artisans (*sarvaprakara karudeyani*), from gamblers (*dyuta*) and dealers in ropes (*rajjupratihara*). It is added that other dues owed to the state are hereby given to the donee of the Brahmadeya. Since dealers in ropes refer to those who measured arable land for purposes of land cultivation, this has been interpreted as a tax on overseers. The tax on gamblers is intriguing and seems to record state sanction to and recognition of gambling as a legitimate profession.

The importance of the Buchireddipalem plate lies in the fact that since it dates back to the sixth century AD, it is the earliest inscription to enumerate a list of professional taxes levied under the Pallavas. For the subsequent centuries, from the eighth/ninth centuries to the twelfth/thirteenth centuries, such lists are available in somewhat larger measure, although the evidence is still limited.

A list of these professional taxes based on inscriptional references is given below.

Professional	*Professional tax*	*Inscriptional reference*	*Remarks*
Potters	*Kushakkanam* *Kambaru dere*	*SII*, Vol. II, part 3, No. 73. *EC*, Vol. XIV, No. 19.	
Tax on the potter's wheel	*Chakra Kanikke* *Tirigai Ayam*	*SII*, Vol. XX, No. 239, dated 1547.	
Goldsmiths	*Tattarpattam*	*SII*, Vol. I, Nos. 59, 61, both from South Arcot district. *SII*, Vol. II, part 3, No. 73.	
Fishermen	*Erimeen kasu*	*SII*, Vol. I, No. 61.	
Fishermen	*Chembadavar kadamai*	*ARE*, 294 of 1911, appendix B, 1911, part II, para 51.	The first seems to be a tax on the profit from the sale of a haul of fish. The second refers to a fixed tax on the professionals who are called by the name '*Chembadavar*'.
On oil mills	*Chekku kadamai*	*SII*, Vol. I, Nos. 59, 61. *SII*, Vol. II, part 5, Nos. 98, 99.	This clearly is not a tax on the professional but on his professional capital since *chekku* means 'oil-mill'.
Oilmongers	*Chakki dere* or *Gaanadere*	*EC*, Vol. X, Km. 36. *EC*, Vol.VII, Sk. 275.	
	Ennaivanigar kadamai	*ARE*, 221 of 1910, 1911, part II, para 51. Also 300 of 1909, appendix B.	The second category is a tax on the professional called '*ennaivanigar*'.
Shepherds *Idaiyar* (shepherds) *Manradi* (shepherds)	*Idaiturai* on the following cattle: *Nallaavu/ Nallerudu Nalkida; Nalpasu*	*EI*, Vol. XVIII, p. 139, and *ARE* 247 of 1915, appendix C, 1916, part II, para 64 from	Here again two categories of taxes can be seen. The first taxes the capital and lists the cow, the buffalo and the goat to be taxed. The rate of taxation is given given as ¼ on each cow; ½ *panam* on each buffalo and ¼ *panam* on 8 sheep/goats.

(*continued*)

	Saadadere	*Srimushnam*, dated 1504. *EC*, Vol. IV, Hs. 137, AD 1162.	
Brokers	*Taragu kasu*	*ARE* 309 of 1968–69 dated in the eleventh century.	It is significant that the find-spot of the inscription is Tiru-Tiruchirapalli, a major centre of craft production in the medieval period.
Barbers	*Navida dere*	*EC*, Vol. X, Mb. 49a, AD 1172.	
Braziers	*Kammaaradere* *Panchakaruka*	*Karnataka Inscriptions*, Vol. IV, No. 9. *EC*, Vol. VIII, Tl. 9.	This was most probably a tax levied on groups of smiths collectively known as *Panchalas, Panchanamuvaru* or *Kammalar*. This also seems to be a collective tax on them.
Carpenters		Ibid.	Carpenters were one of the group of five craftsmen.
Blacksmiths	*Kammaaradere*	*Karnataka Inscriptions*, Vol. IV, No. 9.	Blacksmiths were one of the three categories of smiths (the other two being goldsmiths and braziers or bronze smiths.
Glass (mirror?) makers			There was a Virasaivite woman saint and *vachanakara* by the name of Kannadi Kayakade Remmavve – one who makes a living out of making mirrors[26]
Masons	*Odda dere*	*EC*, Vol. X, Mb. 49.	
Stone cutters	*Kallu-derige*	*SII*, Vol. XVIII, No. 149, dated 1144 AD.	
Shop-keepers Kadaikkarar	 *Kadai irai*	*ARE* 300 of 1909, appendix B. Also *SII*, Vol. I, No. 59 from Veppambattu in Chingleput district dated AD 1406.	Rate is given as 6 *panams* per shop-keeper in the newly created hamlet of Marundakkunaadayapuram in Tirukkachur, Chingleput district.
Market tax[27]	*Angadi dere* and *Angadi sunka*	*EC*, Vol. VII, Ng. 73, dated 1284 and IND 3, dated 1047.	

(*continued*)

Tax on petty shops	*Pasaaradere*	*SII*, Vol. XVIII, No. 377, dated AD 1241.	According to Dr Ritti, this referred to tax on shops erected temporarily in the bazaar.
Tax on merchants	*Banajamaga sunka*	*EC*, Vol. III, Nj 338, dated AD 1530.	
Washermen	*Asaga dere*	*EC*, Vol. XI, Dg. 133, AD 1071.	
Prostitutes	*Soole-dere* *Kannadi vana*	*Karnataka Inscriptions*, Vol. X, No. 55, AD 1255. *SII*, Vol. IX, part I, No. 113, AD 1054.	While the first is a tax on the professional, the second is a tax on her professional tool, in this case, the mirror!
Ferrymen	*Odakooli*		
Beggars (!)	*Ganaachara*	48 of 1915, Appendix C	
Left-hand castes	*Idangai vari / Idangai maganmai* The left-hand/right-hand taxes are also sometimes brought under the broad taxation band called *antarayam*.[28] Such tax-banding seems to have been in use between the eleventh and thirteenth centuries.		Both the categories mentioned at the end constitute communal cesses levied collectively on the artisanal, merchant and service castes of a locality.
Right-hand Castes	*Valangai-vari / Valangai maganmai*		Ibid.
18 *Pattadai*. Refers to18 professional castes as a collective unit.	*Pattadai Ayam*	*ARE*, 221 of 1910, 1911, part II, para 51, dated AD 1397.	This record from the village of Paadi Tiruvallidayam in Kanchipuram, Chingleput-district, is important because of its reference to a collective tax on various professionals, artisans and other service providers.

Notes: *ARE* = *Annual Report of Epigraphy*; *EC* = *Epigraphica Carnatica*; *EI* = *Epigraphica Indica*; *SII* = *South Indian Inscriptions*.
All taxes on weavers have been excluded from this table since the taxes in the textile industry are dealt with separately.

The last three categories mentioned in the above table refer to collective taxes on professional castes. Some of the other taxes, apart from *Pattadai ayam*, referred to under '18 *Pattadai*' are: *maada virutti* (possibly on monthly incomes); *sammadam* (possibly a monthly tax); *pattadai nulayam* (obviously levied on weavers since it means 'tax on silk thread'); *chekku kadamai* (exclusively on oil mills), etc.

Another broad banding of taxes is referred to in the inscriptions as *kizh irai paattam*. This can be literally translated as 'lower order of taxes'.[29] Under this are included *meenpattam*, a tax on catch of fish. This is distinct from the tax on fishermen referred to earlier, although it seems to be similar to the *erimeen pattam* cited in the table. Under *kizh irai paattam* is also included *oor kalanju*, a collective levy on a non-Brahmin settlement, *kumarakachchanam/ kumaragadayanam* and *tattarpaattam*. The last was a tax on goldsmiths and is included in the above table. *Kumaragadayana* (also called *kumarakanikke*) has been defined as a contribution by the people whenever a child was born to the king.[30] Yet another imposition or compulsory contribution, called *darshana kanikke*, was levied whenever revenue inspectors visited a locality.[31] Since completely disparate taxes seem to have been brought under this broad category, scholars have also interpreted it as 'miscellaneous tax collective'. Another collective tax term one comes across in medieval inscriptions is '*chilvari*', which seems also to refer to 'miscellaneous' or 'minor taxes'.[32] Even today, in common Tamil parlance, '*chillairai*' means both petty cash and petty matters. Since these taxes, except for a few, were collected from the entire local populace and not from specific communities, these did not constitute professional taxes per se but additional impositions on the local communities including professional groups.

Reference was made at the beginning of this section to the tax on the tools of various professions. These included loom tax (*tari-irai/magga-dere*); tax on the oil mill (*chekku-kadamai*); on the mirror of prostitutes (*sooleyaralliya kannadivana); chakri dere* on the cart of transporters;[33] and on the hammer of the carpenter called '*kodati vana*'.[34]

Another category of tax seems to have been on the site of production. The tax referred to in the fifteenth-century record from Srirangam as '*akkasale vari*' literally means 'tax on the work-site of the *akkasale*', who were primarily goldsmiths.[35] Another instance of the workplace of smiths being taxed is the inscription of Vira Pandya from Tiruvarangulam in Pudukottai state of Tamil Nadu, dated AD 1456, which states that a tax of two *kasu* (per month or annum is not clear) is to be levied on every smithery in the area.[36] Reference to '*kulume dere*', which can be translated as a tax on the furnace of smiths, occurs in a record dated AD 1396.[37] Another very significant tax mentioned in the records is '*akkasale kammatta dere*'.[38] *Akkasale* is the term for smiths and more specifically goldsmiths, while the term *kammatta* refers to a coin-minter. The *kammatta* constituted specialized professionals within the overarching category of *panchalar/kammalar*. This could indicate a tax either on the coin-minter or on the mint.

Canonical injunctions which suggest that in the case of poorer artisans, what was levied as tax was the fruit of their labour and not their profession, is also borne out by some of the medieval inscriptions. These are the taxes referred to in various inscriptions as *pancha-karuka*, *karuka seva* or *karu dere*. While the term '*pancha*' means five, '*karuka*' refers to labour and *dere* to tax. This category, which can be interpreted as 'service tax', has to be read in conjunction with another term used both in the canons and in inscriptions – the term '*vishti*', referred to in Kannada as *bitti*. An inscription dated AD 1089 from Kolar in Mysore district shows that artisans and other Sudras were required to work free, apparently in lieu of cash tax. It reads: '*Shudirarum karukarum bitti-besam maduvaru.*'[39]

Professional craftsmen seem to have acted as both producers and sellers of their products in the capacity of petty entrepreneurs running their craft shops and production centres within their own homes. These '*manaik-kadaiyar*' – literally, 'those whose homes are shops' – were taxed under the tax law termed *patradai*, i.e. workshop taxes.[40]

Did professional guilds pay corporate tax? Evidence from medieval Andhra appears to suggest so. One of the Amaravati records states that on behalf of the fourteen '*Tapala Panchanamuvaru*' inhabiting the regions between the hills of Kondapalli and Bezawada, a certain Mallaya Mahapatra gifted to Kamatesvara of Dharanikota, the '*pannu*' or tax paid by the *Panchanamuvaru* of Dharanikota and the '*palya pannu*' or tax paid by the *Panchanamuvaru* of Amaresvaram.[41] A second inscription from the same area[42] states that Mallaya Mahapatra assigned the *palayam payindi* of Amaravaram, on behalf of the *Panchanamuvaru* of Srirangarajukondasima and Natavaadi. A third epigraph from Paalakol[43] states that the *Panchana-muvaru* of all the *desas* or of the 74 *ahanas* exempted one Kasha Suraaschari from '*pannu-koodu*' as a reward for his work in the temple of Ramalinga. Narasimha Rao, who has quoted all the above instances, assumes that since the guild itself was gifting away the tax, it had obtained a lease from the state to collect taxes from the artisanal professionals.[44] To quote him: 'The guild must have, on this account, paid the state a fixed amount, as was the usual practice under the tax-farming system' (Rao 1967: 61).

While '*pannu*' is still the Telugu term for tax, its interpretation as a state tax in this context seems somewhat dubious since in all the above instances, it seems to have been more in the form of a community tax/voluntary cess, imposed by the artisanal corporation on itself.

Taxing the Textile Industry

All taxes relating to the weaving industry were paid to the state, unless their proceeds had been specifically granted to the temple by the state. To cite an instance, in Kanchipuram, during the reign of Vijaya Gandagopaladeva, a Pallava chief, Kadavaraya, gifted the tax on looms to the Jvaraharesvara Perumal temple.[45] Kulottunga Chola Sambuvaraya is said to have donated the various proceeds of the village of Achcharapakkam, including the tax on looms, to the local deity.[46] Similarly, Rajanarayana Sambuvaraya gifted the tax on looms within the four limits of the *tirumadaivilagam* for worship in the temple of Tiruppulipagava Nayinar in 1343.[47] This suggests that even the tax levied on weavers within the precincts of the temple went to the state unless it was specifically endowed to the temple.

A variety of taxes was imposed on the handloom industry. The most frequently mentioned in the inscriptions is *tari irai*[48] (loom tax), which begins to find mention in inscriptions from the tenth century onwards as *tari kadamai*.[49] Along with this, *per kadamai* was also levied, which appears to have been a tax on the professional rather than on his tools of production.[50] *Magga dere* is the term used in Andhra and Karnataka to denote loom tax,[51] though the records of the Chola kings belonging to the Andhra region refer only to *tari irai*. Another tax mentioned in the records is *achchu tari*, which probably refers to the patterned loom as distinct from the ordinary loom. The tax on *parai tari* (most probably looms weaving coarse cloth, operated by the Pariah 'untouchable' caste) and on *tusaga tari* is distinctive from the rate on *achchu tari*, which suggests a complicated loom used in weaving luxury cloth.[52] Another oft-mentioned tax is the *tari pudavai*. It is more likely that this was a general tax on cloth since *pudavai* in that period was loosely used to denote lengths of cloth of any kind. Details of the taxes imposed at the local fairs or *santa* on *pudavai* are given in a twelfth-century inscription from Bhimavaram.[53] *Panjupeeli* was the tax on cotton yarn.[54] Cotton was taxed and is referred to as *parutti kadamai*.[55] Tax was levied on cotton thread *(nulayam)* and silk thread *(pattadai nulayam)*.[56] *Kurai taragu ayam* (brokerage fee on textiles) is referred to in an inscription from Vedaranyam, dated 1251.[57] A tax called *kaibanna* or *bannige* was also levied on the dyers in the Bangalore region of Karnataka during the early medieval period.[58]

Inscriptional evidence suggests that the number of looms to be operated within a locality, be it a village or a *nadu* (encompassing more than one village), was fixed by the authorities. These could range from four to twenty looms. A loom tax was levied at Kovilpatti during the period of Jatavarman Srivallabha in AD 1129 on the twenty-four looms in the village of Solapuram, at the rate of 10 *panams* per loom per year.[59] An inscription of Rajaraja I, dated AD 993, refers to *Anniyayavaadanavirai*, which has been interpreted to mean a tax on the unauthorized looms in the village.[60]

Evidence for the incidence of taxation on weavers is rather limited for the early medieval period, though there is sufficient information for the Vijayanagara period. Three inscriptions of the period of Hoysala Ramanathadeva (mid-thirteenth century) give the monthly tax on looms, on an average, as between seven to eight *kasu*.[61] According to an inscription dated AD 1277 of the period of Hoysala king Ramanathadeva, his officer, the *Dandanayaka* Ravideva, reported that the weavers of Kandaradittam in Tiruchirapalli had moved *en masse* due to high taxation. However, in due course, the weavers' desertion induced the king to reduce the taxes to eight *kasu* (per year), in an effort to persuade them to return. The records state that this reduced tax was meant to placate weavers who had earlier migrated in protest against the high levels of taxation. During the period of Jatavarman Sundara Pandya, six *panams* per loom was the annual rate of taxation in Tirukachchiyur in Chingleput district. The loom tax averaged around three *panams* (per month) during the Vijayanagara period.

Inscriptional evidence suggests that the regional authorities issued charters of protection called *nambikkai pattayam* in Tamil – literally, 'charters of trust' – in order to retain the services of weavers.[62]

Broker's Fee in Textiles

Another important factor in the textile trade was the broker. The term *taragu kasu* (brokerage fee) occurs repeatedly in later Chola inscriptions, and there is a specific reference to a brokerage fee on textile trade, *kurai taragu ayam,* in an epigraph of the period of Rajaraja Chola III, who belonged to the thirteenth century.[63] It is possible that these brokers were especially used in foreign trade since problems of communication and negotiations are likely to have arisen due to foreign traders not knowing the native language.

Voluntary Cesses in Textile Trade

Merchant corporations like the *Tisaiayirattu Ainnurruvar* seem to have had both vertical and horizontal monopoly over textiles in some regions in the medieval period, although other patterns of textile trade also existed. Thus, at both Mannargudi and Kulittalai,[65] the merchants made a joint contribution to the temple in the form of a fixed levy on income derived from various items of trade. Here *pudavai kattu* (cloth bundle) is mentioned along with items like paddy, pepper, etc. The record pertains to the thirteenth century. In the period of Jatavarman Vikrama Pandya, merchants made a similar contribution on the sale of paddy and cotton at Velangudi.[66] In the fourteenth century, at Piranmalai, all the merchant corporations headed by the *Tisaiayirattu Ainnurruvar* made a donation on all their commodities of trade per head-load (*talai chumai*), per bag-load (*pakkam*), a unit called *podi* (bigger bundle) and cart-load (*vandi*).[67] Cotton (*parutti*), yarn (*nulu*), coarse

Rates of Taxation on the Textile Industry From Tondaimandalam Region,[64] Fourteenth to Sixteenth Centuries, Vijayanagara Period

ARE Number	*Name of King*	*Period*	*Place Name*	*Taluka*	*District*	*Nature of Taxation*	*Rate of Taxation*
ARE 170 of 1933	Kampana Udaiyar	End of fourteenth century	Tirukkaluk-kunram	Chingleput	Chingleput	*Kattukuttagai* consolidated tax on *kaikkolar*	70 *panams*. If a sum of 3½ *panams* was the average tax per loom, then 70 *panams* must have been the tax levied from 24 weavers.
ARE 221 of 1929–30	Harihara Raya	Fourteenth century	Kunnattur	Ibid.	Ibid.	*Tari Irai* loom tax	4 *panams*
ARE 293 of 1910	Bukka II	1404–05	Pulipparakkoyil	Madurantakam	Chingleput	*Tari Kadamai* on the loom + *Per Kadamai*	2 *panams* + 2 *panams*
ARE 364 of 1908	Virupana Udaiyar Virupaksh I	Beginning of fifteenth century	Vayalur	Kanchipuram	Chingleput	*Tari Irai*	3 *panams*
ARE 294 of 1910	Devaraya I	1418	Pulipparakkoyil	Madurantakam	Chingleput	*Vasal Vari*, i.e. house tax on weavers (remi-ssion of tax)	6 *panams*
						Tari Pudavai (tax on sale of sarees?)	40 *panams*
ARE 272 of 1912	Devaraya II	1436	Nerumber	Chingleput	Chingleput	*Pattadai Nulayam* on silk thread	2 *panams*

(continued)

ARE Number	*Name of King*	*Period*	*Place Name*	*Taluka*	*District*	*Nature of Taxation*	*Rate of Taxation*
ARE 252 of 1916–17	Mallikarjuna	1463	Srimushnam	Chidambaram	South Arcot	*Tari Irai from kaikkolar* living in the Tirumadaivilagam temple precinct	Tax on 5 weavers = 20 *panams* at average of 4 *panams* per weaver.
ARE 201 of 1923	Virupana Udaiyar Virupaksha II	Late fifteenth century	Tiruppulivanam	Kanchipuram	Chingleput	*Kattukuttagai* consolidated tax on each loom	5 *panams* (shows a 20% increase in tax). The record states that the weavers deserted in protest against tax increase but were induced to return on the promise that no additional tax would be levied.
ARE 318 of 1909–10	Saluva Narasimha	1484	Tirukachchiyur	Chingleput	Chingleput	Monthly loom tax – *Tari Irai*	¼ *panam* per month = 3 *panams* annually
SII, Vol. XII No. 221	Ibid.	1491	Tiruvakkarai	Villupuram	South Arcot	Monthly loom tax – *Tari Irai*	Enhanced to ½ *panam* monthly, i.e. 6 *panams* annually
ARE 247 of 1916	Vira Narasimha	1504	Srimushnam	Chidambaram	South Arcot	Loom tax on each *kaikkola* weaver	3 *panams*. Tax reduced to 3 following desertion of village by weavers in protest against heavy taxation.

(continued)

ARE Number	*Name of King*	*Period*	*Place Name*	*Taluka*	*District*	*Nature of Taxation*	*Rate of Taxation*
						Loom tax on each loom owned by the *Chettis*	3 *panams*. An interesting instance of a merchant (*Chetti*) owning looms.
ARE 409 of 1913	Krishnadeva Raya	1513	Aragal	Attur	Salem	Reduced loom tax	3 *panams*. The state lowered taxes to conciliate weavers who had deserted their village.
Local Records, LXI, Nos. 23–24	Krishnadeva Raya	1523	Kontakonda	?	?	Loom tax *Magga dere*	½ *varaha*. According to a record of the period of Krishnadeva Raya, 10 *panams* = 1 *varaha*
SII, Vol. IX, Pt. II, No. 516	Krishnadeva Raya	1526	Velupadige	Gooty	Anantapur	Loom tax	3 *panams*
ARE 2 of 1913	Sadasiva Raya	1561	Pillaipalayam (Big Kanchipuram)	Kanchipuram	Chingleput	Loom tax	5½ *panams*

Note: *ARE* = *Annual Report of Epigraphy*; *SII* = *South Indian Inscriptions*.

cloth (*parum pudavai*), fine cotton cloth (*men pudavai*), *konikkai pattu* and *pattavala* (patola silk) are given as the major items of trade. From the rates levied on each bundle or cart it is clear that a head-load was one-twentieth of a *pakkam*, a *pakkam* was one-tenth of a *podi*, and a *podi* one-fifth of a *vandi*.

Self-imposed levies on textiles from the fourteenth-century Piranmalai inscription:

Yarn (does not specify cotton or silk and presumably includes both)	Per *vandi* (cart-load) Per *podi* Per *pakkam* Per *talaichumai* (head-load)	20 *kasu* 5 *kasu* $2^1/_2$ *kasu* 2 *kasu*
Coarse sarees (*parum pudavai*)	Per *podi*	10 *kasu*
Fine sarees (*nen pudavai*)	Per *pakkam* Per *podi* Per *pakkam* Per *talaichumai*	5 *kasu* 20 *kasu* 5 *kasu* 5 *kasu*
Konikkai pattu	Per *podi* Per *pakkam* Per *talaichumai*	2 *kasu* 1 *kasu* 1 *kasu*
Pattavali pattu	Per *talaichumai*	30 *kasu*

The fact that the levy on *pattavali pattu* is much higher than on *konikkai pattu* suggests that the latter may have been an inferior variety of coarse silk.

In the Piranmalai record cited earlier, the joint donation of all the merchant corporations, like the Chitrameli, Manigramattar and others, is headed by the *Tisaiayirattu Ainnurruvar*. Further, though cotton and cloth did form a part of the general trade of the merchant corporations, these were considered important enough to be vested in specialized textile merchants. While the inscriptional references to the *Chilai Chettis* indicate the possibility of a syndicate controlling the sale of cloth, it is interesting that they also seem to have traded in all items connected with textiles. To illustrate the point, an epigraphical record from Anantapur[70] of the period of the Telugu-Choda king Malladeva, dated AD 1162, states that the Nanadesi merchants of the four languages (Tamil, Telugu, Kanarese and Malayalam) of the Kubera lineage consecrated the temple of Dasisvara by endowing to it a fixed fee on all articles in which they traded, including cotton, cotton thread and sarees. This is shown at greater length in a record pertaining to the period of Kakatiya Ganapatideva (AD 1317), according to which a huge donation was made by the native and foreign merchants to a temple at Mattiwada in Warangal.[71] The contribution or *ayam* is stated to have been levied, among other things, on *nulu*, *pattu nulu*, *dasuri* and *pachchai pattu* (tassore and another kind of expensive silk), and on dyes like *nili*, *manjishta*, etc.

Similar instances have been cited earlier. The evidence indicates the geographical extent of the leading mercantile corporations, pointing to some degree of horizontal commercial control in terms of spatial trade organization. Similarly, the repeated references to the mercantile associations dealing in all items from raw cotton to textiles and dyes are suggestive, to some extent, of vertical control. However, the control exercised by these groups was far from being monopolistic, and there is no doubt that yarn and textiles were also being bought and sold in the local fairs (*santa*), which were outside the purview of these corporations.

Voluntary Community Cess or Tax Farming by the State

Was the collection of taxes farmed out to the communities themselves? It is noteworthy that the weavers, like the smiths mentioned earlier, collected a tax from its members, which may have been occasionally donated to the temple. In Srimushnam, during the period of Sundara Pandya in the thirteenth century, the members of the local Kaikkola community made an agreement among themselves to make over to the temple of Tirunarayanisvaramudaiya Nayanar, certain taxes on looms.[72] Narasimha Rao, in his book *Corporate Life in Medieval Andhra Desa* (1967), has suggested that the collection of tax was farmed out by the state to the artisanal guilds themselves. At the same time, some records suggest that weaver organizations derived the requisite funds for their various activities, such as collective donation to temples, by levying a voluntary contribution on their members. This appears to be not so much the regular tax on looms collected by the state, as a contribution on each loom levied by the organization itself. This cess could either be in terms of a proportionate share of the woven cloth, or on the sale of cloth, or contribution in terms of paddy by the weavers.

It is noteworthy that in most cases desertion on the part of weavers worked as an effective strategy of collective bargaining against arbitrary enhancement of taxes by the state. In an interesting instance from the reign of Devaraya II, the *valangai* and *idangai,* by and large encompassing all professional – especially artisanal and merchant – groups, not only refused to pay the existing taxes, but set forth what they considered to be just taxes on their profession![73] In the case of weavers, they suggested a tax of 4 *panams* on working looms and 2 *panams* on idle looms; 3 *panams* for lace looms in working order and half of that on lace looms that were idle/not in working order; and 2 *panams* as *pattadai nulayam*, i.e. the tax on silk thread. It must also be pointed out here that the periods of both Devaraya II and Sadasiva Raya witnessed a steep increase in taxes, perhaps because of growing militarization.

Computational Problems: Taxing Issues

Many kinds of currencies were in circulation, like the *varaha*, *pon*, *gadayana* and *panam*, to name only some. Their weight, fineness and value fluctuated greatly, and varied from one dynasty to the other, and sometimes even from one king to the other.

The term *panam* occurs very rarely in the coinage of the Chola period. One such reference is its mention in an inscription from Tiruvallikeni (Triplicane in Madras).[74] The *Mitakshara* of Vijnanesvara[75] says that anyone who' maimed breeding bulls was to be fined 100 *panams*. Since the fine for such a minor offence could not have been very high, the value of a *panam* must have been lower than other coins like *varaha* and *pon*. The term was common currency by the fourteenth century, when the Vijayanagara empire was established. But the *panam* became *fanam* in the course of the sixteenth–seventeenth century, and was no longer a gold coin but a much devalued copper coin.

Similarly, several terms are used for taxes, such as *siddhaayam*, *ayam*, *vari*, *kadamai*, *irai*, etc. The inscriptions suggest that taxation was usually annual rather than monthly,[76] although there are exceptions.[77] The record states: '*Prativarsha kuttumbana siddhayavanu*', which means annual tax on a professional/family. Secondly, these rates were flat and fixed.[78] The record says: '*Nitya karvaha siddhayavanu*'. Both these aspects are clarified in epigraphs from Tumkur and Bangalore districts in Karnataka, dated *c*. AD 1200 and 1300 respectively.[79]

Evidence from the early medieval period onwards (i.e. the tenth/eleventh centuries) testifies to levy of taxes both in cash (*kasaayam)* and in kind *(nellaayam)*. *Nellayam* literally means payment of tax in grain. A Kannada inscription dated AD 1284 clarifies this: '*Siddhaaya volagada suvarna aya bhattaayagal inda*', which means that within *siddhaaya* you have both tax in cash and tax in kind.[80]

Not only were tax officials ubiquitous during the medieval period in south India, but quite a few records suggest that they also harassed the people over tax payments. Both the terms *chilvari*[81] and *kiruderelkirukula*[82] refer to petty taxes, probably levied on small-time artisans or shopkeepers. In course of time, in the Kannada language, the word '*kirukula*' itself came to mean harassment![83]

Inscriptions also record the collective protest by tax-payers, who included both farmers and the artisanal communities, against state representatives and inspection officers from the revenue department. A record from Paraiyur, Gopichettipalayam, in the North Kongu region of Tamil Nadu, registers a local protest against corrupt tax officials. The inscription, which is said to belong to the period of Parakesari Tribhuvanachakravartin Konerimaikondan, records the pledge of the village to give the corrupt officers no food, not even a handful of rice, and not to pay more than a *panam* to persons claiming to be tax officials and an additional *panam* to those who actually carried state orders bearing the king's signature.[84]

What comes through by a study of medieval inscriptions pertaining to taxation on artisanal communities and other kinds of workers is a rich tapestry of everyday life in medieval peninsular India. Despite the evidence being disparate and inconclusive, they clearly testify to the presence of vibrant working communities who went through vicissitudes of fortunes, but retained a strong sense of agency vis-à-vis dominant economic groups and the medieval polities.

Appendix: Gautama Dharma Sutra on 'Taxing Professions'

The *Gautama Dharma Sutra* (henceforth *GDS*) is believed to have been written anywhere between the third and sixth century BC. The text is attributed to Gautama Maharshi. *GDS* precedes other well-known *Dharmashastra* texts like the *Manusmriti* and *Yajnavalkya Smriti*.

While most *Dharmashastra* texts follow the usual canonical tradition in laying prescriptive codes pertaining to life-cycle rituals, death rituals, rites of passage and modes of worship, along with more secular matters like the duties of a king (*rajadharma*), etc., hardly any concern themselves with issues of taxation.

Taxation is brought into the *Gautama Dharma Sutra*, *Manusmriti* and *Yajnavalkya Smriti* in the context of royal dharma and the duties of a just king. The concept of just and unjust taxes also finds mention in the *Shanti Parva* of the *Mahabharata*.

The contextual themes in the *Gautama Dharma Sutra* are devoted to the student, orders of life or *āśramas*, the householder, occupations of four classes, the king, impurity, ancestral offerings, women and marriage, property, inheritance and penances.

I shall focus here on the pertinent sections on taxation from the text *Gautama Dharma Sutra* pertaining to the social groups which survive by their physical labour, '*aatmopajeevi*', taking into account the medieval commentator Haradatta's interpretation of the *Sutra*.

31. *Shilpino maasi maasyekaikam karma kuryuhu.*
Each artisan shall monthly do one day's work for the king.

32. *Etena aatmopa jeevino vyakyatah.*
Hereby the taxes payable by those who support themselves by personal labour is explained.

(The commentator adds that these could include jugglers, dancers and others who live by their bodies, apart from the ones who labour for their living)

33. *Nauchakreevantashcha.*

And [the tax] payable by those who make their living from boat and carts [i.e. boatmen and cartiers] should also give one day's labour to the king in the form of tax).

34. *Bhaktam tebyo dadyat.*

He [the king] must feed those persons [who thus give their labour as tax to him].

Notes

1 *Gautama Dharma Sutram*, with the commentary along with *Mitakshara vritti* of the medieval commentator Haradatta, edited by Narendra Kumar (2007).

2 Kane (1958).

3 *'Shanti Parva'*, passage 59, p. 980, cited in Ganguly (1925): esp. 698–99.

4 *Gautama Dharma Sutram*, edited by Narendra Kumar (2007).

5 *Yajnavalkya Smriti* with the commentary of *Mitakshara,* edited by Umesh Chandra Pandeya (1988).

6 Cited at Ganguly (1926): 131.

7 *Gautama Dharma Sutram*, *vritti* for *sutra* 25, p. 106–07. A *nishka* was a gold coin.

8 It is stated: '*Moola, phala, pushpaushadha, madhu-mansa, trna-eendananam shashtah*'.

9 The Orientalist debates foreground the current debates among intellectuals over the 'North' versus the 'South'. For an interesting article 'encapsulating "Orientalism"', see Oldmeadow (2004).

10 Said (2003): 321, 325.

11 Batchelor (1994): 234.

12 I looked at this issue in my review of Burton Stein's book, *Peasant, State and Society in Medieval South India*; see Ramaswamy (1982). Also see the tribute I paid to Stein in my short piece titled 'Burton Stein': Ramaswamy (1997).

13 Yajnanesvara's *Mitakshara,* commentary on the *Yajnavalkya Smriti*, '*Acharadhyaya*', translated by late Rai Bahadur Srisa Chandra Vidyarnava, edited by Wasudev Laxman Shastri Panshikar (2003).

14 Ibid.: 413. The translator has a longish note on the use of the word 'Kayastha' in this *sutra*. Vidyarnava brings in the verse from *Vishnu Smriti* (VII: 3) which states, '*Rajadhikarane tan niyukta Kayastha kritham*'. He also quotes other instances where the word 'Kayastha' occurs.

15 *Yajnavalkya Smriti*, *Mitakshara Sahitam*, *Acharadhyaya*, *sutra* 337. The English translation is provided in *Yajnavalkya Smriti*, edited by Panshikar (2003): 413.

16 In the early medieval period this represented real money, but it is used today as a generic term for cash. It is not unlikely that the English word 'cash' comes from this ancient Tamil word, *kasu*.

17 Cited in Appadorai (1936): 695.

18 *Annual Report of Epigraphy* [henceforth *ARE*], 151 of 1925; *ARE*, 587 and 588 of 1915; *ARE*, Part II of 1916, para 27; Inscriptions of the Pudukottai State, 116, 305.

19 Appadorai (1936): 695.

20 *ARE*, 491 of 1926; *ARE*, 1927, Part II, para 87; *ARE*, 140 of 1915; *ARE*, 1916, Part II, para 66.

21 *Epigraphica Carnatica* [henceforth *EC*], Vol. XI, Dg., 133, p. 75, vide Padma (1993): 157.

22 *EC*, Vol. VII, Sk. 295, p. 150; also see pp. 262 and 343. The tax is termed '*sooleyaralliya kannadivana*'.

23 *EC*, No. 45, Vol. XII, Gubbi, Bangalore district.

[24] *EC*, Vol. IX, No. CP 66; *Mysore Archaeological Report*, 1910, para 86, p. 36, vide Gururajachar (1974): 159.

[25] *Epigraphica Indica* [henceforth *EI*], Vol. XXIV, pp. 141–44. The details of the entire group of inscriptions is to be found in M. Somasekhara Sarma, 'Buchireddipalem Copper Plates of Simhavarman II', *Journal of Madras University*, Vol. XII (I), analysed in Satyanarayana (1999): 200–01.

[26] For a brief note on her, see Padma (1993): 194. For a general overview of women in Virasaivism, a twelfth-century religious movement, see Vijaya Ramaswamy (1996).

[27] Both the taxes on markets and petty shops are referred to in Ritti Srinivas (2000): 46–47.

[28] This explanation of the broad-banding of taxes under '*antarayam*' is provided in J. Sundaram (2009): 414–15.

[29] Ibid.: 414.

[30] *EC*, Vol. VII, Nr. 36, dated AD 1077; and *EC*, Vol. V, Hn. 139, dated AD 1200.

[31] *Mysore Archaeological Report*, 1910, p. 36, para 86; *Karnataka Inscriptions*, Vol. I (19), dated AD 1108; *EC*, Vol. VIII, Sb. 179, dated AD 1189, vide Gururajachar (1974): 165.

[32] *South Indian Inscriptions* (henceforth *SII*), Vol. I, No. 59, dated AD 1406.

[33] *EC*, Vol. II, Sb.142.

[34] *EC*, Vol. VIII, Hn.160, dated AD 1215. In the same series, see Vol. IX, Bn. 6, dated AD 1253.

[35] *EI*, Vol. XVIII, p. 139, dated AD 1434.

[36] *ARE*, 264 of 1914.

[37] *EC*, Vol. VII, Hl. 71.

[38] *SII*, Vol. XV, No. 70.

[39] *SII*, Vol. XV, No. 159, vide Gururajachar (1974): 160.

[40] *ARE*, 59 of 1914; *A.R.E.*, 1915, Part II, para 44.

[41] *SII*, Vol.VI, No. 219.

[42] *SII*, Vol. VI, No. 220.

[43] *SII*, Vol. V, No.158.

[44] See Narasimha Rao (1967). All the above-mentioned instances have been cited here.

[45] *ARE*, 228 of 1910–11.

[46] *SII*, Vol. VII, Nos. 454 and 455. Also refer to *ARE*, 333 of 1935–1936 from Potladurti in Cuddappah district, etc.

[47] *ARE*, 218 of 1910–11.

[48] *SII*, Vol. VIII, Nos. 7 and 8 of the period of Rajaraja Chola I; Vol. VIII (117) of the period of Rajendra Chola; Vol. VIII (123) of the period of Kulottunga Chola I, etc.

[49] *SII*, Vol. V, No. 410 from Tirunelveli, same taluk and district.

[50] *ARE*, 218 of 1910.

[51] *EC*, Vol. VI, Hs. 97 from Kudakkuru in Mysore district; *EC*, Vol. IX, copperplate inscription No. 66 from Yeliyur; and *ARE*, 628 of 1920–21 from Amritalur in Guntur district. For the levy of *Tari Irai* in Andhra by the Cholas, see *ARE*, 64 of 1958–59 from Mundalapundi in Chittoor district of the period of Vikrama Chola.

[52] While *Achchu Tari* alone is referred to in *SII*, Vol. VII, No. 98 of the period of Rajaraja I (AD 1001), all three kinds of looms are referred to in *SII*, Vol. I, No. 64.

[53] *SII*, Vol. V, No. 65.

[54] *SII*, Vol. V, No. 309 from Nilikottai in Madurai, dated 1192; *SII*, Vol. VIII, No. 177 from Ramanathapuram district, etc.

[55] *SII*, Vol. VII, No. 936, the thirteenth-century inscription from Tirukkoyilur in North Arcot district.

[56] *SII*, Vol. VII, No. 109 of the period of Sambuvaraya from Tiruvottiyur in Chingleput; *ARE*, 68 of 1958–59 from Yalamari in Chittoor district of Andhra, etc. This tax has been listed in the taxation table on the Vijayanagar period.

[57] *SII*, Vol. XVII, No. 452.

[58] *EC*, Vol. IX, Cp. 66 from Virupakshapuram in Hubli taluk.

[59] *SII*, Vol. XIV, No. 221.

[60] *EC*, Vol. IV, pp. 137–38. The interpretation of the inscription is vide Appadorai (1936): 476 and fn. 116. The Kuram plates of the Pallava king Paramesvaravarman I state that looms were included among the property owned by the village in common. Appadorai is of the opinion that the weavers may have been maintained out of the village funds.

[61] *ARE*, 311 of 1968–69, dated AD 1261 from Tripattavellur; 152 of 1928–29, dated AD 1267 from Nattamangudi, and 203 of 1928–29 from Kandaradittam, all from Tiruchirapalli district of Tamil Nadu.

[62] *ARE*, 201 of 1923 from Tiruppulivanam, Kanchipuram taluk, Chingleput district of the period of Virupaksha II. See also *ARE*, 454 of 1916, dated 1513, from Ambasamudram, Tirunelveli district; and *ARE* 310 of 1916–17 from the same area.

[63] *SII*, Vol. XVII, No. 452.

[64] Thondaimandalam broadly covered Chingleput, North Arcot and South Arcot districts.

[65] *SII*, Vol. VI, No. 41 of the period of Kochchadaipanmar Sundara Pandya and *ARE*, 88 of 1914–15 of the period of Jatavaraman Vira Pandya.

[66] *ARE*, 507 of 1958–59.

[67] *SII*, Vol. VIII, No. 442.

[68] *Kasu* is a gold coin in currency in early medieval peninsular India.

[69] The fact that the levy on *pattavali pattu* is fairly high suggests that this must have been regarded as an expensive variety of silk cloth, which is logical seeing that it also involved the technology of tie-and-dye weaving.

[70] *ARE*, Nos.15 and 16, Appendix C of 1917–18.

[71] *HAS*, Vol. XIII, No. 14.

[72] *ARE*, 248 of 1915–16.

[73] *ARE*, 59 of 1914–15.

[74] *SII*, Vol. VIII, No. 543.

[75] *Mitakshara* of Vijnanesvara, commentary on *Yajnavalkyasmriti*, edited by J.R. Gharpure (1939): 236.

[76] *EC*, Vol. V, Bl. 140.

[77] See tax table for an instance of monthly tax from the period of Saluva Narasimha, dated AD 1491.

[78] *EC*, Vol. III, TN, No. 98.

[79] Both the inscriptions have been quoted in Gururajachar (1974): 143. They have been interpreted by him as pertaining to fixed annual taxes.

[80] *EC*, Vol. IV, Ng. 38.

[81] *SII*, Vol. I, No. 59 from Poigai, Virinchipuram in North Arcot district, dated AD 1228.

[82] Gururajachar (1974): 146.

[83] Ibid.

[84] *ARE*, 185 of 1910 and para 37 of 1911.

References

Appadorai, A. (1936), *Economic Conditions in Southern India, AD 1000*–1500, Vol. II, Madras: University of Madras.

Batchelor, Stephen (1994), *The Awakening of the West*, Berkeley: Parallax Press.

Ganguly, J.N.C. (1925), 'Principles of Hindu Taxation', *Indian Historical Quarterly*, Part I, Vol. I: 696–702.

——— (1926), 'Principles of Hindu Taxation', *Indian Historical Quarterly*, Part II, Vol. II: 129–46.

Gautama Dharma Sutram, edited by Narendra Kumar (2007), New Delhi: Vidyanidhi Prakashan.

Gururajachar, S. (1974), *Some Aspects of Economic and Social Life in Karnataka,* Mysore: Prasaranga, University of Mysore.

Kane, Pandurang Vamanrao (1958), *Dharmashatras: Ancient and Medieval Religions and Civil Law in India,* Poona: Bhandarkar Oriental Research Institute.

'Mitakshara' of Vijnanesvara, Commentary on 'Yajnavalkya Smriti', edited by J.R. Gharpure (1939), Book II, Bombay: Aryabhushan Press.

Oldmeadow, Harry (2004), *Journeys East: 20th Century Western Encounters with Eastern Religious Traditions*, World Wisdom Inc.; available at www.worldwisdom.com/public/library/default.aspx, accessed 26 January 2012.

Padma, M.B. (1993), *The Position of Women in Medieval Karnataka*, Mysore: Prasaranga, University of Mysore.

Ramaswamy, Vijaya (1982), '*Peasant State and Society in Medieval South India* by Burton Stein: A Review Article', *Studies in History*, Vol. IV, 2: 307–20.

——— (1996), *Divinity and Deviance: Women in Virasaivism,* Oxford: Oxford University Press.

——— (1997), 'Burton Stein', *Studies in History*, NS, Vol. XIII, 1: 147–56.

Rao, R. Narasimha (1967), *Corporate Life in Medieval Andhradesa*, Delhi: University Grants Commission.

Said, Edward (2003), *Orientalism*, London: Penguin.

Satyanarayana, K. (1999), *A Study of the History and Culture of the Andhras*, Hyderabad: Visaalandhra Publishing House.

Srinivas, Ritti (2000), 'Introduction', in *Descriptive Glossary of Administrative Terms in Ancient Karnataka*, Mysore: Directorate of Archaeology and Museums.

Sundaram, J. (2009), *Land System in Tamil Nadu,* Delhi: Bharatiya Kala Prakashan.

Yajnavalkya Smriti, edited by Umesh Chandra Pandeya (1988), *Kashi Chowkhamba Sanskrit Series*, No. 178, Varanasi: Chowkhamba.

Yajnavalkya Smriti, '*Acharadhyaya*', translated by Rai Bahadur Srisa Chandra Vidyarnava, edited by Wasudev Laxman Shastri Panshikar (2003), *Chowkhamba Sanskrit Series* No. CXXIII, Varanasi: Chowkhamba, reprint.

Work Community and Identity

Caste and Work

Weaving in Nineteenth-Century South India

D.W. Karuna Miryam

This essay looks at the handloom industry in nineteenth-century south India in order to examine some questions of work and caste. First, a few general observations. In the existing historiography, research on textile production in India has been almost exclusively focused on the Coromandel coast where production was largely geared towards export, and on so-called specialist weaving castes. It has been argued that, unlike other societies where peasants also wove cloth as a part-time occupation, the weaving industry in south India was more 'highly developed', involving full-time weavers from specialist weaving castes. For example, according to Prasannan Parthasasarathi:

> the majority of cotton weavers in south India were professional weavers; that is, work at the loom represented their sole source of earnings. However, a small number of south Indians took up weaving in order to supplement earnings from other pursuits. This latter group was largely found in the dry or plains areas of south India and their small numbers suggest that they accounted for only a small fraction of total cloth production. Many were primarily agriculturists who followed weaving seasonally.[1]

He refers to these as peasant-weavers and concludes that, considering their small numbers, it must have been rare for south Indian peasants to produce the cloth they wore.[2] 'Barbers, Chucklers (cobblers), Dhers (tanners) and scavengers' are also mentioned as working on looms occasionally.[3]

In a similar vein, Sanjay Subrahmanyam argues that weaving was different from other non-agricultural activities in that it was a full-time occupation:

> These weavers were by no means part-time peasant agriculturists, who turned to manufacturing as a supplementary source of income. With the exception of a few 'coolie' weavers, employed on the looms of others, and some *Pariah* weavers, who typically wove the lower counts of cloth, textile

production was an activity that was not easily combined with the use of the plough.[4]

It is his contention that weaving could not have been a part-time occupation as the demand for textiles peaked at roughly the same time (during the same months) as demand for agricultural labour. Here, again, the focus is on textiles for export from centres located primarily on the Coromandel coast.

Anthropologists also argue that weavers came from specialist castes, grouped together as left-hand castes along with other artisans (and merchants), and were distinct from hierarchically integrated agricultural castes (called right-hand castes). According to this thesis, textile-weaving was a full-time occupation carried out by specialist weaving castes who had no involvement as such in agriculture.[5] Mattison Mines argues that weavers usually lived separately from cultivators in their own communities and took no part in agriculture.[6] He focuses mainly on the Kaikolars, a specialist weaving caste, but also mentions the Devangas. Similarly, Vijaya Ramaswamy, in her study on the textile industry in medieval south India, sees weaving as a specialist occupation carried out by certain castes such as Saliars, Kaikolars, etc. She regards medieval weavers as having been outside the village community, unlike other service castes such as the carpenter, blacksmith, potter, etc., who were integrated into it through the *jajmani* system.[7] She makes no mention of either part-time weavers or Pariah[8] weavers in her monograph.

By contrast, Ian Wendt documents the presence of many weaving castes, noting accurately that four of these have been given pre-eminence in the existing scholarship despite 'there being no strong rationale for excluding the others'.[9] But subsequently he too goes on to differentiate between professional full-time weavers (who, according to him, formed the core weaving groups) and non-professional weavers from 'various agrarian groups and "Pariahs" from different low castes'. Amongst professional weavers he lists Kaikolars, Devangas, Padma Sales, Pedda Sales, Pattu Sales, Togattas, Bilimaggas, Pattvegars, Jadas or Seniyars, and Koliyars. His second category of 'non-professional' weavers 'often wove seasonally or only when there were specific demands or direct orders for cloth', and otherwise worked as agricultural labourers. In this category he lists Paraiyars, Chakkaliyars, Malas, Madigas or Dhers, Whalliaru or Hoyelas, Pallis or Pallans, Agamudaiyars, Balijas, and barbers.[10] What is interesting here is that the Koliyars, whom he lists under 'professional' weavers, were actually a sub-category of Pariahs and thus an 'untouchable' community. My own research shows that Malas and Pariahs, whom he lists under the 'non-professional' category, worked in large numbers as weavers, many of them being employed full time in producing cloth for the Company.

P. Swarnalatha also documents the presence of Pariah weavers in large numbers. According to her, in Godavari district, the Devangas, Padma Sale and Pattu Sale were the predominant weaving communities, apart from weavers belonging to castes such as Karnabattus, Perikas, Bogamvallu and Singammas; while in Masulipatmnam and Guntur districts, 'non-traditional' Pariah weavers were the dominant group in certain areas. Other important castes represented among the weavers were the Sale, Jandra and Togatta castes.[11] Yet, despite documenting the presence of various castes, particularly untouchables (Malas/Pariahs), in weaving, she continues to refer to them as 'non-traditional' weavers.

This equation of particular castes with particular occupations has obscured the wide diversity of production and producers in the weaving industry. In a wider context, the equation of caste with occupation, by colonial observers as well as later researchers, legitimizes some forms of work and dismisses others as aberrations, or simply does not recognize them as work at all. This leads us to the question of exactly which castes worked as weavers in the eighteenth and nineteenth centuries. Most writings on weaving/weavers, be they from the colonial period or in later research, usually give disproportionate prominence to a handful of castes recognized as 'weaving castes'. For Madras Presidency, these would include Pattunoolkarar (later called Sourashtras), Padma Sales and Pattusales, Devangas, Kaikolars, and Seniyars. Now it is true that these castes were present in large numbers, often lived in their own settlements and concentrated exclusively on weaving. This was particularly true of the Coromandel coast where production was on a large scale and oriented towards export. It was also true of many towns and large settlements further inland which produced particular kinds of cloth sold locally as well as in distant markets. But the exclusive focus on these castes has obscured the labour of a large number of weavers belonging to many other castes.

A closer reading of the sources of the eighteenth and nineteenth centuries shows the involvement of people from a wide range of castes in the textile industry, including large numbers of weavers from the so-called untouchable castes. The data are scattered and difficult to compare across districts and regions. Some castes are unique to some districts and absent elsewhere. But looking at the lists of castes, it is clear that quite apart from those identified as weaving castes, many persons from castes associated with cultivation and occupations such as fishing were also involved in weaving. Thus, in the Baramahal region (as well as in other places), Chembadavars (also recorded as Cheniwars) were weavers as well as inland fishers.[12] The Toreas, also known as Bestas in some places, were occasional weavers. They are also found acting as cultivators, ferry-men, armed messengers, burners of lime, fishermen and porters.[13] Members of different castes such as Agamudiyars, Velamavamloo, Balijavanloo, Agamadiahs, Pullee, Gollavars and Iendravars, usually identified as cultivators, are also mentioned as weavers, though in smaller numbers.[14] Coravurs, who were petty traders and appear to have been a nomadic community, also wove. Polavurs, Sevyars, and Andies are some other castes who were employed in weaving albeit in small numbers.[15]

Most important in terms of numbers and their geographical spread are weavers from several untouchable castes often lumped together as Pariah weavers. Here, I will try to document their presence using records mainly from the first half of the nineteenth century; a few references go further back in time and some are from a somewhat later period, in the late nineteenth century or early twentieth century.

The 'Pariah' Weaver[16]

In the Baramahal districts, apart from the 'weaving castes', a couple of Pariah castes were present in substantial numbers: these were the Koliar and Manniwar – the former being concentrated in the southern part of the district, and the latter in the central and northern parts. In the southern division, Koliars constituted between 10 to 18 per cent of the total number of weavers (the variation derives from two different surveys), and in the central and northern division, the Manniwars formed 10 per cent and 38 per cent of the total number of weavers respectively. Clearly, these are substantial proportions. In the three divisions taken together, Koliars and Manniwars constituted about 18 per cent of the total number of weavers. In these three divisions of the Baramahals, the percentages of specialist weaving castes were as follows: 36 per cent (of the total) for Kaikolars, 23 per cent for Jadars and 8.5 per cent for Pattunulkarars.[17] It should be noted that Manniwars were the largest group of weavers (38 per cent) in the northern division, which had very few weavers from the specialist weaving castes.

Similarly, in Madura district, Pariahs were said to constitute as much as 48 per cent of the total number of weavers; in comparison, the main specialist weaving castes were 20 per cent Pattunoolkarars, 7 per cent Kaikolars and 16 per cent Shaiders.[18] A detailed description of the Dindigul area (later part of Madurai district) notes the presence of Pariah weavers in nearly every village. In Dindigul itself there were 93 looms producing different sorts of cloth, both fine and coarse, presumably belonging to specialist weaving castes; but there were also 146 looms in villages adjacent to the 'cusbah talook' (headquarters) where coarse cloths were manufactured by the Pariahs 'which served the purposes of the inhabitants in the country'.[19]

The situation in other districts was not very different. Pariahs constituted 15.5 per cent of the weavers in Coimbatore district.[20] In Tinnevelly, the main castes listed as weavers were Puttagasauliers, Eloovurs (who were also distillers), Keiklers (Kaikolars), Mussalmans, Pariers (Pariahs), barbers and Panisavens.[21] According to the Trichnopoly District Manual, 'dress is provided by weavers and Pariahs in nearly equal numbers, almost to the exclusion of other castes'.[22]

In Guntur district, the number of looms worked by Sales (a specialist weaving caste), and those by Malas (a Telugu untouchable caste roughly equivalent to the Tamil Pariahs) and others, was roughly equal.[23] Mala weavers were present in large numbers in certain areas of Guntur district, while Sales were usually concentrated in other areas. Pariah weavers were found in large numbers in Masulipatam district as well.[24] In Nellore district, it was reported that 'the Sala, the Jaura and Pariah class compose the great body of the weavers'.[25] The looms of Pariahs constituted 38 per cent of the total number of looms there.[26]

Cuddapah, Kurnool and Bellary districts had large concentrations of Mala weavers whose primary occupation is often described as weaving. According to a missionary source, 'the Malas are not mere coolies; the majority of them weave with the handloom, and their wives spin thread; some are cultivators, others field labourers'.[27] The Malas in Nundial (Kurnool) were reported to be 'more industrious and more self-reliant; and besides following the *ordinary* occupation of weaving the common cloth of the country, many of them were engaged in agricultural work, having fields of their own which they till with their own cattle'.[28]

The Malas of this area continued to weave into the late nineteenth and early twentieth century. Thurston, in his *Tribes and Castes*, described them as follows:

> The chief occupation of the Malas is weaving and working as farm labourers for Sudras; a few cultivate their own land. The Malas of the western part of the Telugu country are of a superior type and have largely retained their lands. . . . In the east weaving is the staple industry, and it is still carried on with the most primitive instruments.[29]

Mala weavers were also known as Netpanivandlu (*nethapani* meaning weaving work).[30] Again, according to the Kurnool District Manual, 'Malas live chiefly by weaving, Madigas by tanning leather and making shoes'.[31] In Bellary, it was reported, 'looms are kept not only by the distinct classes of weavers, namely, Pudmasalawar, Davangumwar, Togatewar, Hatakar, Heracooroovany and Chickcooroovany but also by some other castes such as Lublaree/Cubbaree, Momeens, barbers and Pariahs who assume the profession and all these are invariably taxed more or less with Moturpha'.[32]

Buchanan, in his travels through the Mysore country, repeatedly refers to the weavers of the Whalliaru caste whom he equates with the Pariahs of the Tamil region (especially in villages around the towns of Bengaluru, Colar and Silaguta).[33] He also mentions encountering Pariah weavers in the Tamil countryside (in the districts of Salem and Coimbatore).[34]

Thus it is quite clear that Pariah weavers, or rather weavers from several untouchable castes, were present in substantial numbers in most districts of the Presidency. The evidence seems to indicate that they predominated in certain districts, and perhaps in particular areas within these districts. Thus in Guntur district, Pariahs were predominant in some areas and Sales in others.[35] Similarly, Manniwars were present in large numbers in the northern part of Baramahal division where weavers from other castes were comparatively few.[36] Another interesting fact is that while Pariah weavers were found in large numbers in Guntur, Nellore and Cuddapah districts, they were almost absent in Vishakapatnam and Godavari districts.[37] This led Joseph Brennig to argue (in general terms) that weavers came from specific weaving castes (he names three), and that 'there is no evidence of low or outcaste weavers'.[38] Vishakapatnam and Godavari were important textile-producing centres on the Coromandel coast. Even in these, as well as in other textile centres on the coast such as South Arcot, Pariahs though absent as weavers, were found in large numbers as specialist spinners. They often lived in their own settlements and were known to produce the finest thread.[39]

From the evidence it seems reasonable to assume that Pariah weavers were present in much larger numbers in dry areas, where the agricultural season was much shorter, and particularly in cotton-producing areas with easy access to cotton and yarn. This hypothesis is borne out by their numbers in Cuddapah, Kurnool, Guntur, Coimbatore, Baramahal (Salem) and Madurai districts – all dry cotton-producing regions. This also fits in with the thesis that the bondage of untouchable castes as agricultural labourers was most prevalent in areas of irrigated agriculture.[40] But even in the large textile centres on the Coromandel coast, which were also irrigated agricultural areas, Pariahs were present in large numbers as specialist spinners, and thus played a prominent role in the weaving sector as a whole.

Untouchable weavers also seem to have been widely scattered, living in villages (or more often in their own settlements outside villages) rather than in towns or weaver settlements. In Dindigul district, nearly every village was said to have a few Pariah weavers. Buchanan reported that in the Bengaluru region, 'weavers of this kind [Whalliaru] live scattered in the villages'.[41] Similarly, for the region around Colar, while weavers from the Devanga and Shayniga castes (specialist weaving castes) lived in the town, the Whalliaru were found in surrounding villages.[42] In Silagutta, the specialist Padma Shalay weavers lived in the town, while Whalliaru weavers occupied the hinterland.[43] But they were not always scattered in this fashion across the countryside. In Guntur they were concentrated in certain centres of production; and similarly, Ian Wendt refers to larger settlements of untouchable weavers in the Kaveri delta region.[44]

What did Pariah or Untouchable Weavers Produce?

In brief, Pariahs wove mostly plain coarse cloth. It is this pattern of production that has led many historians to dismiss them as unskilled and therefore, by implication at least, unworthy of close attention. But what untouchable weavers produced was what a majority of the population wore; moreover, the kind of cloth they wove was not very different from that produced by many sections of professional weavers. My research shows that different groups of weavers within a particular region produced particular kinds of cloth. Some might specialize in women's cloths, others in men's cloths, and some in turbans.

Let us look at the evidence in more detail. According to Buchanan: 'The Whalliaru make a coarse, white, strong cloth called Parcalla. It serves the poorer male inhabitants, throughout the country, as a covering for the upper parts of their bodies.'[45] This cloth was made in three different degrees of fineness. The cloths woven by Togattas (professional or specialist weavers) and by the Whalliaru were essentially similar in quality.[46] It was coarse, thick, white cotton cloth. These cloths were durable and as such used by the majority of the population.

Similarly, in the Tamil countryside, what Pariahs wove does not seem to be very different from what some specialist weavers such as the Kaikolars wove. According to two reports from 1794 and 1796, Kaikolars in the Baramahal division wove coarse cloth from 12 to 72 cubits in length, sold under different names – *selampore nedumulum* was 72 cubits, *kaili* 36 cubits, *pachoram* 18 cubits.[47] They also produced *mota khadis*, a coarse cloth suitable for making tents, *vastis* and *salamburies*. But Pariahs are also described as producing similar kinds of cloth.[48]

In some regions they also produced fine cloth. In Baramahal, Koliyars are reported as weaving *parkallies*, described as long cloth or fine white cloth.[49] Manniwars (an untouchable caste) were reported to 'weave the finest kinds of turbans and none of the other cloths of the Jadars but all those made by the Kaikolas. Their manufacture excels in fineness that of all other castes of weavers.'[50] They also wove coarse cloth such *motakhadis*, *vastis and sailumbaries*, similar to that woven by Kaikolars. A Dutch Company servant reported the presence of many Pariah weavers who made 'very good textiles' in some villages in the Kaveri delta.[51]

Coarse, durable cloth (produced by different groups of weavers) was what most of the population wore, and it was therefore sought after. While discussing possible exemptions from duties for coarser kinds of cloth (those of value not exceeding Rs 2 per piece), the Collector of Nellore district estimated that it would lead to a loss of about one-fourth of the total *sayer* revenue (shorthand for duties on trade). He went on to add that though this exemption would be a relief for the poorer classes,

> cloths of the value above mentioned (1½ rupees) are not exclusively worn by the poorer classes. Though persons in good circumstances and those generally in the public employ will not use such cloths when they appear in public it is notorious that they are used by them in their houses.[52]

Munro, reporting on the production of cloth in the Ceded Districts in 1804, remarked that 'by far the greatest proportion of the looms are employed in the fabrication of the coarser and low priced cloths'.[53] According to his detailed report, the cloth category produced by the largest number of looms was *kaudie*: the coarsest kind of cloth. *Kaudie* was woven by 49 per cent of looms producing white cloth, and as many as 40 per cent of the total number of looms did so. In terms of value, *kaudies* constituted 40 per cent of the value of white cloth produced and 29 per cent of *all* cloth produced.[54]

Similarly, 70 per cent of the cloth produced in Coimbatore district was of a value below Rs 2 (per piece); and in Chingelput this per centage was 41 per cent.[55] A similar situation prevailed in the Central Provinces where Rivett-Carnac reported that a coarse and strong cloth, greatly favoured by the Kunbis (farmers) of Berar, was entirely produced by the Dhers (a local untouchable caste) who both spun the thread and wove the cloth. He counted as many as 350 Dhers (compared to 110 Koshtee or specialist weavers making much finer cloth) selling cloth in the weekly market of Jamoorghotta where, according to him, 'the peasantry flock[ed] for the cloth made by the Dhers'.[56]

Thus it is clear that the kind of cloth which Pariah weavers produced was not very different from what many specialist weavers did. However, this has been dismissed or ignored in most academic writing as unworthy of attention. Another implied justification for the dismissal of untouchable weavers as 'non-traditional' or 'non-professional' stems from the fact that they are assumed to be part-time weavers whose 'actual' or 'real' occupation was something else. This view is influenced by the colonial anthropological outlook which, in its attempt to categorize Indian society, slotted different castes into different occupations, and saw anything that did not fit this picture as an anomaly or deviation.

Part-time Weaving

It is perfectly true that in many areas Pariah or untouchable weavers worked part-time and were also involved in work other than weaving. But this does not necessarily mean that, taken in total, the amount of cloth they produced was in any way negligible. The Whalliaru from around Bangalore would 'hire themselves out as day-labourers to farmers, or other persons who will give them employment'.[57] But though they were part-time weavers, Buchanan reported that 'in the country villages much coarse cloth is made by [them]'. Munro, discussing cloth production in the Ceded Districts, says that 'many of the looms belong to Barbers-Chucklers and Dhers who only weave occasionally and many of the weavers themselves have not always employment in their own profession and are engaged several months in the year as field labourers'.[58] Some Koliars were also *totis* or village servants who worked part-time as weavers: they 'do not constantly apply to their trade as weavers but as they have time to spare from their ordinary occupation or ability to purchase the raw materials'.[59] Hurdis, reporting from Dindigul, says that the Dhans (an untouchable caste) 'are taxed in proportion to the time they work at their looms and the produce of the time since in the months of cultivation they leave their craft to attend on that particular business'.[60] But it should be remembered that this kind of 'part-time' weaving might last as long as eight months of the year, given the intrinsic character of the agrarian economy in regions of dryland cultivation. For example, Mala weavers from Cuddapah were said to weave for eight months of the year, being involved in agricultural work only for the remaining four months.[61]

And it was not just the Pariah or untouchable weavers who were part-time weavers. Many professional weavers were also often part-time cultivators. In those census years when this fact is noted, it is usually regarded as a deviation: a sign of the decline of the weaving industry in general, with weavers abandoning their profession. And this may have been the case from roughly the second quarter of the nineteenth century. But even at the beginning of the nineteenth century it was noted that many Kaikolars were cultivators.[62] In 1824, the Collector of Nellore reported that many of the weavers of his district had land which they cultivated.[63] The Jaders of Coimbatore, who constituted the largest community amongst the weavers, also cultivated land: '[M]any of these persons if not all employ half their time in weaving and the other portion in cultivation.'[64] Thus it was not exceptional for weaving to be combined with other forms of work, most obviously for untouchable weavers, but also for an unknown proportion of specialist weavers. This brings us to the whole question of the organization of textile production.

How Was Production Organized?

A close examination of the records shows that production of cloth by Pariah or untouchable weavers was organized in several ways. The most common arrangement was one where the weaver got his thread (or even cotton) from a customer, for whom he wove the cloth in return for a wage. A report from Cuddapah district says that

> at present the thread used for the hand shuttle is spun by the Mala women from ordinary cotton produced in the district. The Mala weavers do not provide their own cotton for the clothes they weave, but the Kapus give them the cotton from their own fields, pay the women a few annas for spin-

ning it, and then pay the men a regular wage for weaving it into cloth.[65]

Moreover, 'each weaver has his own customers, and very often one family of Malas will have weaved for one family of Sudras for generations'.[66]

Giving cotton or thread to the weaver to be spun into cloth was a common practice, and not just in the case of 'Pariah' weavers. According to Buchanan, the Togattas were too poor to make cloth on their own account, and 'in general receive the thread from the women in the neighbourhood, and work it up into cloth for hire'. In Chingleput district, cloths of low value were made by the 'commoner classes of weavers, on their own account and that of others, who make their own thread, and pay the hire of weaving it into cloth'.[67] In North Arcot district, the Collector reported that 'the lower orders of cultivators . . . were in the habit of preparing the thread, getting the cloths made for their own use'.[68] According to the Collector of Cuddapah, 'the practice of supplying the material and getting cloths made for home use obtains to a great extent in this district'.[69] A similar practice was reported from Coimbatore and Rajamundhry districts.[70]

A servant of the Dutch East India Company who toured the Kaveri delta reported that Pariah weavers used yarn spun by their women and children.[71] It was quite common for labourers picking cotton (often from the untouchable castes) to be paid in kind.[72] This was later cleaned and spun by them. The Dhers of the Berar region in the Central Provinces cleaned cotton and spun their own yarn, which they then wove into cloth.[73]

Other systems of production existed. Pariah weavers were also hired by merchants or different European companies to weave cloth for them, and provided with advances for the purpose. Merchants in the Baramahal division would give advances to Koliyars to produce cloth.[74] But in general, weavers (of whatever caste) were provided with advances only when there was a specific and sustained demand for their goods.[75] Otherwise weavers bought yarn from local markets or received yarn directly from cultivators. In Silagutta, in the Mysore country, the cloth chiefly exported was the very coarse kind made by the Whalliaru and was collected from neighbouring villages. 'When any considerable quantity is wanted, advances are made by the merchants; but more than the price of one piece at a time is never given in advance. There are no intermediate agents between the merchant and the weaver.'[76]

Thus cloth production by Pariah weavers was organized in different ways – they might weave for particular clients who gave them cotton or thread for the purpose; or weave on their own account and sell in local markets; or, more rarely, weave for merchants who provided advances. The last mode was not very prevalent as these weavers were usually very poor and merchants feared to give them advances that might never be recovered.

Indeed Pariah weavers were amongst the poorest weavers. There are a few, admittedly unreliable, accounts of the earnings of different kinds of weavers. These show the income of Pariah weavers as being the lowest.[77] More importantly, they also paid the lowest rates as loom tax.[78] The loom tax was roughly proportional to quality of cloth produced and/or the estimated earnings of the individual weaver. However, even though the untouchable weavers were poor and did not usually work for merchants, they, like weavers from other castes, produced either directly for customers or for the market, and worked for wages (sometimes in the form of grain, especially when the customers were poor).[79] They were not, in any case, normally part of *jajmani* system of reciprocal obligations, that is, they were not provided part of the harvest for the weaving they did. Thus it would appear that though Pariah weavers were sometimes employed by merchants, they usually produced cloth using yarn supplied by their customers or bought/spun by themselves.

Changes in the Nineteenth Century

Towards the end of the nineteenth century and particularly in the twentieth century, these Pariah or untouchable weavers gradually disappeared. So much so that no association remains in popular memory between 'Pariahs' and 'weaving'. It is noteworthy that the same period sees the decline and disappearance of decentralized forms of yarn-spinning and cloth production (a subject discussed elsewhere in my research).

The handloom industry in the nineteenth century is usually discussed in the context of the 'deindustrialization' debate. However, it is necessary to differentiate between different periods within the nineteenth century and between different sectors of the industry. In the mid-nineteenth century, immediately after the withdrawal of the East India Company from the textile export trade, the worst affected weavers were those who produced fine cloth for the export market. Weavers who produced coarser cloths for local markets were reported to be faring relatively better in most districts. At this time most of the yarn used was hand-spun and locally produced.[80]

But by the 1880s, the situation had been inverted. E.B. Havell, who was appointed to study the state of industries in the Madras Presidency, reported in 1884 that the worst hit by competition from imports were the coarser, ordinary varieties of cloth worn by most people and woven by the poorer weavers (many of whom came from the Pariah castes). This time it was the weavers of finer varieties of cloth who were reported to be doing better.[81] Also, cloth produced for women survived better. Thus the earlier situation had been reversed. In this period, the greatest decline was in the cheaper, coarser, plain cloth, using yarn spun locally, either by the weaver's family or by women of cultivating and labouring castes, and woven by the poorest weavers. In Havell's opinion, 'the whole industry must disappear . . . so far as low caste or purely cotton goods are concerned, the only part likely to be able to hold its own being a small remnant in the shape of the finer manufactures wherein silk is used either solely or partially'.[82] He was partly right and partly wrong; but it is significant that this decline in coarse cloth production coincided with the replacement of hand-spun yarn by imported mill yarn. This was to prove one of the determining factors in the decline of the untouchable weaver.

Tirthankar Roy cites observations like Havell's to argue that the less skilled and inefficient ('obsolete') parts of the weaving industry, its 'backward segments', disappeared, while the 'progressive segments' (those that were 'viable') that could adapt and restructure production along capitalist lines and capture niche markets by reorganizing their labour more efficiently, survived.[83] There is another way of looking at the whole question. The faceless, inefficient and obsolete parts of the weaving industry which Roy deplores consisted of untouchable weavers, women who spun yarn, whether from untouchable or other castes, and an unknown number of poorer weavers from specialist weaving castes. It was their labour and their earnings that dried up and vanished with their exclusion from the world of weaving.

For Roy, the driving force behind all these changes was the market. However, he ignores the political element, i.e. the policies of the colonial state which influenced this apparently neutral market during the second half of the nineteenth century. Colonial tariffs encouraged the export of cotton which peaked during the American Civil War, and caused local scarcities of cotton and yarn, throwing poorer weavers out of work.[84] From this period onwards, the import of mill yarn increased rapidly, displacing localized and decentralized spinning, and, along with it, weaving (particularly of the poorer weavers) that depended on it.

But the disappearance of this sector was long drawn out, at least in some regions. Various reports from the beginning of the twentieth century still refer to Pariah weavers. In 1915 the Malas were still estimated to constitute 9 per cent of the weavers in Cuddapah.[85] Narayana Rao, in his *Survey of Cottage Industries* conducted in the late 1920s, reports the presence of Adi-Andhras and Adi-Dravidas in remote villages in parts of Cuddapah, Kurnool and Nellore districts: these 'weave cloths only when their customers supply them with raw material'.[86] Venkatraman, in his study of the handloom industry in 1935, alludes to Panchamas and Malas (untouchable castes) along with other non-traditional castes such as Vellalas and Musalmans.[87] Narayanaswami Naidu, asked to report on labour conditions in the handloom industry in 1948, noted the extreme poverty of the 'Harijan' weavers of Kumbakonam.[88] But by the 1970s, they seem to have disappeared. A study on the weaving industry in Madurai (which once had, as we have seen, a large number of Koliyar weavers) conducted in the late 1970s does not even mention them. Its weaving castes are the familiar Sourashtras, Mudaliars and Saliyars.[89]

As interesting as the disappearance of Pariah weavers is the disappearance even of the memory of Pariahs having ever *been* weavers: this is true of the community itself. It is interesting that most major studies on weaving either leave out Pariah weavers or cite them as some kind of anomaly, though they survived several decades into the twentieth century, in pockets at least. Nor do Pariahs themselves remember having been weavers: this might be more understandable given their geographical dispersion, the fact that weaving had been one of an ensemble of occupations for them, and the passage of time.

'Pariah' Weavers: Work and Caste

What does the presence and subsequent disappearance of Pariah weavers contribute to our understanding of the weaving industry, and more generally about notions of work and caste? To begin with, it adds something to the evolving discussion on caste, and the logic and roots of the caste system. As we know, there have been innumerable attempts to explain and define caste. Race, occupation, ritual hierarchy based on concepts of purity and pollution, etc., have all been used as a basis for explanation. The concept of purity–pollution as well as 'clean' and 'unclean' work has, despite challenges, come to colour the general and academic understanding of caste. In the general perception and in a lot of academic discourse (Louis Dumont is an example), untouchable castes are associated with unclean work such as tanning, scavenging, etc., and rarely with work such as weaving.

Nicholas Dirks has shown how modern understandings of caste have been influenced by the colonial archive and acts of the state, especially from the late nineteenth century onwards when anthropological understandings of Indian society became reflected in the policies of the colonial state.[90] Though many colonial observers as well as Indian intellectuals rejected the occupational explanation of caste, pointing to numerous anomalies (reflected in the censuses), a link between occupation and caste in most understandings has remained, as in the explanations of *varnashrama* adopted by Gandhi (among others). In addition to this, there has been a conflation of ritual purity to occupational purity/status. From this stems the view that certain occupations were regarded as clean and others unclean, the latter being associated with the untouchable castes. Thus untouchables are seen as either menial workers, landless labourers, or as performers of unclean occupations such as tanning or scavenging. But many unclean occupations associated with the untouchable castes are in fact modern ones. Scavenging on a large scale emerged only with the proliferation of large cities. Similarly tanning as a modern workshop/factory-based industry emerged only in the twentieth century.

Shahana Bhattacharya, in her doctoral thesis on tannery workers, has shown how tannery owners as well as colonial bureaucrats actively encouraged the recruitment of Pariahs into factories, arguing that they were suited to the work *because* they had been traditionally associated with it (all that this meant in practice was that they had experience of handling carcasses, and were suitable because they were untouchables and therefore peculiarly qualified to do supposedly polluting work). In actual fact, she shows, Pariahs were new recruits to this industry.[91] Ramnarayan Rawat argues that the association of Chamars with the ritually impure occupation of leather-working was largely constructed in the nineteenth and twentieth century through Hindu, colonial and post-colonial representations of untouchability. He shows that in the early nineteenth century Chamars were primarily agriculturists, also involved to a certain extent in occupations such as weaving and tanning; the subsequent identification of Chamars with their imagined traditional occupation of leather-work led to, and perhaps was designed to, reinforcing their untouchability.[92]

It is now widely recognized that the censuses were not a passive recording of information about the people of this country; on the contrary, its categories influenced the evolution of the social structure in terms of how people represented themselves and others. It should therefore be of interest to look very briefly at some census data in the context of Pariah weavers. Interestingly, the census cannot be used to track their changing numbers simply because they are not represented as such in it. From the very first census, the population of India was sought to be categorized on the basis of caste. In the 1871 Census, the entire population was divided into eighteen broad caste categories which were seen as synonymous with various occupations. Thus, in the Madras Presidency, castes which were considered to be cultivators were enumerated under the head Vellalar (a dominant caste of cultivators); several castes considered to be labourers under Pariahs (the largest caste of labourers); and castes considered to be weavers under Kaikalar (the most prominent caste of specialist weavers).[93] A similar classification was followed in the Census of 1881 despite the acknowledgment that 'the lines of occupation and of caste no longer enclose identical spaces'.[94]

All castes considered to be weavers were grouped under the heading Kaikolar on the logic that the Kaikala (or Kaikolar) was the predominant weaving caste in the Presidency. Pariahs or Malas find no place in this list. The only caste listed under this category that has elsewhere been identified as a sub-caste of the Pariah is the Koliar/Koliyan. However, of all the groups enumerated under this category (the Kaikolar or weaver category contained many castes/sub-castes), only 47.4 per cent were actually employed in the occupations defined as 'Dress' (a category that included those making cloth as well as those making shoes), while 21.3 per cent were employed in *cultivation*.

Meanwhile the Pariahs are categorized as a menial caste of labourers, the Malas and many sub-castes being grouped under this heading, though the actual occupation of 26.4 per cent of the Pariahs was recorded as 'Dress'. As already mentioned, the occupational categories in this census included 'Dress' (those involved in the production of clothes/textiles as well as those involved in making shoes). Significantly, it was assumed by Cornish, the compiler of the final report of the census, that Pariahs whose occupation was recorded as 'Dress' had to be shoe- and slipper-makers, or cobblers.[95] However, many Pariahs recorded under the occupational category of 'Dress' lived in the districts of Cuddapah and Nellore, where we know from other sources that Malas were involved in weaving in large numbers.

As in the earlier lists, the 1891 list of castes grouped under Kaikolar (weavers) does not have any name (except Koliar) that could be recognized as being an untouchable caste. The Malas in particular are significant by their absence. Time and again the mismatch between occupations and castes was noted, but considered a sign of changing times, the erosion of traditional patterns of employment, though, as we have seen, these traditional patterns were more complex than is usually assumed.

Hand in hand with the identification or fixing of particular castes with particular occupations through the census went the actual disappearance of untouchable castes from occupations such as weaving. It has already been noted that this was a long drawn out process in some regions (mostly remote villages in cotton-producing areas), but it is significant that the exclusion of these groups was most pronounced in newly emerging, modern versions of the weaving industry, be it the new textile mills or handloom factories. Gail Omvedt describes how untouchables were excluded from the spinning sections of Bombay's textile mills as the licking of broken threads before joining them was held to be 'contaminating'.[96] Similarly, Pariah weavers were totally absent from the handloom factories that emerged in cities such as Madurai, though later this sector did witness the entry of other non-weaving castes such as Vanniyars, Vellalars, etc. Thus, even though the industry in its more modern forms was opened to new entrants, it seems to have been closed to untouchable castes. It could be that the creation of new spaces of work where workers worked in close proximity to each other had a role to play in this kind of exclusion. Earlier the Pariah weaver worked in his own home on his own loom, while in factories and mills he had to share work-space with other-caste weavers who wished to exclude him/her on grounds of prejudice.

Perhaps it is the absence of Pariahs in the modern weaving industry, combined with an unconscious linkage between caste and occupation, particularly between untouchable castes and polluting work, that leads to the historical presence of Pariahs as weavers being regarded as an anomaly. This is perhaps what impels scholars such as P. Swarnalatha and David Washbrook to explain their 'entry' into weaving. According to Washbrook, the political chaos of the eighteenth century and the expansion in commerce during this period provided opportunities for Pariahs to enter different occupations such as soldiering and weaving; some even became landholders or petty merchants. But soon this topsy-turvy world was turned right-side-up again, and 'the golden age of the pariah' ended with the tightening of colonial rule and the end of the era of textile exports.[97]

Against the argument that it was the expansion of the textile industry, prompted by the commercial activity of European companies, that led to the entry of weavers from non-weaving castes into the profession, Swarnalatha traces their 'entry' to the Bhakti and Virasaiva movements of the twelfth and thirteenth centuries which, thanks to their inherent egalitarianism, made the caste system more flexible.[98] Thus, for her (as for Washbrook) the presence of Malas and Pariahs in the weaving profession is an anomaly that needs to be explained.

While it might well be the case that more Pariahs took advantage of the increased opportunities for employment in weaving and soldiering created by the economic and political conjunctures of the eighteenth century, there is little reason to assume that Pariah weavers were an entirely new phenomenon, certainly in the decades preceding this period. Stray references, including an eleventh-century inscription in the time of the Tamil Chola king Raja Raja, mentioning '*nesavu paraiyans*' (*nesavu* means weaving), another inscription dating from 1522 in Dharmavaram taluk mentioning four important communities associated with weaving including Mala and Pariah weavers mentioned in the records of the Dutch East India Company,[99] indicate their presence in a much earlier period – though more research is needed to establish the extent of their involvement, including possible changes in the ways in which they produced cloth, and the impact of the political and economic changes of the seventeenth and eighteenth centuries upon them.[100]

The basic problem here is an unthinking equation of caste with occupation. Thus, for example, Vijaya Ramaswamy, in her monograph on weaving, equates the two in a strikingly literal fashion (referring to weavers as 'professional caste groups'), and treats all inscriptional references to the Kaikolar, Devangar or Saliar, whether or not they mention textiles/looms, as references to weavers. She says:

> it must be noted that in the inscriptions the caste name and the professional name were considered synonymous. If the inscription mentioned 'Banajiga' or 'Chetti' it could be assumed automatically that the reference was to a merchant, and if it mentioned 'Saliya' or 'Kaikkola' it would be quite natural to assume that the reference was to a weaver.[101]

This procedure is adopted despite the fact that she herself describes how Kaikolars are often referred to as soldiers, and many of them (and presumably members of other 'weaving' castes) owned land and cultivated. It is therefore entirely possible that some at least may have been cultivators or combined cultivation with weaving. Similarly, Pariahs are equated in a unilinear fashion to menials or agricultural labourers.[102] Thus an eleventh-century inscription referring to Pariahs as weavers finds no mention in her work.

Perhaps this explains the reluctance of observers and researchers to draw out the implications of the presence of Pariahs as weavers. Weaving was (and is) not seen as a polluting occupation or a menial one. Therefore it is implicitly assumed that it could not have been a legitimate occupation for Pariahs. Therefore their presence as weavers is seen as 'non-traditional' and their work as secondary: they are dismissed as producers of coarse cloth, unskilled and part-time weavers, etc. However, the evidence shows there were whole communities of supposedly untouchable castes such as the Koliars, the Manniwars and the Malas who wove extensively and even specialized in weaving. The connection of Malas with weaving is also expressed in some of the legends associated with the community, such as the story of Lakshmi disturbing a Mala who was busy at his loom and cursing him when he spurned her.[103] And also in such customs as the Mala bride placing her foot on the weaver's beam and the groom placing his foot on hers during marriage ceremonies.[104]

The Impediments of Social Status

However, my discussion of the problem should not be taken to imply that caste had no influence on occupation and work, or that caste itself was a kind of colonial invention. Caste as it exists now is certainly different from what it used to be in the eighteenth and nineteenth (as well as earlier) centuries. But the *jati* that an individual belonged to had a strong, even determining, effect on his or her working life, closing off certain choices, and imposing structural limitations and disabilities on the poorest groups. We have already seen that Pariahs were invariably the poorest weavers and that they had to depend on other sources of income as well. Their poverty and inferior social status made merchants wary of providing them with advances. From the evidence available it does not seem that they threw up head weavers or merchants from their own caste, as was the case with several of the specialist weaving castes, and this fact is in itself an index of their social subordination.

Though the evidence shows that these weavers worked for a wage and were not part of the *jajmani* system (where service castes received a fixed portion of the harvest), their caste and social status almost certainly had an impact on their bargaining power over wages. There is evidence to show that some zamindars got weavers (particularly Pariah weavers) to weave cloth free for them in exchange for an exemption from the loom tax.

Thus, in four villages belonging to a zamindar in Nellore district, 'the banias and the pariahs who have looms do not pay any tax because they work for the poligar without receiving any hire or remuneration'. In another zamindari where the *poligar* had been collecting tax from Pariah weavers, when they declared their inability to pay, 'he exempted them from paying it but in lieu thereof he makes them perform any work'.[105] In another zamindari, no tax was collected from the people who wove 'as the poligar gets the cloths he requires woven without paying any hire, only furnishing thread for that purpose'.[106]

Given that the loom tax was a relatively small amount for Pariahs, it is not clear how much the exemption worked to their advantage. Even when these weavers did not work for zamindars, they often worked, or had to work, for the locally dominant cultivating caste (apart from producing for local markets). Thus in Cuddapah district, Kapus would get their cloth woven by Malas, providing them with the cotton. According to the gazetteer, 'each weaver has his own customers, and very often one family of Malas will have weaved for one family of Sudras for generations'.[107] Here again, social inequality undoubtedly influenced the wage paid. Some of these weavers were also village servants such as Totties and Taliars. As a result, they were sometimes allowed to keep one loom free of tax, and also to collect loom tax from other weavers of their own community. But their obligations as village servants and their inferior status may have intertwined, affecting the wages they earned. The real advantage as far as income from weaving was concerned would have been when they could sell their cloth in local markets, or when there was an increased demand for the cloth they wove. All other arrangements smack of a certain amount of social coercion. Hence it is possible that increased demand for textiles in the eighteenth century may have widened their opportunities of producing for the market.

The lack of bargaining power of Pariah weavers can also be observed in their relationship to merchants and the Companies for whom they occasionally seem to have worked. Merchants in Baramahal, contracted by the English East India Company, complained of their inability to make any profit at the rates stipulated as the Koliar weavers they employed were so poor that they could not be trusted with advances (but at the same time could not survive without those advances if they were expected to work full time for the Company). The possibility that they might abscond with advances can be interpreted as a factor working to their advantage; it may even indicate greater occupational mobility in the late eighteenth and early nineteenth century. The obverse of this is lack of bargaining power when it came to wages, for it can safely be assumed that merchants held the upper hand in this respect. Also, it is striking that while one comes across many instances of weavers (from the specialist weaving castes) uniting along caste lines to demand better wages or more control over the production process,[108] I have not come across a single instance of collective bargaining by Pariah weavers.

The other area in which caste played an obvious and damaging role was in the organization of the work-space. As long as Pariah weavers worked in the confines of their own homes, not coming in contact with any 'caste' persons, the cloth they produced had no stigma, and was in fact often sought after for its durability and strength. But when systems of production and the very arrangement of work-spaces changed, creating situations where Pariahs or individuals from other untouchable castes had to work in close proximity to caste workers (particularly in textile mills as well as modernized handloom workshops), they were promptly excluded from the industry.

Conclusion

In this essay I have tried to document the widespread presence of weavers from several untouchable castes, commonly referred to as Pariah weavers, in colonial records. They may have been part-time weavers, mostly producing coarse cloth, but they produced significant quantities of cloth of the type and quality used by a large section of the population. In addition, they were also skilled spinners. Thus they played a considerable role in the weaving sector as a whole, a fact almost ignored by historians thus far. As a result of the economic and political changes of the nineteenth century, they virtually disappeared from the weaving sector.

The loss of weaving as an occupation affected their lives in several ways. Economically, they lost a source of income, however small, which might have helped sustain them, especially in times of scarcity. Their plight was similar to that of women spinners who lost their source of income from weaving in the nineteenth century. Arguments to the effect that this loss was not very significant since women were grossly underpaid do not hold much water: they may have been underpaid, but what they earned was crucial to the family income (a fact established by Ian Wendt).[109] For the Pariahs, in particular, the shrinkage of available occupations and earning opportunities must have been damaging. It is generally accepted that in the nineteenth century, an increasing number of people were thrown solely upon agriculture: this would be particularly true of Pariahs. Inevitably, they formed a large proportion of those who migrated overseas as indentured labourers.

This exclusion of Pariahs from the textile industry must be seen in the context of much wider developments in the nineteenth and twentieth centuries. In the European context, the inevitability, and indeed the desirability, of the Industrial Revolution as it occurred in Britain has been strongly challenged. It is now accepted that there is no one linear form of industrial development culminating in the establishment of large-scale, mechanized industries.[110] Different countries/regions followed different trajectories of industrial development for various reasons, ranging from state policy to environment, choice of technology, class conflict, etc. In the case of India, a combination of factors, including state policy, global factors, technological choices and social forces, pushed the handloom industry (and the textile industry in general) towards a much more centralized structure wholly dependent on mill-produced yarn. This automatically led to the exclusion of the poorest weavers (among them the Pariahs) and hand-spinners. This is not to argue that spinning and weaving could have, or should have, survived in the old forms. But the particular path that was taken was by no means an inevitable or natural one. Similarly, I am not arguing that women spinners and Pariah weavers had a 'golden age' followed by a decline. But certainly, a possible avenue of economic advancement that might have remained open to them, if the industry had developed in a different way, was closed.

Socially, too, their exclusion from weaving had long-term effects. Particularly significant is the exclusion of Pariahs from the modern textile industry, handloom as well as powerloom. This may be linked to the transfer of concepts of pollution and purity to modern work-spaces, but it is also, in many ways, linked to the fossilization or fixing of caste identities through public discourse and colonial projects such as the census. Again, this is not to argue that Pariah weavers (and Pariahs in general) were not stigmatized, but it is incontestable that they were at one time in one of the avenues/occupations that was *not* stigmatized and in the nineteenth century they were gradually excluded; this contributed to the fixing of their identity as those performing menial and unclean work. That this has had long-term consequences is demonstrated by the way in which Pariah weavers have been dealt with in various works of history as well as anthropology.

Acknowledgements: I would like to thank Dr Prabhu Mohapatra, Dr Chitra Joshi, Dr Ravi Ahuja and Shashank Kela for reading various drafts of this paper, and for important criticisms and suggestions that have helped improve my arguments. It goes without saying that all errors and omissions are mine alone.

Notes

1 Parthasarathi (2001): 10.
2 Ibid.: 11.
3 Ibid.: 10.
4 Subhrahmanyam (2004): 29.
5 Mines (1984): 3–10, 18, 37–38, 41.
6 Ibid.: 151.
7 Ramaswamy (1985): 36.
8 For the sake of uniformity and historical context, I use the word 'Pariah' to refer to those belonging to the caste group variously referred to as Paraiyar, Parayar, Paraiyah, etc., while at the same time acknowledging that in present times the term Dalit is more appropriate due to the demeaning connotations attached to the word 'Pariah'.
9 Wendt (2005): 216.
10 Ibid.
11 Swarnalatha (2005): 31.

[12] Baramahal Records, Section VII, Imposts: 18 and 27.
[13] Buchanan (1807): 152, 116.
[14] *Proceedings of the Board of Revenue* [hereafter *PBR*], Vol. 1906, No. 30, 29 February 1844: 3825–26.
[15] *PBR*, Vol. 1942, No. 49, 25 November 1844: 16133–35.
[16] I use the term 'Pariah weavers' to refer to weavers from several 'untouchable' castes. This is the term used in most colonial records. But in some cases the actual caste or sub-caste is mentioned, and where it is possible to be more specific, I have used specific caste names such as Mala, Walliyar, Koliar, Manniwar, etc.
[17] Figures based on tabulations in Baramahal Records, Section VII, Imposts: 18, 19, 2765.
[18] *PBR*, Vol. 1325, 21 May 1832, No. 44: 4901 onwards. The figures here are not very reliable as they were based upon an estimate rather than an actual survey; the weavers of this district were resisting enumeration as they feared imposition of a loom tax from which they had until then been exempted. But the large numbers of Pariah weavers is significant.
[19] Madurai Collectorate Records, Vol. 1258, 1816, Tamil Nadu Archives [henceforth TNA].
[20] *PBR*, Vol. 1325, No. 47, 24 May 1832: 5011.
[21] *PBR*, Vol. 1820, No. 31, 29 September 1842: 11118.
[22] Moore (1878): 105.
[23] *PBR*, Vol. 1929, No. 29, 5 September 1844: 11761
[24] Swarnalatha (2005): 31.
[25] *PBR*, Vol. 1931, No. 47, 23 September 1844: 12521.
[26] *PBR*, Vol. 1334, No. 22, 13 August 1832: 7768–69.
[27] Pascoe (1901): 566b.
[28] Lewis (1879): 12; emphasis added.
[29] Thurston (1909): 350.
[30] Ibid.: 345.
[31] Chetty (1886): 142.
[32] *PBR*, Vol. 1925, No. 42, 8 August 1844: 10276.
[33] Buchanan (1807), Vol. I: 218, 302, 313, 314, 327, 355; Vol. II: 33, 151.
[34] Buchanan (1807), Vol. II: 261.
[35] Swarnalatha (2005): 31.
[36] Baramahal Records, Section VII, Imposts: 65.
[37] Swarnalatha (2005): 31.
[38] Brennig (1986): 345–46.
[39] Wendt (2005): 135–37.
[40] Dharma Kumar (1992): 35.
[41] Buchanan (1807), Vol. I: 218.
[42] Ibid.: 302.
[43] Ibid.: 327.
[44] Wendt (2005): 219.
[45] Buchanan (1807), Vol. I: 218.
[46] Ibid.: 217–18, 355.
[47] Baramahal Records, Section VII, Imposts: 27.
[48] Ibid.: 64, 65.
[49] Ibid.: 64, 108.
[50] Ibid.: 27.
[51] Quoted in Wendt (2005): 219.
[52] *PBR*, Vol. 1554, No. 18, 10 April 1837: 1848–50.
[53] *PBR*, Vol. 382, 21 June 1804: 5075.

[54] Calculation based on figures in the above report.
[55] *PBR*, Vol. 1583, No. 23, 23 November 1837: 15073; *PBR*, Vol. 1583, No. 34, 16 November 1837: 14917–18.
[56] H. Rivett-Carnac, 'Report of the Cotton Commissioner for the Central Provinces and the Berar on the Operations of His Department for the Year 1867', *House of Commons Records*: 17–18.
[57] Buchanan (1807), Vol. I: 218.
[58] *PBR*, Vol. 382, 21 June 1804: 5075.
[59] Baramahal Records, Section VII, Imposts: 115.
[60] *PBR*, Vol. 383, 25 June 1804: 5285.
[61] Thurston (1909): 350.
[62] Baramahal Records.
[63] *PBR*, Vol. 987, No. 27, 5 July 1824: 5732.
[64] *PBR*, Vol. 1942, No. 49, 25 November 1844: 16131.
[65] Thurston (1909): 351.
[66] Ibid.: 350.
[67] *PBR*, Vol. 1583, No. 23, 23 November 1837: 15070.
[68] *PBR*, Vol. 989, No. 25, 22 July 1824: 6341.
[69] *PBR*, Vol. 1494, No. 16, 7 March 1836: 4088.
[70] *PBR*, Vol. 984, No. 42, 17 May 1824: 4439–40, and *PBR*, Vol. 380, No. 7, 31 May 1804: 4499.
[71] Wendt (2005): 219.
[72] Baramahal Records, Products: 34. Also see 'Return to an Order of the Honourable the House of Commons', dated 15 February 1847, for a return 'of papers in possession of the East India Company, showing what measures have been taken since 1836 to promote the cultivation of cotton in India, with the particulars and result of any experiments which have been made by the said company, with a view to introduce the growth of American cotton, or to encourage the production of native cotton in India', *House of Commons Records* (1847): 161.
[73] Report of H. Rivett-Carnac, 'Return to an address of the Honourable House of Commons', dated 13 May 1869: 18.
[74] Baramahal Records, Section VII, Imposts: 22.
[75] Buchanan (1807), Vol. I: 218.
[76] Ibid.: 327.
[77] *PBR*, Vol. 1942, No. 49, 25 November 1844: 16129.
[78] *PBR*, Vol. 1325, No. 47, 24 May 1832: 5011; *PBR*, Vol. 1942, No. 49, 25 November 1844.
[79] Havell (1909): 19.
[80] I discuss this in greater detail in my dissertation. See *PBR*, Vol. 1955, No. 21, 10 February 1845: 1853; *PBR*, Vol. 1931, No. 47, 23 September 1844: 12519; *PBR*, Vol. 1929, No. 29, 5 September 1844: 11761.
[81] Havell (1909): 4–5.
[82] Ibid.: 15.
[83] Roy (1993): ix, x, 2–5, 73.
[84] Harnetty (1965): 333–49.
[85] Brackenbury (1915): 108.
[86] Narayana Rao (1929): 17.
[87] Venkataraman (1935): 181.
[88] Naidu (1948): 28.
[89] Sundar Singh (1981): 158.
[90] Dirks (2002).
[91] Bhattacharya (2012).
[92] Rawat (2012).

[93] Cornish (1874).
[94] *Census of India, 1881*: *Madras* (1883): 104.
[95] Cornish (1874): 170.
[96] Omvedt (1994): 141–42.
[97] Washbrook (1993): 73, 81.
[99] Swarnalatha (2005): 39–44.
[99] For the two inscriptions, see ibid.: 39–40, and the 'Report of the Dutch East India Company' in Wendt (2005): 219.
[100] Washbrook, as well as Ravi Ahuja, argue that labour scarcity in the eighteenth century may have created relatively favourable conditions for the social, occupational and spatial mobility of Pariahs. See Ahuja (2002): 795.
[101] Ramaswamy (1985): 15.
[102] Ibid.: 37.
[103] Ibid.: 363.
[104] Ibid.: 361.
[105] The *banias* also paid no tax as they brought articles of consumption for the *poligar* without charging hire for transport.
[106] *PBR*, Vol. 1327, No. 25, 11 June 1832: 5352.
[107] Thurston (1909): 350.
[108] Parthasarathi (2001): 101–20, and Swarnalatha (2005): 123–45.
[109] Wendt (2005): 144–74.
[110] This discussion began with the introduction of the concept of proto-industrialization but has developed beyond it. For some stimulating explorations of this theme, see Liu (1994): Chapter One; and Sabel and Zeitlin (1985)

References

Ahuja, Ravi (2002), 'Labour Relations in an Early Colonial Context: Madras, *c.* 1750–1800', *Modern Asian Studies*, Vol. 36, 4: 793–826.

Bhattacharya, Shahana (2012), 'Labour in the Leather Industry in India, 1870s–1970s', unpublished Ph.D. thesis, University of Delhi, Delhi.

Brackenbury, C.F. (1915), *The Cuddapah District Gazetteer*, Madras: Government Press.

Brennig, Joseph J. (1986), 'Textile producers and production in late seventeenth century Coromandel', *Indian Economic and Social History Review*, Vol. 23, No. 4.

Buchanan, Hamilton Francis (1807a), *A Journey from Madras through the Countries of Mysore, Canara and Malabar*, Vol. I, London: Bulmer and Co.

——— (1807b), *A Journey from Madras through the Countries of Mysore, Canara and Malabar*, Vol. II, London: T. Cadell and W. Davies.

Chetty, Narahari Gopalakristnamah (1886), *A Manual of the Kurnool District*, Madras: Government Press.

Census of India, 1881: *Madras* (1883), Vol. I: Report, Madras: Government Press.

Cornish, William Robert (1874), *Report on the Census of the Madras Presidency, 1871*, Madras: Government Press.

Dirks, Nicholas B. (2002), *Castes of Mind: Colonialism and the Making of Modern India*, New Delhi: Permanent Black.

Harnetty, Peter (1965), 'The Imperialism of Free Trade: Lancashire and the Indian Cotton Duties, 1859–1862', *The Economic History Review*, New Series, Vol. 18, No. 2: 333–49.

Havell, E.B. (1909), *Reports Submitted by Mr E.B. Havell during the years 1885–1888 on the Arts and Industries of Certain Districts of the Madras Presidency*, Madras: Government Press.

Kumar, Dharma (1992), *Land and Caste in South India*, New Delhi: Manohar.

Lewis, Edwin (1879), *History of the Telugu Missions of the London Missionary Society in the Ceded Districts*, Madras: Addison and Company.

Liu, Tessie P. (1994), *The Weavers Knot: The Contradictions of Class Struggle and Family Solidarity in Western France, 1750–1914*, Ithaca: Cornell University Press.

Mines, Mattison (1984), *Warrior Merchants: Textiles, Trade and Territory in South India*, Cambridge: Cambridge University Press.

Moore, Lewis (1878), *A Manual of the Trichinopoly District in the Presidency of Madras*, Madras: Government Press.

Naidu, Narayanaswami (1948), *Report of the Court of Enquiry into Labour Conditions in the Handloom Industry*, Madras: Government Press.

Omvedt, Gail (1994), *Dalits and the Democratic Revolution: Dr Ambedkar and the Dalit Movement in Colonial India*, New Delhi: Sage Publications.

Parthasarathi, Prasannan (2001), *The Transition to a Colonial Economy: Weavers, Merchants and Kings in South India, 1720–1800*, Cambridge: Cambridge University Press.

Pascoe, C.F. (1901), *Two Hundred Years of the S.P.G: An Historical Account of the Society for the Propagation of the Gospel in Foreign Parts 1701–1900*, London: Society for the Propagation of the Gospel.

Ramaswamy, Vijaya (1985), *Textiles and Weavers in Medieval South India*, New Delhi: Oxford University Press.

Rao, D. Narayana (1929), *Report on the Survey of Cottage Industries in the Madras Presidency*, Madras: Government Press.

Rawat, Ramnarayan S. (2012), *Reconsidering Untouchability: Chamars and Dalit History in North India*, New Delhi: Permanent Black.

'Return to an Order of the Honourable the House of Commons' (1847), dated 15 February 1847, *House of Commons Records.*

Rivett-Carnac, H., 'Report of the Cotton Commissioner for the Central Provinces and the Berar on the Operations of His Department for the Year 1867', *House of Commons Records.*

——— (1869), 'A return to an address of the Honourable House of Commons', dated 13 May 1869, *House of Commons Records*. Subrahmanyam, Sanjay (2004), *The Political Economy of Commerce in Southern India, 1500–1650*, Cambridge: Cambridge University Press.

Roy, Tirthankar (1993), *Artisans and Industrialization: Indian Weaving in the Twentieth Century*, New Delhi: Oxford University Press.

Sabel, Charles and Jonathan Zeitlin (1985), 'Historical Alternatives to Mass Production: Politics, Markets and Technology in Nineteenth-Century Industrialization', *Past and Present*, No. 108, August: 133–76.

Sundar Singh, John D.K. (1981), *The Handloom Industry in Madurai City*, Madurai: Publications Division, Madurai Kamaraj University.

Swarnalatha, P. (2005), *The World of the Weaver in Northern Coromandel, c. 1750–1850*, New Delhi: Orient Longman.

Thurston, Edgar (1909), *Castes and Tribes of Southern India*, Vol. IV, Madras: Government Press.

Venkataraman, K.S. (1935), *The Handloom Industry in South India (Supplement to the Madras University Journal)*, Madras: Diocesan Press.

Washbrook, David (1993), 'Land and Labour in Late Eighteenth-Century South India: The Golden Age of the Pariah?', in Peter Robb (ed.), *Dalit Movements and the Meanings of Labour in India*, New Delhi: Oxford University Press.

Wendt, Ian C. (2005), 'The Social Fabric: Textile Industry and Community in Early Modern South India', unpublished Ph.D. thesis, University of Wisconsin-Madison, 2005.

State and Working-Class Identity in the Ottoman Empire and Turkey

The Zonguldak Coal Basin

E. Attila Aytekin and H. Tarik Sengul

Since the second half of the nineteenth century, Zonguldak has been one of the most important coal-mining areas of the Ottoman Empire and Turkey. It developed as a 'workshop' region for productive activities, although it later partly assumed administrative and redistributive functions. Despite the dramatic decline in coal mining since the late 1970s, mining is still a very important economic activity for the city of Zonguldak as well as the eponymous region. With more than 10,000 workers currently employed, there is a heavy concentration of industrial workers in the Zonguldak coal basin. Moreover, despite the fluctuations in the fortunes of industry, Zonguldak has been perceived as a 'working-class town' by its inhabitants and outsiders. One of the factors that foment this perception is the tradition of worker militancy which surfaced from 1908 to 1990–91 – occasionally, but when it did, very strongly. At the moment, the future of the region is in the doldrums, and the miners as well as the local population in general are not optimistic about their future.

Based on preliminary findings of field research carried out in Zonguldak from 2009 to 2011, this essay problematizes the relationship between the state and the working-class population of the region by placing an emphasis on the local perception(s) of the (rise) and decline of the region, and the role of the state in this process.

The following section deals briefly with the question of identity, and its current crisis through a stress on its relational and spatial nature. The next three sections provide a discussion of the three phases in the development of the region. The final section provides a discussion on the perception of decline of Zonguldak coal mining, drawing upon preliminary findings of the field research carried out.

Crisis of (Working-Class) Identity?

In line with the recent decline of coal mining in Zonguldak, a widespread belief has emerged that the importance of class identity is also in decline. On the other hand, such a decline is hardly unique to the region or even to the working class in general. When one looks at the sociology and political science literature of the last three decades, there is stress not only on the decline of working-class identity, but it is also alleged that there has been a wider crisis of identities. It has become almost commonplace to argue that the old identities that had defined the individual in the modern world are in crisis. The safe meanings attributed to identities, such as race, gender, ethnicity, nationality and class, so the argument goes, are being increasingly fragmented and dislocated (Hall 1996: 275). Some theories developed along these lines suggest that the crisis of 'old' identities and their concomitant dislocation constitute a challenge to the notion of the modern individual as an autonomous subject.

The crisis of class identity, on the other hand, has been discussed largely in the context of a number of social and political changes that took place in the last decades of the last century. Some of the developments that are emphasized are social and economic, such as the rise of the service sector and the decline of the industrial proletariat; the increasing importance of white-collar employees as opposed to blue-collar ones; the embourgeoisement of the working class; the dominance of immaterial labour; and globalization (for the less known theory of immaterial labour, see Lazzarato 1996). Political developments such as the dissolution of actually existing socialisms in Central and Eastern Europe are also mentioned as part of the processes that created the alleged crisis of class. Whatever these social, economic and political processes are held to be, it is problematic to argue that class identity was once 'finished', unproblematic and fixed, and is not so now.

There is indeed a body of literature which emphasizes that all identities are by definition fluid, and are constantly contested, negotiated and reconstructed. Class identity has always been of this character and for this reason, in order to understand the concrete forms of contestation, negotiation and reconstruction of working-class identity, it is necessary to look at the concrete local histories of working-class formation along with the broader socio-economic and political processes which condition the local contexts (Kirk 2007). In that sense, we need to look at 'particular responses to wider national and regional developments, and of changing local ideas of the nature of community' (Gilbert 1992: 47).

In his seminal work on the urbanization of consciousness, David Harvey provides us with a fruitful set of concepts to study the question of identity with reference to the spatialized forms of consciousness. One of the advantages of his approach is that Harvey relates the question of identity to the question of consciousness, thereby emphasizing the relational nature of identities. He identifies five primary loci of consciousness formation, namely, individualism, class, community, the state and the family:

> *Individualism* attaches to money uses in freely functioning markets. *Class* under capitalism reflects the buying and selling of labour power and the social relations embodied in the socio-technical conditions of production under conditions of surplus value extraction. *Community*, as we shall see, is a highly ambiguous notion that nevertheless plays a fundamental role in terms of the reproduction of labour power, the circulation of revenues and the geography of capital accumulation. *The state* also impinges on consciousness as a centre of authority and as an apparatus through which political–economic power is exercised in a territory with some degree of popular legitimacy. *The family*, finally, has a profound effect upon ways of thought and action simply by virtue of its function as a primary site of social reproduction through child rearing. (Harvey 1985: 252; emphasis added)

Harvey goes on to argue that no one locus of consciousness formation can be understood independently of its interaction with the others. Perhaps one can define a particular identity, be it individual or community, as an overdetermined outcome of the interaction of these different loci of consciousness. Although we do recognize the complexity and the high degree of interaction between the loci of consciousness, our focus in this essay will be on the interaction of class and state.

The national state is certainly part of the wider context in which the working class develops those 'particular responses' that Gilbert mentions. It is indeed being increasingly recognized that the state plays an important role in the formation of class and class consciousness (Katznelson 1981). In the case of mono-industry areas where the state is the main 'entrepreneur' and employer, the state's role in class formation becomes even more accentuated. This essay focuses on class formation processes in such a setting, where coal mining has been the key industry since the second half of the nineteenth century and the state-owned Turkish Coal Company the main employer since 1940.

Rise and Decline of Zonguldak Coal Basin

Zonguldak lies at the centre of a rather compact coal basin that stretches from Akçakoca in the west to Cide in the east. The basin can be seen as a long and narrow strip; most of the active or abandoned mines are situated along the Black Sea coast that stretches around 200 kilometres from west to east, but is only 25 kilometres wide. Geologically speaking, the basin mostly consists of fractured and twisted strata running parallel to the coast, which makes extracting coal difficult and brings about the presence of quite different types of coals belonging to different geological eras next to each other (Quataert 2006).

The advent of coal mining in Zonguldak brought about a sea change in the landscape. A predominantly agrarian region was gradually transformed into a container of heavy industry, also creating a new urban centre. Before coal mining began in the region in the second half of the nineteenth century, Zonguldak was merely a neighbourhood in a rather obscure village. It was transformed into a town in a matter of decades and became the biggest urban settlement in a rather large region. Thus the city of Zonguldak owes its existence entirely to coal mining. The urban growth trend continued in the Republican era as well and the city became the centre of the eponymous province. Later, Zonguldak became a crucial part of the country's import-substituting industrialization strategy.

Although the mines were operated by private entrepreneurs before 1940, both the Ottoman and the Turkish states showed an interest in the basin as coal was a strategic asset. They actively tried to ensure a steady supply of coal, and to this end, they also enacted some protective measures for the workers. Since the biggest problem in the basin was labour scarcity, it was one issue the Ottoman and Turkish states were particularly concerned with. Forced labour was imposed twice on the inhabitants of the region, first after 1867 and then during World War II. One of the very first acts of the Ankara government, established in 1920 following the collapse of the empire, was to regulate labour processes in the coal basin. The nationalization of all mines in the basin in 1939–40 heralded a new era in the relationship between workers and the state, making the state a direct employer of all workers rather than an overseeing external regulator.

Based on archival documents located in Zonguldak and Istanbul for the Ottoman period, and in-depth interviews with workers and other people living in the area for the Republican period and for the present, we seek to provide preliminary remarks about the role of the state in identity formation among miners in the Zonguldak coal basin. We do not treat the state as an external actor or structure to working-class identity. Rather, we consider it as one of the loci of consciousness around which a distinctive identity has been built in the Zonguldak region.

In such an analysis, it is possible to identify three distinctive periods: the Ottoman and early Republican period (1848–1940), characterized by minimal involvement of the state in the region; the period of nationalization and the 'golden age' (1940 – *c.* 1980), defined by massive and direct involvement of the state in the region; and the period of decline (from the 1980s to the present), marked by a strategic withdrawal of the state from coal mining.

The Ottoman and Early Republican Periods, 1848–1940

The operation of the mines in the basin started in 1848, when Sultan Abdülmecid endowed the revenues of the mines to a religious charity. The mines were managed first by the Privy Purse (*Hazine-i Hassa*), which was responsible for overseeing the operations of private pit owners and collecting the revenue, and then, in 1865, by the Naval Ministry, which needed coal for warships.

In the early years, mining in the basin was carried out through primitive methods. Mainly due to the lack of investment on the part of the mine operators, contemporary coal-mining technology was not introduced. The production levels, therefore, remained very low and unstable. Trying to change the situation, the Ottoman government decided in 1882 to abolish the Naval Ministry's purchasing monopoly, and announced measures – such as tax reductions, reductions in export duties and customs duties exemptions – to support private Ottoman capital (Quataert 1983: 47). As a result, from the 1880s onwards, large-scale capital was invested in the mines, which led to both an increase in production and a concentration in ownership. Small-scale operators were rapidly eliminated, and by 1893, four big companies accounted for three-quarters of the total production.

The concession to exploit the coal mines given to the French *Sociéte d'Heraclée* (*EreðliSirket-i Osmaniyesi*) in 1896 was a major event, not only for the region but for the late Ottoman Empire as well. The investment capital of the company was enormous in comparison with that of other foreign companies in the mining sector. The company soon eliminated most of its rivals: in 1902 it represented 79 per cent of the total production of the coal mines (Quataert 2006: 29). On the other hand, the company had to deal with foot-dragging by the government, and hostility from local entrepreneurs and the populace. The Ottoman government's attempts to control the mines increased under the constitutional (post-1908) regime, but the company managed to preserve its dominant position until the advent of war in 1914 (Aytekin 2006: 36–39).

The operation of the French company came to a halt during World War I, which threw France and the Ottoman Empire (later the Ankara government) into opposite camps. The war years (1914–22) and the entry of government-controlled private capital companies in the basin in 1926 did not, however, end the presence of foreign capital in the mines. On the contrary, in 1931, approximately two-thirds of total coal production came from pits controlled by foreign capital, while individually owned mines accounted for only 10 per cent of the total sales of coal produced in the basin (Çýladýr 1977: 160–61). By the early 1930s, production was heavily concentrated in the hands of few large companies of French, Italian and Turkish origin.

The beginning and intensification of mining in the area has meant much change for the people of the region, which had been predominantly agricultural for centuries. The mines and the range of commercial activity involved gradual but irrecoverable transformation of their lives. Immigrant workers, who were usually employed overground and worked full-time, arrived. The great majority of local miners were rotational workers; they worked underground on and off, at biweekly or monthly intervals. Their lives were now very different from the lives of peasants elsewhere in the country. They entered the new world of mining where they had an additional source of income, and socialized with co-workers in and around the workplace; but they also suffered the hardships of mining.

Indeed the miners found themselves in a very unhealthy and dangerous working environment. Fatal accidents in the pits were a common occurrence (Aytekin 2006: 71–83). The first government attempt to regulate labour relations in the mines took place in 1867, when a regulation concerning various aspects of mining in the basin was promulgated. The so-called *Dilaver Pa°a Nizamnamesi* officially classified workers according to their jobs, provided protection and improvement for workers relating to pay schedules, work hours, labour conditions, medical care, dormitories, off-days, etc. Moreover, it created a forced labour system for the fourteen districts in or surrounding the coal basin. It seems that the goal of the regulation was to ensure a steady labour supply and preserve a degree of social stability by offering some protection to the labourers. However, whether the regulation was implemented thoroughly and to what extent it changed working conditions is not clear. There is indication that the accidents, health concerns and the problem of irregular payments continued. Moreover, labour shortage continued to preclude government attempts to increase coal production. Thus forced labour was not sufficient for the government to solve the problems of workforce scarcity. Nevertheless, the regulation stands a milestone in the relations between miners and the state. The government became relevant to miners' lives to such a degree for the first time. The few remaining memoirs or biographic accounts from the period suggest that the imposition of forced labour on the inhabitants of the region was registered in the collective memory of the people as a government policy that was much resented. Especially during the harvest time, a high degree of coercion was necessary to keep the miner–peasants in the pits.

The Republican government closely monitored the Zonguldak coal basin from the earliest years of its rule. It enacted legislation about the basin even during the War of Independence, passing three laws between 1920 and 1922. There were other laws enacted in the course of the 1920s and the 1930s, some of these aiming to improve the working and living conditions of miners. Among these, the creation of *Amele Birliði*, a solidarity and emergency fund, in 1922 is noteworthy. Albeit a positive step towards improving the working conditions of the miners, *Amele Birliði* was directly linked to the mine administration bureaucracy and headed by the director of the administration himself. The fund could be considered as part of the government's attempts to stabilize the workforce in a crucial mining region. Yet, the move to establish it must also have stemmed from pressure coming from the workers themselves, whose activism was visible even during World War I (Sengül and Aytekin 2011: 165).

After the foundation of the Republic in 1923 and increasingly during the 1930s, the Republican government adopted a corporatist–solidarist ideology that denied class divisions – or even the existence of social classes. As elsewhere in the country, there were severe limitations on labour organization and activity in Zonguldak. Legal labour activity took place only within the narrow boundaries determined by the state (Koç 1998). The early Republican period did not see much change in the working conditions of miners either. Accidents were frequent (Nichols and Kahveci 1995), and health-care facilities for victims of accidents and work-related diseases were inadequate. The problems of irregular payments, arbitrary fines and absence of overtime payments continued. Despite certain government attempts to regulate labour practices in the coal basin, in this period the miners perceived the state as a negative force in their lives.

Nationalization and the 'Golden Age', 1940 – c. 1980

The crucial moment in the history of the Zonguldak mines came in 1939–40 when the government nationalized the mines. Turkey had not initiated nationalization schemes for coal mining until that time, and this relatively late date seems to be related to the concentrated ownership structure in the basin. The nationalization of the Zonguldak mines, then, should be understood in relation to the economic crisis of the 1930s and the government's attempt to alleviate the effects of the crisis through a programme of state-led industrialization.

Nationalization did not improve the fortunes of the majority of the miners since a chronic labour shortage in the basin led the government to impose forced labour on the local people during World War II. As we have seen, the local population had been obliged to work in the mines during the late nineteenth century as well, making it the second period of forced labour they experienced. This time the labour requirement lasted seven years and took a heavy toll on the rural population. The number of fatal accidents increased during these years, and the gendarmerie and state company officials implemented the forced labour regime using heavy-handed methods. Conscripted soldiers were also intensively used as forced labour in the mines (Çatma 1998). The miners thus paid a heavy price for the operation of the Turkish war economy, although Turkey did not join the war until near its very end.

The period from 1940 to 1947 was extremely important in terms of the way miners related to the state. Nationalization, which made the state the miners' boss and provider of services hitherto provided by large companies, drastically increased the importance of the state in miners' lives. On the other hand, nationalization was immediately accompanied by forced labour. The forced labour practices of 1940–47 alienated a significant portion of workers. The generation of workers who suffered the forced labour period related to the state as an important yet largely negatively perceived entity. The Democratic Party (DP), the new opposition party that won the second multi-party elections held in 1950, got more than 60 per cent of the vote in Zonguldak, a fact that could be related to the alienation as well as the reaction of a significant part of the local population to wartime labour practices.

From the early 1960s, the relationship between the miners and the state started to change. In fact, for more than two decades following nationalization of the coal mines in 1940, up until 1965, state investments in the region increased. Major coal-processing facilities and the local railroad network were built, and mining equipment renewed (Tüylüoðlu and Karakaþ 2006: 207). With the establishment of a giant, state-owned steel company in Ereðli in 1965, in addition to the already existing one in Karabuk, the triangle formed by Zonguldak, Karabük and Ereðli became the spatial focus of Turkey's industrial strategy of import substitution. As a result, the state became the unrivalled actor in the economic and social life of the region. At its peak, the company employed more than 40,000 people, and was heavily involved in the social and cultural life of the inhabitants. It built roads, sports facilities and dormitories for workers; operated supermarkets; provided cheap or free food to the poor; and organized cinema and theatre shows, and concerts. It acted almost autonomously in the region, and the director of the company was at times considered to be more powerful than the provincial governor.

The Period of Decline, c. 1980 to the Present

There are various signs of the decline of coal mining industry in the Zonguldak coal basin from around 1980. From 1923, when the Turkish Republic was founded, to the mid-1970s, coal production in Turkey recorded a steady increase. It began to fall in 1975 and declined steeply from that point onwards. The production figures are more or less parallel to employment and demographic data. Employment in coal mining fell from more than 40,000 in 1980 to just over 10,000 in the 2000s. The population of the city of Zonguldak followed a similar course. After steadily increasing from 1950 to 1985, it began to fall from that point onwards. As of 2009, Zonguldak was one of the provinces with the highest rate of out-migration in the country.

Moreover, the process was accompanied by increasing privatization of the mines. For roughly half a century, following the completion of nationalization in 1940, coal was extracted only by the state company. Coal production by private companies began in the early 1990s and has expanded since then. After fifteen years of ups-and-downs, production by coal companies began to increase steeply in 2005. Combined with the continuing decrease in the production of the Turkish Coal Company, the production figures of the public and private sectors has converged noticeably in the recent years.

In the late 1980s, the government announced its intention to close down the mines. The workers' response was a strike in 1990 and a climactic march on Ankara in the winter of 1990–91. As a result, the government had to drop its plans to close down the entire basin, and instead switched to a policy of phasing out coal production through early retirement of workers, not hiring new personnel and suspending investment. The phasing-out policy was followed by all subsequent governments during the 1990s, and early and mid-2000s. Currently, some pits are closing down while others are being privatized; yet, at the same time, the state coal company has recently hired new workers. Zonguldak is stuck amidst this contradictory policy, and there are hardly any comprehensive regeneration plans in sight.

The state investment figures show that the state has been gradually withdrawing from Zonguldak. From 1983 to 2001, the average state incentives to the mining sector in general declined almost 50 per cent in nominal terms. The share of incentives offered to the mining sector within total state incentives also fell, from 4 to 1 per cent. Moreover, the proportion of public-sector investment in the mining sector in Zonguldak to total public-sector investment has visibly declined since 1999. Similarly, the investment in Turkish Coal Company, once the sole extractor of coal, declined in the 1970–2000 period.

Despite government attempts to initiate stimulus plans for trade, tourism and maritime transport, and the recent hiring of workers, the fact and the perception of economic decline in the region persist. As a result of the continued closure of state-owned mines, the privatization of others and its general failure to invest in the region, the state is becoming increasingly irrelevant to the lives of the miners and the people of Zonguldak.

The state is withdrawing in terms of physical landscape, too. The land around mines that are no longer in operation lies idle with machines and equipment rotting. Unused rail tracks are visible even in the city centre. The state coal company is liquidating its real estate assets. While some of the former company buildings are now used for other purposes, others have been demolished. Some of the land sold or transferred by the company now houses residential or commercial buildings. It seems that the government and capital in Zonguldak are in agreement to eliminate all traces of industry in the city. The company, of course, does not declare its intention as such, but emphasizes the need to liquidate its extra land and buildings to help the economy of the city. It has rented, privatized, transferred to other public bodies or otherwise liquidated tens of buildings and plots of land in the last decades. The process continues with a visible carelessness about buildings that could be considered part of the industrial heritage.

In the analysis presented above it is seen that early presence of the state in the region took the form of repressive measures such as forced labour. The few remaining memoirs or biographic accounts from the period suggest that the imposition of forced labour on the inhabitants of the region registered in the collective memory of the people as a government policy that was much resented. Especially during harvest time, a high degree of coercion was necessary to keep the miner–peasants in the pits. In addition to forced labour, the miners found themselves in a very unhealthy and dangerous working environment, and this factor also contributed to the resentment of the miners towards the state.

This negative relationship between the state and the miners started to change towards the 1960s as the state became a direct and sole coal producer in the region in the course of World War II. Thus the period from 1940 to 1980 witnessed the most significant presence of the state in the lives of miners as well as other inhabitants of the coal basin. The heavy involvement of the state company in providing social services might have created some sympathy among the workers towards the state, decreasing the impact of the bad memories of the war years, but also increasing expectations and labour militancy directed to the state.

The relationship between the state and the miners took another dramatic turn starting from the early 1980s as the region started to experience a steady decline, thanks to the strategic withdrawal of the state from the mining sector. While privatization and deregulation has paved the way for private companies, their involvement in coal production brought along with it lower wages and declining working conditions for the miners rather than a recovery of the local economy.

The rise and decline of state intervention in the region and its coal-led economy have had an important impact on the consciousness and identity formation of the working-class population of the region. In what follows, we deal only with the working people's perception of the presence of the state in the local economy, as there are various other dimensions that need to be considered for a fuller account of the state's impact on identity formation processes.

The Rise and Decline of State Intervention in the Eyes of Locals

In this section, using empirical material from our field research, we would like to look at the perception of the local people regarding the state withdrawal, and the following decline of the region and economy. It is a striking but not surprising fact that in the interviews conducted with local people, there was little reference to the conditions of the region and mines in the Ottoman and early Republican period. That period is almost completely missing in the local people's history of the Zonguldak mines. As this period is a distant past for them, the history of the region often starts with the glamorous days of direct involvement of the state in the region.

Nevertheless, the present perception of the period, i.e. after the decline of the industry, by the local people is quite variegated as the interviews exemplify different modes of remembering the past prevalent among the people of Zonguldak. In this context, one of the striking findings of the field research which should be reported at the outset is the bifurcation of opinions and perceptions between workers, and office employees and professionals, as well as the middle class in general.

In the case of professionals and office employees, a general sense of nostalgia pervades most narratives about Zonguldak. Often, the problems of the present are compared with an idealized past when the company 'took care' of the region. The nostalgia is all the more strong because there seems to be a realization that the 'good times' of the past will not come back. The narrative about the good times is based, above all, on the strength of the state company in the past and the role it played in the development of Zonguldak. 'Clean', 'socially developed', 'full employment'and 'tidy' are some of the attributes of the old Zonguldak according to the interviewees.

This is a view not limited to office workers of the coal mining company, but also shared by a diverse group of people, from an urban-based left-wing worker (A4) to a businessman (L20) and the head of the local chamber of architects (N2, N20). An 80-year-old shop owner (M9) says: 'When the Turkish Republic was founded, we were ahead of Ankara in terms of intellectual people. We had doctors, engineers, lawyers; all professions. There were foreigners, too.' The younger son of a very rich family in the city confirms (L20):

> When there were no movie theatres in most provinces in Turkey, there was one in Zonguldak. There were theatres; ballets were performed. One of the first marine clubs in Turkey was founded in Zonguldak. People in most other places did not know how to swim, but there were boat races in Zonguldak.

On the other hand, while the dominant narrative idealizes the former strength of the company and its social contribution to the city, class-based tensions emerge from time to time. One of the miners (F17) considers the money spent on social services by the company as an unnecessary cost: 'We had a tennis court here; what business does the company have with the tennis court?' Another miner (A10), whose father was also a miner, talks positively about the role of the company in the city, but when asked whether his family benefited from the services, he says: 'those who resided in the company housing [mostly white-collar employees] benefited more from certain services and their social environment was better than ours. . . . we had to create [our social spaces] ourselves.'

This difference between working-class and middle-class attitudes becomes even more accentuated when the issue comes to the present of the city of Zonguldak. While the middle class displays a visibly strong attachment to the city, the working class finds hardly anything that would keep them there after retirement. In this sense they have an indifferent attitude towards the future of the city. It seems that Zonguldak has two social landscapes with which different social groups associate themselves. We have tried to understand this difference using Zukin's concepts of 'landscape of the powerful' and 'vernacular of the powerless' (Zukin 1991). Yet, these concepts apply more easily to Zonguldak for the period before 2000. In recent years, the changing economic relations and the alliance of the state coal company with private capital to erase the remnants of industry from the landscape of the city have complicated the picture. The landscape of the powerful is increasingly being redefined as the middle class finds itself in opposition and increasingly less powerful.

The middle class and the professionals on the one hand, and the miners on the other, have quite different approaches to the actions and policies of the state during the deindustrialization period. In the case of the working class, there are still important expectations from the state. Yet their concerns and expectations are quite different from those of the middle class. They are not concerned that much about the future of the city and what the company provided for it in the past. Instead, the miners mention the guarantees provided by the state as the best aspect of their jobs.

> Nothing compares to working for the state. . . . Thank God. You get your salary every month. When a guy working somewhere else buys something for 1–2 thousand liras, the shop owner asks 'When are you going to pay?' He doesn't ask that to me. He knows that the money will come [from the state]. (E25)

The workers also want the state to have a more active role in economy:

> The state could work on the untouched areas, increase the number of workers and contribute to the national economy; there could be more coal and more workers for less. I also know that it gets more expensive as we go down, I admit it. Then give lower ones to private firms, not these ones. None [of the private firms] are below 200m; we are at 630m below sea level, they are all at 100m, untouched areas. Then the state should take them and employ more workers. The people, the youth here are unemployed and going to Istanbul and other places to find a job. (H15)

The middle class has a more confused and at times contradictory view of the state's historical role in the region. They yearn for a past long gone, and accuse the state of abandoning the region and its inhabitants. Moreover, they do not expect much from the state for economic improvement or at least to ward off the negative consequences of recession. This seems to be related to the widespread idea that Zonguldak has already relied too much on the state and that, as a result, an entrepreneurial spirit has not developed.

In fact, the withdrawal of the state seems to be leading to the rise of a form of entrepreneurial spirit in the region. As we have seen above, private employment in the mining sector is increasing. Moreover, the wages are higher in state mines and lower in private ones; thus there is significant discrepancy between the earnings of public- and private-sector employees. Whether or not this is the kind of entrepreneurialism the middle class laments, many workers realize the declining standards of work and living as a result of the entry of private capital, and are therefore not keen on celebrating the rise of such entrepreneurialism. They see the entry of private capital into mining as a threat to the security of their jobs and income levels:

> – *Do you consider the entry of private sector [into mining] a threat?*
> – Of course, what else could it be? I'm now retired, entitled for retirement. I'm not thinking about myself, I'm thinking about the next generation. (E14)

Many interviewees think that the working conditions in the private mines are worse than in the state coal company:

> My elder son worked for a while [in a private pit]. He has missed two days of work and they have written it down as eight days. If it is so, why do you work at all? Here in the company, if I don't go to work for two days, I lose two days of wage. There you lose eight days of wage; how does it happen? You can't be right there, it's not like here; either you [like it and] work or they kick you out. (E27)

> The conditions in the state company are a little bit better. Private sector doesn't make people as content as the state does, in terms of either wages or work. The state works regularly, everything is set in advance. But private companies pay on time only if they want; so it's irregular. And of course, private sector always wants to make money. This is not the state company's goal. (H6)

> It's different in the private sector; you don't have the right to organize. 'Take it or leave it.' With so much unemployment, with such bad conditions in the market, and when people agree to work almost only in exchange for social security payments, of course private companies make profit and the state loses money. (N25)

> This place was privatized in 2004; for the first time the company privatized one of its areas. There was much demand at the time; there were, if I'm not mistaken, 5,000 applications for 130–140 positions. Everyone had the same hope: 'if we work here [in this privatized area], they would hire us in the state company when they begin employing again.' (I3)

Conclusion

The state played a two-fold role in the coal basin from the late nineteenth century to the 1980s. On the one hand, it failed to provide a safe working environment, imposed forced labour, tried to break strikes, imprisoned and shot at workers. On the other hand, it introduced legislation to protect workers, defended them against the mine operators and provided social services to the employees. This double role began to change as a result of the decline of coal mining industry from the 1980s as the degree and quality of protection and services provided by the state declined visibly. The most serious confrontation of workers and the state in the post-1980 period was the strike during the winter of 1990–91. When the negotiations ended in a deadlock, thousands of workers and their families, supported by other inhabitants of Zonguldak, hit the road to march to Ankara, but were stopped halfway by troops. The strike still lingers in the workers' perception of the state.

Since then, through continued closures of state-owned pits, privatization of others and the general failure to invest in the region, the state has become increasingly irrelevant to the lives of the miners and the people of Zonguldak. The coal basin, therefore, especially in the last two decades, has witnessed a gradual yet unmistakable withdrawal of the state. Moreover, given the long-term engagement of the region in coal mining, an alternative sector that would replace the mining industry has not emerged yet. Given the absence of an alternative, many among the local people are still turning to the state for a solution, which creates even more ambiguity about the role of the state in the region. Although the private sector began to play a more important role in running the pits as contractors, the state's withdrawal from the region as the owner and manager of the coal mines was not followed by the flocking of private enterprises to take control of the mines.

There have been important effects of the withdrawal of the state on the working people of Zonguldak, their identity and sense of belonging. As we have seen, the middle classes and the miners have responded to the physical and social gap created by the withdrawal of the state in different ways. The former responded, above all, with a deep sense of nostalgia, for a reconstructed version of the past where the state figures in a positive role and which has become a crucial component of their identity. On the other hand, when they turn to the current situation, given that no alternative seems to be viable, they tend to blame the long-term state involvement in the region as responsible for the absence of an 'entrepreneurial spirit'.

The longing for the past is not as strong among the workers. Indeed, they do not seem to be much interested in the fate of Zonguldak as a city. Yet, perhaps paradoxically, they still have important expectations from the state as an employer. As private coal companies offer less-secure and less-paid jobs, they expect and demand that the state continue to be the main actor and employer in the mining sector.

It would not be wrong to argue that the attitudes of these two major groups are different due to the divergence in their concrete experiences. The urban middle class was the major beneficiary of the services provided and improvement in urban life brought about by the massive intervention of the state company especially after the 1960s. The miners hardly benefited from such advantages. Their gains remained limited to the workplace, given the fact that a sizeable proportion of them continued to live in rural areas. Even the urban-based workers did not often make use of the services that the state company provided. This is one of the reasons why their present expectations and demands from the state are related to 'work' in the narrow sense, concerning wages, job security, workplace security, etc. This bifurcation between the two groups has an important negative consequence. While the region has undergone an immense decline, the local people have so far failed to develop a common position towards the future of the region. This renders them increasingly weak vis-à-vis the emerging alliance between the state and capital, which has the potential to generate a quite bleak future for the middle class as well as the working class.

References

Aytekin, E.A. (2006), *Tarlalardan Ocaklara Sefaletten Mücadeleye: Zonguldak-Ereğli Kömür Havzası Isçileri 1848–1922* (From Fields to Pits, From Misery to Struggle: The Workers of the Zonguldak-Eregli Coal Basin, 1848–1922), Istanbul: Yordam Kitap.

Çatma, E. (1998), *Asker İşçiler* (Soldier-Workers), Istanbul: Ceylan.

Çıladır, S. (1977), *Zonguldak Havzasında Isçi Hareketlerinin Tarihi, 1848–1940* (History of Workers' Movements in the Zonguldak Coalfield, 1848–1940), Ankara: Yeraltı Maden-Is.

Gilbert, D. (1992), *Class, Community, and Collective Action: Social Change in Two British Coalfields, 1850–1926*, Broadbridge: Clarendon.

Hall, S. (1996), 'The Question of Cultural Identity', in Stuart Hall, David Held, Don Hubert and Kenneth Thompson (eds.), *Modernity: An Introduction to Modern Societies*, London: Blackwell: 595–634.

Harvey, D. (1985), *Urbanization of Capital*, Baltimore, MD: John Hopkins University Press.

Katznelson, I. (1981), *City Trenches: Urban Politics and the Patterning of Class in the United States*, New York: Pantheon Books.

Kirk, J. (2007), *Class, Culture and Social Change: On the Trail of the Working Class*, London: Macmillan.

Koç, Y. (1998), *Türkiye'de Isçi Sınıfı ve Sendikacılık Hareketi* (Working Class and Union Movement in Turkey), Istanbul: Gerçek.

Lazzarato, M. (1996), 'Immaterial Labor', in Paulo Virno and Michael Hardt (eds.), *Radical Thought in Italy: A Potential Politics*, Minnesota: University of Minnesota Press: 133–47.

Nichols, T. and E. Kahveci (1995), 'The Condition of Mine Labour in Turkey: Injuries to Miners in Zonguldak', *Middle Eastern Studies*, Vol. 31 (20): 197–228.

Quataert, D. (2006), *Miners and the State in the Ottoman Empire: The Zonguldak Coalfield, 1822–1920*, New York: Berghahn Books.

——— (1983), *Social Disintegration and Popular Resistance in the Ottoman Empire, 1881–1908: Reactions to European Economic Penetration*, New York: New York University Press.

Şengül, T. and E.A. Aytekin (2011), 'Zonguldak Coalfield and the Past and Future of Turkish Coal-Mining Communities', in John Kirk, Sylvie Contrepois and Steve Jeffreys (eds.), *Changing Work and Community Identities in European Regions: Perspectives on Past and Present*, Hampshire: Palgrave Macmillan: 154–83.

Tüylüoglu, S. and D.N. Karakaş (2006), '*Bölgesel Kalkınma ve Ekonomik Durgunlasma Süreci: Zonguldak Örnegi*' (Regional Development and Economic Stagnation: The Case of Zonguldak), *Amme Idaresi Dergisi*, 39/4: 195–224.

Zukin, S. (1991), *Landscapes of Power: From Detroit to Disney World,* Berkeley: University of California Press.

Family, Neighbourhood and Community

Working Lives of Weavers in Colonial United Provinces

Santosh Kumar Rai

This essay analyses the embedded hierarchies and informal relations of work that shaped the handloom-weaving industry in the north Indian province of Uttar Pradesh under colonial rule. Globalization and modernization gave only two options to the weavers, either to get excluded or to be included in the growth model of modernity with its terms and conditions. This essay discusses how the family-based production system, and the ways in which the social relations of productions were entangled by the household, neighbourhood and community, led to differentiation in the structure of production. A dominant premise in the *Julaha* notion of work is the disciplining of the worker by the division of time and space within the local context. The basic process of reproduction of the household through community/locality expressions provided the social meanings of the economic processes. Therefore the changes had also to be defined through this collectivity only. Historically unequal connections operated through the social power balance of community, and those in families (husbands and wives, parents and children) found new meanings of work in the bargaining processes of labour markets.

In recent times, major reinterpretations of artisan history in the nineteenth–twentieth centuries have been published by Tirthankar Roy and Douglas Haynes.[1] These works suggest that while the handloom weavers faced adversities from the market, many of them coped with these by using a variety of strategies, including migration, reapplication of skills and strengthening of social ties, and that some of them succeeded to such an extent that new hubs of small enterprise emerged upon a foundation of artisanal industry. The commercialization-through-modernization paradigm given by Douglas Haynes and Tirthankar Roy pursues the idea that historically, community cohesion has been congruent to technological progress and knowledge diffusion among community-based weaving clusters and groups in India. This essay suggests otherwise, which is that there are functional limitations beyond which the detriments of 'community social capital'[1] and the rigidities associated with inherited networks set in, hindering knowledge diffusion and technological advancement in favour of the status quo. This essay brings out the specific features of weavers' experience in the middle Gangetic plains, which Roy, Haynes and others have not studied in detail, as opposed to the well-researched western India and southern India.

I discuss here the family-based production system and the ways in which hierarchical social relations of productions entangled the household, neighbourhood and community, leading to differentiation in the structure of production, in the context of weaving industries of colonial United Provinces. Notions of neighbourhood and community have a long history of interconnectedness with family-based production and traditional forms of apprenticeship. Globalization of the market system and capitalistic modernization of textile industries were the two major challenges before the traditional work process. A significant transformation happened within the household production process due to its struggle to adapt to the fluctuating demands of the market. But the whole process of exclusion and inclusion within the weaving industry cannot be explained just in terms of 'organization', 'network', 'institution' and 'technology'. These were the inevitable effects of 'change'. So the process of community formation rather than the enumeration of features of a reified community structure transcended the notion of the *Julaha* community as a pre-given entity; rather, it was constituted and reconstituted with shifting boundaries and in interaction with the living context.

Age and gender were two major factors which constituted labour relations in the process of the weaving cycle. In this tradition of weaving, women workers had a subordinate role. Everyday dynamics of hierarchy, authority, class and gender at the household and neighbourhood levels constantly influenced the relations of production. Primordial ties and traditional culture had their own frames of hierarchy and dominance with an exploitative nexus. Instead of a direct transformation of new institutions and mechanisms, the weaving sector in eastern Uttar Pradesh functioned in socio-cultural contexts of inherent necessities and shared hierarchical understanding. The specific structures and relations of production prevalent in the region had an inbuilt capacity to produce various hierarchies of producers. The pyramid of producers began with invisible labour in the family and went on to comprise paid workers, weavers on contract, independent weavers and the authority of *grihasta*[2] – the interface between production and marketing. The system of advances ensured the viability of this exploitative mechanism over the period under consideration. Skill, the quality of products and opportunities created different variables for the rural and urban weavers in the region.

By the second half of the nineteenth century, due to major economic depression, and subsequent famine and unemployment, weaving communities, especially rural *Julaha*s, were compelled to give up their sole profession of handloom-weaving. Some of the rural weavers became agricultural labourers, and a major section migrated to eastern and western India, faced with the problem of underemployment in their sole occupation. It was only the option of agriculture that gave considerable relief to the rural weaver from the trauma of leaving his roots. During the famine of 1868–70 in the North-Western Provinces it was observed that 'it is a famine of labour rather than of food'.[3] The worst affected section of the 1868–70 famine were village artisans, especially the weavers of famine-affected districts such as Jhansi, Muradabad, Hamirpur, Banaras, Budaon, Barielly and Bijnore.

The demand for indigenous cloth goods remained in only two forms. The market for the cloth made by these indigenous weavers was limited, and the poor sections of the society constituted the major part of the market for this indigenous cloth. First was the demand for the 'roughest production for the use of the very poor classes'. But the problem for the *Purabiya* (eastern) weavers was that their rough cloth needed raw material which was not locally produced and was expensive. The second demand was for 'articles of great artistic and intrinsic worth',[4] which could be afforded only by the very rich classes and produced by only specialized skilled weavers.

The experiences of Raza, a non-specialized *Julaha* weaver from Ghazipur district in the late nineteenth century, would explain the nature of family life and the livelihood of weavers in rural United Provinces (hereafter UP). While reporting to the Dufferin Enquiry of 1888, the Collector of Ghazipur stated that seventy-year-old Raza's family consisted of his wife, and two married sons with their three wives and three small children. One of his sons had left for Calcutta in search of work and the family had no information from him since his departure. Raza had no land and was entirely dependent on the proceeds of weaving. Moreover, Raza and his wife were too old to weave, and their second son could not weave more than 5 yards of cloth daily. There was nothing to supplement their income beyond the little work the women used to get when they were employed in harvesting. Such a family did not often know what the meaning of a feast was. A few such families could undoubtedly be found in every populous village. According to Raza, 'fifty years ago he was far better off than he is now and . . . the consumption of country cloth had much diminished of late in consequence of the import of European goods'.[5]

The story was almost similar for non-specialized, young rural weavers in western UP. Nanhe of village Nabhipur in Mathura had no relationship or connection with Raza *Julaha*, except that they shared the same fate as weavers. Nanhe's grievance was that there had been no sale of cloth the previous year, and in the scarce winter of 1887–88 he took recourse to being a labourer to survive. But at the time of Dufferin Enquiry demand for cloth had sprung up again and Nanhe resumed his old trade. However, his wife and twelve-year-old son were still working in the fields so that his family could eat two meals a day.[6]

In comparison to their rural counterparts, the weavers living in *qasba*s like Mau and Mubarakpur in Azamgarh, who specialized in the manufacture of some specific varieties of cloth, had better chances of survival. Silk cloth was only one among the many types of cloth produced in eastern UP till the early nineteenth century. From the late nineteenth century, some localities of this region increasingly focused on silk products, and gradually their fame and survival, both became solely dependent on silk. These changes in the production process need to be viewed against the totality of the complexities of the colonial economy – including industrialization, modernization and deindustrialization, loss of traditional skills, along with changing patterns of cloth consumption and use of raw material – to explain the rise of *grihasta*s in the new hierarchy among producers.

By the first decade of the twentieth century, the shifts in specialized production led to hierarchies of production structure being entrenched in silk-weaving. These hierarchies resulted in segmentation of the industry according to type of cloth, cost of raw material, and degree of organization of investment and marketing. Availability of costly yarn and gold thread made skill-based work remain subordinate to the mediators active in the industry. Urban weavers did not have the option of pursuing agriculture,[7] and the only option was migration in order to run their households. Generally, weaving remained household production. A government official, A.C. Chatterjee, commented about Tanda in 1907: 'there is practically a system of small factories'.[8] The master-weaver's loom might be in a ground-floor room of his residence or in a building nearby, or even in a different part of the town. In some cases, the *grihasta*s installed their looms in the houses of individual paid workers. In Benaras, Mau and Mubarakpur, the *bani* and independent weavers had their own looms.[9] The nature of space for work also ensured informality. An important function of the weavers' organizations was to maintain sizing yards. In many parts of the country, warping and sizing were done in the open streets, making the streets in weavers' quarters wider than elsewhere. The weaving community also made sure that shady trees were planted on both sides of the road. Maintenance of such cloth-sizing facilities was one of the traditional duties of the weaving organizations.[10]

Home-based production had many advantages like avoiding space constraint, as well as the use of unaccounted-for and unpaid labour of wives and children. The members of a weaver's family, irrespective of age or sex, supplied all the labour needs of this family occupation. The preparatory processes prior to actual weaving were usually done by women, and sometimes even the weaving was done by them. The production of Benarasi saris involved a number of pre-weaving and post-weaving activities. The yarn, called *katan*, had to be reeled, bleached and dyed. The dyed yarn was then prepared for the *tana* (warp) and *bana* (weft). Four to five people were needed to reel the warp. The length of yarn reeled on a five-feet-long warp cylinder could be sufficient for up to six saris. Yarn for the weft was reeled on a small, cylindrical object in a process locally known as *nari bharna* (filling the bobbin). A *charkha* (spinning wheel) was used for reeling the yarn on *nari* (bobbins), and this was usually done by women. *Nari bharna* was a continuous process as long as the loom is running. Women performed the tasks of reeling, bleaching, dyeing and warping of the yarn, winding the thread on bobbins for use as weft yarn, embroidering saris, and sizing – i.e. applying starch paste on the warp thread. This unusual joint participation of men and women in a single industry led to the emergence of a broader, gendered division of labour which was far from being equal, even prior to the arrival of modern technology, due to the kind of surrogate tasks allotted to the women of the family.

In the Muslim weavers' tradition in eastern UP, women were never treated as legitimate *karigar*s to work on *kargha*. *Janana* weaving has been traditionally opposed on the basis of the Islamic law that women should be kept away from the responsibility of earning a livelihood.[11] Elders always construed the practice of *janana* working on *kargha* as a *lanat* (insult) which arose due to economics dominating over the social ethos with the passage of time. The dominance of husbands and fathers in families, and the lack of job alternatives for women other than time-consuming household tasks, gave them little opportunity to develop their capabilities or skills. Another way in which this gender differentiation worked was among the weavers of Barabanki, where there existed a distinction between quilt-making and weaving of cloth. While cloth for everyday use was marketed, quilts made for everyday life were meant solely for the use of hearth members (joint family). The focal point of the *zanana*s was the quilt room, while that of the *mardana* was the work-shed (*karkhana*).[12] In the case of Barabanki this scenario was explained in terms of weaving as masculine work. But in the last decade of the nineteenth century it was noted that 'the employment of women would probably mean a further lowering of wages, and – what is worse – it would increase the opportunity for man to sit idle'. *Janana* weaving is basically a post-1960s trend[13] that started from Mau. People from Mubarakpur acknowledged the practice of women's weaving, but at the same time argued that they were the last ones to accept this practice, following the trend set by other weavers from Mau, Mohammdabad, Khairabad and Ibrahimpur. In their perception, '*Janana ki kamai haram hai*' ('Dependence on the income of women is a sin'). In fact, it appears that women's weaving was a double-edged weapon. On the one hand, it was liberating, making women self-sufficient based on their knowledge of a *hunar* (vocation) that could be used during adverse times to earn money. At the same time *janana* weaving was also related to the practical requirement of collecting money for dowry, but, unfortunately, a girl's hard work on the loom might lead to tuberculosis even before her marriage.

Sometimes, when the cost of thread was high in the market, woman had to also perform the work of a spinner.[14] This segmentation of work was reflected in terms of earnings also; spinning was often unpaid work when performed by wives.[15] The Census Report of 1911 observed: 'The women of the artisan classes generally offered relief to their husbands of the lighter and simpler forms of labour . . . the weaver's wife spins the thread'.[16] An official similarly observed:

> In all ages and in all countries the spinning of thread has been the woman's function, and almost as generally the task of weaving has been allotted to the man. According to Muhammadan tradition, this immemorial division of labour dates from our first parents, for after the fall and the expulsion from Paradise, Gabriel taught Eve to spin and Adam to weave.[17]

Serving the household by cooking, washing and nursing the children, was women's 'natural' work. In Abdul Bismillah's novel *Jhini Jhini Bini Chadariya*, when Aleemun dies of tuberculosis, Rehana falls victim to illiteracy, poverty and superstition. Her epileptic seizures are treated through prayers or witchcraft.[18] Womenfolk who toiled all their lives in helping their men weave fabulous Benarasi saris often died in poverty – never draping themselves in the saris they had helped to weave. Though important, their tasks were not given the status and value they deserved, and were usually not included when the pricing of the sari or labour wage-fixing was done. This unpaid labour of the womenfolk of households thus reduced them to the status of invisible workers.

A shift to the *karkhana* meant the exclusion of women from some of their prescribed duties, as the *parda* system ensured that women did not visit the neighbourhood *karkhana*, which was an unfamiliar, men's domain. The survival of weaving as household work was linked to the reluctance of male weavers to abandon the aid of unpaid labour in enhancing their productivity, i.e. the labour of their wives and children. The use of new technology was to be accommodated in this set-up.

At Moradabad, a local difficulty related to the training of weavers arose when the *Julaha* women, who earlier gave considerable assistance in connection with the *kargha*, were unable to assist in the Serampore loom. Most of the weavers refused to use the fly-shuttle looms as they found that their womenfolk were unacquainted with this loom, whereas using the '*kargha*' loom they could take a considerable share in producing the cloth. Thus, the weaving school committee started to offer scholarships to 'women who will accompany their husbands and learn the use of fly shuttle loom'.[19] During his visit to several localities in Shahjahanpur district, J.M. Cook saw many ex-students of the school at work both on the fly-shuttle loom and the *kargha*. He also noticed many women and children at work preparing the yarn: 'Here, as in other places, the women folk take a large share in producing the cloth. Even when the male member of a family was weaving on a fly shuttle loom I noticed there were also "karga" looms on which the women weave.'[20] Thus, it was suggested that in the existing *zenana* school two or three fly-shuttle looms might be included, which, in time, might help in setting aside the objection of the male weavers that their womenfolk were unable to aid them on the improved looms.

Despite of playing such a vital role in the production process, in the male-centric accounts of Sheikh Abdul Majid's diaries or police intelligence reports, women appeared only when they were accused of adultery or social mis-demeanours.[21] The *panchayats* had only male members who played a significant role in fixing role models for the females of the community. In the neighbouring Shahabad district of Bihar, the most severe offence for *Julaha panchayats* was marriage outside the caste – an offence to be dealt with severely, to the extent of ostracizing from the community. Widow remarriage was another serious offence which was punished in rural areas by permanent excommunication from the caste. *Panchayats* in towns were more lenient on the issue. The 1911 Census observed: 'even teenage daughters who are widowed are not given in marriage by respectable *Julaha* in rural area'.[22] Adultery, however, was not punished with 'honour killing'. A secret police report of 1922 observed that in Azamgarh, inter-community relations became tense as a *Julaha* man who was living with an *Ahir* (milkmen's community) woman was not ready to abandon her.[23] This issue became a point of communal mobilization and ill-will between the *Julaha* and *Ahir* communities. Sheikh Abdul Majid of Mubarakpur, who generally remained silent about women, gave a detailed description of an affair between a married woman of Pura Sofi and a 'sepoy' (constable), and the resulting friction within the family that culminated in disgrace of the woman and transfer of the sepoy by May 1916.[24]

The training of labour was in the form of a traditional, informal apprenticeship system, usually confined to family and caste. In 1906 it was reported that: 'What their earnings are is very difficult to estimate as the price they receive for their clothes include the earnings of women and children on the preliminary operations of wrapping and sizing.'[25] In Kopaganj, a male weaver with the help of two children could earn six *annas* daily.[26] The weft-yarn was used in a shuttle called *dharki*, which was thrown from side to side while weaving. Children in the household helped in the weaving process by throwing the shuttle while sitting beside the adult weaver on the loom. In the *doria* system children began by working on the spinning mill or in wrapping yarn. Once they developed these skills they were allowed to become assistant weavers, and they became skilled weavers by their late teens. Weaving as a skill required a long process of training, and the family setting of weavers provided the required atmosphere for the training process. In a 1921 memorandum submitted by E.B. Havell to the Industries Department, on Improvement of

Indian Art and Crafts, it was recommended that the 'government must try to reach fathers and uncles . . . rather than take their sons and nephews away from them'.[27] The shift from household production to wage *karkhana* labour meant a transformation of familial apprenticeship to forms of child labour. The practical difficulty in obtaining boys to attend the government's weaving classes was reflected in the high premium given in the form of an advance to the boys' parents, which was paid by weavers in Benares to secure boys for their factories.[28] The child thus became, in a sense, a commodity, exchanged between his/her parents and the employer. The parents or guardians who received the money were often destitute, and had no other means to obtain credit. They used the loans to pay for weddings or funerals, childbirth or treatment of illnesses; to pay off other loans; or just to arrange food. The employers used the loans to secure indefinitely the cheapest possible form of labour.[29] The artisans often moved to other workshops when they got better wages. The *karkhanadar*s began to pay these apprentices their wages either when they had learnt to make the articles or after a period of apprenticeship.[30]

The proportion of such full-time weavers working with the support of family labour was 75 per cent in the United Provinces, and weavers constituted a considerable proportion of the population in Benaras, Barabanki, Mirzapur and Mau.[31] In fact, family and community support were found to be so crucial to run weaving as a home industry that non-weavers trained at the weaving schools could not succeed in their endeavour. The weaving schools committee, established in 1924 by the Industries Department of the United Provinces, did not come across a single non-weaver ex-student who was carrying on the profession independently at his own house. The main reason cited for the failure of non-weavers to carry on hand-weaving as a home industry was the supposed lack of assistance from various members of his family in the conduct of his business. With no community to help him, his margin of profit from the business would therefore have been lower than that of a weaver. This was the limitation restricting weaving to a family and community business.

Independent weavers, i.e. those who owned their own looms and at times had capital to buy yarn, remained a minority as they could survive only in a flourishing market. When the product was sub-standard or lost its demand in the market, the weaver had to sell it at a price that might not even cover his labour cost. In 1942 it was officially observed that:

> among the types of weavers theoretically, the economic position of the independent weaver is excellent. He is free to produce what he wants and works when it is convenient to him. He works in the midst and with the assistance of his family. But all this does not help him in his business. He has only a limited market and when there is no demand for his cloth he is not able

> to hold back his prices until prices improve. He often sells his cloth in the bazaar on the gujari [direct sale] basis because he cannot wait, and therefore when he is pressed for money he would even sell his cloth at anything above the cost of yarn.[32]

At the beginning of the twentieth century, when the government of UP tried to introduce improved weaving contraptions, it faced the problem of *Julaha* weavers having 'a religious prejudice against the paying as well as receiving of interest'.[33] This was one among many other excuses the *Julaha* weavers gave to resist the introduction of new techniques by external agencies. This situation kept the Muslim worker-weaver bound to the *grihasta* through community spirit and religious commonality. This situation also gave the master-weaver a chance to exploit the worker-weaver. If a weaver wanted to change his employer but had no money to repay his debt, the new employer paid his debt to the old one, keeping the weaver ever-indebted while he worked for the new employer. To escape this obligation, the only option for the worker was to resort to the moneylender, eventually paying exorbitant interest rates. In the early twentieth century, the organization of the production–marketing mechanism was taken over by Muslim mediators who used the claims of their religious identity to counter the exploitation of their Muslim brethren by 'Hindu' brokers. For the Muslim weavers, their relationship with the master-weaver had a stronger sense of solidarity as the master-weaver, being a Muslim, generally would not practise usury as it was prohibited by Islam.

These *grihasta*s supplied their workers with raw materials and paid them for the finished product on a piece-rate basis. The *grihasta* was the essential design and marketing link in the system: he selected the design (according to market preference), determined the structure of production, provided all costs relating to the design maker, suggested the colours, purchased the silk and gold yarn, even set up the loom and ensured the quality of the product. A weaver could only function well if the *grihasta* understood the constraints of the loom, and appreciated and provided quality yarn. The *grihasta*'s capability in supplying the raw material and providing the weaver with regular work even in off-seasons ensured the continuity of a patrimonial bond with the weaver. The paid and independent weavers were given advances or interest-free loans to be deducted from their piece-work payment. Even if the workers remained in debt to the master-weaver, this relationship acquired the status of a 'moral debt or moral economy' as the master-weaver was the only person on whom a weaver could fall back in case of an emergency.

By the 1920s, increasing commercialization led to the redefinition of the role of community institutions and leadership. The resurgence of the community was not limited to the negation of modern techniques or restrictions on its members, for even the existing commercial alliances were reviewed and reformulated. On Friday, 12 December 1919, weavers of *atthaisi* (twenty-eight) *mauza*s of Mubarakpur met at Haji Abdur Rehman's place in Gajhadha village, and decided that they will not transact any further with Babu Mahabir, Babulal and Kamta Prasad Aggarwal (prominent cloth merchants) in yarn and silk. Further, it was resolved that Muslims would trade exclusively among themselves.[34] On 9 January 1920, the *panchayat* of *atthaisi* was held at a house in the Pura Dulhan locality of Mubarakpur for opening the shop by Mahabir Chaudhary, Kothi Babulal and Babu Kamta Prasad. On the issue of selling of cloth in certain houses by weavers, fines were imposed and Abdul Majid was also fined Rs 101 – the heaviest fine of the whole lot. On the night of Saturday, 8 February 1920, another *panchayat* assembled in Gola Bazar. The shop of Chaudhary (probably Mahabir Chaudhary, mentioned earlier) was opened and Chaudhary paid a fine of Rs 200 to the *panchayat* along with Rs 25 for the expenses incurred in assembling the *panchayat*. Moreover, among the weavers themselves, the *panch* collected a fine of Rs 200 from Karim Baksh Dalal of Sariyain village. He was also made to stand for two hours along with *gosh maali* (pulling of ears), and only then was he forgiven. Sabir, son of Ismail of Sarayain, was expelled from the *biradari* for his offence.[35] The realm of productive activity was to be defended and controlled at 'the community' level since the whole process of production was also the ultimate site of identity formation and source of prestige for 'the community' of *Julaha* weavers. Thus the weavers of Mubarakpur gave priority to this issue. However, migration and political action were activities where 'the community' could not decide the collective course of action, which diluted the authority of 'the community'. Thus the use of boundaries of 'community' by resourceful individuals with commercial concerns was behind major community actions.

The traditional role of the *panchayat* could also be reinvented for altogether different purposes. In 1929–30, associations known as *panchayat*s, representing only middlemen, were in existence in different weaving *mohalla*s of Benaras, where they exercised a great influence and there was a compact sense of brotherhood among different members of the *panchayats*. If it was found that a weaver working under a particular *karkhanadar* left his service without repaying the complete amount advanced to him and joined a new *karkhanadar*, the latter was bound to pay the dues to the old master in case he employed the worker for more than three days after it was reported to him. If he did not pay, the *panchayat* took up the case and decided in the old *karkhanadar*'s favour. But there was no such association or *panchayat* of workers against middlemen dealers, and 'If cases, where the workers absconded with money were not frequent, cases where the workers were not paid or underpaid by middlemen dealers were also not rare.'[36]

Thus, in their traditional strongholds, community *panchayat*s of the

Julahas still insisted on numerous restrictions resembling the Hindu caste system.[37] These restrictions were more instrumental in the reinvention of 'the community' as this was the only way in which 'the community' (which was certainly controlled by the affluent) made its presence felt. Fines and expulsions were the instruments used by 'the community' in its attempt to strengthen its hold over its members. The moments of crisis were already proving to be a big challenge for the community to change their perception, and 'their temper and general outlook on life has been soured by the very severe losses they have suffered from plague'.[38]

Weavers were also affected by the seasonality of their occupation, which peaked from the month of *Phalgun* (February–March) to *Vaishakh* (April–May), and again after Durga Puja (October), corresponding to the marriage seasons.[39] The work time was not fixed. In 1837, a hindsight view from Azamgarh reflected that the cloth was made 'at looms erected in the private houses of the weavers'.[40] The working hours fluctuated according to demand and the season. The tendency was to freely manage the time as payment was by piece. On average, the weavers worked throughout the year with few holidays, except for some religious festivals that were observed. It was not unusual for them to be required to put in up to 10 hours a day, and in rare cases even up to 14 hours. The normal daily and weekly working hours (on all seven days of the week) were 8 to 9 and 48 to 54 hours, respectively, for time-bound wages. But if the weaver was working under per-piece *bani* obligation, he could put in up to 10 to 12 hours per day, or 60 to 72 hours a week. The average number of working days in a year varied between 275 and 300. There was great diversity in the practices prevalent at various centres and even in different establishments. The work, however, was done under circumstances very different from that in powerloom factories.[41]

Certainly, the artisans did not enjoy a romanticized, liberated lifestyle. Issues of subsistence haunted them. Being followers of Islam, *namaz* five times a day, the month of *Ramadan* and *Id* festivities were some of the obvious adjustments embedded within their working hours and days. The timings for the daily *namaz* – *Fajr, Dhuhr, Asr, Maghrib* and *Isha* – fluctuated according to seasonal changes, which in turn led to flexibility in work time. The gap between *Asr namaz*, i.e. afternoon prayer, and *Maghrib namaz*, i.e. sunset prayer, is very short during the winter season, and so there was no point in coming back to work after the *Asr namaz* during winter. Thus calling off work for the day used to be early in winter. Similarly, on the day of *Jumma* (Friday), a weekly off had to be taken. During the month of *Ramadan*, contrary to the general perception, weavers increased their working hours in order to earn more money so that they could afford the expenditure on clothes, sweets, etc. for the forthcoming festival of *Id-ul-Fitr*. During *Ramadan*, as women started midnight preparations for pre-dawn meals, i.e. *Sahur* or *Saheri*, men also woke up early for prayer, which also advanced the time for work to earlier in the day. For the *Julahas* the pious month of *Ramadan* meant moral performance of work to the rhythms of *naat*s, the religious songs. The month-long fast could not suppress the overwhelming human desire for religious celebration. Ultimately, the *Id* festivals – *Id-ul-Fitr* and *Id-ul-Zoha*, and for Shia weavers *Muharram,* meant week-long holidays to visit relatives and friends. These practical realities of day-to-day existence guided the weavers' notion, style and time of 'work'.[42] The ideal working environment for an ordinary weaver family was as follows:

> There is nothing to rack the nerves or fatigue the mind. A good deal of the work is done in the open in the courtyard of the worker's house or even in the public street or lane. There is no discipline to observe rest and recreation are taken whenever the need is felt. Contact with the home and the familiar surroundings is seldom interrupted. The usual amenities of social life are not disturbed. The training of apprentices (members of the family or relatives and craftsmen) goes on along with the regular work.[43]

In the official perception, due to this homely work culture, evenness and uniformity of handloom products were difficult to achieve. One textile expert opined that 'there will always be a difference in a weaver's work before and after to smoking his *hukka*'.[44]

Leisure and everyday life found expression in usual forms. The drinking habit among *Julaha* weavers was on record since the beginning of British rule in this region. C.R. Crommelin complained that there was slow progress in obtaining cloth up to 30 April 1803, and the reason given by him was that manufacturers and others were 'so much taken up with marriage ceremonies and so greatly given to drinking toddy' that their occupations were neglected.[45] The Commercial Resident recorded that 'the weaver appears to be industrious except during what is called the drinking season, in March and April, when general intoxication takes place from the effect of a liquor distilled from the fruit of the Mova tree [*sic*] which falls during those months'.[46] Almost a hundred years later, Abdul Majid described the leisurely lifestyle of the Muslim *Julahas* of Mubarakpur as follows:

> [They are] very sober and devout and thoroughly follow their *roza* and *namaaz* but they also enjoy the worldliness. They also know arts of worldliness i.e. wine, adultery, theft, dance and deceit very well. There are certain *namazis* who after spending the whole day in *roza* and *namaaz* used to spend leisurely nights with wine and women of the *mohalla*.[47]

Defiance of authority and drunkenness are revealed in another incident in which a Sikhti zamindar *Safar* and *Sakhavat* weaver married into Sikhti were convicted for beating up, under the influence of toddy, a constable who had come to serve a warrant on them.[48] In the year 1919 business at Mubarakpur led to prosperity of the *qasba* – so much so that in each *mohalla* people purchased buffaloes even if they were not producing milk. They wasted their money. In the same year as many as 1,082 persons of the brotherhood performed *Hajj-i-Kaaba*, indeed a pious work.[49] Bonds of community were helpful on certain occasions. In 1877, the Settlement Officer observed about the *Julahas* of Mau:

> A day is fixed every year and all marriages in the brotherhood are celebrated on that day. The object of the custom is to save expense, the guests, whom it is necessary to invite from among the caste, being distributed over a number of households; and it proves the unanimity that exists among the weavers.[50]

To conclude, beyond the facilitation by the community networks and 'small-town capitalism', this essay argues that due to the basic requirements needed 'to live' or for reproduction of one's household, autonomy of the weavers and their control over production processes and time may be treated as merely hypothetical. They were neither independent nor was the informal system of production free from control of the hierarchies from above. Yet home-based production created independent notions of work, time, space and leisure for the weavers amidst their own cultural context. Household production was a distinguishing characteristic of handloom weaving and the involvement of family labour was crucial for its sustenance. In the basically labour-intensive, low-cost production of households, the structure of the production process was defined by the need to purchase yarn, and the living expenses of the weaver and his dependants while the cloth was being woven. Yet the very basic process of reproduction of the household through community/locality expressions provided social meaning to the economic process. Thus the changes also had to be defined through this collectivity. The historically unequal connections operated through the social power balance of the community, and families (husbands and wives, parents and children) found new meanings in the bargaining processes of labour markets (between capitalists and workers), changes in the components of production (competition between British and Indian mills), uniqueness of the product, mediators and the demand. Together these shaped the social relations of production for weavers in eastern United Provinces. This transformation happened because of the interaction between the capitalist economic process under colonialism and the already existing economic activities of the weaving community. What unfolded over the years was the birth of a 'community economy' of *Julahas* that was neither 'capitalist' in terms of its modern functions, like availability of 'free labour', a wage system and a 'factory'-type managerial system, nor a typical caste-based occupation system. It was instead the development of a 'community economy' that had the characteristic features of both the traditional caste-based occupations and features of the capitalist system of production. This simultaneous process produced the 'exclusive' space of a 'community economy' to operate for *Julaha*s, and for weaving to remain a caste-based occupation. It also provided the necessary space for the community to withstand the aggressiveness of modernization under colonial capitalism. In effect, this became an alternate sphere of the economy as an interface to mainstream capitalist economic processes by remaining a 'marginal economy' exclusively of the *Julaha*s. Yet the prism of community solidarity ultimately worked as an agency to build material hierarchies.

Acknowledgements: An earlier version of this essay was presented at the XI International Conference on Labour History organized by the Association of Indian Labour Historians in March 2012 at the V.V. Giri National Labour Institute, New Delhi. I acknowledge valuable comments and suggestions shared by the discussant, Prasannan Parthasarathi, and my research supervisor, Prabhu P. Mahapatra. I would also like to express my special gratitude to Justin Mathew, N.R. Levin and Shalin Jain for their contribution in giving a final shape to this essay.

Notes

1 Roy (1999); Haynes (2012).

2 Alam (2011).

3 The term *grihasta* comes from the ancient terminology for a Hindu householder. By the late nineteenth century, in the weaving hubs of eastern United Provinces, the Hindi word *grihasta* meant a senior member of a weaving caste community with extra resources, and a mediator between the community and the traders and merchants. In this context, the term *grihasta* (referring to the master-weaver) was used for organizers or trainers of handloom production, as a parallel to the 'guild master' and 'merchant manufacturer' of the 'putting-out' system. It is a matter of speculation whether it was due to a desire to become an 'independent' prosperous householder or to subvert the status of the exploitative Hindu merchant-householder (*grihast*) that, from the late nineteenth century, Muslim master-weavers or *karkhanadar*s started using this connotation of the term.

4 Henvey (1871): 2. Also see *Narrative of the Scarcity during 1874* (1875): 83.

5 *Report on the Railway-Borne Traffic of the North-Western Provinces and Oudh* (1883): 30.

6 *Reports on the Condition of the Lower Classes of the Population of India*; *Report from the Benaras Division*, paragraph 17; E. Rose, Collector Ghazipur, Letter No. 2420/ VII-49, dated 10th April 1888, in *Famine Proceedings* (1888).

7 'Notes from Mathura', paragraph 20, in *Reports on the Condition of the Lower Classes of the Population of India, Famine Proceedings* (1888).

8 'Information regarding the Slackness of Demand for European Cotton Goods', Art. 4, in *Selection from the Records of Government, North Western Provinces* (1864).

9 Chatterjee (1908): 19, 21.

10 *Bani* is an occupational term for handloom weaving and for weft. *Bani* consists of a putting-out system by which a master-weaver provides his labourers with handlooms, raw materials and sari designs. The weavers are bound to give the woven saris to the master-weaver and receive a fixed wage in return, which represent payment for the previous sari given to the master-weaver. The *lagaar* system was introduced in the post-independence period when, due to increased demand, the relation between the *grihasta* and his *karigar* changed. Instead of *bani*, from then on the

system of *lagaar* prevailed in Mubarakpur. In this system the *karigar* also has a share in the profit made out of sale of cloths, especially saris. It is a kind of partnership during days of prosperity, though even now, if any defect is detected in the product, the profit of the *karigar* is reduced.

[11] *Report of the Fact-Finding Committee (Handloom and Mills)* (hereafter *RFFC*), *1942* (1942): 69.

[12] Silberrad (1898): 13, 45.

[13] Mehta (1997): 40.

[14] Interviews with weavers, Mubarakpur and Maunath Bhanjan, May 2007.

[15] Silberrad (1898): 13; interview with Qazi Zafar Masud.

[16] *Royal Commission on Labour in India, Evidence*, Vol. III, Part I: Central Provinces and United Provinces (1930): 137, 173.

[17] *East India (Census): General Report of the Census of India, 1911* (1914): 411.

[18] Morison (1911): 137–38.

[19] Bismillah (1986).

[20] *Annual Report on Industrial Education in the United Provinces for the Year 1912–13*, File No. 232/1913, Box No. 31: 10.

[21] Ibid.: 3.

[22] Sheikh Abdul Majid (1864–1934?) was a weaver of *muhalla* Pura Sofi in Mubarakpur. His diary recording events from 1902 onwards to the last entry of 1934 establishes his credentials as a prosperous member of the weavers' community, in all probability a *grihasta*.

[23] O'Malley (1913): 491.

[24] Secret Police Abstracts of Intelligence of the United Provinces of Agra and Oudh (Weekly) (PAI), No. 15, 22 April 1922.

[25] Sheikh Abdul Majid, diary entry, April 1916.

[26] Fremantle, *Report on the Supply of Labour in the United Provinces and Bengal*: 108.

[27] 'Memorandum by E.B. Havell on Improvement of Indian Art and Crafts'.

[28] Ibid.

[29] The practice of giving loans to secure child labour aggravated over a period of time. A November 2000 survey of 324 households in the Varanasi area, sponsored by the V.V. Giri National Labour Institute (Ministry of Labour), found that 23.5 per cent of silk handloom workers were boys, and of them, 27 per cent were non-family labour. Based on this data, the researchers estimated that roughly 106,000 boys (6.4 per cent of the total workforce) were working for non-family employers in Varanasi district. Although girls work in silk-weaving as well, the researchers were not able to document their work because they were often confined to and worked from their homes. About 80 per cent of sari-weaving households in the Varanasi area are Muslims, about 15 per cent are 'backward caste' Hindus, and about 6 per cent are Dalits; while Muslims have traditionally engaged in sari-weaving, backward caste Hindus and Dalits have recently entered the profession, both as weavers and as traders. See Sharma and Nikhil Raj, *Child Labour in Sari Units of Varanasi (Draft Report)*: Sec. III, Tables 3.1 and 3.6. There are about 120,000 looms in Varanasi and 35,000 looms in Mubarakpur (Azamgarh). Most of the weaving is done in homes, although there are also workshops with multiple looms. An estimated 200,000 children under the age of fourteen are working in the silk industry in the Varanasi area, about half of whom are bonded to a non-family member. The rest of these children, while not individually bonded, are likely working with their families, most of whom bonded to a trader. See Juyal and Jha (1999): para 2.3.

[30] 'Witness, Sheo Narayan Juneja, Principal, Government Central Weaving Institute Benaras', in *Report of the United Provinces Provincial Banking Enquiry Committee, 1929–30* [hereafter *RUPPBEC*], *Evidence*, Vol. III (1930): 383.

[31] *RFFC* (1942): 63, 66.
[32] Ibid.: 79–80.
[33] Chatterjee (1908): 30.
[34] Sheikh Abdul Majid, diary entry, 12 December 1919.
[35] Ibid., 9 January 1920 and 8 February 1920.
[36] Choudhury, 'Extracts from a Survey of the Small Urban Industries of Benaras', *RUPPBEC*, Vol. II: 371.
[37] O'Malley (1913): 491.
[38] 'Mubarakpur Riot Case, Proceedings for January 1905', Serial No. 10, File No. 254/1904, Box No. 662.
[39] Interviews with Maulvi Kamaruzzaman Mubarakpuri and Asrar Ahmad, Mubarakpur, Azamgarh; Muhammad Shamim, Khairabad, Maunath Bhanjan, May 2008.
[40] Thomason (1837): 9.
[41] *Royal Commission on Labour in India, Evidence*, Vol. III, Part I (1930): 173.
[42] Interviews with Maulvi Qamaruzzaman Mubarakpuri, Qazi Zafar Masood and others, Mubarakpur, 12 April 2007; Maulana Rashid Ahmad, Dr Masud Ahmad, Pathan Tola, Ishrat Kamaal Azmi, Mirza Hadipura, Mahshar Azmi, Chattarpura and others, Maunath Bhanjan, June 2007; Danish Qadah, *Urdu MS*, Ansari Library, Khairabad, Azamgarh.
[43] *Royal Commission on Labour in India*, Vol. III, Part I (1930): 174.
[44] *Administration Report of the Department of Industries and Commerce, United Provinces, for the year ending 31 March 1939* (1940): 17.
[45] C.R. Crommelin, Resident Mow and Azimghur, to President and Members Board of Trade, 16 August 1803, *Board of Trade (Commercial) Proceedings*, Vol. 166, Part II, No. 66, para 2, 22 to 29 August 1803, microfilm, West Bengal State Archives (hereafter WBSA).
[46] Report on the Commerce and Customs of the Ceded Provinces, 27 April 1804, *Board of Trade (Commercial) Proceedings*, Vol. 172, para 78, 3 to 27 April 1804, microfilm, WBSA.
[47] Sheikh Abdul Majid, diary entry, 2 May 1916.
[48] Ibid., February 1919.
[49] Ibid., 10 August 1919.
[50] Reid (1881): 147.

References

Administration Report of the Department of Industries and Commerce, United Provinces, for the year ending 31 March 1939 (1940), Allahabad: Government Press.

Alam, Arshad (2011), *Inside a Madrasa: Knowledge, Power and Islamic Identity in India,* New Delhi: Routledge.

Annual Report on Industrial Education in the United Provinces for the Year 1912–13, File No. 232/1913, Box No. 31, Industries Department, Uttar Pradesh State Archives (UPSA).

Bismillah, Abdul (1986), *Jhini Jhini Bini Chadariya*, New Delhi: Rajkamal Prakashan.

Board of Trade (Commercial) Proceedings (1803), Vol. 166, Part II, No. 66, 22 to 29 August, microfilm, West Bengal State Archives (WBSA).

Board of Trade (Commercial) Proceedings (1804), Vol. 172, para 78, 3 to 27 April 1804, microfilm, West Bengal State Archives (WBSA).

Chatterjee, A.C. (1908), *Notes on the Industries of the United Provinces,* Allahabad: Government Press.

Choudhury, S.N. Majumdar (1930), 'Extracts from a Survey of the Small Urban Industries of Benaras', in *Report of the United Provinces Provincial Banking Enquiry Committee, 1929–30* (*RUPPBEC*), Vol. II.

Das, Shyamsundar (ed.) (1951), *Kabir Granthavali*, Kashi.

East India (Census): General Report of the Census of India, 1911 (1914), London: H.M. Stationery Office.

Fremantle, S.H., *Report on the Supply of Labour in the United Provinces and Bengal*, File No. 167/1906, Box No. 47, Revenue Department, Uttar Pradesh State Archives (UPSA).

Haynes, Douglas E. (2012), *Small Town Capitalism in Western India: Artisans, Merchants, and the Making of the Informal Economy, 1870–1960*, Cambridge: Cambridge University Press.

Henvey, Frederick (1871), *A Narrative of the Drought and Famine which Prevailed in the North West Provinces During the years 1868, 1869 and beginning of 1870*, Allahabad: Government Press.

Hoey, William (1880), *A Monograph on Trade and Manufacture in Northern India,* Lucknow: American Methodist Mission Press.

Indian Industrial Commission Report and Minutes of Evidence 1916–18 (1918), Calcutta: Superintendent Government Printing.

Juyal, B.N. and M.K. Jha (1999), 'Executive Summary', *Child Labour Involvement in Sericulture,* submitted to U.P. Diversified Agricultural Support Project, April.

Majid, Sheikh Abdul, 'Diary' (1904–1930s), unpublished Urdu manuscript, Maulvi Kamaruzzaman Mubarakpuri, Muhalla Sufipura, Mubarakpur, Azamgarh.

Mehta, Deepak (1997), *Work, Ritual, Biography: A Muslim Community in North India*, New Delhi: Oxford University Press.

'Memorandum by E.B. Havell on Improvement of Indian Art and Crafts', File No.172/1921, Box No. 239, Industries Department, Uttar Pradesh State Archives (UPSA).

Morison, Theodore (1911), *The Economic Transition in India,* London: J. Murray.

Mubarakpuri, Qazi Athar (1974), *Tazkira-e-Ulema-e-Mubarakpur,* Mubarakpur: Daira Millia.

Narrative of the Scarcity during 1874, in the Eastern Districts of the North-Western Provinces of India, with District Reports (1875), Allahabad: Government Press.

O'Malley, L.S.S. (1913), *Census of India, 1911,* Vol. V: Bengal, Bihar and Orissa and Sikkim, Part I, Report, Calcutta: Bengal Secretariat Book Depot.

Parthasarathi, Prasannan (2001), *The Transition to a Colonial Economy: Weavers, Merchants and Kings in South India, 1720–1800*, Cambridge: Cambridge University Press.

Qadah, Danish, *Urdu MS*, Ansari Library, Khairabad, Azamgarh.

Reid, J.R. (1881), *Reports on the Settlement Operation in the District of Azamgarh: As also in Parganas Sikandarpur and Bhadaon*, Allahabad: Government Press.

Report of the Cottage Industries Committee, United Provinces (1938), Allahabad: Superintendent, Printing and Stationery.

Report of the Fact-Finding Committee (Handloom and Mills) (*RFFC*) (1942), Delhi: Ministry of Commerce.

Report of the Indian Famine Commission, 1898 (1901), Simla: Government Central Printing Office.

Reports of the Registrar for Co-operative Credit Societies in the United Provinces (1906–20), Allahabad: Government Book Depot.

Report of the United Provinces Provincial Banking Enquiry Committee, 1929–30 (*RUPPBEC*)*, Evidence* (1930), Vol. III, Allahabad: Government Press.

Reports on the Condition of the Lower Classes of the Population of India (1888), *Famine Proceedings*, Nos. 1–24, Revenue and Agriculture Department, Government of India, December.

Report on the Railway-Borne Traffic of the North-Western Provinces and Oudh, during the year ending 31 March 1882 (1883), Allahabad: Government Press.

Report on the Survey of the Handloom Weaving Industry in United Provinces (1949), Allahabad.

Roy, Tirthankar (1999), *Traditional Industry in the Economy of Colonial India*, Cambridge: Cambridge University Press.

Royal Commission on Labour in India, *Evidence* (1930), Vol. III, Part I: Central Provinces and United Provinces, London: H.M. Stationery Office.

Secret Police Abstracts of Intelligence of the United Provinces of Agra and Oudh (Weekly) (1920–49), Police Intelligence Department/Criminal Investigation Department Office, Lucknow.

Selection from the Records of Government, North Western Provinces (1864), Part XL, Allahabad: Government Press.

Sharma, Alakh N. and Nikhil Raj, 'Child Labour in Sari Units of Varanasi (Draft Report)' (undated).

Showeb, M. (1994), *Silk Handloom Industry of Varanasi: A Study of Socio-Economic Problems of Weavers*, Varanasi: Ganga Kaveri Publishing House.

Silberrad, C.A. (1898), *A Monograph on Cotton Fabrics, Produced In the North-Western Provinces and Oudh*, Allahabad: Government Press.

Thomason, J. (1837), *Report on the Settlement of the Ceded Portion of the District of Azimgurh, Commonly called 'Chuklah Azimgurh'* (1837), Agra: Government Press.

Village Crime Register (1900–59), Mubarakpur Police Station, Mubarakpur, Azamgarh.

Soldiers and Sailors at Work

Three Case Studies

Beyond Asiatic Despotism

Soldiers, Mercenaries and Peasants in Eurasia

Alessandro Stanziani

Warriors, Mercenaries and Peasants in Empire-building: Questions and Methodology

In economic history, a recurring question since decades consists in asking why and how the 'west' had been so successful vis-à-vis China or India.[1] This question is biased in itself: we already know the end of the story and seek arguments to justify the supremacy of the west. These attitudes are not new (they were already widespread in the eighteenth century, if not before), but they are not the only possible ones. I do not intend to summarize these debates here; rather, I would discuss the relationship between technical innovation, recruitment and economic growth. Thus, many historians explain the difficulties of China and India in terms of the lack of a 'military revolution' in the western style. The Chinese (and in part Indians) are said to be deprived of the 'practical' knowledge that can convert inventions into innovations, both in the sphere of economic activity and military performance. The problem is that these arguments ignore two facts: first, the 'western art of war' has for a long time proved to be ineffective outside of Europe and other solutions were perfectly rationale elsewhere; second, unlike traditional judgments, the military revolution occurred in the west only in the nineteenth century, and therefore it was much less a source than a consequence of the Industrial Revolution.[2]

If the military 'revolution' in the west has to be relativized, at the other end, the Eurasian empires were definitely less reticent to military innovation than is usually held. The cavalry and its role evolved, and so did the infantry. Firearms were spread across the steppes and the Indian peninsula – certainly less than in Europe, but for what reasons?

These dynamics were partly dictated by local conditions. In the steppes horses maintained their importance, and the Mongol skills were efficiently transmitted to the Chinese, Russian and Mughal armies. European techniques of fighting and weapons were hardly successful in the steppes, the Indian mountains of Kashmir and in Bengal.

If not the 'military revolution', another argument which seeks to justify the difficulties confronted by China, Russia and India with the 'rise of the west' is that these countries were unable to introduce (or import) new military techniques because their administration lacked unity and was highly corrupt. This argument can be turned upside down, however, for right up to present times, military development often has been supported precisely by corruption and lack of centralism. In other words, the link between military performances and administrative organization seems difficult to justify and generalize.

Therefore, the relevant question is not why Muscovy, India or China did not act as an idealized west, but for what specific reasons recruitment, supply networks of the army, military organization and skill evolved in one way or another; how reciprocal influences among these powers intervened (for example, in horse-riding, horse-breeding, iron-making, etc.); and why the encounter with the west took place in certain ways and not in others. The answers are related not only to military techniques, but also to overall relationships between peasants, landlords and bureaucracies. Indeed, the well-known passage from the cavalry to the infantry, and from archers to infantrymen, requires a reconfiguration of all these relations. Cavalry military elites in China, Inner Asia and India were perfectly aware that the diffusion of firearms and the infantry could strongly undermine their military, political and social roles. Yet these understandable resistances did not give the same results in China, India and Russia. Why was this so?

First, some historians have argued that because China had been quickly unified, war skills and the economy there had evolved poorly. On the other hand, persistent divisions and wars in Europe encouraged technical, military and economic innovations.[3] This argument is a product of the last ten to fifteen years. Before that, in the aftermath of World War II and through the Vietnam War, historians actually argued the opposite, stressing the negative impact of wars on economic growth.

Indeed, the link between war and economic growth is not univocal: if the growth of the United States since the 1930s is undoubtedly linked to the military industry, history is full of counter-examples, either because war produced decadence (as in modern Spain) or because economic growth relied upon peace (like in nineteenth-century Europe). Russia constitutes a perfect example of the shortcomings of this easy link between war and growth: some consider that the military burden lowered the economic growth of Tsarist and Soviet Russia,[4] while many others argue that Russia and the USSR were successfully competitive with the west mainly in military issues.[5]

The link between war and economic growth therefore requires explanation. Even if one refrains from making generalizations about war being always good or always bad for economic growth, one still needs to explain why war has affected different regions differently. An immediate solution would consist in affirming that war in Europe was based on efficient economic institutions, correct taxation and a centralized state, while these elements were lacking in India, Russia or China. Thus, following this line of reasoning, modern war sustained economic growth in Europe, but not in China or in India.

Yet, it was precisely starting from these elements – decentralized taxation and a decentralized army – that the Mughals and Qing built up their empires. How did they do so? In other words, we cannot take the highly centralized nation-state as the unique way to modern military performance. This was true in particular areas in a given historical period, not everywhere and at all times. For example, there is nothing to prove that England won in India because of its fiscal organization or because of the strength of its army. Over the years, in fact, the opposite was true, for the East India Company (EIC) preserved a strong financial and military autonomy vis-à-vis the British state. The difficulties the English parliament had in controlling the EIC were not necessarily less weighty than those faced by the Mughals and, after them, the Marathas, when collecting taxes and controlling their military elites. Thus, the efficiency of institutions and neo-institutionalist approaches hardly explain such historical issues.

Another explanation recently advanced is that institutions were not necessarily inefficient in Asia and efficient in Europe; they were both efficient and inefficient, and as such, they cannot explain different developments. From this perspective, the only difference between the English, Mughal and Qing empires lies not in their institutions or economic outlook, but in relative costs. Thus Robert Allen, providing an extreme version of Pomeranz's argument, argues that England benefited more from the availability of energies than China or India; war increased everywhere the cost of labour, but the west was able to overcome the problem thanks to capital-intensive innovations (in economy and war). This outcome was in turn possible because of available and cheap sources of energy. The industrial revolution was a kind of derivative of the military revolution, rather than the other way round. Conversely, in China, the absence of war and the burden of a heavy population would have encouraged the adoption of labour-intensive techniques and delayed both industrialization and the military revolution.[6]

The logic of this argument is strong and the model itself is amazing, but it does not advance by even an inch our understanding of military and socio-economic dynamics. We have a perfect *post facto* justification, not a historical explanation. The argument of energy availability as advanced by Allen, Pomeranz and Wrigley is highly contested for it is hard to measure such a thing, and also because a direct causal link between energy, war and the overall economy is lacking.

A widespread solution to this problem consists in focusing on the population–land ratio. Forms and rates of conscription and coercion depend on this ratio. For example, the low population in Russia explains both serfdom (coercion) and early (compared to other powers) general conscription. On the contrary, in India and China, the excess of population compared to land would explain the early (compared to Russia and even Europe) diffusion of free labour and the lack of military conscription.

Unfortunately, available archival sources do not confirm this long-standing argument. The fact that the density of population is higher in India than in the Russian steppes is not enough to transform peasants into soldiers. One may even suppose that constant and long-term recruitment will be less difficult where the population is abundant compared to land, instead of the other way round. The simple fact is that population density is not the answer to our problem, but the problem itself: why and how was population density so high in the supposedly 'backward countries'? The same can be said for sources of energy: what does it mean to say that energies are available? Difficulties in extracting energies in Siberia (as nowadays in Alaska) are not necessarily synonymous with backwardness. We need much more than tautologies.

For this, we need to get away from the simple confrontation between the west and the east. The question is to understand how Ming and Ching China, Muscovy and Mughal India were successfully settled in the sixteenth and seventeenth centuries, and why they evolved differently after that period. Circulation of knowledge between these entities certainly played a major role: it was true for religion, war-making, horse-breeding, metal-making and organization of the bureaucracy. At the same time, circulation of knowledge, people, horses and armies did not guarantee a similar base; fiscal organization and policies were indeed related to the territorial organization of the army. Economic dynamics and social hierarchies were linked to the supply of the army and the cities, on the one hand, and to social and economic equilibrium in the countryside, on the other. In Eurasia, trade and war were much less antagonistic than complementary. European representations of feudalism have linked the hierarchical order to the protection that cavalrymen offered to the peasants. This link, already doubtful in medieval Europe, does not find any confirmation in early modern Eurasia. Territorial instability and war did not kill trade but sustained its growth. This does not mean that war and instability *as such* enhanced the economy, but only that, in order to understand the Eurasian empires, we need to stop thinking of peasants, soldiers, the military, landed elites and bureaucracies as separate entities ordered in a hierarchy similar to that of France or England.

Starting from this, it is possible to challenge the well-known Tilly's model. Trade and capital both played a major role in early modern and modern Eurasia, and it is simply not possible to contrast a despotic and coercive Asia to a capitalistic Europe. Capital and coercion interacted and often overlapped in both Asia and Europe. Coercion was financed by capital. The question is rather to understand how these elements interacted in the social organization, military strategies and state-building of different areas. I intend to show that Russia was definitely less coercive than it is usually affirmed, while China mostly relied for its army's supply on merchants and trade, and Mughal India built up its strength on forms of decentralized capital and coercion. If in Europe the transition to modernity has been found in the centralized nation-state, it does not mean that this was the only possible solution or that in Asia despotism was the only available solution.

Yet, we still need to identify the historical forms of the state in the above-mentioned areas. If the nation-state is not pertinent to understanding the relationship between war, growth and social dynamics in Eurasia, does it mean that 'empire' is a better paradigm?

The focus on empire is a strong trend in recent historiography.[7] However, one needs to be careful to use empire as a heuristic to question historical diversities and not as a new black box. In our case, the notions and practices of empire were not the same in the Muscovy, Mughal India and Qing China, and they also changed over time.The concept of empire, historically located, questions territorial entities which are fluid and mobile, and in which different ethnicities, religions and social entities (the family, the clan, the administration, peasants, soldiers, etc.) interact on a hierarchical basis following procedures of different integration and/or assimilation. For example, the diffusion of Islam in Africa–Eurasia constituted a powerful factor of unification between these various parts of the world. At the same time, this process took different outlines in different areas. Islam was not the same in Central Asia, the Ottoman Empire, Mughal India, Indonesia and Africa. Relations between Moslems and Hindus, Manchus and Russians were not what one might expect today – starting from the recent tensions in India, the forms of exclusion launched by the Russian state since the end of the nineteenth century (not forgetting Stalinist ethnic cleansing), and the current Chinese attitudes towards Tibet or Muslim minorities. Most of these tensions belong to the twentieth century, and it would be misleading to look for them in early modern and modern Eurasia, at least in present-day forms and intensities.[8]

The presence of ethnicity and religious markers in army hierarchies is a good test and a starting point to discuss these questions in Eurasia between the sixteenth and early nineteenth century. Warrior elites were not integrated in the same way in each of the mentioned empires, and the military and political role of the Cossacks was not the same as that of the Rajputs or Marathas in India, or the Manchus in China. The problem thus consists in understanding how these forms of insertion interacted with imperial constructions and produced the overall political and social dynamics. My answer would be that, in the short and medium term, the Mughal attitude of giving relative autonomy to the armed elites and peasants of various political entities of the subcontinent was an essential ingredient of their success. This strategy worked even better than the contemporary attempts at centralization in the Muscovy and China. However, from the eighteenth century onwards, the effectiveness of these strategies changed: the Mughal solution became ineffective against the commercial expansion of the west and the development of centripetal tendencies in India, while the Chinese and especially Russian centralization proved to be a successful answer to these new dynamics. Why was it so?

My answer to this question is located not in the efficiency of institutions, but on the historically defined notions and practices of territory, frontier, town and state in each of the mentioned empires. Neither size nor sources of energy or mere demographic numbers can explain the strength of Eurasian empires. To affirm that the strength of India, China and Russia lies in the extent of their territory means to take the issue for its cause. This all the more important because size is not inevitably a source of strength, but can easily be the origin of political and institutional weaknesses. The decadence of imperial China, Byzantine and other ancient empires has often been explained by the excessive size of their territories. Indeed size in itself cannot be presumed to be either a factor of strength or of weakness; it is the way in which this size is achieved and kept that counts. This process was not the same in India, China and Russia. The relationships between lords, peasants and the army heavily influenced these issues.

Population is also often evoked to justify the strength of India and China, and, conversely, the weakness of Russia. This argument goes back in time at least to the arithmetic policy of the eighteenth century and ever since has constantly surfaced in public debates. However, according to the period and the area, population has been alternatively indicated as a source of growth and as the cause of poverty. In the case of India, both these interpretations have coexisted. I do not intend to discuss this point at length here. Instead of questioning the link between population and economic growth, I will discuss the relationship between demographic dynamics and military organization. What is the link between the numbers and dispersion of population, on the one hand, and forms of military organization, on the other? How are populations mobilized? What is the relationship between the labour market and the market of war, between peasant–soldiers and cavalrymen–landowners?

I will develop two major points in this essay. First, I will examine the relations in Inner Asia between trade and war, devoting particular attention to captives of war and the horse trade as a ground for imperial expansion besides military conscription. Second, I will take a closer look at the Muscovite expansion, and the solution it found to recruitment and supplies to the army. In conclusion, I will use the Muscovy as a heuristic to question China and India. I do have not the skills to study Mughal and Qing China through primary sources; however, I argue that instead of examining each of these areas – Russia, India and China – starting from a comparison with the west (rather an idealized image of it), it is worth exploring on the basis of an implicit comparison between Russia and India as well as Russia and China. For example, why did the Mughals not act like Ivan IV? Why did they not organize a system of local collection to feed the army?

An advantage of this approach is that I could make use of several documents translated into Russian from Persian, Kazakh, Mandarin and Manchu, since the seventeenth century. Many edited collections of these documents are available, in particular, on the relationships between the Russians, Tatars and Chinese in the seventeenth century,[9] and the commercial links of Inner Asia in the sixteenth and seventeenth century.[10] In the local archives in Orenburg, Tashkent and Samarkand there are several documents – many of which were edited in the Soviet period – relating to the relationship between Russia and China,[11] Russia and Central Asia,[12] and Afghanistan and India.[13]

Besides sources in Russian, there are several documents that have been translated from Persian, Hindi and Turki into English.[14] It is important to know the conditions of production of these sources. Yet the 'colonial obejective' is not reason enough to reject *en masse* these collections and translations. Cross-checking sources is one way to escape this danger.

Recruitment through Colonization: The Case of the Muscovy

Russia is often described as a land of despotism, corruption and serfdom; only repression, centralization and the country's large land-mass could make it pass for a great power. These arguments deserve an explanation. To start with, the issue of size: could Russia have dominated simply through the extension of its territory? If yes, then are we not taking the result to be the cause? Large spaces are never empty spaces, they have to be conquered and held. After all Moscow was a tiny duchy and then a principality, starting from the north of current Russia and progressing towards the centre, i.e. the south and the steppes. It was surrounded by much stronger powers, such as the Safavids of Persia, the Ottoman Empire, the Mongolian Khanates, the kingdom of Poland-Lithuania and Sweden. How did Muscovy succeed against these powers?

If we look at the population: since the eighteenth century at least, many commentators have stressed the large empty plains and vast spaces of Russia. In 1550, Muscovy had a land area of approximately 1 million square kilometres with 6.5 million inhabitants. By the beginning of the eighteenth century its territory had widened considerably and the population reached 15 million people.[15] In the same period a country like France, far smaller than Russia, consisted of a population of approximately 10 million individuals. Thus we need to explain how the Muscovites managed to mobilize a significant number of troops as compared to the available population, and that too for relatively longer periods than its rivals.

One of the most widespread arguments in military history and in the history of Russia in general is that, before Peter and the western military revolution, Russia had a limited military capacity and resorted to backward methods. This line of reasoning suggests that the western military revolution, namely, massive conscription, recourse to light cavalry, firearms, etc., would have been introduced very late in Russia. The reasons of this delay are identified in inefficient and limited taxation, corruption and privileges and bureaucratic inefficiency, in addition to the general cultural backwardness of the Russian population. According to this view, the real military history of Russia – as also Russian history in general – begins only with Peter the Great. This myth finds a broad consensus both in Russia and in the west, where it is used to show that any progress outside of Western Europe could be achieved only by adopting western techniques.[16] On the Russian side, this myth makes it possible to mystify the Mongolian influence and add a further layer to the myth, making it one if not the most lasting myth in Russian nationalist history. However, this interpretation forgets two major aspects: first, that the western military revolution occurred long after Peter and was strongly influenced by the methods of Russian conscription;[17] second, most of the Muscovy expansion took place before Peter. The question is, how?

We have to look at weapons, tactical organization, and the army's modes of supply and recruitment. Indeed, Moscow did not adopt the same type of weapons, soldiers and tactics on its various war fronts. In particular on the western front, in its confrontation with Poland-Lithuania, Moscow was pushed, because of the climatic conditions and the equipment of its enemy, to extensively borrow from European military art. It was quite different in the south and along the steppe frontier, where Moscow relied on long-tested Mongolian tactics and weapons, duly adjusted in view of an increasingly territorial power. If, in these areas, there was nothing like a western military revolution, it was because firearms and the infantry adjusted badly to the steppe conditions.[18]

This explains why firearms were only gradually introduced in the Muscovy and then in Russia, and that too mostly on the western front. Artillery and firearms were largely employed during the siege of towns – the first Muscovite body of infantry equipped with firearms, i.e. the *pishchal' niki* (initially Swedish and Polish mercenaries), appeared in the early sixteenth century, and was employed not only in seizing Pskov in 1510, but also against the Cossacks and Tatars. Similarly, the *strel' tsy* (a kind of musketeers), armed with harquebuses, constituted the first permanent army corps in Russia and played a big role in the fall of Kazan in 1552. Artillery was set up during the first half of the sixteenth century, but it developed only towards the end of that century. Guns (cannons) were already widespread in the mid-sixteenth century, and continued to increase. The estimated numbers are about 3,500 cannons in 1600 and 5,000 by the end of the century.[19] This process accelerated during the years 1630–40 when the firearms were massively used by the Muscovite army, thanks to the discovery of the mines of the Urals.

Against the populations of Central Asia and the Crimean Khanate, the Muscovites had recourse to light cavalry equipped for archery. They borrowed the tactics of war from the Mongolians, i.e. sudden raids and escape, but they added new elements to it, in particular dragons and European artillery. In turn these methods of warfare required more trenches and fortifications, and thus more drudgeries and labour services provided by the soldiers and the local population.[20] In the sixteenth century, the Muscovites built a line of defence known as Abatis, which protected Moscow from Tatar invasions via Ukraine and also connected the latter to the Volga. Several fortified cities were built in these areas, in order to reinforce this line of defence. Between 1520 and 1550, these were accompanied by improved defences to forestall seiges of the forts, i.e. more solid constructions, more important reserves and more men on the spot who were better armed.[21]

Under Ivan IV, between 1551 and 1568, a new set of fortresses was built; this expansion continued until the end of the century. However, the majority of these fortifications declined and were even abandoned during the 'time of trouble', i.e. the beginning of the seventeenth century. Even when stability was recovered, the initial attention of the new dynasty of Romanov (1613–1917) turned towards the western front; resources were focused on this area with a decline of the southern fortifications.[22]

It was only after 1635 that Russia decided to improve its defences in the south, by reconstituting the existing fortifications and constructing new defence lines. It began (at the end of the 1630s) with the repair of the Abatis line. Financial resources and men were assigned to this task. The military chancellery estimated that it would require 27,400 workers, 3,500 horses and 16,900 soldiers in all to repair the line and defend it effectively. Despite the fact that finally only a total of 20,000 men could be found and that the supply was often lacking, in six months the line of defence stretching 600 kilometres was rebuilt and placed under protection.[23]

At this same time, tensions arose again with the Ottoman Empire and the Crimean Khanate. The Russians realized that they were still vulnerable on that front and undertook to build another line of defence, the Belgorod line, located in the southeast. It was equipped with a wall, near the European new lines of defence. The remainder of the line of fortifications was supplemented during the 1650s, along the Voronezh river – until, finally, a line of defence of 800 kilometres protected the southernmost and eastern sides. Thus the raids of Crimean Tatars were strongly reduced, while Moscow made use of its new fortifications for launching raids against the Kalmyks and the Nogays.[24]

It is necessary now to advance an additional step, i.e. how could these tactical and military results be achieved? Was it thanks to a particularly powerful military bureaucracy, due to financial and material resources, or both?

Mobilization and Coordination

A centralized military chancellery was established only during the third quarter of the sixteenth century. In the following decades, this endeavour was weakened by the creation of other chancelleries in charge of the management of fortifications, supplies, arms and officers' remuneration. Attempts made by the military chancellery to subordinate and coordinate these other chancelleries proved unsuccessful. Yet one has to be careful when criticizing this development. Detailed historical analysis of bureaucracies in different countries (Prussia, France, Britain, etc.) from the seventeenth century up through the twentieth century have shown the extreme difficulties in coordination, if not the tensions, in both vertical hierarchies and horizontal connections between institutions. Therefore, the issue is not so much to evaluate them starting from an ideal model, but to clarify where these tensions were located, why they existed and what was their impact. From this we may advance further and understand how a rather limited coordinating military organization was weakened. Muscovy had to face serious problems in feeding the army and in routing enormous quantities of corn over very long distances. Unlike contemporary China, the Muscovy did not try to solve this problem by building 'corridors' linking the regions of production to areas under military activity.[25] This was because, given the local climatic conditions and available techniques, the construction and maintenance of roads was excessively expensive while the use of the roads themselves depended on the season. Mud and/or freezing temperatures made the use of such routes impractical during a good part of the year. Thus, when the Russian troops moved towards the south of Ukraine, they were confronted with important problems of supply of provisions. For example, in 1686, in the campaign against the Crimean Khanate, the Russians mobilized one of the most important armies of that time: 132,000 men accompanied by 2000 *kholopy*.[26] They moved with 100,000 horses from Samara to Crimea over a distance of 300 kilometres. The chancellery calculated that for a four-month campaign these men needed 23,000 tons of corn, and their horses required 9,000 tons of oats. The chancellery managed to collect these resources, and the corn was conveyed from European Russia using boats and tanks. However, this initial logistical victory was exhausted because of the prolongation of the operations. In 1680, the number of troops rose to 200,000 men. Their commander-in-chief, Prince Golitsyn, was confronted with a lack of provisions. Moscow tried to cope with these difficulties by injecting more and more resources into its military activities: 1 million roubles only in 1663.

Historians have repeatedly stressed the excessive military burden of Russia. In 1680, the 1 million roubles Moscow devoted to the Crimean campaign covered half of its whole budget. During the same period, France and Britain spent much more than their resources to make war and were forced to take recourse to loans from abroad. In 1689, 70 per cent of the Britain's budget was devoted to military activity. Thus, comparatively speaking, Russia did not devote more resources to war than the other European states. Unlike them, it relied upon a system of capitation from 1714.[27] This method of taxation was calculated starting from the requirements of the army, to which the contributions of the peasants and urban groups subjected to taxation were to adapt.[28] Besides capitation, Peter relied also on indirect taxation and rouble devaluation, which acted as a tax on the bulk of the population. Even if these forms of financing have been discussed in the relevant historiography, they were not the only ones and perhaps not even the most important in sustaining the Russian expansion. As massive recruitment and firearms, taxes and devaluation developed mostly under Peter if not after him, it cannot explain previous Muscovy expansion. To understand this, we need to take a closer look at the links between recruitment, production and storage.

Feeding the Army

Not just soldiers but even officers and cavalrymen were not necessarily remunerated in money: remuneration in kind, honours and spoilation of villages also played a major role. Again, this was not specific to 'backward' Muscovy, for these were common practices in Europe and Asia at that time. In Muscovy, until the mid-sixteenth century, cavalrymen had to themselves finance their campaigns. It was only with the introduction of 'service cavalrymen' and the infantry that remuneration became a problem. If not on the western front (where the important problem was of transporting food from elsewhere), in the southern front the Muscovites quickly adopted the principle that 'the land nourishes the soldier', i.e. local resources were to be used to feed the local army.

As regards the eastern front, Moscow decided that one-tenth of the harvest of central Russian areas had to be seized and stocked for provision to the military. Indeed this was a general principle for in practice, in case of war, on the one hand further requisitions of cereals were made, and on the other, civil granaries (meant for civil populations in times of bad harvests) were also seized by the military chancellery. Granary stocks resembled those that were in place in China since before the Mings, although the methods of calculation were much less sophisticated than in China (they developed in Russia only towards the end of the nineteenth century). As in China, these granary stocks were conceived not only as a buffer against bad harvests but also as local banks, lending seeds and eventually cereals to local landowners and peasants in villages.[29] But, unlike in China, the Muscovy leaders appealed to private merchants only in extreme cases. In both Ming and Qing China, two policies were put in place: the army purchased cereals either directly from merchants, or through intermediaries. In the first case it gave fixed prices, but it was likely to be faced with insufficient supply. In the second case the risk was that the merchants indulged in highly speculative pricing. These two policies were alternatively practised and eventually coexisted, even when, in the eighteenth century, a 'market orientation' seemed to prevail.

In Muscovy, then in Russia, such changes in economic policies did not take place: the authorities purchased from merchants only in particularly bad years, and even then, only at fixed prices. The prices were fixed by the authorities themselves by taking into account the market price, their own budgetary constraints, and the needs of the population and the army. However, it would be misleading to conclude from this that the Muscovite authorities were hostile to the market. The expansion of the Muscovy largely relied upon markets and trade, and fixed prices were mostly the practice in military concerns and not in all fronts of the rising empire. Indeed Muscovy economic policies were dictated by general political and social considerations. In the sixteenth and early seventeenth centuries, cereals were purchased above all to feed the cavalry. However, with the diffusion of service cavalry and infantry, this connection between purchase of cereals, military concerns and the social order was blurred. Extraordinary purchases and later requisitions were effective for short-term campaigns, but had no real significance in long campaigns – as on the southern front, or when a relatively stable army had to be regularly fed. The first attempt in this direction was made with the musketeers, the first stable army unit in Russia. Instead of relying upon local taxes, the special chancellery of musketeers decided to pay a fixed price to the merchant in exchange for regular supplies. Such an arrangement could be made because the musketeers were relatively few in number: 7,000 to 10,000 at the end of the sixteenth century, 33,775 in 1632, and 65,000 in 1663.[30] However, with territorial dispersion of the musketeers, the chancellery found it necessary to establish contracts with merchants in many different localities. The hostility of other military chancelleries and of various local civil authorities also contributed to the difficulties. In the end, the musketeers were regularly fed only when the military elites were able to establish a regular and successful relationship with local merchants and local civil authorities.[31]

Despite this the Muscovite authorities decided to generalize the system across the whole army, assuming that the difficulties mostly related to competition between the different chancelleries, and that when all of them were centralized and coordinated, the problem would be solved.[32] In addition, by the last quarter of the seventeenth century, the infantry had become the largest unit (80 per cent of the army), while the use of firearms required skills and thus stability of those recruited. The central military chancellery set up a grain department (*khlebnyistol*) in 1663. Calculation of needs (and of local taxes to meet them) were made by the central authorities, while collection of cereals was left to the local authorities. However, with the increasing number of soldiers, agreements were only occasionally reached, here and there, and the supply to the army remained unstable. In the 1690s, therefore, the Russian leaders conceived of a scheme to transform the annual tax into several seasonal taxes, so as to ensure a certain quantity of corn reserves throughout, while reducing the cost of storage and limiting speculation. This system, known as *zaprosnyikhleb*, sought to coordinate the requirements of the various armies with local-level production.[33] Until this time, the southernmost areas, for example, had been expected to produce corn for the local troops, except in the event of war or of other crises, wherein compensation was requested from other areas. Now, on the contrary, these compensations were required to be constant so as to overcome local difficulties, and to also constitute and feed the army in times of peace.[34]

Yet, at the turn of the seventeenth century, this system had to face several challenges. The multiplication of local taxes increased the gap between urban and rural tax-payers. Not only peasant communities but also landowners of supposedly surplus areas protested against the tax burden introduced to finance Russian territorial expansion. Landowners and village communities also protested against conscription. Last but not least, protests arose also because the expansion towards the southern frontier was believed to empty central Russia and blur social identities.

Mobilization and Colonization: The Frontier as Social and Political Experiment

In terms of manpower in the army, large European countries such as France or Spain had 40,000 men around the middle of the sixteenth century; this gradually increased to approximately 150,000 in the 1630s. Muscovy began the Thirteen Year War (1654–67) with Poland-Lithuania with an army of 40,000 men and finished with 100,000. The infantry, which accounted for a quarter of the manpower in 1654, rose to more than one-third in the 1660s. Towards the end of the century, Russia had a regular army of about 100,000 men, which, in terms of the population of the time (approximately 15 million) made it one of the countries with the highest percentage of conscripts (1 to 1.5 per cent). Finally, by about the middle of the eighteenth century, Russia and France had 1.3 per cent of their population in uniform, close to England with a conscription percentage of 1 per cent but far behind Prussia with a percentage of 2.5–3 per cent.[35]

Before the phase of general conscription under Peter the Great, Russia, like other powers of that time, drew upon foreign mercenaries and 'armed' populations like the Cossacks. Mercenaries (mostly German and Swedish) were used especially on the western front, and much less in the wars against Mongolian Khanates. Mercenaries systematically provoked strong disagreements and tensions among the Russian military and political elites; some favoured them because they were considered better equipped and trained than Russian soldiers, while many others underlined the mercenaries' lack of trustworthiness and loyalty.[36] Among officers, in 1663 (i.e. during the Thirteen Year War), there were 54,448 foreigners in the army, that is, 79 per cent of the forces on the ground. In the infantry, their proportion was 55.3 per cent. During the 1660s, out of 227 high-ranking officers (colonels, lieutenant-colonels, majors, etc.), Russians numbered only 18, while foreigners accounted for 648 out of 1,922 captains and lieutenants. Russians constituted the overwhelming majority of the lower-grade officers and, of course, most of the infantry.[37] The Russian state paid foreign officers well above the European standards of the time. Colonels received between 250 and 400 roubles per month. The salaries paid to army officers represented approximately one-third of the silver expenditure on the army in 1663 (approximately 1 million roubles). Problems with the mercenaries emerged during prolonged conflicts as a consequence of lack of food as well as inflation. Moreover, as these circumstances were even harsher for the Russian troops, hostility against the mercenaries grew within the army. The Thirteen Year War brought this issue even more urgently to the fore, and led to the gradual disappearance of mercenaries in the Russian army. To this also contributed the supremacy of the infantry and the first attempts to introduce general conscription, between the last quarter of the seventeenth century and the 1710s.

However, in discussing this issue it is not sufficient to speak of the monopoly of violence being in the hands of the Russian state, for other forms of recruitment were also practised, particularly among 'warrior' groups such as the Cossacks (or in India among the Rajputs and the Marathas).

Cossacks

In the case of the Cossacks, Muscovy had to face a quite standard problem: they were relatively independent and efficient warriors, and Moscow would have liked to mobilize them without having to fully integrate them within its own elites.[38] Moscow also wished to deploy them against its neighbours while absolving itself of any responsibility for this, as was the case with the Cossacks' raids into Poland-Lithuania, the Ottoman Empire or the Crimean Khanate. The risk – which was revealed to be concrete on several occasions – of this approach was that the Cossacks could also make raids against Russian settlements. Thus Moscow initially had to negotiate its 'monopoly of violence'. The Cossacks had a stable military organization with growing recruitment due to the inflow of populations of Tatar origin, in addition to peasants and ordinary criminals from central Russia and Ukrainian areas.[39] The Cossacks refused any formal submission to Moscow, above all in terms of taxes and conscription. However, unlike the Tatar Khanates, the Cossacks did not have a fully developed administrative organization, and they were consequently left with very unstable resources to feed their people and horses. This left the door open to Moscow, and it started to control the commercial routes and protect the populations that owed tributes to the Cossacks. Further, from the 1620s, Moscow worked to establish a kind of political organization among the Cossacks, giving funds and resources to some Cossack elites and dividing them from other chiefs. This strategy was successful in increasing the dependence of Cossacks on Moscow.

This strategy was close to that of the Manchus vis-à-vis some Mongol raiders, or that of the Mughals who also drew on professional warriors in India. However, unlike the Manchus, Moscow gave a kind of military autonomy to the Cossacks for a longer time, while, unlike the Mughals, it never introduced financial autonomy. The Cossacks could fight, make raids and not pay taxes, but they did not have their own resources. In other words, Moscow cut off the unity of the Cossacks, and their links with local producers and traders. Ultimately, the southern fortification stopped not only the raids of the Crimean Tatars into Russian territory, but also those of the Cossacks in Crimea and the Ottoman Empire, which had previously been a powerful threat in the hands of Cossacks to win concessions and resources from Moscow, the Khanate and the Ottoman Empire. Last but not least, like in the case of the mercenaries, development of the infantry and massive conscription also contributed to ensure Moscow's monopoly of power over the Cossacks. However, in the steppes, more than ordinary conscription, it was massive colonization and recourse to the *peasant–soldier–colon* (peasant–soldier–colonizer) paradigm that ensured Moscow's success.

Military Service and Social Order

Indeed, during the period under study, distinctions between nobles, service officers, soldiers and administrative personnel were often fuzzy, and existed according to parameters different from what we are accustomed to. Administrative and military centralization started under Ivan III (1462–1505) bringing with it the obligation on nobles to serve only the prince of Moscow, whereas earlier they could profess their allegiance to any local prince.

Since the fifteenth century, the princes of Moscow had required the nobility's exclusivity in their military services. Muscovy aristocrats and cavalrymen were no more free to sell their services to other princes. Ivan III conquered Novgorod and exiled its aristocracy; he introduced obligatory service for the Muscovite elites, and, in exchange, he provided them with land and titles. It was at the time of Ivan III and Vasilli III (1459 to 1533) that the legal definition of Muscovite landed elites was specified: besides hereditary ownership (*votchina*), the law introduced properties given in exchange for military services carried out (*pomest'e*). This resembled the Mongolian and Muslim institution of the *iqta* in Central Asia, which could be transferred only if at least one descendant served the prince. Otherwise, at the death of the officer, the land returned to the state. The *pomest'e* could neither be sold nor mortgaged; it could only be exchanged against another *pomest'e*. By this rule, the Muscovite leaders sought to achieve two aims: to control the elites and to ensure a relatively stable cavalry.

Around the middle of the sixteenth century, owners of *votchina* were not numerous (approximately 2,000), while those having a *pomest'e* numbered approximately 5 per cent of the population, that is to say 25,000 persons. On average they had five to six peasants, and so their social status was precarious. These institutions were the pillars of the Muscovite expansion: social and political frontiers were linked to each other. In order to encourage the service and reinforce the army, the Muscovite princes multiplied the granting of *pomest'e* in the border regions, particularly in the south. Unlike in other Russian areas, in the south the *pomest'e* was issued not only to nobles, but also to people coming from different social and legal conditions. These included peasant-soldiers, as well as officers of urban garrisons (*gorodovaiasluzhba*) and rural military outposts (*polkovaiasluzhba*) who did not belong to the nobility. Initially, the former were supposed to be cavalrymen and the latter just peasants. However, because of the difficult conditions of many cavalrymen, it was not rare that they took part in agrarian activities alongside the peasants.[40] Although this led to some improvement in the well-being of cavalrymen, the fact that the distinction between the legal status of a peasant and a cavalryman became so porous provoked negative reactions from many Muscovite top-ranking aristocrats, as well as from provincial landowners who feared that the trend could get generalized.

In 1678, the Muscovite leaders decided to restrict access to hereditary service status, and thus nobility, to 'well-proven' aristocrats. This appeared to be an appropriate response to the increasing tensions between cavalrymen and landowners. At the same time, it was barely implemented and was even countered by other rules, due to the simple fact that the massive introduction of firearms and new tactics was increasing the role of the infantry and thus of the peasantry in the army. This tendency developed furher with the legal creation of the *odnodvortsy*: unmarried small-holders identified as owners in both the tax and military rolls, as well as according to the ordinances adopted between 1710 and 1724. At this time, the *odnovortsy* included 600,000 Muscovites and their domestics, the majority of them settled along the Belgorod line and in the province of Sevsk. The *odnodvortsy* had a legal status close to that of state peasants: they paid a tax (in money or in kind) and offered no labour service, but at the same time, they were considered landowners and had to perform military obligations.[41] As for peasants–soldiers–colonizers, this implied that land-ownership was no more a privilege of aristocrats and 'hereditary' nobles. This fluid social boundary was the price that had to be paid to colonize the steppe and create an empire. The problem with the freshly conquered areas was that they had very few Russian peasants. The first wave of colonization took place in the sixteenth century, i.e. immediately after the conquest of Kazan in 1552; a second wave occurred during the1580s–1590s, as a consequence of the withdrawal of the Crimean Tatars and Nogays, but also due to the agricultural crisis in central Russia. The emigrants were fugitive peasants and deserters, but also service elites whose possessions (*pomest'e*) were insufficient to guarantee them a high enough income corresponding to their political and legal status.[42]

Thus the Muscovite authorities accepted that peasants willing to move to the southern and eastern frontiers could transfer their land to their descendants. These policies, in open contrasted to those officially enforced in central Muscovy, nevertheless had to face the hostility of landowners. Thus, who were the peasant-soldiers who migrated?

Recruitment and 'Serfdom': A Reappraisal

Peasant-soldiers along the southeastern frontier came from the southern areas, but also from Ukraine and central Russia. If, in the beginning, they were state peasants, nothing came in the way of their emigration except the agreement between military and state officials in the new colonies, and those of the areas they migrated to. Documents show that, despite protests by local authorities of emigration areas, the strong Muscovite interest in colonization of the steppe ultimately won.

The issue was more complicated when private peasants, that is, serfs, emigrated. In this case, landowners claimed them, while local authorities of emigration regions tended to resist and keep the emigrants. The central authorities adopted contradictory rules. An ordinance of 1635 authorized southern chief commanders of garrisons as well as governors to retain fugitive peasants and not return them to their owners as scheduled by the law. The following year a new ordinance went further to state that all intermediate and lower ranks of cavalrymen who had experienced degradation of their social status, and whose legal status had been turned into that of a peasant, were also excluded from the general rules for fugitive peasants. This provision was interpreted by many state officials and, of course, peasants as an agreement to free all peasants who had been put under legal constraints (on mobility in particular) after 1613. Protests by the nobility were so intense that in 1636 it was ordered that all fugitive peasants had to be returned to their legitimate masters.[43] Indeed, this rule was hardly implemented and, except for a few 'exemplary cases', peasants moving to the frontier were not returned. The nobility's protests turned into open opposition to the central power, and during the 1640s petitions multiplied so much that in 1649, the famous *Ulozhenie* – the legalization and generalization of serfdom – was adopted.

Contrary to common interpretations, much of this text is devoted to the documentary evidence that nobles had to provide in order to have peasants returned. On this subject, the regulation does not refer in any way to ownership rights and titles over peasants, as would be the case for serfdom or slavery, but rather to land registry certification concerning noble estates. As was the case for regulations adopted from the sixteenth century, this text aimed first and foremost to impose upon nobles, state certification of their ownership rights over land. Only on that basis would they have a right to transfer land along with the resident population, and be able to claim labour services and raise credit. This explains why the regulation placed less emphasis on punishing fugitive peasants than on sanctioning the nobles who took them in.[44]

This also explains why peasants who settled on an estate continued to sign a contract with the lord. Such contracts reflected a different legal status for master and peasant, which was a source of inequality, dependence and a particular form of servitude. The fact that the norms defined the landowners and avoided mentioning 'serfs' did not mean that servitude did not exist, but only that it was given more flexible characteristics. This aspect was to play a crucial role in the working and evolution of the Russian rural world. Within the framework of these provisions, landowners continued to authorize widespread marriages outside the estate[45] and the emigration of entire families, which was encouraged by the Tsarist authorities to further colonization. Thus, in 1678, 3.7 million migrant men populated the new areas (Siberia, southeastern steppes and the Volga area).[46]

In short, the territorial expansion of the Muscovy and then of Russia, passed through officially fixed but actually flexible legal and social boundaries. Peasant-soldiers were colonizers of the steppes and this undermined the whole Tsarist apparatus. It is in these terms that we can understand Peter's reforms.

Confronted by Sweden, a big player and military power of the time, recruitment widened after 1700. Between 1700 and 1713, the number of men conscripted were 335,000, out of a population of 15 million. A permanent army stabilized at about 160,000–200,000 soldiers. Peter's conscription aimed at drawing one soldier from every twenty tax-payers (that is, peasants and lower urban groups). To reach this target, Peter sought to coordinate the demographic, tax and recruitment rolls. Periodical censuses (*reviziia*) were introduced, while capitation replaced imposition per household. The Western European powers had built a similar system just a century later, i.e. under Napoleon or immediately after its wars.

These features help to understand why historians have often considered Peter as the 'modernizer' of Russia: he had not only taken recourse to western methods (the infantry), but generalized and rationalized them through massive conscription. However, this view misses the main points: first, that Peter achieved his reform a century before Europe did; second, that Russian serfdom and thus military conscription were far from being a 'feudal vestige'; and third, that the evolution of Russian military skills owed much to the geopolitical conditions of the steppes and the Mongol heritage.

Power in the Steppes, Power of the Steppes

Muscovy was not simply a latecomer but the last entrant in the steppes and Eurasia; yet it took a lead in territories which, far from being empty, were filled with powerful polities such as the Ottoman and Safavid Empires, the Mongolian Khanates, Poland and Sweden. These territories were difficult to seize and even more difficult to hold on to. Muscovy played above all a perfect diplomatic game: it drew its neighbouring powers against one another while being alternatively financed by one or the other in its military effort. For decades if not centuries, these polities complied, for they considered Moscow too weak to eventually turn into a dangerous enemy.

In domestic affairs, the Muscovite princes found their strength in the way they won and practised the monopoly of violence; they wished to subordinate the military and landed elites. On the military plane, this goal was initially achieved by taking recourse to European mercenaries, then to Cossacks and finally to peasants (with the help of the 'military revolution'). Military and landed elites never felt the need to exercise a monopoly of violence and thus a strong control over the state elites.

In official texts, the success of Moscow is explained in terms of increasingly fixed social borders, and more social flexibility in social and administrative practices. The typical example cited is the difference between hereditary landowners and service elites: this distinction changed not only in time, but also in daily practices and in different areas of Russia.

The same coexistence of closing and opening of social frontiers was true for peasants. They were officially subjected to increasingly heavy legal constraints in terms of mobility; these rules were adopted in order to satisfy the intermediate levels of the administration, small landowners and, partly, the state's requirements in terms of conscription. At the same time, the territorial expansion achieved through these policies undermined these constraints; peasants were encouraged to emigrate and colonize the new areas in spite of the protests of landowners of the areas of emigration. In the emigration areas, the legal status of peasants was immediately placed under attack and the limit of the low cavalry and *pomest'e* often vanished. Legal, military and social experimentation spread from the frontier to the whole of Russia.

By these policies, Muscovite leaders achieved two aims: they controlled the nobility and made the new peasant-owners loyal to the crown. In turn, territorial expansion, to which the nobility was opposed, was encouraged.

Unlike China, Russia did not develop markets and routes in order to mobilize and feed the army, nor did it develop a precociously centralized bureaucracy. Instead it relied on peasant–soldier–colonizers so as to dispose of a permanent army without having to move both soldiers and provisions. As a consequence, merchants in Russia played a minor role in supplying the army in comparison with China. This does not mean that merchants and markets were absent in the Muscovy; quite the contrary, for its territorial expansion was dictated by both commercial and geo-political interests. Not a tribute system but development of Eurasian markets under the control of Russian merchants was the goal of these politics. In the long run, the Muscovy and then Russia made a more appropriate choice than Qing China in that they did not let merchants control the supplies to the army nor allow local bureaucracies to take the lead. However, the Muscovite approach was not particularly successful or more efficient than that of the Qings until the turn of the eighteenth century and the nineteenth century, when monetary inflation and market development led by the European powers destabilized the markets. This was possible in China and in India, but not in Russia.

On the political side, the growth of Moscow never went along the path of exclusion of local merchants. On the contrary, following the previous Mongol powers, Moscow sought to gradually integrate them in its empire. The same attitude was expressed when dealing with local political and religious elites. The Russification of the steppes was a late phenomenon, dating to the end of the nineteenth century.

Notes

1 Parker (1988).
2 Black (1994).
3 Hoffman (2009, 2010).
4 Duffy (1981).
5 Holloway (1994).
6 Allen (2009).
7 Burbank and Cooper (2010).
8 Alam (2005).
9 Demidova and Miasnikov (eds.) (1969–72); Demidova (ed.) (1995, 1996, 2000).
10 Chekhovich (1974); Mukminova (1985); Levi (trans.) (2002), Appendix One.
11 Chimitdorzhiev (1978); Zlatkin and Ustiugov (eds.) (1959).
12 *Kazakhsko-russkieotnosheniia v 16–18 vekakh, Sbornik Dokumentov i Materialov* (1961, 1964): n. 88, 209; n. 33, 64; n. 76, 181, 184. *Mezhdunarodnye Otnosheniia v Tsentral'noi Azii: 17-18vv, Dokumenty I materialy* (1989).
13 Antonova and Goldberg (eds.) (1965).
14 *Akbarnama of Abul Fazl* ([1875] 1989–93); *Baburnama*, trans. Thackston (1996); *Muntakhab al-Lubab* by Khafi Khan (1975); *Muntakhabu-t-Tawarikh* by Bada'uni ([1898] 1986); *Maathir-al-Umara* ([1888] 1911, 1979).
15 Moon (1997).

[16] Ralston (1990).
[17] Black (1994).
[18] Hellie (1971); Keep (1985); Stevens (1995); Davis (2007).
[19] Hellie (1971): 157, 185.
[20] Stevens (1995).
[21] Kostomarov (1994).
[22] *Akty, sobrannye v bibliothekakh i arkivakh Rossiskoi Imperii arkheograficheskii ekspeditsieiu imperatoskoi akademiia nauk* (1836, 1858); in particular, volume 3.
[23] Lakovlev (1916).
[24] Khodarkovsky (2002).
[25] Zagorovskii (1969).
[26] Hellie (1976).
[27] Le Donne (1991): 276–67, Table 15.1.
[28] Anisimov (1989); Anisimov (1982); Bushkovitch (1978).
[29] *Rossiikii Gosudastvenny Arkhiv Drevnikh Aktov* (Russian State Archives of Ancient Acts; hereafter *RGADA*), fonds 210 (Razriad), *Belgorodskiistol*: 643, 772.
[30] Stevens (1995): 45.
[31] *RGADA*, fonds 210, *Belgorodskaiakniga*: 118, 152.
[32] Ibid.: 118, 156.
[33] Vazhinskii (1973).
[34] Davis (2007).
[35] Dixon (1999).
[36] Razin (1994).
[37] Hellie (1971): 191, 227.
[38] Witzenrath (2007).
[39] Hrushevsky (2002), Volumes 7 and 8.
[40] Zagorovskii, *Belgorodskaia Cherta*.
[41] Thomas Esper, 'The Odnodvortsy and the Russian Nobility', *Slavonic and East European Review*, Vol. 45, 1967, pp. 124–35.
[42] Zagorovskii (1969).
[43] Hellie (1971).
[44] Hellie (1988); in particular, see Chapter 11, n. 10.
[45] Thousands of certificates were delivered every year: *RGADA*, fonds 615.
[46] Moon (1997); Sunderland (1993); Bruk and Kabuzan (1982).

References

Akbarnama of Abul Fazl by Abul Fazl Allami ([1875] 1989–93), 3 volumes, Delhi.

Akty, sobrannye v bibliothekakh i arkivakh Rossiskoi Imperii arkheograficheskii ekspeditsieiu imperatoskoi akademiia nauk (*Documents collected in the libraries and archives of the Russian Empire by the archaeological expedition of the Imperial Academy of Sciences*) (1836, 1858), 4 volumes, Saint Petersburg.

Alam, Muzaffar (2005), *The Language of Political Islam, c. 1200–1800*, Chicago: Chicago University Press.

Allen, Robert (2009), *The British Industrial Revolution in Global Perspective*, Cambridge: Cambridge University Press.

Anisimov, Evgenii V. (1982), *Podatnaia Reforma Petra I: Vvedenie po Dushno Ipodati v Rossii 1719–1728* (*The Tax Reform of Peter I: The Introduction of the Poll Tax in Russia, 1719–1728*), Moscow: Nauka.

——— (1989), 'Remarks on the Fiscal Policy of Russian Absolutism during the First Quarter of the Eighteenth Century', *Soviet Studies in History*, Vol. 28 (1).

Antonova, Katia A., N.M. Goldberg (eds.) (1965), *Russko–Indiskie Otnosheniia v XVIII veke: Sbornik Dokumentov* (*Russian–Indian Relations in the Eighteenth Century: Collection of Documents*), Moscow: Nauka.

Baburnama (1996), translated from Persian by W.M. Thackston, New York: Oxford University Press, 1996.

Black, Jeremy (1994), *European Warfare, 1600–1815*, New Haven: Yale University Press.

Bruk, Serguei I. and Vladimir M. Kabuzan (1982), '*Dinamika chislennostii rasselenie russkogo etnosa, 1678–1917*' ('The Dynamics of Number and Location of Russian Ethnics, 1678–1917'), *Sovetskaya Istoriografiya*, 4: 9–25.

Burbank, Jane and Frederick Cooper (2010), *Empires in World History*, Princeton: Princeton University Press.

Bushkovitch, Paul (1978), 'Taxation, Tax Farming and Merchants in Sixteenth-Century Russia', *Slavic Review*, Vol. 37 (3): 381–98.

Chekhovich, Oleg D. (ed.) (1974), *Samarkandie Dokumenty, XV–XVI vv* (*Documents of Samarkand, Fifteenth and Sixteenth Centuries*), documents in Persian, translated into Russian, Moscow.

Chimitdorzhiev, Sh. B. (1978), *Vzaimootnosheniia Mongolii i Rossii v 17–18 vekakh* (*Relations between Mongolia and Russia in the Seventeenth–Eighteenth Centuries*), Moscow: Nauka.

Davis, Brian (2007), *Warfare, State and Society on the Black Sea Steppe, 1500–1700*, London: Routledge.

Demidova, Natalia F. (ed.) (1995, 1996, 2000), *Materialy po Istorii Russko-Mongol'skikh Otnoshenii: Russko-Mongol'skie Otnosheniia, 1654–1685, Sbornik Dokumentov* (*Materials for the History of Russian–Mongol Relations: Russian–Mongols Relationships, 1654–1685, Collection of Documents*), Moscow: Izdatel'skaia Firma Vostochnaia Lietartura.

Demidova, Natalia F. and Viktor S. Miasnikov (eds.), (1969–72), *Russko-kitaiskie otnosheniia v xvii veke: Materialy i Dokumenty* (*Russian–Chinese Relations in the Seventeenth Century: Materials and Documents*), 2 volumes, Moscow: Nauka.

Dixon, Simon (1999), *The Modernization of Russia, 1676–1825*, Cambridge: Cambridge University Press.

Duffy, Christopher (1981), *Russia's Military Way to the West: Origins and Nature of Russian Military Power, 1700–1800,* London: Routledge.

Esper, Thomas (1967), 'The Odnodvortsy and the Russian Nobility', *Slavonic and East European Review*, Vol. 45: 124–35.

Hellie, Richard (1971), *Enserfment and Military Change in Muscovy*, Chicago: University of Chicago Press.

——— (1976), *Slavery in Russia*, Chicago: Chicago University Press.

——— (1988), *The Muscovite Law Code (Ulozhenie) of 1649*, Part 1, Irvine, Ca.: Charles Schlacks.

Hoffman, Philip (2009, 2010), 'Why Was it the Europeans Conquered the World?', Working Paper, Caltech; available at http://federation.ens.fr/ydepot/semin/texte0910/HOF 2010WHY.pdf.

Holloway, David (1994), *Stalin and the Bomb: The Soviet Union and the Atomic Energy, 1939–1956*, New Haven: Yale University Press.

Hrushevsky, Mykhail (2002), *History of Ukraine-Rus*, Volumes 7 and 8 (*The Cossack Age to 1625 and from 1626 to 1650*), Edmonton: Canadian Institute of Ukrainian Studies.

Iakovlev, Aleksandr'I (1916), *Zasechanaia cherta Moskovsko gogosudarstva v XVII veka* (*The Defence Maps of the State of Moscow in the Seventeenth Century*), Moscow.

Kazakhsko–russkieotnosheniia v 16–18 vekakh, Sbornik Dokumentov i Materialov (*Russian–Kazakh Relations in the Sixteenth–Eighteenth Centuries, Collection of Materials and Documents*) (1961, 1964), Alma-Ata: Akademia nauk Kazakhskoi SSSR.

Keep, John (1985), *Soldiers of the Tsar: Army and Society in Russia, 1462–1872*, Oxford: Clarendon Press.

Khodarkovsky, Mikhael (2002), *Russia's Steppe Frontier: The Making of a Colonial Empire, 1500–1800*, Bloomington and Indianapolis: Indiana University Press.

Kostomarov, Nikolai'I (1994), *Smutnoe Vremia Moskovskovo Gosudarstva v Nachale XVII Stoletiia, 1604–1613* (*The Time of Troubles in the State of Muscovy at the Beginning of the Seventeenth Century, 1604–1613*), Moscow: Charli.

Le Donne, John (1991), *Absolutism and Ruling Class: The Formation of the Russian Political Order, 1700–1825*, Oxford: Oxford University Press.

Levi, Scott (trans.) (2002), *The Indian Diaspora in Central Asia*, documents in Persian, translated into English, Leiden: Brill.

Maathir-al-Umara by Nawab Samsam al-Daula Shah Nawaz Khan ([1911] 1979), translated from Persian, Delhi.

Mezhdunarodnye Otnosheniia v Tsentral'noi Azii: 17–18 vv, Dokumenty i materialy (*International Relations in Central Asia, Seventeenth–Eighteenth Centuries, Documents and Materials*) (1989), 2 volumes, Moscow: Nauka.

Moon, David (1997), 'Peasant Migration and the Settlement of Russian Frontier, 1550–1897', *The Historical Journal*, Vol. 40 (4): 859–93.

Mukminova, Rozia G. (1985), *Sotsial'naia Differentiatiia Naseleniia Gorodov Uzbekistana v XV–XVIe vv* (*Social Differentiation of the Urban Population in Uzbekistan, Fifteenth–Sixteenth Centuries*), Tashkent.

Muntakhab al-Lubab by Khafi Khan (Khafi Khan's History of Alamgir) (1975), translated from Persian, Karachi.

Muntakhabu-t-Tawarikh by Bada'uni ([1898] 1986), translated from Persian, Delhi.

Parker, Geoffrey (1988), *The Military Revolution and the Rise of the West, 1500–1800*, Cambridge: Cambridge University Press.

Ralston, David (1990), *Importing the European Army: The Introduction of European Military Techniques and Institutions into the Extra-European World, 1600–1914*, Chicago: University of Chicago Press.

Razin, E.A. (1994), *Istoriia voennogo iskusstva, XVI-XVII vv* (*Military History, Sixteenth–Seventeenth Centuries*), Saint Petersburg: Poligon.

Sunderland, Williard (1993), 'Peasants on the Move: State Peasant Resettlement in Imperial Russia, 1805–1830', *Russian Review*, Vol. 52 (4): 472–85.

Vazhinskii, Viktor M. (1973) '*Vvedenie Podushnogo Oblozheniia Na Iuge Rossii v 90-kh Godov XVII Veka*' ('The Introduction of Poll Tax in the South of Russia during the 1690s'), *Izvestiia Voronzhskogo Gospedinstituta*, 127: 88–103.

Witzenrath, Christopher (2007), *Cossacks and the Russian Empire, 1598–1725*, London: Routledge.

Zagorovskii, Viktor P. (1969), *Belgorodskaia Cherta* (*The Belgorod Defensive Line*), Voronezh: Voronezhskii Gosudarstvennui Universitet.

Zlatkin, Igor Ia. and Nikolai V. Ustiugov (eds.) (1959), *Materialy po Istorii Russko-Mongolskikh Otnoshenii: Russko-Mongol'skie Otnosheniia 1607–1636, Sbornik Dokumentov* (*Materials for the History of Russian–Mongol Relations: The Russian–Mongol Relations 1607–1636, Collection of Documents*), Moscow: Izdatel'estvovostoc hnoiliteratury.

The Rise of the Asian Sailor?

Intra-Asiatic Shipping, the Dutch East India Company and Maritime Labour Markets (1500–1800)

Matthias van Rossum

In contemporary maritime industry, Asian sailors have become indispensable. Sailors from China, Indonesia and the Philippines together make up almost half of the labour force manning the world merchant fleet.[1] The role of Asian sailors even extends to sectors where their employment would seem less likely at first sight, for example, in Dutch river shipping, which is reported to be increasingly manned by sailors from the Philippines and other nationalities.[2]

The rise of the Asian sailor is often traced back by historians to the internationalization of maritime labour markets in the nineteenth and early twentieth century, referring to the enormous expansion of European shipping in the nineteenth century and the resulting demand for labour which led to internationalization and recruitment of Asian maritime labour. In recent years, some excellent scholarship has begun to excavate the histories of Asian sailors in this emerging stage of a global maritime labour market, focusing especially on South Asian sailors or *lascars*.[3]

No matter how revealing and important this research has been, the focus on the nineteenth century, however, distracts scholarly attention from an earlier chapter in the history of Asian maritime labour and its rise on the world stage. This chapter concerns the history of early modern maritime Asia, its shipping and maritime labour markets. It is in the intra-Asiatic shipping of the early modern period that the internationalization of Asian maritime labour markets seems to have received its first acceleration. Furthermore, it seems that it was in exactly this period that Asian sailors expanded from already well-established Asian maritime labour markets into newly emerging global labour markets created with the increasingly worldwide shipping of European powers.

For long, the maritime dimension of Asian history has been ignored as of little importance. In recent years, increasing attention has been given to the history of the Indian Ocean and the surrounding seas.[4] This renewed attention, however, focuses mainly on trade routes, traders and the products. The crucial activity underlying this exchange, the actual shipping and the maritime labour involved, is to a large degree still unexplored terrain. As a result, information on Asian shipping and maritime labour markets is not superfluous. This is in contrast to the information on the European (and Atlantic) maritime industry for which we can not only find extensive academic literature, but also comprehensive reconstructions of both shipping and the labour market. This inequality may, to some extent, be explained by the availability of sources. It seems, however, that it is also directly related to the still resounding echoes of older 'official' discourses of Asian empires and their prevailing disregard for maritime trade. Or, as has been stated in relation to early modern China: 'Little effort has been made so far to compare the imperial myth . . . with the real situation along the maritime frontier.'[5]

This essay, therefore, aims to open up renewed interest in the early maritime history of Asia, and the history of maritime labour markets and sailors in particular. First, it will study the concepts presently used for maritime Asia and Asian maritime labour. As a second step, this essay will present a tentative reconstruction of the size of shipping in Asian waters. Based on this reconstruction, it will be possible to establish an indication of the size of the (continuous) demand for Asian maritime labour – and through this the existence of large pools of Asian maritime labour and labour markets, both before and after the ascendance of European maritime power in Asian waters. Thirdly, this essay aims to provide several first indications of the character of these labour markets by exploring the level of internationalization, patterns of recruitment and more detailed information derived from the experience of the Dutch East India Company (VOC) in its employment of Asian sailors.

Taken together, the conclusions in this study provide evidence to rethink several assumptions with regard to early modern maritime Asia and Asian maritime labour. Based on this evidence, it will be argued that the rise of the Asian sailor must not solely be seen as a product of the nineteenth-century expansion of European maritime activity and imperialism. The essay will bring forth, on the contrary, another history in which the rise of the Asian sailor found its roots in an earlier phase of internationalization of maritime labour markets occurring in Asian waters, in particular in Southeast Asia and the Indian Ocean region. It will furthermore propose that the evidence indicates that Asian sailors made their appearance on this early stage of internationalizing labour markets as skilled maritime workers, operating in circumstances rather similar to those known for European workers. This is in contrast to the perception of Asian sailors for later periods of high colonialism emphasizing their position in *lascar* (or 'coolie') type labour relations.

Perceptions of Asian Maritime Labour

So first, let us turn to the concepts and the resulting assumptions relating to early modern maritime Asia and Asian sailors. At least two influential concepts have left their mark: the notion of 'peddler trade', introduced by J.C. van Leur to describe Asian trading patterns; and that of 'lascar' labour, used to describe working and recruitment conditions of Asian sailors.

The notion of 'peddler trade' was introduced by J.C. van Leur in his work on Indonesian and Asian trade and society in the 1950s. Although it received its fair share of criticism, it still seems to have left its imprint on the conceptualization of (early modern) Asian maritime labour.[6] According to van Leur, maritime Asia was characterized by 'a large number of peddlers with small cargoes and a small capital, a limited number of ships and a reluctant overabundance of "shipper-passengers"'.[7] It was a world of 'countless' 'isolated' markets, 'an international trade of person-to-person haggling'. This was a world of travelling petty traders, joining each other for purposes of transport. 'When the traders were gone and the money brought along had been put to use or spent, trade came to a standstill.'[8]

In this perspective, *sailors* have disappeared. The need for their labour seems to have disappeared when trade came 'to a standstill'. And, when maritime labour power was needed, they were either replaced by masses of petty traders sailing their own ships or became sailor-traders themselves – their sailing occupation became merely a means that enabled them to trade. The continuous emphasis on the role of personal or private trade for Asian seafarers – and the claim that this would make them stand apart from European sailors – seems to be the main mark left by this perspective.[9]

This is an understandable consequence of the long prevailing notion of 'peddler trade' and the tendency to disregard the importance of maritime Asia.[10] But where the underdeveloped character of Asian maritime activity is being seriously challenged in recent years, this seems not yet the case for the perspective on maritime labour. Here the concept of *lascar* labour has come to fill the gap for the early modern period.

Michael Fisher provides a definition of *lascars* as Asian sailors, very often from different backgrounds, working 'in a single maritime labour-gang under a *serang*', brought and kept together via specific recruitment patterns and conditions of employment. In an important study bridging employment of Asian sailors for the East India Company in the eighteenth and nineteenth century, Fisher briefly mentions that 'there were many pre-colonial patterns of recruitment and service in the Indian Ocean'. He however continues to stress that the *lascar* developed 'most extensively'.[11]

It seems that this holds true not only *historically* for the development of the *lascar* pattern from late eighteenth century into later periods, but for the development of our *historical imagination* as well. The *lascar* concept as it functions for the nineteenth and twentieth century has increasingly been projected on the early modern period. This has been done in multiple ways. Michael Fisher does this implicitly by portraying *lascar* 'modes of labour recruitment and service' as 'historically common in the Indian Ocean'.[12] Others, like René Barendse, employ the *lascar* concept in more explicit ways by describing the working conditions of eighteenth-century '*lascarins*' in similar ways as *lascars* in later periods.[13]

This is important not merely as an argument on the labels assigned to Asian sailors, but because the *lascar* concept is intrinsically linked to assumptions about extra-economic bonds, informality and underdevelopment. This has led to an explanation of characteristics of Asian sailors in a way similar to that of a *stereotype*. Asian crews are stated to be large and inefficient, less well-trained, lazy, cheap and occupied with their own private trade. Barendse, for example, states that: '*nakhuda*s of Indian ships were men of dignity. They were wont to take a large number of retainers along, even if this did not benefit the effective compliance with tasks aboard'.[14] Elaborating on European shipping in Asia, Barendse claims that both the ships of the VOC and the French Compagnie des Indes 'rarely had Asian crews on board' as 'they were often insufficiently trained and were thought lazy'. He continues his portrayal of the Asian sailor with the claim that 'a *lascarin* was paid much less than a European sailor'.[15] He explains this by the fact that they would have been 'largely remunerated' with the allowance 'to take some freight along, "to benefit their family", which they could sell at the destination'.[16]

Here the concepts of 'peddler trade' and *lascar* labour have strengthened each other in the characterization of the Asian sailor. Both concepts seem to set apart European and Asian labour as inherently different, and in a way, even seem to reproduce older, colonial perceptions of difference between the European 'free' 'wage earner' and the Asian un-evolved petty trader, or 'unfree' or 'semi-free' worker. This might be related to the tendency to disregard the importance of maritime Asia.[17] Since maritime activity was viewed as underdeveloped, so was labour. Following recent renewed attention on the dynamics of maritime Asia, however, this essay will argue otherwise. Based on a reconstruction of the size of shipping in Asian waters, it will emphasize the large and continuous demand for maritime labour. Furthermore, it will deal with evidence pointing towards the internationalized character of maritime labour markets involved. And it will study evidence that provides several first indications of the character of these labour markets, mainly based on the experience of the company that for most of the seventeenth and eighteenth century served as largest single maritime employer in Asia, the VOC.

Asian Shipping

It is an interesting observation that despite the increasing attention on the Indian Ocean region as the oldest of maritime networks, the 'world's oldest oceanic "world"', only limited attention has been paid to the size and development of its shipping. While several reconstructions have been produced of the size of European merchant fleets in the early modern period, this is not the case for Asia.[18]

Although a reconstruction of the size of shipping in Asia is very useful in assessing the relative importance of the maritime sector, it has to be approached with caution. Estimations of the size of Asian shipping are difficult due to lack of sources. European sources are important for tracing European as well as Asian shipping. Except for a first tentative indication of the size of Asian trade for the early seventeenth century by J.C. van Leur, there are no overall reconstructions. Some authors provide estimates in the form of cross-sections for specific regions. Most authors, however, simply focus on the shipping movements of one port, often for limited periods.

The data on these shipping movements often originates from scattered references in qualitative sources like travel accounts, or – somewhat more reliable – from quantitative sources such as shipping lists or harbour registrations produced mainly by European trading companies.[19] For most shipping data there is some indication of the size of the ships involved, although for most ships it is not possible to indicate the exact tonnage. A very rough estimate can be produced by combining information on type of ship, the owner and different traditions of shipping.

Based on this information, a first attempt has been made to reconstruct the size of early modern shipping in Asia. For this, the many fragmented references in the literature to available ships in ports and to specific ship movements have been listed and taken as a foundation for assessing the size of fleets in different parts of the Asian seas. The approach taken for reconstruction could be labelled as 'modest' as the estimations are based only on the available references to ships and ship movements that have been recovered so far. The reconstruction, therefore, is a minimalist account of shipping traced in Asia. For regions and periods where too little data was available to make a reliable reconstruction, 'intrapolations' have been made to fill the gaps (in bold). These intrapolations are based on surrounding reconstructions and on the assumed development of trade and shipping in a certain period and region as described in the available literature.

Again, it has to be emphasized that this should be seen as a tentative reconstruction and a starting point for further debate and reconstructive work. In the meantime, however, it does provide us with an initial indication of the size of shipping, and also – by adding tentative data on early modern

TABLE 1 ***Reconstruction of Shipping and Labour Demand in Asia***

			1550		*1600*		*1650*		*1710*		*1750*		*1790*	
			Ships	*Tonnage*	*Ships*	*Tonnage*	*Ships*	*Tonnage*	*Ships*	*Tonnage*	*Ships*	*Tonnage*	*Ships*	*Tonnage*
Intercontinental	Europe			3.000		4.858		12.147		19.868		34.001		50.130
	VOC		–		–			9.896		15.278		19.525		21.165
	America		?		?		?		?		?		?	
Intra-Asiatic	European	Portuguese	20	15.000	30	25.000	20	6.000			30	7.500	30	7.500
		VOC	–		–			40.987		37.975		26.056		32.373
		Dutch private	–		–		?		10	2.500	20	5.000		
		EIC	–		?			**15.000**		**15.000**		**25.000**		**60.000**
		English country trade					10	2.500	60?	15.000	100	25.000	575	175.000
		French	–		–		–				20	5.000	30	7.500
		Other European	–		–		?		10	2.500	20	5.000	30	7.500
	Asian													
	South China Sea	Overseas	?		180	60.000	140	48.000	175	65.000	150	40.000	200	60.000
		Intern	?			**80.000**		**60.000**		**80.000**		**100.000**	900	100.000
	Southeast Asia	Mainland and Sumatra	?		85	13.000		**10.000**		12.000		**10.000**		10.000
		Java	?		375	30.000		**25.000**		18.000		**20.000**		20.000
		Rest	?		200	20.000		**20.000**		20.000		**25.000**		25.000
	Bay of Bengal		?			**40.000**		**40.000**		35.000		**35.000**		35.000
	Arabian Sea		?			50.000		**50.000**		50.000		40.000		**40.000**
Coastal			?		?		?		?		?		?	
Intra-Asiatic total **estimate:**						200.000		100.000		260.000		150.000		450.000
						350.000		**350.000**		**400.000**		**400.000**		**600.000**
						?		?		?		?		?

Note: This reconstruction is based on a collection of references of fleet sizes and ships engaged on various routes in Asia. The references are available in collection structured as lists of references per region. Bold estimates are intrapolations, provided for parts that could not be reconstructed due to lack of references.

labour productivity – a first tentative indication of the size of the demand for maritime labour.[20]

Labour Markets and Internationalization?

Shipping in Asian waters was a significant and structural phenomenon. While European shipping in Asia was on the rise, Asian shipping stagnated but certainly does not seem to have disappeared or declined. Taking this rough indication of the size of shipping in Asia as a starting point, a first estimate can be made for the size of the labour force needed to operate these merchant fleets.

Assessing labour productivity in the form of manning ratios (tons per man) for the many different segments of this reconstruction is an impossible task, due to lack of sources and the diversity of shipping traditions. However, since we are dealing with a total reconstruction and are aiming for a rough indication of the size of labour force involved, it seems reasonable to use an overall indication for the labour productivity based on general knowledge for this period.[21] If we assume that 5 tons per man would be a rather general but reasonable indication for the average of early modern maritime labour productivity, it would provide us with a demand for some 70,000 sailors around 1600, growing to 120,000 sailors around 1790. Even though this reconstruction builds on a 'modest' approach, these seem to be significant numbers for the early modern period.

How then were the many ships and vessels manned; how did the maritime labour markets function? Again, it is impossible here to chart all local and regional maritime traditions. More work on specific regions will be necessary. One characteristic of shipping in Asia, however, stands out: international composition of crews seems to have been not an exception but a rather normal phenomenon in Asian waters. This is remarkable especially when we look at available data for European recruitment patterns. As Jelle van Lottum, Jan Lucassen and Lex Heerma van Voss have shown, early modern European maritime nations tended to recruit their maritime labour force primarily in a national way. The Dutch Republic was one of the main exceptions to this rule, relying on large numbers of foreigners engaged via more or less free recruitment.[22]

Available data for Asia is fragmented. Almost no structural registration of ships crews are available for early modern shipping in Asian waters. The extensive administration of the Dutch East India Company for its personnel engaged in intra-Asiatic shipping (the *Generale Zeemonsterrollen*) is one of the main exceptions, providing yearly information on the composition of crews of VOC ships in Asian waters from 1691 to 1791.[23] Other exceptions are the *Tôsen Fusetsu-gaki* and *Oranda-sen Fusetsu-gaki* statements given by Chinese and Dutch officers of junks arriving in the port of Nagasaki, containing information on overseas news, the ship and its journey, and for many of the statements, also the crew.[24] Japanese control of trade in Nagasaki, however, was very strict, and the Chinese and Dutch counterparts seem not to have been allowed to take 'strangers' on board, turning this into a less representative branch of shipping when it comes to the composition of crews.[25] Other ways available for further inquiry into the recruitment patterns of Asian and European shipping often provide more fragmented evidence. Three lines of research are explored here: references in literature (based on various, dispersed source material), the so-called *Prize Papers* and VOC sources.

From the literature we can establish two clear cases of international recruitment strategies for the European shipping in Asia: the Portuguese from the beginning of the sixteenth century onwards, and the English private trade in the (later) eighteenth century. Although no systematic study exists on the crews of Portuguese ships in Asia, it seems safe to conclude that the Portuguese made extensive use of mixed crews consisting of European and Asian sailors already from the early sixteenth century onwards.[26] As the first Europeans arriving in Asian waters, they recruited sailors in Macau, Malacca and India.[27] These mixed crews have been depicted by Japanese artists in their paintings of arriving Portuguese ships on folding screens – called *Namban screens*.[28] For some ships the composition of the crew has been preserved through the list of crew members: for example, the *Fé de Christo Salvador nosso* departed from Macau in 1640 with a crew consisting of 16 Portuguese, 2 'Castelhanos', 2 Mestizos, 13 Chinese from China, 4 Chinese from Macao, 6 sailors from Bengal, 5 from Malabar, 3 'Ballalas', 3 'Cafres', and one sailor each from Canarin, Acheh, Malaya, Solor, 'Indios Papangos', Timor and Iaos.[29] The Portuguese appear to have continued this strategy of international recruitment throughout the seventeenth and eighteenth century.[30]

At the end of the eighteenth century, English private merchants gained hegemony over Asian maritime trade, the so-called 'country trade'. The English are reported to have engaged Asian or European-Asian crews.[31] Dermigny, for example, refers in his study of Canton to 54 British country ships in Cochin in 1785, carrying some 2,000 *lascars*.[32] This was also the case in earlier decades. In 1729, 18 Moors were interrogated who claimed to have been recruited three months before at Madras by a captain William Plumble as sailors on the brigantine *Anna*, '*bemand met 31 coppen waar onder 24 mooren*'.[33] In 1761, the Batavia-born inland sailors Simon Joseph and Pieter Vermin testified that they had sailed with a Dutch burgher to Madras and from there on worked on English ships for two years.[34] In 1780, the British privateer *Hornby* sailing in Asian waters near Macao had on board a crew consisting of English and '*lascars*'.[35]

But what was the composition of the crews of ships of other nations in the period in between? What do we know about recruitment patterns of

Asian shipping? And did other European nations follow this pattern? To begin with the European nations: just like the Portuguese and the English, the VOC employed both European and Asian sailors on board their ships that were active in intra-Asiatic shipping.[36] The VOC archive contains interesting information on the employment of Asian sailors, which will be further elaborated later in this essay. For the French Compagnie des Indes too, it seems, in contrast to what has been stated in the literature, the employment of Asian sailors was a common phenomenon.[37] For the period 1745–81, information on the crews of eight ships sailing in Asia has been recovered in the *Prize Papers*. On board these ships French sailors amounted to only 10 per cent of the total crew. Besides their own nationals, the French employed sailors from other European nations who were born in Europe and in Asia. These mixed European crews, totalling to somewhat less than 15 per cent, were completed with mixed Asian crews comprising more than 85 per cent. Also, for earlier periods, there are references to employment of Asian sailors on board French ships.[38]

This strategy of mixed crews employed by Europeans within Asia might be very similar to recruitment patterns that seem to have been employed by Asian traders. Again, findings from the *Prize Papers* might be indicative here, as all Asian ships that have been found thus far made use of a mixed Asian crew in one way or another (Table 2). For example, the Chinese vessel *Juffrouw Gogua*, sailing with a pass of the VOC from Palembang to Samarang in 1799, was manned with 12 Chinese and 32 Javanese sailors, as well as two young slaves. Another illustrative case is the aforementioned *Santa Reta*, sailing from Manilla to Macau in 1780, with a Portuguese mate and a crew of Chinese, Indians and natives of Macau. In 1750, the Armenian-owned vessel *Mahajoub* sailed from Cochin via Mocha for Bengal with a French captain, 3 Portuguese and 38 Indian sailors, indicated as 'natives of different ports of India'.[39]

TABLE 2 *Crews in Asiatic and Intra-Asiatic Shipping, 1744–1810 (Prize Papers)*

		N Ships	*N Ships with mixed crew*	*Nationals*	*Europeans*	*Unknown / Non-European*
France	Europe – Asia	19	2	97.5%	98.8%	1,2%
	Intra-Asiatic	8	7	9.8%	14.6%	85.4%
Dutch Republic	Europe – Asia	5	5	–	76,6%	23.4%
	Intra-Asiatic	17	16	4.2%	11.3%	88.7%
Portugal	Intra-Asiatic	1	1	7.1%	12.9%	87.1%
Asian traders	Intra-Asiatic	4	4	13.6%	4.5%	95.5%

Source: *Prize Papers* (June 2009).

These patterns are confirmed by ships found in VOC-related sources.[42] The references to the compositions of crews of both Asian and European ships seem to indicate two things. First, most ships seem to have enlisted mixed crews. Table 3 provides an overview of the information recovered on the composition of crews of ships sailing in Asian waters. Some crews were marked by a large degree of diversity: for example, the Chialoup of Carel Carelsz, a burgher from Samarang, sailing from Batavia to Samarang in 1748 with a Chinese captain, a Macau foreman ('bootsman') and a crew consisting of one sailor from Macau, one from Macassar, one Malayan, one Javanese and two 'Bataviase Mahometaanse inboorlingen' (Batavian Muslim born). The two Macau sailors, foreman Constantijn Dias and sailor Emanuel Wiera, were noted to have come into service on Batavia around a year before ('*beide in dienst op Batavia, een jaar geleden*').[43] Other crews were marked by diversity as well, but in a less abundant way. For example, the ship of '*nachoda*' (captain) Malim was manned with a crew consisting mainly of sailors from Batoebaroe (including the brother of the *nachoda*, Soedin), but complemented with a sailor from Banjan and Siantang.[44]

Second, based on the references found it seems reasonable to establish that the sailors on both European and Asian ships in Asia were engaged, often individually, in labour relations in which wage was the main form of remuneration. Workers on board ship were referred to as '*huurlingen*', i.e. hired persons: for example, the three 'free' Javanese sailors from Cheribon – Jamin, Benata and Raka – declared to have been *huurlingen* (hired men) on board the ship of Louw Tjaijko coming from Cheribon under the command of the (Chinese?) '*annachkoda*' Paun Tjaik.[45] Even the aforementioned inland sailors Simon Joseph and Pieter Vermin declared 'to have engaged themselves in the service' of an English captain at Madras ('*zig in die zelve qualiteit [als matroos] in dienst hebben begeeven*').[46]

This, of course, is not to say that local conditions or traditions could not vary. Recruitment patterns and the conditions of engagement often did: as for instance in the case of the Balinese ship sailing to Batavia with a clearly 'national' recruitment pattern, with a crew consisting of exclusively Balinese sailors. These Balinese sailors, however, did state themselves to be 'hired' workers – they claimed '*alle mael huurlingen van 't vaartuijg geweest [te zijn]*' (that they were 'all hired men of the ship'). On the conditions of engagement there appears to have been contrasting views from the sailors, claiming to be 'hired', and the VOC, claiming that it was common among the Balinese to engage 'in equal condition' ('*van eene aguale conditie*'), with everything in common. This might however have been a strategy to pursue all Balinese on board – who were seen as illegal slave traders and smugglers.[47]

One of the main established exceptions that should be dealt with here seems to be the Chinese sailors. Commonly, historians claim that 'junk

Table 3 *The Composition of Crews of Asian and European Ships, Excluding the VOC, 1618–1788 (VOC and other sources)*

Year	*Ship*	*Crew*	*Route*	*Owner*	*Captain*	*Crew*	*Type*	*Labour relation*	
1618	St. Louis	?	[Asia-Europe]	French (CdI)	French?	France, [Asia]	m		[PvD, dl.1.2, 609]
1621	–	70	Basrur-Bengal	Chatim	Mapilla	[Malabar], [Asia]	m		[Subrahmanyam 1990]
[1630s]		?	[Asia]	Golkonda	?	[Asia], [Europe]	m		[Subrahmanyam 1988]
1639	–	?	[Pulicat]	Portuguese	Portuguese	[Asia], [Europe]?	m		[GM, dl.2, 63]
1651	[Junk]	?	Amoy-Taiwan	Chinese	Chinese?	China, Dutch Republic	m		[DZ, dl.3, 246]
1669	–	11	[Machilipatnam]	Dutch private	English?	England, [Asia]	m		[GM, dl.3, 672]
1671	–	?	Mocha-Bantam	Bantam	?	England, [Asia]?	m?		[GM, dl.3, 744]
1683	[Chialoup]	?	[Palembang]	Siam	Portuguese	Dutch Republic, [Asia]	m		[GM, dl.4, 535]
1685	–	?	[Dela Goa Bay]	Portuguese	Portuguese	Portugal, Mozambique, Goa	m		[Barendse, 22]
1691	–	10?	Batavia-Atjeh	Dutch private	?	China, Java, Batavia?, [Europe]	m		[De Roy, 10]
1699	–	?	[Arabian Sea]	[Pirate]	English?	[mixed: 'white, yellow and black']	m		[GM, dl.6, 88]
1710	Lamboe [bark]	?	Johor-Nagapatnam	Johor	Johor?	Java, Johor?	m?	h	[GM, dl.6, 868]
1722	[Brigantijn]	14	Ansjenga-Madras	English?	English	['swart']	m?		[GM, dl.7, 623]
1723	–	?	[Calate]	French	?	[Asia], [Europe]?	m?		[GM, dl.7, 623]

TABLE 3 (*contd.*)

Year	Ship	Crew	Route	Owner	Captain	Crew	Type		Labour relation
1744	–	*21*	*Bali-Batavia*	*Bali*	*Bali*	*Bali*	*s*	*h*	*[VOC 9408.20]*
1744	[Prauw]	14	Sia-Samarang	[Asian?]	Sia	Java, [Malaya]	m		[VOC 9408.21]
1744	–	13		[Asian?]	Batoebaroe	Batoebaroe, Banjan, Siantang	m		[VOC 9408.23]
1744	–	9	Cheribon-Samarang	Jehor	?	?	u		[VOC 9408.27]
1746	[Prauw]	?	Cheribon-Batavia	[Asian?]	Chinese	Javanese	m	h	[VOC 9410.27]
1748	[Chialoup]	9	Samarang-Batavia	Samarang	Chinese	Macao, [Indonesian archipelago]	m		[VOC 9414.21]
1748	–	6	Batavia-?	[Asian?]	Java?	Javanese?	s?		[VOC 9414.18]*
1748	–	6	Batavia-?	[Asian?]	Mandhaar	Sumbauwa, [Boegis]	m		[VOC 9414.18]*
178x	–	76	Goa-Madras	Portuguese	Portuguese?	[Asia], [Europe]	m		[Campbell van Barbreck]
1788	[Bark]	>15	Queda-Malacca	Macao	Macao	Macao, Java, [Malaya], [Moor]	m	h	[VOC 9515.13]

Notes: PvD = Pieter van Dam, *Beschrijvinge*; GM = *Generale Missiven*; DZ = *De dagregisters van het kasteel Zeelandia, Taiwan 1629–1662*; *This ship was taken over by the slaves on board. The original crew appears to have been killed. Both crews – before and after – are mentioned.

sailors were not given fixed wages but rather shared in the profits from the cargos'.[48] This seems to have applied mainly to Chinese ships leaving from – and returning to – China.[49] This claim, however, seems to be based on evidence that has been repeated in several cycles of historical attention for Chinese sailors. For his assessment that 'no wages were paid, and everyone carried his own merchandise', Blussé refers to Cushman. She in turn states that 'crew members of a Chinese junk were merchants first and sailors second'.[50] This statement is based on a rich but rather romantic description of some journeys made by Gutzlaff on several Chinese junks in the 1830s, in which he states that the crew's

> principal object in going to sea is trade, the working of the junk being only a secondary object. Every one is a shareholder, having the liberty of putting a certain quantity of goods on board; with which he trades, wheresoever the vessel may touch, caring very little about how soon she may arrive at the port of destination.[51]

To strengthen this conclusion, Cushman refers to claims made by Raffles on similar practices that would have been 'developed to an even greater degree on Malay vessels in that none of the officers received a salary and "every person on board [had] some commercial speculation in view, however small"'.[52] This statement of Raffles, however, should be seen in its context: it is an observation accompanying a translation of the *Malacca Maritime Codes*, a *judicial* code created in the late thirteenth century during the reign of Sultan Mahmud Shah, and copied by later Southeast Asian maritime states. Also important is the observation preceding Raffles' statement that 'there is no *description* [in the code] of persons who receive wages on board a Prahu'.[53]

Two things are important to note here. First, however important and possibly accurate the contributions on Chinese sailors may be, more research is required in order to arrive at conclusions on the relation between wage and trade as an incentive for Chinese sailors. The evidence concerning the absence of wage labour and wage as a form of remuneration on board Chinese ships seems thin. Second, it should be noted that private trade by sailors was not unique and did not in itself eliminate the importance of wage labour relations. European sailors and officers were allowed private trade as well, as evidence for both the Dutch and the Portuguese shows.[54]

Recruiting Sailors

Wage labour and international recruitment of crews seem to have been common for the Asian maritime labour markets under review here. But how did these labour markets function? Actual examples of recruitment and careers of Asian sailors can be helpful in providing a better insight. An incident in Malacca in February 1735 is intriguing in that sense. Lying at the port of Malacca, the Batavian burger, Gıdion Schrijver, had sent out his '*moor bootsman*' Aldsie with '*40 rijksdaalder en 12 stuivers*' to recruit ten new 'Moor' sailors in Malacca. Once employed at the ship, however, one of the sailors had been discovered to be the inland soldier Joan de Choisa, who had fled the service of the Dutch East India Company.[55]

Both the soldier and the foreman, Aldsie, were taken into custody, and before the *Raad van Justitie* an interesting controversy developed around the recruitment of Joan de Choisa by Aldsie. Joan de Choisa claimed that Aldsie had been aware of him being a soldier. The two supposedly met in a Chinese bar in Malacca and it was the foreman – according to de Choisa – who told him to meet him again in the same bar in two days' time. Aldsie assured de Choisa that he could arrange transport away from Malacca and Aldsie took the soldier to the house of 'Moor Aboe Backar'. There they cut off his hair and Aldsie gave him sailor's clothes worth the value of nine rupees.[56] In the evening they brought him on board the ship of Gidion Schrijver as a sailor – where he was discovered to be a deserter soldier within two days.

The Moor foreman Aldsie was also taken into custody after Joan de Choisa was interrogated. Aldsie, however, denied the charges of having consciously recruited a deserter. On being interrogated with force ('*ad torturam*'), Aldsie persisted that he had met Joan de Choisa in no other place than the house of Aboe Backar. Contrary to the claims of de Choisa, Aldsie stated that he had not met the soldier earlier (in a Chinese bar) and had not made any agreement on his transport. Aldsie did not deny having bought de Choisa his clothes and recruited him as a new sailor ['*als een nieuw aangeworben matts*'], but he held on to his declaration that he did not know that de Choisa had been in the service of the Company ['*sonder kennisse bevoorens gehad te hebben dan den selve ten dienste der E: Comp: is geengageert geweest*'.].[57]

This example is an illustrative instance of easy recruitment of 'Moor' – probably Indian – sailors in one of the main ports of the Malaysian peninsula. It shows a European captain employing European and Asian labour, and thus making good use of the local maritime labour markets. Furthermore, it is interesting that the foreman and sailor might have met either at a Chinese bar or at the house of the Moor Aboe Backar. There seems to have been no established relation between the recruited (Joan) and the foreman (Aldsie) in the sense of social or financial bonds (debts, family ties, regional connections, etc). The advance or investment provided to the new recruit, in the form of a hair-cut and sailor's clothes, is rather similar to patterns of recruitment known for European sailors. As far as the description of the middleman, the Moor Aboe Backar, goes, his role seems to have been limited to perhaps providing clothing (Joan's version) or temporary lodging (as might be the conclusion from Aldsie's version, who claimed to have met Joan at Aboe Backar's house).

The Armenian-owned *Mahajoub*, sailing from Mocha to Bengal in

1750 under the French captain Francis Monsimett with three Portuguese and an Asian crew, might be another illustrative and rather argumentative case. After the capture of the vessel, the French captain was interrogated together with the *sarang* Hodjee Subdee and the Portuguese first mate, Theodore Lobe. What is interesting about this case is the difference in 'knowledge' between the three persons interrogated. The captain could state the tonnage of the vessel precisely but was unable to provide the exact number of sailors on board. The *sarang*, Hodjee Subdee, on the contrary, did not know the ship's tonnage but was able to state that 'at the time she was taken and seized [the ship had on board] forty-two mariners, besides ten passengers'. They were 'all natives of different ports of India, except the captain, and he was a French Man'. It was reported 'that they all came on board at Chardanagore' [Chandernagore]. The *sarang* seemed better informed than the captain about the size of the crew and the place of recruitment. But Hodjee Subdee's information was contradicted by the Siam-born Theodore Lobo, who stated that *Mahajoub* had, besides eleven passengers, 'thirty four mariners, including himself and the rest of the officers, on board the said ship' and 'that the people had come on board at different places, and their complement was last compleated [*sic*] at Chardanagore'.[58]

It cannot be said with certainty who was correct and therefore who would have had responsibility for crew and recruitment, i.e. the Bengali *sarang* or the Asian-Portuguese first mate. Normally we might expect the *sarang* to be in control of the *lascar* crew. The vague reference to the place of recruitment is puzzling however, even more so because the statement of the first mate – that recruitment was only completed at Chandernagore – corresponded with the statement of the captain who declared that the crew 'came on board at different parts of the river of Bengal'.

Both cases problematize the supposed *lascar* labour and recruitment patterns for early modern maritime Asia. They indicate that it was apparently possible to recruit skilled maritime workers in a large number of port cities, and that these sailors could be engaged individually and possibly also through direct recruitment done by European or Asian ship officers. They also indicate that these sailors were engaged in labour relations in which wage was the main form of remuneration. Sailors were referred to, and referred to themselves, as 'hired' and 'wage workers'. They took service on board ships, making use of the employment opportunities and changing employers. Furthermore, advances seem to have been made not merely as part of a supposed 'debt culture' (or relations of indebtedness) but also, as in the case of the Malacca recruitment presented here, as the start of a labour agreement and as an investment in production means, sailors' clothing.

This is of course not to say that coercion or violence was never present within the labour relations described here. This is illustrated, for example, in the story of eleven Javanese from different ports, a Malayan and a Moor sailor. They left the service of the Dutch East India Company without permission, went into employment in 1783 on a Macau barq ('*hadden dienst genoomen*') from Queda to Malacca, and there they asked for their dismissal ('*hadden verzogt hun ontslag te moogen hebben*'). The captain answered that he would let them go once they arrived at Macau. But shortly after the departure from Malacca, rumours started that the captain planned to hand them over to the local authorities at Macau and press them into military service. The sailors revolted, fled with the small boat and went to VOC-controlled ports – where they were discovered and brought before the Court of Justice.

Asian Labour and the VOC

As this example shows, the VOC was one of the players to be reckoned with in maritime Asia. We have seen that the demand for labour for shipping in early modern Asia was significant and structural, both before and after the arrival of European seafaring nations. We have also seen that many different maritime traditions were present in Asia, but the evidence points towards a few characteristics of Asian maritime labour markets involving an emphasis on wage labour, employment of 'diverse' labour crews, often international recruitment, and also recruitment of individual sailors.

The VOC forced its way into this already well developed and international Asian maritime world from the early seventeenth century onwards. For most of the seventeenth and eighteenth centuries it was the largest single maritime employer in maritime Asia and in shipping between Asia and Europe. In this position, the VOC paved the way for the first steps of 'the Asian sailor' into global labour markets. Detailed evidence based on VOC sources provide us with more information on aspects of this history, especially patterns of recruitment, wages and some first indications for labour efficiency.

The VOC was not only active in intercontinental shipping between Europe and Asia. Participation in Asian trading networks was indispensable.[59] For most of the seventeenth century, the size of VOC fleet active in intra-Asiatic shipping was three to four times larger than the fleet returning to Europe (Table 4). During the eighteenth century the intra-Asiatic shipping of the VOC stagnated and then declined, slowly. It was however still twice or equal to the size of the intercontinental shipping in this period.[60]

Intercontinental shipping between Europe and Asia was chiefly manned with a European labour force throughout the seventeenth and eighteenth century. The exclusively European crewing of intercontinental shipping lasted until 1781, when the VOC started to systematically recruit non-European sailors in five Asian ports for voyages to the Republic. On the

TABLE 4 *Tonnage of fleets active in Asian and intercontinental shipping, 1600–1790*[61]

Year	Intra-Asiatic fleet		Return fleet	
	VOC (per July)	VOC (incl. hired ships)	VOC (whole year)	Europe total
1600			2.550	4.858
1610	6.866		2.640	5.820
1620	18.830		3.130	7.919
1630	13.224		5.000	7.598
1640	19.553		5.400	6.858
1650	29.802		7.690	11.291
1660	40.987		9.896	12.147
1670			14.596	12.514*
1680			9.926	17.211
1690			10.840	17.154
1700	[30.000]		12.367	15.017
1710	35.698	37.975	15.278	19.868
1720	40.831		20.038	26.140
1730	34.037		24.305	34.802
1740	35.919		15.860	36.737
1750	26.056		19.525	34.001
1760	29.000		28.135	41.736
1770	18.466		22.580	43.383
1780	29.747		19.680	46.172
1785	22.200	32.373	22.744	
1790	25.355		21.165	50.130

Note: * de Vries (2010) provides us with totals per decennium. The indications in Table X are yearly averages derived from these totals. These figures are, therefore, indicative, and do not reflect the exact yearly tonnage of the European fleet. This accounts for the deviation in the year 1670 in which the 'real' size of the VOC fleet is higher than the indication (based on an average) for the European return fleet.

Sources: *Dutch-Asiatic Shipping*; de Vries (2010); van Rossum, *Database Generale Zeemonsterrollen* (10–2010).

returning voyages to Asia, the Asian sailors travelled back as passengers.[62] However, for the large fleet of ships engaged in intra-Asiatic shipping, the VOC did not only rely on European labour sent over from the Republic; this shipping was manned with a mixed labour force of both European and Asian sailors.

The recruitment of Asian sailors for the intra-Asiatic shipping can be traced back to early in the seventeenth century. An apt example is the ship *Delft*, which sailed to Batavia in 1627 with an 'inland' navigator.[63] In the 1630s and 1640s, the VOC frequently used crews consisting of European, Chinese and 'black' sailors.[64] The junks *Alckmaer*, *Qulangh* and *De Goede Hoop* were all manned with 5 European sailors, 11–15 Chinese and 40 soldiers.[65] In July 1654 the VOC authorities at Formosa (Taiwan) complained that Chinese captains hid their sailors even though the Company was desperate for Chinese sailors.[66] In 1653, the ship *De Reijger* was complemented with '*10 inlantse bootgesellen*' at Paliacatte (Pulicat, India).[67] In 1664, it was reported by the captains that sailed with 'inland' sailors that they were '*kloeke seeluyden*' (good or courageous sailors) when the weather was good, but that they used to hide themselves during storms.[68]

Local sailors seem to have been used by the VOC for local maritime work in and around its Asian factories from early on. They rowed boats in rivers, sailed small vessels to load and unload cargo, and performed other maritime and shore-work tasks. An interesting example of this more localized maritime work is the work done on *panchalangs* patrolling in the Indonesian archipelago ('*kruisende*'). These ships were used to control the Southeast Asian waters and to patrol against trade that violated the VOC monopoly. The crews of these small boats often consisted of a few European and Asian sailors. The Asian sailors originated from various places in the Indonesian archipelago.[69] The sailors were often labelled as '*inlands matroos*' (inland sailor), or '*inlands marinjo*' or '*inlands marine*' (inland marine), probably referring to their combined maritime and patrolling functions.[70]

From the 1670s onwards, the VOC started to recruit Asian sailors systematically for its (larger) ships engaged in intra-Asiatic shipping. The personnel employed on these ships have been recorded in the so-called *Generale Zeemonsterrollen* – the 'maritime' part of the administration that gives a yearly account (every July) of VOC personnel employed in Asia (*Generale Land-en Zeemonsterrollen*) for the period 1691–1791. These sources enable us to study the European and especially Asian sailors working for the VOC, the composition of crews, their place of origin or recruitment, categorization, wages, and other information. For some reason, Asian sailors have been left out of the record for the period 1756–81, although they were employed in the service of the VOC during these years.[71]

The Asian sailors employed by the VOC were recorded in different sections, often at the end of the list of European crew members. The administration, in that sense, made a clear distinction between 'European' and 'non-European', or 'Asian'. The categories used for Asian sailors were often 'Inlands', 'Moors' or '*Toepassen*'. *Toepassen* were the most distinct category, referring to 'dark half-caste Christians, claiming to be of Portuguese descent'.[72] The category of 'Moor' might refer to religious classification (Muslim), but this seems not necessarily the case here. The categories 'Inland' and 'Moor' are used in different ways and are often interchangeable. It is, for example, possible to find sailors with 'Christian' or Portuguese names under the label 'Moor sailor'.

The Asian sailors of the first half of the eighteenth century were mainly recruited in Bengal, and to a lesser extent, in other places in India (Nagapatnam, Ceylon, Cochin, Surat). References to places of origin of Asian crews become less frequent during the mid-eighteenth century, but the few references available point towards Bengal as the main place of recruitment for the early 1750s, with Surat coming up as a good second. Due to the gap in the administration for the period 1756–81, information on the second half of the eighteenth century is fragmented. Towards the end of the eighteenth century, however, the VOC switched to the recruitment of Chinese, Javanese and Malayan sailors. These sailors seem to have been recruited often in Batavia. Indian sailors did not disappear but were less omnipresent as before, and were now mainly recruited in Surat and Cochin.

Skilled Labour?

By the end of the eighteenth century, the VOC had almost two centuries of experience in sailing with Asian sailors. The perspective of historians on this experience seems to have been influenced to a large extent by 'managerial' or 'administrative' sources, in which the use of Asian sailors has often been formulated in the form of complaints or even discarded as a marginal phenomenon. It is however important to realize that these discourses came into being within the organizational dynamics of the Company.

In 1716, for example, it was proclaimed in Batavia that the *Heren Zeventien* had given the order to forbid the recruitment of 'blacks' or 'inlands' in the service of the VOC ('*speciael hebben gelieven te verbieden het plaatsen van eenige swarten of inlanderen in den dienst van d'E. Comp.*'). In 1717, a prohibition was stated against the recruitment of '*mixtisen*' (persons of mixed European–Asian descent) if Europeans were available in Batavia.[73] Both prohibitions were explicitly ordered by the *Heren Zeventien* who had, settling in the Republic, only limited grip on the organization in Asia.[74] The recruitment of Asian sailors had been taking place for dozens of years and was also to continue in the eighteenth century. Even though the positioning of the *Heren Zeventien* may not have had a real effect on the policy of Batavia, it does seem to have influenced the communication between Batavia and the Republic.

References to the recruitment of Asian sailors at the end of the seventeenth century were almost always accompanied by complaints of the lack of European labour.[75] After the prohibitions from the Republic in the 1710s, the references to Asian sailors came to a halt in the yearly reports from Asia to the Republic (*Generale Missiven*) and in the regulations (*plakaten*). Only with the coming of Van Imhoff as governor-general in 1743 did the topic again receive attention. In the second half of the eighteenth century, references and complaints were about both the lack of skills of Asian sailors and the lack of European labour. It seems likely, however, that some of these complaints were probably made with the intention to convince the *Heren Zeventien* to send larger numbers of European personnel in order to satisfy the unceasing and large demand for labour of the Asian organization of the Company.

Some complaints also seem to be related to transitions in the Asian maritime labour market and the position of the VOC. After having recruited 'Moor' sailors in India for decades, first in Bengal and then in Surat, the VOC seems to have been looking for new ways to recruit Asian sailors in Southeast and East Asia. In this process, Javanese and Chinese sailors were sometimes explicitly compared. In 1789, Javanese sailors were called 'lazy' and 'fat' ('*te lui en te vadzig van aard*') and the Company preferred Chinese sailors. In 1794 this perspective changed completely when the Company stated with clear satisfaction that it had been possible to recruit some hundred Javanese sailors for a longer period for service on the return fleet. The Company appears not to have been blind, in this period, to (individual) differences in skills and quality within ethnic groups. Unskilled sailors, for example, received lower wages than skilled Javanese.[76]

Given these organizational dynamics, the administrative or 'managerial' sources provide only a limited and, perhaps, too negative perspective on the experience of the VOC in the Asian maritime labour market. The negative tendency found in Dutch 'managerial' sources was not always reproduced elsewhere.[77] The administration of personnel can complement this perspective in various interesting ways. As shown above, the VOC depended heavily on Asian maritime labour both in and around its factories, as well as in its intra-Asiatic shipping. The *Generale Zeemonsterrollen* provides us with information on the intra-Asiatic shipping of the VOC. Here, the share of Asian sailors increased steadily from the late seventeenth century onwards, increasing up to a third in mid-eighteenth century and to one-half towards the end of the eighteenth century (see Figure 1).

Asian sailors were employed in mixed European–Asian crews. The share of ships with mixed crews (as against ships with completely European crews) rose sharply during the eighteenth century. Figure 2 shows this rising trend (black line): the share of ships with mixed crews rose from approximately 10 to 20 per cent at the end of the seventeenth century, and to around 30 per cent in the 1720s. From 1735 onwards, the share rose above 40 per cent, with peaks of almost 80 per cent for some years.

At the same time, the size of the Asian part of the crew was rising on board ships with mixed crews. In the period 1691–1730, the share of Asian sailors in the total crew varied between a quarter and a third. From 1730

FIGURE 1 *Personnel of the VOC Employed in Intra-Asiatic Shipping, 1691–1791*

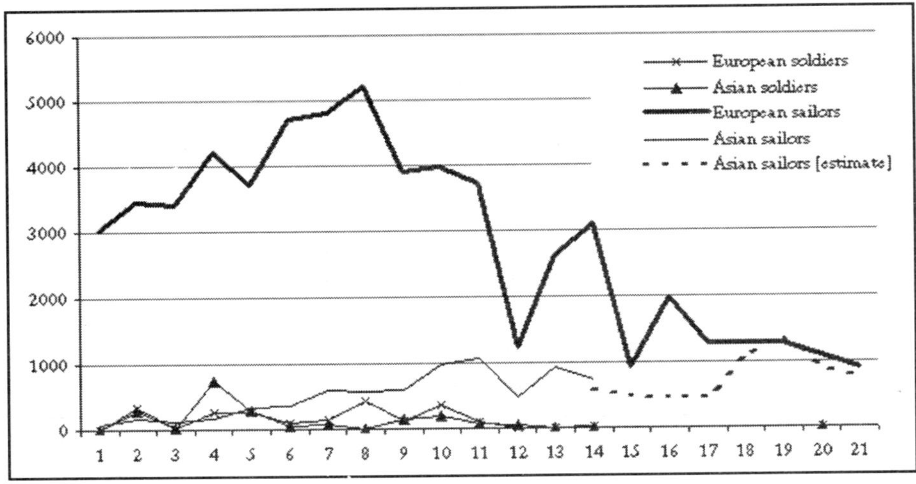

Source: van Rossum, *Database Generale Zeemonsterrollen* (10–2010).

FIGURE 2 *Mixed crews on VOC ships, 1691–1791 (averages in percentages)*

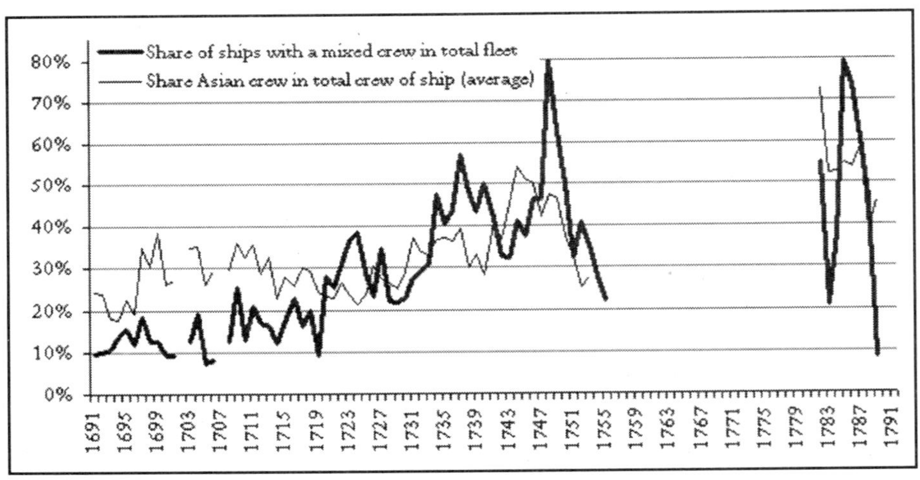

Source: van Rossum, *Database Generale Zeemonsterrollen* (10–2010).

onwards, this share rose to an average of 40 to 60 per cent, with peaks of 70 per cent for some years. To illustrate the impact of this development: in July 1691 the ship *De Groote Visserij* was manned with a crew of 52 European and 21 Asian sailors; in July 1784 the ship *Europa*, had on board only 18 Europeans, and no fewer than 25 Chinese and 51 Javanese sailors. The increased employment of mixed European–Asian crews and the simultaneous rising share of Asian sailors within these crews seem to indicate a certain level of trust from the side of the VOC regarding the usefulness of Asian sailors.

The usefulness of Asian sailors seems to be confirmed by indications of labour productivity. Ships of the VOC engaged in shipping in Asian waters were relatively efficient. Table 5 presents an overview of the labour productivity of VOC ships in intra-Asiatic shipping. For these overviews yearly weighted averages have been used and are differentiated between ships in various tonnage classes (as size influences efficiency).

Sailing with mixed crews seems not to have hindered the VOC in intra-Asiatic shipping in a serious way. Ships with completely European crews

TABLE 5a *Weighted Average Labour Productivity per Tonnage Class of VOC Ships with 'Mixed Crews' in Intra-Asiatic Shipping* (tons per man), *1691–1791*

Jaar	*>0 <140*	*>=140 <=340*	*>340 <=700*	*>700 <=1.000*	*>1.000 <20.000*
1695	3.1	6.2	7.8	9.0	15.6
1700	3.2	5.9	8.2	9.1	11.5
1710		4.2	8.5	9.0	8.1
1720		4.3	6.6	7.2	7.6
1730			7.3	8.8	11.7
1740		2.9	8.8	10.3	13.1
1750			9.2	10.6	13.0
1785	4.4		13.1	12.5	15.4

Source: van Rossum, *Database Generale Zeemonsterrollen* (10–2010).

TABLE 5(b) *Weighted Average Labour Productivity per Tonnage Class of VOC Ships with 'European Crews' in Intra-Asiatic Shipping* (tons per man), *1691–1791*

Jaar	*>0 <140*	*>=140 <=340*	*>340 <=700*	*>700 <=1.000*	*>1.000 <20.000*
1695	4.3	8.1	9.7	10.5	13.0
1700	4.3	8.2	9.6	9.7	11.8
1710	5.7	6.7	9.1	9.7	10.2
1720	9.2	6.7	8.0	8.6	10.5
1730		8.3	8.8	9.4	11.1
1740		9.0	11.3	11.3	14.8
1750		7.7	10.4	12.3	12.5
1785			15.2	10.9	11.5

Source: van Rossum, *Database Generale Zeemonsterrollen* (10–2010).

seem to have been slightly more efficient, but overall the use of a certain type of crew (mixed or European) does not seem to have had a great impact on labour productivity. Especially for ships of large tonnage categories, the difference in labour productivity between mixed European–Asian crews and exclusively European crews was rather small, and sometimes to the advantage of mixed crews.[78]

In comparison to ships of other nations active in intra-Asiatic shipping, the VOC appears to have operated in an efficient way. French ships in Asia reached an average labour productivity of only 5.9 tons per man at the end of the eighteenth century.[79] Chinese junks are estimated to have had an average labour productivity of 2.5 tons per man.[80] The labour productivity of English and Danish ships engaged in intercontinental shipping between Europe and Asia in the eighteenth century varied between 5 and 7 tons per man.[81] Ships in intra-Asiatic or intercontinental shipping on average were marked by lower labour productivity than ships in Europe. The productivity on board VOC ships in intra-Asiatic shipping, manned with both European and mixed European–Asian crews, could very well measure up to the productivity of ships of other nations sailing outside Europe.[82]

Can this be seen as a indication of the quality, reliability and equal position of Asian sailors in comparison to European sailors? The remuneration of sailors in Asia seems to confirm this picture. For most of the eighteenth century, the VOC paid Asian sailors 7.50 guilders per month. Asian foremen earned either 12 guilders as a *sarang* (*zarang*) or 10.50 guilders as a *tandel* (*zarangsmaat*). The Asian sailors employed as 'inland marines' on smaller ships – *panchalangs* used for patrolling the Southeast Asian waters – earned 9 guilders per month, probably due to their complementary military tasks. Towards the end of the eighteenth century, in the 1780s, the wages of Asian sailors had risen to 9 or sometimes 12 guilders. The wages for Asian officers seem to have become more flexible. Foremen received sometimes 13.50 guilders, but more often 22.50, 23 or even 24 guilders per month. Foreman mates mostly earned 12 or 18 guilders.

These wages did not differ much from wages earned by European sailors employed by the VOC. Until the second half of the eighteenth century, European sailors were recruited in the Republic for a starting wage of seven to eight guilders; younger sailors ('*jongen*', '*jongmatroos*', '*hooploper*') started at wages ranging from 5 to 7 guilders per month. Once in Asia, they had the possibility to raise their wages by extending their service overseas, leading to wages ranging from 8 to 13 guilders. Most of the wage of European sailors, however, was paid out in Europe. In Asia – where the money was of more value to the Company – European sailors only received partial advances.[83]

The VOC was not unique in this more or less equal payment of European and Asian maritime labour. Information available for wages paid by

TABLE 6 ***Wages Paid by European Companies to Sailors in Asia, Mid-Eighteenth Century***[84]

	Area of recruitment	*Function*	*Wage (guilders)*	*Wage (original)*
Asian sailors				
VOC	Asia	Sailor (fighting skills)	9	
VOC	Asia	Sailor	7.5	6 Rp
CdI	Asia	Sailor	7.3	6 Rp
EIC	Asia	Sailor 1	7.3	6 Rp
EIC	Asia	Sailor 2	5	4 Rp
European sailors				
VOC	Europe	Sailor (fighting skills)	9 to 12	
VOC	Europe	Sailor	7 and onward	
VOC	Asia	Sailor	7 and onward	
VOC	Asia	Young sailor	5 and onward	
VOC	Europe	Young sailor	5	
CdI	Europe?	Sailor	9.40 to 14.10	20 – 30 L
CdI	Europe?	Young sailor	3.3	7 L

other European Companies in the middle of the eighteenth century indicates that wages did not differ much between Asian sailors working for different Companies (6 rupees seems to have been the standard), and that wage levels of Europeans and Asians were rather equal.

Conclusions

Asian sailors dominate modern-day maritime labour markets. This essay aims to show that this was not only the result of the nineteenth-century expansion and internationalization of the European maritime industry, but that the rise of the Asian sailors found its roots in an earlier phase of internationalization of Asian maritime labour markets.

It has shown that the demand for maritime labour created by Asian and European shipping in early modern maritime Asia was significant and structural. Furthermore, it has brought forward evidence which indicates that shipping with mixed crews was a common phenomenon in Asia. Maritime labour was recruited from the many different port cities of maritime Asia, often also internationally. It has been indicated that Asian sailors could be recruited as individuals, possibly also through direct recruitment done by European or Asian ship officers. The evidence indicates that the Asian sailors were engaged in labour relations in which wage was an important form of remuneration. Sailors were referred to, and referred to themselves, as 'hired' and 'wage workers'. Seeking service on board ships, they made use of employment opportunities and changing employers.

The experience of the largest single maritime employer of early modern maritime Asia, the Dutch East India Company (VOC), is indicative of the fact that not only Asian, but also European employers depended on Asian labour markets. Other Europeans sailing in Asia, like the Portuguese and later the English private traders, after the VOC employed large numbers of Asian sailors as well. The VOC employed Asian sailors in and around its factories, on small vessels patrolling the Southeast Asian waters, and on its larger vessels engaged in intra-Asiatic shipping. Local recruitment of Southeast Asian and Chinese sailors seems to have happened almost immediately at the start of the presence of the VOC in Asia. At least from 1670 onwards, the VOC employed Indian sailors in intra-Asiatic shipping, initially recruited mainly from Bengal and later mostly from Surat. In the second half of the eighteenth century the focus of the VOC shifted, probably due to increased competition from other European nations, towards sailors from Southeast and East Asia, i.e. Chinese, Malayan and Javanese sailors.

The experience of the VOC seems to have been rather good. European and Asian sailors were employed together in mixed crews. During the eighteenth century, the use of these mixed crews grew drastically as compared to the use of completely European crews. At the same time, the share of Asian sailors in the total crew of ships with mixed European–Asian crews rose sharply as well. Furthermore, the available indicators for labour productivity show that the use of mixed crews barely hindered the VOC. The ships of the VOC in intra-Asiatic shipping were relatively efficient compared to Asian shipping, and compared to shipping in and to Asia by the French, English and Danish.

Asian sailors come to the fore as qualified wage workers. It is interesting, in that respect, that they also seem to have occupied a comparatively equal position on the level of remuneration. Wages of Asian sailors seem not to have differed between different (European) employers. Even more, wages of Asian sailors were more or less the same as the wages of European sailors. Asian and European shipping depended heavily on apparently relatively well-functioning maritime labour markets in which wage labour was the main mode of labour relations.

This evidence and its implications seem to be in contrast with some of the concepts commonly used for Asian maritime labour. The *lascar* concept, as we know it for the nineteenth and twentieth century, appears to be not applicable for this earlier period – as has been done by, for example, Barendse. The same seems the case for the implications of the model of 'peddler trade', introduced by van Leur to describe early modern Asian maritime trade. Asian sailors were not primarily merchants or coolies; they seem to have been qualified wage workers operating in often internationalized labour markets. It seems that even the long-established historical wisdom concerning early modern Chinese sailors – seen as 'sailing merchants' receiving no wage but receiving part of the trade as their payment – is in urgent need of critical examination.

This is of course not to say that the Asian maritime world was one of completely free labour markets in which sailors could happily jump from job opportunity to job opportunity. Local conditions and arrangements in maritime labour markets could vary. And coercion and violence were often present as well, in ports and on board ships. That was the case in Asia, just as it was in Europe.

What might be stressed here, however, is that the labour relations involved may not have been very different from the maritime labour relations we know for early modern Europe. In this period, maritime labour markets seem to have been already well-established and functioning. Further, these maritime labour markets seem to have been rather internationalized, both on an 'Asian' scale as well as – with the involvement of European companies – on a 'global' or 'intercontinental' scale. This was the starting point of the story of the rise of the Asian sailor on the global maritime labour market.

This essay aims to open up new questions concerning this history and to provide a first contribution. It has presented an initial, tentative reconstruction of the size of shipping in Asian waters. This is intended as a starting point for further debate and reconstructive work. More research is needed to unravel the histories of Asian sailors and Asian maritime labour markets. In addition, this will open up the way to larger questions concerning the context of these new insights. How did these early modern, multicultural 'floating' workplaces function? How did this shape the development of intercultural

A small vessel of the Dutch East India Company with Asian crew, Jan Brandes, 1779, Collection: Rijks museum Amsterdam, NG-1985-7-2-60 (public domain).

relations between Europeans and Asians? How did this change under the influence of increasing colonialism? And how does this history of Asian maritime labour and labour markets relate to the diverging economic development of Europe and Asia? These are questions that challenge us to further explore the histories of early modern maritime Asia. All this will require not only more quantitative work, but qualitative research as well. At the same time, it will be important to reflect on the implications of the new horizons in sight.

Notes

1 Information from *SIRC Global Seafarers Database* (2003); Amante (2003): 5.

2 *NRC Handelsblad*, 30 May 2007; *Volkskrant*, 6 October 2011.

3 Ahuja (2006); Balachandran (1997); Balachandran (2002); Broeze (1981); Ewald (2000); Fisher (2006); Frost (ed.) (1994); Tabili (1994). For Asian sailors on board the German fleet: Küttner (2000). For the Dutch merchant fleet: van Rossum (2009).

4 Among others: Chaudhuri (1985); Borsa (ed.) (1990); McPherson (1993); Mukherjee and Subramanian (eds.) (1999); Barendse (2002); Das Gupta (ed.) (2001); Kearney (2003); Pearson (2003). For an earlier 'wave' of academic attention to the maritime dimension of the history of (Southeast) Asia, see van Leur (1967); Meilink-Roelofsz (1962).

5 Blussé (2008): 11–12. Blussé continues: '"Out of sight, out of mind" is an apt saying when it comes to the problematic relationship between the imperial administration and Chinese entrepreneurs in Monsoon Asia during the Ming and Qing periods. Contrary to European expansion overseas, the Chinese flag did not follow the trade, and as a result the importance of this creeping overseas expansion and economic penetration, which adapted itself to local conditions wherever it went, has been underestimated and misunderstood in current scholarship.'

6 A. Das Gupta (2001)): 88–101.

7 van Leur (1967): 214.

8 Ibid.: 218–19.

9 For example, Cushman (1986).

10 'The Europeans also participated to some extent in trade within Asia, especially between Japan and elsewhere. This intra-Asian "country trade" was marginal for Asia but nonetheless vital for Europe, which earned more from it than from its own trade with Asia.' Frank (1998): 127.

11 Fisher (2006): 23.

12 Ibid.: 25.

13 Barendse (2002).

14 Ibid.: 434. Barendse compares 'Asian ships' with English private traders. It must be mentioned, however, that English private traders were also mostly manned with Asian crews and European or Indo-European officers.

15 Ibid.: 436–37.

16 Ibid.: 434.

17 For example, in Frank (1998): 127, cited above.

18 For reconstructions of the tonnage of European merchant marines, see Lucassen and Unger (2000); Maddison (2003): 59; van Zanden (2001). For an overview, see Broadberry and O'Rourke (eds.) (2010). For an overview of the number of sailors, see Lucassen and Lucassen (2010).

19 Mainly EIC and VOC administrations. Especially the preserved copies of the VOC shipping lists are useful here, as they provide information on European and Asian

ships entering and leaving (Company-controlled) ports throughout Asia for much of the seventeenth and eighteenth century.

[20] The explanation of this reconstruction, and the literature and sources behind it, will be published in a forthcoming working paper that is intended as part of the IISH Working Papers. This paper is not attached as it is not yet finalized. The concept of reconstruction is presented here to make the point that shipping in early modern Asia was significant, and that the demand for maritime labour in Asia during this period was large and continuous. Furthermore, this reconstruction shows the VOC as the largest single maritime employer during most of the seventeenth and eighteenth century.

[21] The most recent work on this can be found in Unger (ed.) (2011).

[22] van Lottum and Lucassen (2007); van Lottum (2007); van Voss, van Lottum and Lucassen (2011).

[23] van Rossum (2011).

[24] A selection of the *Tôsen Fusetsu-gaki* is available for the period 1674–1723 in Ishii (ed.) (1998).

[25] These restrictions on enlisting 'foreigners' or 'mixed' crews seem likely as apparently none of the VOC ships sailing to Deshima in the late eighteenth century carried Asian sailors on board. This has been shown by Koetsier (2010). Restrictions on taking 'foreigners' or 'strangers' are also mentioned in the account of ship numbers, 75 (counted as number of arrivals in that year), in the year 1693. 'As we proceeded adverse winds continued to blow so that we were not able to progress and instead were adrift when we saw a small boat in the distance in which someone was waving a cloth. . . . Slowly, the small boat approached us and we found them to be Guangnan people. We tried to ask them about their situation, but we were unable to communicate with them. One man among us spoke a little of Guangnan language. When he uttered one or two words he was understood. Then we were certain that they were Guangan people. . . . They had encountered a storm which had broken their mast and blown away their sail. Since then they had been adrift and were about to starve to death when fortunately they noticed our ship which came to rescue them. All the boat's passengers were crying and thanking us and pleading with us to save their lives. Since we were going to Nagasaki and not in a position to carry any strangers on board, we explained to the men on the boat the following: "We would like to have you aboard, however, we already have many tôjin, and a ship bound for Japan cannot take foreign people like you aboard. Instead we will give you a new mast, a sail and essential food and other supplies so that you can proceed to Guangnan." Despite our repeated explanation, these Guangnan people insisted that they had been afloat for several days and did not know where they were. Even with new equipment, they did not know how to orient themselves and were not sure where to go. Whatever the truth on that point may have been, they pleaded strongly that having seen us their lives should be saved. So we decided to help these 18 people who are aboard our ship. We ask your special favour to send them back on board a ship bound for Guangnan. Should there be no ship bound for Guangnan, then we would like to take them back to Siam. This is why we brought them here. . . . You might be suspicious of us for carrying foreigners on board this time in addition to tôjin and Siamese. But the truth is as we have just told you and there is no other reason. We just wanted to save the lives of the 18 people who were on the verge of dying, and that is all there is to it.' From Ishii (1998).

[26] Ruiz-de-Medina (ed.) (1990): 14; Loureiro (2011); McPherson (1993): 187–90.

[27] Loureiro (2011): 202.

[28] For example, the Japanese folding screen in *Museo Nacional do Reis* in Porto.

[29] Cardim, Antonio Francisco, *Embaixada de Macau ao Japão em 1640*, published and

annotated by C.R. Boxer (1933). With sincere gratitude I thank Professor Reinier H. Hesselink for this reference.

[30] Take, for example, the Portuguese ship, *Antonio e Almas Santas*, that sailed in 1747 via Calcutta to St. Thome with a crew consisting of 'Black Christians' or 'Black Christians and Lascars of different ports of India'. Quoted from the interrogation of Captain Antonio Fernandez and Supercargo Francisco da Cunha de Essa of the ship *Antonio e Almas Santas*, The National Archives, Kew, High Court of Admiralty, 32, 97. But also other ships in early and late seventeenth century, as well as late eighteenth century, are reported to have had mixed crews. Barendse (2002): 22; Coolhaas, van Goor, Schooneveld-Oosterling and Jacob (eds.) (1964): 63; van Barbreck (undated).

[31] Barendse (2002): 434–36.

[32] Dermigny (1964).

[33] Nationaal Archief, Den Haag, Archief van de VOC (henceforth NA, VOC), 8521, folio 97.

[34] NA, VOC, 2998, folio 349.

[35] National Archives, Kew, High Court of Admiralty (henceforth TNA, HCA), 32/440.

[36] van Rossum (2011); van Rossum, van Voss, van Lottum and Lucassen (2010).

[37] Barendse (2002): 436–37.

[38] In 1618, the ship *St. Louis*, returning from Asia to Europe, was reported to have engaged Asian sailors. See van Dam (1929): 609. In 1723, several Asian sailors deserted from a French ship lying before Calate. See *Generale Missiven*, Vol. 7: 623.

[39] TNA, HCA 32/712, HCA 32/342, HCA 32/440, HCA 32/133.

[40] For Dutch intercontinental shipping between Europe and Asia it has not been possible to reconstruct the share of Dutch sailors, since most interrogations mention only Europeans of 'different nations'.

[41] The results for Dutch shipping between Europe and Asia are limited to the period 1781–95. The lower share of Europeans is the consequence of the decision to systematically recruit non-European sailors in five Asians ports from 1781 onwards.

[42] It should be mentioned that this overview is *not* based on an a-selective sample from structural sources. References are comprised from various sources, such as the *Generale Missiven*, the *Beschryvinge* and judicial sources of Batavia. These sources have been studied for several reasons, but also have been scanned systematically for references to Asian sailors. All references to the composition of the crews of Asian (and European) ships have been noted as consequently as possible.

[43] On board were also two children and several slaves. The ship was stopped due to suspicion of smuggling. NA, VOC, 9414, folio 21.

[44] NA, VOC, 9408, folio 23. See also, for example, the inland '*prauw*' sailing from Sia to Samarang, with a 'Malayan' crew and complemented with a 'Javanese' crew member (NA, VOC, 9408, folio 21).

[45] NA, VOC, 9410, folio 27.

[46] NA, VOC, 2998, folio 349.

[47] NA, VOC, 9408, folio 20. There seems to be a contrast between the sailors identifying themselves as '*huurlingen*' and the VOC claiming the sailors to have been 'in equal condition' with the captain. The sailors: '*Seggende voorts de overige gevangens soo te samen, als ieder in 't bijsonder, dat zij alle onlangs van Balie alhier zijn overgekomen . . . en zijn de verdere alle mael huurlingen van 't vaartuijg geweest*'. The VOC prosecutor: '*twintig matroosen als met den soogenaemde schipper van eene aguale conditie*' (equal in condition) and persecuting the crew as well as the captain for smuggling slaves – as it is, according to the VOC, '*nae den inlandschen gewoonen trant van vaert onder welke er altoos maar een, die best laet en ommegang kundig is, den schippersnaem word opgedraegen, daar alles in tegendeel gemeen sonder commando, gagie, salaris, off randsoen, onder malkander behandelt en uijtgevoerd*

word, dienvolgende in een bijna gelijken graet schuldig met den anachoda off schipper'. It might, however, be a (judicial) strategy to pursue all Balinese on board. This suspicion is raised by the negative statement on Balinese in general in the indictment: '*hoe dese soort van natie, meest in slaven handelende, met hun vertrek niet schroomen een parthij schuijm van weggeloopen lijfeijgenen weder na hun land te rug te voeren*'.

[48] van Dyke (2011): 223–48, 238.

[49] As, for example, studied by Cushman (1993); Blussé (1986).

[50] Blussé (1986): 110; Cushman (1993): 99. Also see van Dyke who refers in his most recent study on Chinese shipping to this passage of Blussé, van Dyke (2011): 238.

[51] Cushman refers to Gutzlaff (1833): 46. My quote here is from the journal of the first voyage printed in a later revised edition: Gutzlaff (1834): 96.

[52] Cushman (1993): 105; Raffles (1879): 67.

[53] Raffles (1879): 66. 'There is no description of persons who receive wages on board a Prahu, with the exception of persons who may act as substitutes for such as may be obliged to quit the Prahu on account of illness or otherwise.'

[54] Some private trade was permitted for European sailors in India working on Portuguese and Dutch ships. See Magelhaes-Godinho (1969): 809; Prakash (ed.) (1997); van Dyke (2011); Bruijn and Lucassen (eds.) (1980).

[55] '*Door een van zijn mattroosen in presentie van zijn schrijver en stuurm: wierd g'rapporteert dat zig aan boord op hield een zoldaat in dienst der E: Comp:*'; NA, VOC, 9373.

[56] '*Dat hij gev: voorm: bootsman verzorgt heeft om hem van hier te vervoeren als dat niet konde doen hij gev: weder naar zijn post zoude gaan dat die bootsman hem gev: verzekering deede van hem gev: weg te zullen helpen gaande*'; NA, VOC, 9373.

[57] Ibid.

[58] TNA, HCA 32/133. See also van Rossum, van Voss, van Lottum and Lucassen (2010).

[59] Gaastra (2003); Jacobs (2010).

[60] For a more elaborate explanation, see van Rossum (2011).

[61] This overview compares the size of the intra-Asiatic fleet of the VOC with the return fleet from Asia to Europe of the VOC and the combined European Asian trading companies. The figures for the intra-Asiatic fleet are based on a reconstruction provided in van Rossum (2011), i.e. on the basis of *Database Generale Zeemonsterrollen*. The figures for the return fleet of the VOC are derived from *Dutch-Asiatic Shipping*. There the total tonnage of ships arrived in the Republic is used. The figures for the European return fleet are derived from de Vries (2010).

[62] Lucassen (2004); Bruijn (1976).

[63] Parthesius (2010): 103.

[64] The daily records (*dagregisters*) of Fort Zeelandia (Taiwan) contain many references to Chinese sailors in the service of the VOC. See Blussé, van Opstall and Yung-Ho (eds.) (1986–2000). In 1643 and 1644, several Company junks were stated to have '*swarten*' ('blacks') on board. Other sources mention the use of Chinese sailors as well. For example, the account of Antonio van Diemen in the *Generale Missive* refers to a hired junk with 36 Chinese and 19 Dutch sailors (18 December 1639); see Coolhaas, van Goor, Schooneveld-Oosterling and Jacob (eds.) (1964), Vol. 2: 7–8. Pieter van Dam refers to '*inlantse soldyen, verdient op de schepen . . . in Indien gevaren of aan land gelegen hebben*' for the year 1646 in his *Beschrijvinge van de Oostindische Compagnie* (Vol. 1.1: 705; Vol. 2: 299) .

[65] Blussé, van Opstall and Yung-Ho (eds.) (1986–2000), Vol. 2: 61.

[66] Ibid., Vol. 3, p. 381. In Dutch the complaint was that the Chinese sailors '*door de schippers verborgen [worden] gehouden*', '*dewijle wij seer om . . . Chineesche matroosen verlegen sijn*'.

[67] Parthesius (2010): 103.

[68] Coolhaas, van Goor, Schooneveld-Oosterling and Jacob (eds.) (1964), Vol. 3: 463–64.

[69] Various places of origin are mentioned, as for example, Batavia, Pangoloangh, Wadjo, Bougies, Lajoe, Tienorongh, Hoesavangh, Toadjo, Boone, Timorang, Macassar, etc.

[70] The wages these sailors of patrolling *panchalangs* received indicate a military role in addition to their maritime role, as the wage standard for these sailors (9 guilders) was more similar to that of soldiers than of other (Asian) sailors (7.5 guilders).

[71] On this, see van Rossum (2011).

[72] Price and Rangachari (trans.) (2006): 59.

[73] van der Chijs (ed.) (1885–1900), Vol. 4: 71, 80, 102.

[74] Bruijn, Gaastra and Schöffer (1979–87); Witteveen (2011).

[75] Also: '*soo oock moeten de schepen in tyden van oorlogh swaarder werden bemant als in vredige tyden. By gebreck van matrosen, en waarover die van Indiën doorgaans klagen, gebruycken sy mede Moorsche bootsgesellen*'. From van Dam (1929), Vol. 3: 316–17.

[76] van der Chijs (ed.) (1885–1900): Vol. 11: 190, 817; Vol. 12: 862. Here there is reference to unskilled Javanese sailors who '*op de straaten worden opgepakt of, uit de boeyen komende, direct op de schepen en houtvlotten geplaatst*'.

[77] 'The Gujarati ships bound for Malacca, whose crews must have been mainly Gujarati – they were known as accomplished seamen – also carried a very international company of travelling merchants.' See Meilink-Roelofsz (1962): 62.

[78] Further research to labour productivity could be done in order to investigate whether these figures are a good indication, and what would be the best explanation for differences in labour productivity.

[79] van Rossum, van Voss, van Lottum and Lucassen (2010): 19.

[80] van Dyke (2011). The estimates of labour productivity of VOC ships in Asia by van Dyke seem not to be useful here as they are based on information on the intercontinental shipping of the VOC based on *Dutch-Asiatic Shipping* (Bruijn, Gaastra and Schöffer 1979–87) instead of information on intra-Asiatic shipping of the VOC as provided in this article.

[81] Bruijn and Gaastra (eds.) (1993).

[82] Lucassen and Unger (2011).

[83] All references are based on the *Database Generale Zeemonsterrollen* (10–2010). Also see van der Chijs (ed.) (1885–1900), Vol. 10: 424. For an overview see van Rossum (2011): 60.

[84] TNA, HCA, 32/114: 193; Fisher (2006): 70; van Rossum (2011): 60.

References

Ahuja, R. (2006), 'Mobility and Containment: The Voyages of South Asian Seamen, *c.* 1900–1960', *International Review of Social History*, 51, supplement: 111–41.

Amante, M.S.V. (2003), *Philippine Global Seafarers: A Profile*, Cardiff.

Balachandran, G. (1997), 'Recruitment and Control of Indian Seamen: Calcutta, 1880–1935', *International Journal of Maritime History*, 9: 1–18.

——— (2002), 'Conflicts in the International Maritime Labour Market: British and Indian Seamen, Employers, and the State, 1890–1939', *Indian Economic and Social History Review*, 39: 71–100.

Barendse, R. (2002), *The Arabian Seas: The Indian Ocean World of the Seventeenth Century*, Armonk: M.E. Sharpe.

Blussé, L. (1986), *Strange Company: Chinese Settlers, Mestizo Women and the Dutch in VOC Batavia*, Dordrecht: Foris Publications.

——— (2008), *Visible Cities: Canton, Nagasaki and Batavia and the Coming of the Americans*, Cambridge: Harvard University Press.

Blussé, J.L., M.E. van Opstall and Ts'ao Yung-Ho (eds.) (1986–2000), *De dagregisters van het kasteel Zeelandia, Taiwan 1629–1662* (*The Daily Registers of the Fortress Zeelandia, Taiwan, 1629–1662*), Vols 1–4, Den Haag: Nijhoff.

Borsa, G. (ed.) (1993), *Trade and Politics in the Indian Ocean*, New Delhi: Manohar.

Broadberry, S. and K.H. O'Rourke (eds.) (2010), *The Cambridge Economic History of Modern Europe*, Vol. 1, Cambridge: Cambridge University Press.

Broeze, F.J.A. (1981), 'The Muscles of Empire – Indian Seaman and the Raj, 1919–1939', *Indian Economic and Social History Review*, 18: 43–67.

Bruijn, J.R. (1976), '*De personeelsbehoefte van de VOC overzee en aan boord, bezien in Aziatisch en Nederlands perspectief*', *B dragen en mededelingen betreffende de geschiedenis der Nederlanden*, 91: 218–48.

Bruijn, J.R. and F.S. Gaastra (eds.) (1993), *Ships, Sailors and Spices: East India Companies and their Shipping in the Sixteenth, Seventeenth and Eighteenth Centuries*, Amsterdam: NEHA.

Bruijn, J.R., F.S. Gaastra and I. Schöffer (1979–1987), *Dutch-Asiatic Shipping in the Seventeenth and Eighteenth Centuries*, Den Haag: Nijhoff.

Bruijn, J.R. and J. Lucassen (eds.) (1980), *Op de schepen der Oost-Indische Compagnie: Vijf artikelen van J. de Hullu* (*On the ships of the Dutch East India Company: Five articels by J. de Hullu*), Groningen.

Chaudhuri, K.N. (1985), *Trade and Civilization in the Indian Ocean*, Cambridge: Cambridge University Press.

Coolhaas, W.Ph., J. van Goor, J.E. Schooneveld-Oosterling and H.K. Jacob (eds.) (1964), *Generale missiven van Gouverneurs-Generaal en Raden aan Heren XVII der Verenigde Oostindische Compagnie* (*General Reports of the Governors-General and Council of India to the Heren 17 of the Dutch East India Company*), 2, Den Haag: Nijhoff.

Cushman, J.W. (1993), *Fields from the Sea: Chinese Junk Trade with Siam During the Late Eighteenth and Early Nineteenth Centuries*, Ithaca.

Das Gupta, A. (2001), 'The Maritime Merchant of India, *c.* 1500–1800', in Das Gupta (ed.) (2001): 88–101.

Das Gupta, U. (ed.) (2001), *The World of the Indian Ocean Merchant 1500–1800: Collected Essays of Ashin Das Gupta*, New Delhi: Oxford University Press.

de Vries, J. (2010), 'The Limits of Globalization in the Early Modern World', *The Economic History Review*, 63 (3): 710–33.

Dermigny, L. (1964), *La Chine et l'Occident: Le commerce a Canton au XVIIIe siècle 1719–1833* (*China and the West: The Canton Trade in the Eighteenth Century*), Paris: Touzot.

Embaixada de Macau ao Japão em 1640 (*Embarking from Macau to Japan*) by Cardim, Antonio Francisco, published and annotated by C.R. Boxer (1933), Lisboa: Imprensa da Armada.

Ewald, J.J. (2000), 'Crossers of the Sea: Slaves, Freedmen, and Other Migrants in the Northwestern Indian Ocean, *c.* 1750–1914', *The American Historical Review*, 105: 69–91.

Fisher, M. (2006), 'Working across the Seas: Indian Maritime Labourers in India, Britain, and in Between, 1600–1857', *International Review of Social History*, 51, supplement: 21–45.

Fisher, Michael H. (2006), *Counterflows to Colonialism: Indian Travellers and Settlers in Britain 1600–1857*, second edition, New Delhi: Permanent Black.

Frank, A.G. (1998), *Reorient: Global Economy in the Asian Age*, Berkeley: University of California Press.

Frost, D. (ed.) (1994), *Ethnic Labour and British Imperial Trade: A History of Ethnic Seafarers in the UK*, London.

Gaastra, F.S. (2003), *The Dutch East India Company: Expansion and Decline*, Zutphen: Walburg Pers.

Gutzlaff, C. (1833), *The Journal of Two Voyages along the Coast of China in 1831 and 1832*, London.

——— (1834), *The Journal of Three Voyages along the Coast of China in 1831, 1832 and 1833*, London.

Ishii, Y. (ed.) (1998), *The Junk Trade from Southeast Asia: Translations from the Tôsen Fusetsu-gaki 1674–1723*, Singapore.

Jacobs, E. (2010), *Merchant in Asia: The Trade of the Dutch East India Company during the Eighteenth Century*, Leiden: Leiden University Press.

Kearney, M. (2003), *The Indian Ocean in World History*, London: Routledge.

Koetsier, T. (2010), '*Het varend vermogen van de Compagnie: Een onderzoek naar de relatie tussen menselijk kapitaal en arbeidsproductiviteit op de Deshimavaart van de VOC (1780–1795)*' ('The Sailing Capital of the Company: A Research into the Relation between Human Capital and Labour Productivity on the Deshima-Shipping of the VOC, 1780–1795'), unpublished MA thesis, Vrije Universiteit, Amsterdam.

Küttner, S. (2000), *Farbige Seeleute im Kaisserreich. Asiaten und Afrikaner im Dienst der deutschen Handelsmarine* (*Coloured Seafarers in the Empire: Asians and Africans in the Service of the German Merchant Navy*), Erfurt: Sutton Verlag.

Loureiro, R.M. (2011), 'The Macau-Nagasaki Route (1570–1640): Portuguese Ships and their Cargoes', in Unger (ed.) (2011): 189–206.

Lucassen, J. (2004), 'A Multinational and its Labor Force: The Dutch East India Company, 1595–1795', *International Labor and Working-Class History*, 66: 12–39.

Lucassen, J. and L. Lucassen (2010), 'The Mobility Transition in Europe Revisited: Sources and Methods', *IISH Research Papers*; available at http://www.iisg.nl/publications/respap46.pdf, accessed in February 2012.

Lucassen, J. and R.W. Unger (2000), 'Labour Productivity in Ocean Shipping, 1450–1875', *International Journal of Maritime History*, 12 (2): 127–41.

——— (2011), 'Shipping, Productivity and Economic Growth', in Unger (ed.) (2011): 3–46.

Maddison, A. (2003), *The World Economy: Historical Statistics*, Paris: OECD.

Magelhaes-Godinho, V. (1969), *L'économie de l'empire Portugais aux Xve et XVIe siecles* (*The Economy of the Portuguese Empire in the Fifteenth and Sixteenth Century*), Paris: SEUPEN.

McPherson, K. (1993), *The Indian Ocean: A History of People and the Sea*, Delhi: Oxford University Press.

Meilink-Roelofsz, M.A.P. (1962), *Asian Trade and European Influence*, Den Haag: Martinus Nijhoff.

Mukherjee, R. and L. Subramanian (eds.) (1999), *Politics and Trade in the Indian Ocean*, Delhi: Oxford University Press.

Parthesius, Robert (2010), *Dutch Ships in Tropical Waters: The Development of the Dutch East India Company (VOC) Shipping Network in Asia 1595–1660*, Amsterdam: Amsterdam University Press.

Pearson, M.N. (2003), *The Indian Ocean*, London: Routledge.

Prakash, O. (ed.) (1997), *European Commercial Expansion in Early Modern Asia*, Aldershot.

Price, J.F. and K. Rangachari (trans.) (2006), *The Private Diary of Ananda Ranga Pillai*, Vol. 1, New Delhi.

Raffles, S. (1879), 'The Maritime Code', *Journal of the Straits Branch of the Royal Asiatic Society*, Vols. 3 and 4.

Ruiz-de-Medina, J. (ed.) (1990), *Documentos del Japon* (*Documents on/of Japan*), Rome.

Tabili, L. (1994), 'The Construction of Racial Difference in Twentieth-Century Britain: The Special Restriction (Coloured Alien Seamen) Order, 1925', *The Journal of British Studies*, 33: 54–98.

Unger, R.W. (ed.) (2011), *Shipping and Economic Growth 1350–1850*, Leiden: Brill Publishers.

van Barbreck, esq., D. Campbell (undated), *Landreize naar de Oostindien langs eenen tot heden nog nooit door Europeers bereisden weg* (*Travelling by Land to East India through Ways Never Travelled by Europeans*).

van Dam, P. (1929), *Beschryvinge van de Oostindische Compagnie* (*Description of the Dutch East India Company*), Vol. 1.2, Den Haag: Nijhoff.

van der Chijs, J.A. (ed.) (1885–1900), *Nederlandsch-Indisch Plakaatboek* (*The Dutch-Indies Orders*), Vol. 4, Batavia: Landsdrukkerij.

van Dyke, P.A. (2011), 'Operational Efficiencies and the Decline of the Chinese Junk Trade in the Eighteenth and Nineteenth Centuries: The Connection', in Unger (ed.) (2011): 223–248, 238. van Leur, J.C. (1967), *Indonesian Trade and Society. Essays in Asian Social and Economic History*, second edition, Den Haag: W. van Hoeve Publishers.

van Lottum, J. (2007), *Across the North Sea: The Impact of the Dutch Republic on Labour Migration, c. 1550–1850*, Amsterdam: Aksant.

van Lottum, J. and J. Lucassen (2007), 'Six Cross-sections of the Dutch Maritime Labour Market: A Preliminary Reconstruction and Its Implications (1610–1850)', in R. Gorski (ed.), *Maritime Labour: Contributions to the History of Work at Sea, 1500–2000*, Amsterdam: Aksant: 13–42.

van Rossum, M. (2009), *Hand aan hand (Blank en bruin): solidariteit en de werking van globalisering, etniciteit en klasse onder zeelieden op de Nederlandse koopvaardij, 1900–1945* (*Solidarity and the Dynamics of Globalization, Ethnicity and Class Among Sailors on the Dutch Merchant Navy, 1900–1945*), Amsterdam: Aksant.

——— (2011), '*De intra-Aziatische vaart: Schepen, "de Aziatische zeeman" en de ondergang van de VOC?*' ('The Intra-Asiatic Shipping: Ships, "the Asian Sailor" and the Demise of the Dutch East India Company?'), *Tijdschrift voor Sociale en Economische Geschiedenis*, 8, 3: 32–69.

van Rossum, M., L. Heerma van Voss, J. van Lottum and J. Lucassen (2010), 'National and International Markets for Sailors in European, Atlantic and Asian Waters, 1600–1850', in M. Fusaro and A. Polonia (eds.), *Maritime History as Global History: Research in Maritime History*, Vol. 43, St. John's.

van Voss, L. Heerma, J. van Lottum and J. Lucassen (2011), 'Sailors, National and International Labour Markets and National Identity, 1600–1850', in Unger (ed.) (2011): 309–52.

van Zanden, J.L. (2001), 'Early Modern Economic Growth: A Survey of the European Economy 1500–1800', in M. Prak (ed.), *Early Modern Capitalism*, London: Routledge: 69–87.

Witteveen, M. (2011), *Antonio van Diemen: De opkomst van de VOC in Azië* (*The Demand for Labour of the Dutch East India Company Overseas on Board its Ships, seen from an Asian and Dutch Perspective*), Amsterdam: Amsterdam University Press.

The Native Soldiers in the British Indian Army

Fighting Men

Sabyasachi Dasgupta

This essay deals with the attitude of the pre-Mutiny Bengal *sepoy* (a native soldier in the army of the English East India Company) towards his work and status. Did he perceive his work as a *sepoy* as labour or would he have considered such a description demeaning? Did he view the vocation of a soldier as a means of upward mobility where he could clearly distinguish himself from those who earned their living by manual labour? While the Bengal *sepoy* mostly hailed from an upper-caste background he generally came from middling or impoverished economic circumstances, thus rendering the question of upward mobility vital for him. While upward mobility involved a concrete process of bettering his lifestyle and prestige in society, it also possibly implied a change in the self-perception of the sepoy. The essay asks whether it was vital for the *sepoy* or the *soldier* to establish an identity distinct from and superior to that of those who made their living from *manual labour* in civilian society and in the army. Why was the appellation of a 'fighting man', with its implied connotation of a profession distinct from manual labour, important to the *sepoy*?

Service in the army had allowed him to escape performing manual labour as men hailing from a typical Bengal *sepoy*'s economic background had no choice but to till the land themselves. This seriously blighted their standing in society, and came in the way of asserting influence or exercising the leverage which would have otherwise accrued to them on account of their high-caste status. Did this, therefore, render it vital for such men to acquire the identity of a company *sepoy*? Emboldened by official recognition of their caste sentiments and practices, or what was construed as so, the *sepoys* often stated that they would not dig trenches as high-caste men were not supposed to pick up the shovel and engage in manual labour. The situation reached ridiculous proportions when they even refused to sound the gong at the quarter-guard, arguing that it was beneath their status as high-caste soldiers.

This essay explores why the Bengal *sepoy* exhibited such an obsessive reluctance to perform any duty remotely resembling manual labour. The

Bengal *sepoy* was also very sensitive to perceived equalization of perks and allowances with camp followers and other non-combatant personnel employed in the army, whom he regarded as lowly labour. To cite an instance, one of the grouses of the Bengal *sepoy* during the Barrackpore mutiny was that while even lowly camp followers and drivers of carriages were being paid handsome allowances, he was being denied his due. The *sepoy* considered this to be positively degrading;[1] his superior calling in the army and indigenous society were under threat.

Recruitment and Status

The recruitment policy of the East India Company's Bengal Army had a pronounced high-caste bias from the very outset. It recruited mainly from Oudh and Bihar, as high-caste recruits from these areas were perceived to be loyal, obedient, faithful and ideal soldiers.[2] Sleeman praised the deference of the Bengal *sepoy* towards constituted authority. According to him, it was unthinkable for a son of the families from which the Bengal Army drew its recruits to utter a disrespectful word to his parents. He commented: 'Such a word from a son to his parents would shock the feeling of the whole community in which the family resides and the offending member would be vested with their highest indignation.'[3] Company officers believed that the high-caste Bengal *sepoys* were morally and physically superior to troops of other Presidencies.[4]

Caste became a major factor in the functioning of the Bengal Army because of this high-caste preponderance; and caste sentiments and prejudices came to be tolerated and, at times, even encouraged as Company officers came to believe that its predominantly high-caste recruits' caste sentiment was immutable. For instance, when the Bengal *sepoy* refused to strike the gong at the quarter-guard fearing a loss of status, men called *ghanta pandeys* were specially recruited and paid to do the job.[5] Similarly, taking into consideration high-caste sentiments regarding sea voyages, overseas service remained voluntary until 1856 when a general order made such service within or beyond the territories of the Company compulsory.[6]

The general mode of recruitment was to ask *sepoys* and Indian officers leaving for home on furlough to bring back recruits from their village.[7] In extreme circumstances, recruiting parties were sent to Bihar and Oudh.[8] A closed-shop system originated, in which ties of clan, caste and residence ensured inter-relationship among the *sepoys* and Indian officers. Douglas Peers argues that this system of recruitment and residence reinforced the *sepoys*' sense of primordial exclusivity, and the English officers' lack of authority and subsequent failure to manage regiments. He also says that the internal cohesiveness of these regiments was further entrenched by the tendency of the *sepoys* to extend their contracts beyond the initial period of three years.

Approximately 35 per cent of *sepoys* in the 1830s had between ten and seventeen years' service. Peers further points out that a sense of continuity and corporateness evolved because personnel turnover was so low and because the army depended on the *sepoys* for recruitment. The Bengal Army became a military family that increasingly excluded officers, both British and Indian. This indigenous, high-caste, corporate identity was further strengthened by the system of residence. Instead of living in the barracks where socialization would have been encouraged, the *sepoys* arranged for their own room and board.[9]

The present study agrees with Peers only partially. The mode of recruitment in the Bengal Army, its marked high-caste bias and the native soldiers' manner of residence undoubtedly led to a strong sense of corporate identity based on primordial ties of caste and clan. However, going by Samuel Huntington's description of a corporate identity, the personnel of a fighting force can be described as having developed such an identity if they have a sense of organic unity and consider themselves a group apart from laymen, and if their collective sense of identity originates in lengthy training and discipline necessary for professional competence, the common bond of war, and the sharing of a unique social responsibility. While the Army no doubt exposed *sepoys* to discipline and training, its recruitment policy ensured that they did not consider themselves a group completely separate from laymen. The Bengal *sepoy* did not have a corporate identity by this index.[10]

However, army life and discipline must have moulded him to an extent. While retaining strong vestiges of their civilian identity, the Bengal *sepoys* also entered into conflict with the non-privileged peasantry and the traditional elite of the Indian society. They were a terror to both these sections. They often misused their access to the Resident of Lucknow to establish fraudulent claims. Sleeman mentions an invalid *subedar*, Sheik Mehboob Ali, who fraudulently acquired a village from a big landlord by influencing the Resident. Thus, while *sepoys* had strong links with civilian society, they often came into conflict with the peasantry and the traditional elite. The Bengal *sepoys* were by no means peasants in uniform, as Rudrangshu Mukherjee puts it; rather, they had a dichotomous mentality.[11]

The Notion of Status and the Bengal Sepoy

The Bengal *sepoys* had a very strong notion of status. Though high up in the caste hierarchy, they were by no means elite. Upward mobility held great importance for them and they aspired to be part of the elite. Company service gave them the leverage to aspire to this role. Service in the army helped the *sepoys* shed their tag of being agriculturalists who wielded the plough themselves. Aspiring elites could hardly afford to have any association with manual labour, even if it meant labouring on their own land. While this in no way equated them with the class of agricultural labour, it did not qualify them as an elite class either. The *sepoys* looked askance at any task that had even a whiff of manual labour. They considered it a serious impediment in their endeavour to be the new elite. Their anxiety about the odium of manual labour often bordered on paranoia.[12]

The fear of being clubbed with the category of manual labourers led them to strenuously oppose equalization of their allowances with that of *doolie*-bearers or drivers. For example, one of the main grouses of the Bengal *sepoys* during the Barrackpore mutiny was that their allowances had been equalized with that of *doolie*-bearers and carriage drivers of the Madras Army.[13] This was construed as a severe insult and added to other existing grouses. It was as if the very core of their identity had been attacked. Everything that army service meant to them was at stake. Any perceived equalization of their status with that of manual labourers seemed to elicit a hysterical reaction from the *sepoys*.

This anxiety in a way shaped the Bengal *sepoys*' attitude towards the contentious issue of flogging. On 24 February 1835, a General Order by the Governor-General abolished corporal punishment for Indian soldiers, and laid down that any regimental or brigade court-martial could sentence a soldier of the Indian Army to dismissal from service for any offence for which the punishment formerly was flogging. However, a sentence of dismissal could not be carried out unless confirmed by the general officer or any other officer commanding the division.[14] Bentinck, while defending the decision to abolish corporal punishment, affirmed that corporal punishment was injurious to the feelings of the native soldiery, bred discontent and was inimical to the *sepoys* developing a sense of allegiance towards the state. He claimed that the general strand of opinion in the three Presidencies was against the abolition of corporal punishment, and though some favoured its restriction, the practice could no longer be defended with regard to the high-caste Bengal *sepoys* particularly when it was prohibited in the general regulations of the Bengal Presidency.[15]

Flogging in the Bengal Army acquired an extra dimension since it was composed predominantly of high-caste men from so-called respectable sections of society. The incidence of flogging was low in the Bengal Army and was only one-sixth of that in the Madras Army.[16] Douglas Peers argues that the preponderance of high-caste *sepoys* in the Bengal Army was the reason why the lash was sparingly used. As evidence he cites the opinion of British officers who were convinced that use of the lash on Bengal *sepoys* was counterproductive. These officers felt that to strike a man in India was considered an act of great dishonour, and the higher the caste, the greater the dishonour.[17] Peers says that the Company's preferred mode of punishment for *sepoys* in the Bengal Army was dishonourable discharge, dismissal being seen as challenging the *sepoys*' sense of honour in a caste-ridden army. Even in Bengal, flogging was followed by immediate dismissal. Peers says that dismissal for flogged *sepoys* was bound with questions of status. Flogging meant ignominy, and reflected the British belief that flogging a high-caste *sepoy* destroyed his pride and confidence. Peers quotes Bentinck, who considered discharge to be so severe a punishment as to make the application of corporal punishment unnecessary. He argues that by emphasizing the caste of the *sepoy* over the crime when fixing punishments, the British were conforming to the Indian legal tradition as they understood it. Officials like Mountstuart Elphinstone concluded from studies of pre-colonial regimes that caste was more important than crime in determining the punishment.[18]

The ramifications of the decision to abolish corporal punishment are beyond the purview of this essay. It would suffice to say that a vigorous campaign to reintroduce flogging was started, and the pro-flogging lobby scored a victory when Lord Hardinge reintroduced it on a limited scale in 1845.[19] The story goes that when one of the generals of a division was inspecting a native regiment, one of the best recruits of that regiment, a Brahmin, stepped out and demanded to be discharged. When asked why, the *sepoy* replied that he might be forced to work on the roads for any crime he might commit, chained to someone of a low caste. When Lord Hardinge heard of this incident, he decided to reintroduce flogging.[20]

This incident of a Brahmin wanting discharge on the grounds that he might be forced to perform labour on the roads chained to a 'half-caste' is of interest to us for what it reveals of the *sepoy*'s attitude. The prospect of the punishment held out a twin terror for high-caste *sepoys* like the Brahmin who complained to Lord Hardinge. The threat to his status was a double-pronged one: the misery of performing menial labour on the roads, which was demeaning enough, was compounded by the possibility of having to work side by side with a lower-caste person. This prospect, even if hypothetical, was enough for the Brahmin *sepoy* to demand a discharge. The loss of an attractive job which admittedly bestowed on him a distinct status was acceptable if it mitigated the threat of an acute loss of status by being forced to do degrading manual labour, and side by side with a 'half-caste' to boot.

The Company responded, as the story goes, by reintroducing flogging. Though there were notions of status that were bound with flogging too, the Company believed that being flogged for select offences was preferable to the *sepoy* than performing demeaning manual labour, for the latter had the potential of equalizing his status with that of the manual labourer. The *sepoy*, as mentioned before, viewed the army as a tool for upward mobility, and to be required to perform manual labour would set him back drastically in his endeavour to rise in social status.

Contextualizing the Term Military Labour

The category of military labour seems to have been problematic as far as the Bengal *sepoy* was concerned. Various historians though have used the category to describe the vocation of the soldier. Eric van Zurcher while discussing the Turkish army, and Orlando Figes and Richard Pipes while studying the Red Army, have sought to investigate whether the vocation of fighting can be described as a kind of labour. Can the soldier be placed within the larger family of men and women who earn their living by labour?[21]

These historians also alert us to the possibility that soldiers often hailed from the labouring sections of the populace. They were often recruited from among agricultural labourers or from the industrial proletariat in more modern times, and it is possible that they retained vestiges of their old identity. In the Indian context, Rudrangshu Mukherjee and Eric Stokes have sought to establish links between the *sepoys* and the peasantry, as large sections of especially the Bengal *sepoys* had peasant origins. Rudrangshu Mukherjee goes so far as to call the Bengal *sepoy* a 'peasant in uniform'.[22] He argues that the Bengal *sepoy* who hailed from the peasantry retained strong emotional and physical links with his parent society, and remained at heart a peasant. The annexation of Oudh and the imposition of an arbitrary land settlement by the British therefore severely discomfited the Bengal *sepoys*. Certain latent professional grievances of the *sepoys* added grist to the mill. Discontent over service conditions and their identification with the anxiety of the peasantry produced an explosive condition, and only a spark was need to ignite the fire. While that is true, the question is whether the sections of the peasantry from which the Bengal *sepoy* hailed can be categorized as agricultural labour even though they tilled their own land . The *sepoy*, as we have seen, maintained a grim resolve to distinguish himself from those who were classified as labourers.

Dirk Kolff discusses the military labour market in the context of the Indian subcontinent where a large market existed for mercenaries from the medieval till the colonial period, i.e. up until the British Raj sought to progressively disarm indigenous society, especially in the countryside. Kolff argues that the Company sought to achieve an absolute monopoly of coercive capability and to neutralize potential avenues of armed opposition in indigenous society. Disarming indigenous society was part of this grand design.[23] This thesis seems to be incontestable. However, in considering the fighting men as belonging to the category of men who earned their living by a distinct kind of labour, we must also pay attention to the question, how did these fighting men perceive themselves? Kolff does touch on the fringes of that question. He points out that state recruitment for military service from the Purbiya region – which corresponds roughly to the Awadhi and Bhojpuri Hindi-speaking areas of present-day eastern Uttar Pradesh and western Bihar – had a long tradition of military recruitment, and that the region continued to supply troops to the

Bengal Army though the British modified these traditions somewhat. That ended after the rebellion led by *sepoys* in 1857. Kolff argues that centuries of honourable '*naukari*' as fighting men thus ended abruptly, dealing the region a severe blow. The term '*naukari*', according to Kolff, now lost its former sheen, and denoted menial rather than proud, independent service.[24]

If one were to take a brief look at some examples outside the subcontinent it appears that questions of status were inextricably bound with the vocation of fighting, and any allusion to menial service detracted from the status brought on by military recruitment. The Bolivian army in the twentieth century is an apt example. While the government sought to engage troops in projects of what they termed as national reconstruction, the most menial of tasks were reserved for troops of indigenous origin. For instance, road building would mostly feature soldiers of indigenous origin.[25] In the late 1940s, a leftist government (MNR) came to power in Bolivia. It sought to impart a halo to the non-martial tasks of soldiers, such as setting up schools, farms, building roads, airports, etc., which were deemed integral to the task of nation-building. The soldier by assisting in these tasks was performing a vital role for the nation. In a way, the government was thus trying to blur the distinction between the martial and non-martial roles of the soldier. By blunting the emphasis on the fighting role of soldiers the government was trying to negate the threat from the army.[26] Yet finer distinctions and hierarchies did not go away. Even the avowedly progressive MNR government employed mostly indigenous soldiers in non-martial tasks. So the notion of non-martial tasks being of inferior mould was engrained in the mind-set of even the more progressive elements of Bolivian society. And outright menial tasks figured at the bottom of the pile. Thus, although they were ostensibly trying to demystify the halo associated with martial men, they nevertheless ascribed a superior status to fighting. The more mundane and less attractive tasks were assigned to the indigenous soldiers, who figured at the bottom of the social pyramid even for the left-oriented MNR government.

The other example worth looking into is the military system in German East Africa in the concluding decades of the nineteenth century where, apart from the German colonial troops, African troops known as the '*Askari*' were extensively employed. The *Askari* evolved into a indigenous elite who commanded resources of their own, and, in addition, employed and supervised indigenous labour on behalf of the German colonists. These tasks were usually coordinated by senior soldiers in the *Askari* who had accumulated considerable resources and were among the elite of indigenous society.[27] Yet junior members of the *Askari* were not exempt from performing menial tasks. They had to put in manual labour in roadworks and other building projects. They also had to work on agricultural farms. With a gradual rise in the hierarchy, members of the *Askari* moved from being labourers themselves to being supervisors of labour. They were thus a force whose junior ranks participated in manual tasks while at the same time performing supervisory roles. Clearly, manual labour signified an inferior status. One of the markers of a superior calling was that you were exempt from manual labour, and moved from contributing labour to supervising and employing labour for such work. *Askari* members, as they moved up the social scale, exempted themselves from manual labour as a sign of their enhanced status. Their tasks would be strictly military. The roles they eked out for themselves were mainly martial apart from their function as supervisors of indigenous labour.[28]

To return to the main object of this study, i.e. the pre-Mutiny Bengal *sepoy*, we have considerable evidence to show that the Bengal *sepoy* had grievous objections to being included among men who earned their living by labour. That would have defeated the very rationale of his taking up service with the Company. His dreams of elite status would come to nought. Perception was important to him, both his self-perception and the way indigenous society looked at him. We have a revealing passage in the memoirs of a sepoy, Sitaram, who left his village in Oudh to join the Bengal Army in 1812:

> My father had a brother by name Hanuman who was in the service of the Company Bahadur and was a Jemadar in an infantry battalion. He came home on leave for six months and on his way home, he stayed with my father. My uncle was a very handsome man and of great personal strength. He used . . . [every] evening [to] sit on the seat before our house and relate the wonders of the world he had seen and the property of the great Company Bahadur he served, to a crowd of eager listeners who with open mouths and starry eyes took in all his marvels as undoubted truths. None of his hearers were more attentive than myself, and from these recitals I imbibed a strong desire to enter the world and try the fortune of a soldier. Nothing else could I think of day or night. The rank of Jemadar, I looked on as quite equal to that of Ghazi-ud-din Hyder the king of Oudh himself, in fact of even more importance. He had such a splendid necklace of gold beads and above all, he appeared to have an unlimited supply of gold *mohurs*. I longed for the time when I would possess the same which I then thought would be directly mine if I became the *Company bahadur*'s servant.[29]

The Company's military service in concrete ways enhanced the *sepoy's* power and leverage in indigenous society, and the way native society looked at him. Company service and uniform added to his prestige. Sitaram's account gives us a glimpse of the way indigenous society perceived the *sepoy*, the aura that distinguished his uncle who was a low-grade, non-commissioned native officer in the Bengal Army, and the respect inspired in Sitaram's village for that uncle who sat in the village square every evening to narrate wondrous tales. For the *sepoy* this perception of indigenous society was importat. Service in the Company's army seemed to confer a high status. And that reinforced the *sepoy*'s perception of himself as a person of high status who was miles away from the world of the labouring man.

Notes

[1] *Report of the Enquiry Committee of the Barrackpore Mutiny*, Military (Misc.), Vol. 11, 1824: 479, National Archives of India [henceforth, NAI].
[2] Ibid.: 502.
[3] Ibid.: 520.
[4] *Russell Select Committee for Indian Affairs, 1831–32, Minutes of Evidence*, Vol. 13: 567, West Bengal State Archives, Kolkata [henceforth, WBSA].
[5] Jacob (1855): 38.
[6] Roberts (1897): 256.
[7] An important break the Company achieved as far as recruiting was concerned was when the East India Company stopped the practice of recruiting matchlock men under their own jobber-commander or *jemadar*, who would join directly as an officer, a practice prevalent in Indian armies. Henceforth, Indian officers would rise from the ranks, joining service in the capacity of a *sepoy*. Indian officers would, however, continue to play an important role in recruitment. See Kolff (1990): 178.
[8] Major General Sir Jasper Nichols, *Select Committee for Indian Affairs, 1831–32, Minute of Evidence*, Vol. 13: 113.
[9] Peers (1991): 551–52.
[10] Huntington (1972): 10.
[11] See Mukherjee (2002): 167.
[12] Jacob (1855): 38.
[13] *Report of the Enquiry Committee of the Barrackpore Mutiny*, Vol. 11: 550.
[14] General Orders, Governor General, Fort William, 24 October 1834, NAI.
[15] General Orders, Governor General, Fort William, 24 September 1835, NAI.
[16] *Report of H.M. Commissioners for Enquiring into the System of Military Punishments in the Army*, Parliamentary Papers, XXII (1836): 285.
[17] Peers (1995): 229.
[18] Ibid.: 229–30.
[19] General Orders, Commander-in-Chief, Fort William, 20 June 1845, NAI.
[20] Evidence of Philip Melville, *Peel Commission for Reorganization of the Indian Army, Minutes of Evidence*, 24 September 1858: 83, NAI
[21] For details, see Pipes (ed.) (1968); Figes (1989); Zurcher (1999).
[22] Mukherjee (2002): 167.
[23] See Kolff (1990).
[24] See Gommans and Kolff (2001): 13–17.
[25] See Sheshko (2011).
[26] Ibid.
[27] Moyd (2011).
[28] Ibid.
[29] Sitaram ([1873] 1970): 4. Sitaram was born in the village of Tilowee in erstwhile Oudh and modern Uttar Pradesh in 1797. His father was a yeoman farmer who owned about 150 acres of land. Sitaram joined the army in 1812 at the behest of his uncle who was a *jemadar* in the Bengal Army. Sitaram was a typical Bengal Army soldier, high caste and coming from a yeoman peasantry background.

References

Figes, Orlando (1989), *Peasant Russia, Civil War: The Volga Countryside in Revolution, 1917–1921*, Oxford, Oxford University Press.

Gommans, Jos J.L. and Dirk H.A. Kolff (2001), *Warfare and Weaponry in South Asia, 1000–1800*, New Delhi: Oxford University Press.

Huntington, Samuel (1972), *The Soldier and the State: The Theory and Politics of Civil-Military Relations*, Harvard: Harvard University Press.

Jacob, John (1855), *A Few Remarks on the Bengal Army and Furlough Regulations with a View to their Improvement*, London.

Kolff, Dirk (1990), *Naukar, Rajput and Sepoy: The Ethno-history of the Military Labour Market in Hindustan, 1350–1850*, Cambridge: Cambridge University Press.

Moyd, Michelle (2011), 'Making the House, Making the State: Colonial Military Communities and Labour in German East Africa', *International Labour and Working Class History*, No.80, Fall: 53–77.

Mukherjee, Rudrangshu (2002), *Awadh in Revolt, 1857–58: A Study of Popular Resistance,* New Delhi: Orient Blackswan.

Peers, Douglas (1991), 'The Habitual Nobility of Being: British Officers and the Social Construction of The Bengal Army in the Early Nineteenth Century', *Modern Asian Studies*, Vol. 25 (3).

——— (1995), 'Sepoys, Soldiers and the Lash: Race, Caste and Army Discipline in India, 1820–50', *The Journal of Imperial and Commonwealth History*, Vol. 23, No. 2, May.

Pipes, Richard (ed.) (1989), *Revolutionary Russia*, Harvard: Harvard University Press.

Roberts (Field Marshall) (1897), *Forty-One Years in India*, Vol. 1, London: Longmans and Green.

Sheshko, Elizabeth (2011), 'Constructing Roads, Washing Feet, and Cutting Cane for the Patria: Building Bolivia with Military Labour, 1900–1975', *International Labour and Working Class History*, No. 80, Fall: 6–29.

Sitaram ([1873] 1970), *From Sepoy to Subedar*, translated by Lieutenant-Colonel Norgate, edited by James Lunt, Lahore and New Delhi.

Zurcher, Eric Jan (1999), *Arming the State: The Military Conscription in the Middle East and Central Asia, 1775–1925*, London: I.B. Tauris.

Perception of Work

Unpopular Assam

Notions of Migrating and Working for Tea Gardens

Nitin Varma

At the turn of the twentieth century a group of labourers from Chhota Nagpur working on the Duars tea plantations were persuaded by their manager to cross over to the Assam tea gardens, where the manager held certain interests. These labourers described Assam to be *Agreement ka jagah* (place of agreement/contract), where they would never want to go.[1] Around the same time, a colonial official persuaded the leader of a labour-gang from Allahabad (North West Provinces) working on railroad construction in Assam, regarding the possibility of shifting their services to the tea gardens. The leader feared that even a mere mention of the word 'tea garden' would create havoc among his people.[2] The panic took grave proportions in the case of a few hundred Gandas lodged in a district prison of Sambalpur in Orissa who were proposed to be relocated to Assam to work in the tea gardens. The Gandas threatened to slit their throats if forcibly taken there.[3]

These geographically separated, socially differentiated and seemingly isolated episodes in fact hint at a range of anxieties that came to be associated with, and in many senses signified, the Assam tea gardens. This has to be situated in the context of the changing nature of work organization in the plantations and the intensified strategies of work. Such anxieties as the incidents suggest engendered a sense of apprehension, fear and resistance in the people willing to go there. It came to be acknowledged by the colonial officials, tea agents and missionaries stationed in the recruiting districts that Assam was extremely 'unpopular' and generally had a 'bad name'.[4] This was a startling admission in light of the positive colonial constructions of Assam tea gardens throughout the nineteenth century – as an attractive avenue for the overpopulated districts of eastern and northern India, perpetually trapped in a vicious cycle of deprivation, starvation and famine.[5] The realization, however, was necessitated by mounting concern that the reluctance and resistance in the migrating regions could threaten the sustained production of cheap, disciplined labour (*coolie* labour) for the plantation work process. It had become imperative to comprehend, control and counter it.[6] Such comprehensions were predominantly framed in stereotypical notions of the irrational and ignorant mind-set of the 'inferior' castes and 'primitive' tribes migrating to Assam, and their gullibility to disinformation spread by the moneylenders and the local landed elites (their creditors and tenants) who deterred them from migrating. The unscrupulous private recruiters, i.e. *arkattis*, were particularly singled out for perpetrating the fear, anxieties and distaste for Assam.

Keeping such concerns in mind, this essay suggests how the various concerns collapsed in the overarching category of 'unpopular' attest to a general disruptive impact of the Assam tea gardens – accentuated by the abuses in recruiting and intensification of plantation life and work, which became an enduring legacy of the 'free system'. Notions about the *cha-bagaan* (Assam tea garden) ranged from it being a metaphor for hope and loss, to a site of fear and deception.[7] The following sections which specifically focus on the nature and substance of these perceptions, while not suggesting that such concerns were 'absent' in an earlier period of migration and work on the tea gardens, argue that they gained a greater urgency and resonance in the late nineteenth century.

Understandably, such constructions/negotiations were informed by the geographical, social and economic profile of the migrant groups and the histories of their migration, but points of overlap and intersections came to manifest over a period of time. Here, I find Sabyasachi Bhattacharya's emphasis on a 'fuzzy' concept of labouring poor particularly useful, where he emphasizes a 'commonality among labouring poor in cultural terms, as it tries to cut through the various divides (especially wage/non-wage)'. In the language of this culture, as Bhattacharya argues, 'value is attached to poverty, indigence, destitution and hunger'.[8]

Assam as a Lost World

A recurring anxiety associated with the Assam *cha-bagaan* in the recruiting regions was a deep sense of loss. Concern was voiced regarding the many family members, friends and acquaintances who were taken there, and of whom only a very few actually returned.[9] Apart from rampant abduction and kidnapping practised with impunity by the recruiters, the 'decision' to move for some seemed to be a 'short-term strategy' or even an 'act of desperation' induced by an inability to make a living at home or honour mounting debts. The generous advances made by the recruiter and the hope of earning and saving some money in Assam addressed that immediate crisis. Unlike some other destinations where labour often 'circulated' in search of employment and earning for varying degrees of time, the *cha-bagaan* seemed to be a more permanent change – a point of no return.[10]

This sense of immobility, as already discussed, was induced by the contract regime in Assam and the assumption of magisterial roles by the managers – where the discipline and punishment of the workers were claimed almost as their 'right'. Also, repatriation, an integral feature of the overseas indenture contract, was never allowed to be made mandatory for the Assam.[11] Often, the time-expired labourers, even if they managed to get a discharge certificate (*hathchit*) or considered 'useless' for future engagement by the manager, were left stranded with little means to make the journey back home even if they wished to.[12] There were fears expressed of people being forced and kept against their consent and will. Renewal of contracts was particularly perceived to be made under duress and threat. Many futile efforts were made to establish contacts, but the repeated assurances of the local tea 'agents' of a good 'settled' life in Assam rarely calmed apprehensions.[13]

The hope of establishing contracts in some regions of coastal Orissa came to be expressed in a belief that the God of Wind (*Ringesum*) would blow pieces of bones of those who were 'lost' and died in Assam back to their villages.[14] A rumour circulating in the district of Sambalpur (Orissa) more explicitly visualized the Assam tea managers as systematically tying their *coolies* to trees, lighting a fire beneath, and roasting and eating them. On being told by some recruiting agents about the 'improbability' of such a practice, the locals reasoned that how could they explain the thousands of individuals being taken to Assam without anyone ever coming back and neither the province (Assam) ever 'filling up'.[15] The rumour graphically connected the overlapping anxieties of the loss of family members and acquaintances, and the insatiable demand for fresh recruits for Assam.[16] Another rumour from the district of Jabalpur (Central Provinces) portrayed *coolies* on tea gardens being regularly boiled down for oil extracted from their bodies.[17] The symbolism of extraction of oil from the *coolie* paralleled the sapping of the vitality of body and life on account of the grinding, machine-like work regime in the tea gardens. A common perception in the district (Jabalpur) of the kind of work expected in Assam was that *coolies* worked in waist-deep water which would result in their death in not more than six months.[18]

The notion of 'loss' in these rumours was also an allusion to the rampant sickness and death in the tea gardens, in line with the idea of 'unhealthy' Assam. In contrast to the colonial understanding of 'unhealthiness' which was framed almost exclusively in a climate/race/disease paradigm, these stories hinted at the complicated yet connected repercussions of an exacting work regime and gruelling conditions of life to account for it. The symbolic visualization of 'roasting' and 'boiling' further stressed the excessiveness and unreasonableness of the practices of discipline and work of the *cha-bagaan*, which were expressed in cultural idioms describing 'exceptional' circumstances.

Problems of Life and Work on the Tea Gardens

The nuanced symbolism of the stories about Assam found resonance in the anxieties about *dukh* (state of unhappiness) and *taklif* (problems) that animated various 'anecdotes' about life in the Assam tea gardens and the 'experiences' of people who had been there.[19] Such accounts do unravel an unmediated subaltern/*coolie* perspective of plantation life, but also indicate a deepening anxiety in these regions that the conduct of everyday life was outraged and rendered difficult in the tea gardens. *Dukh* and *taklif* as the perceived conditions of life in the tea garden were not only informed by the 'alienness' of Assam, but also induced by the strategies of work, life and discipline in place in the plantation.

There were specific issues brought about by the circumstances of a new place and a changed climate, as expressed by some of the time-expired *coolies* from Chhota Nagpur. Unlike the usual practice, they were unable to consume the rice cooked overnight for their morning meal. They found the water to be 'different' and saltish, and believed it to be the reason for their frequent bowel complaints.[20] There was anxiousness too about the persistent rains and excessive fever affecting their health. Leeches in the tea gardens were seen as a nuisance and interference in work and there were demands of boots for protection.[21]

Dukh and *taklif* induced by the changed context of place and climate were compounded by certain practices of the *cha-bagaan* that were interpreted as a threat to social/cultural norms. For instance, common boarding and dining among members of different castes/communities during the long journeys to Assam (in depots and on steamers) and in the cramped residential quarters of the tea gardens (barracks/lines) was perceived as conducive to a potential 'loss' of status.[22] There were stories in circulation in the United Provinces about this lack of 'caste consciousness' of the *cha-bagaan* where a single individual was delegated to cook food for everyone during steamer journeys, and that 'outsiders' were allowed free access to their kitchens in the gardens. The colonial state 'responded' by legislating 'dry rations' for some of the steamer routes, but this did not put an end to these apprehensions. Such fears were primarily but not exclusively voiced by the 'upcountry' migrants, who held similar objections during their service in the army and journeys to the overseas plantations.[23] The threat of social ostracism due to transgressions in Assam often had to be mitigated through the performance of purification rites, as was the case with a ritual called *jati mandi* among the Ho tribe (of Chhota Nagpur). This ritual was marked by a communal feast arranged by members of the tribe who had been Assam to regain their lost status.[24]

The nature of the tea garden had other possible implications for the conduct of everyday life. Some returnees felt that on the *cha-bagaan* they usually had very little time for mid-day meals, except during *Chaith* and

Baisakh, i.e. the cold season and the non-manufacturing season.[25] Others had to subsist on a single meal as against the customary two meals and being put to task at the end of the day.[26]

Kamjari or the daily work routine (literally translated as continued work) of the tea gardens systematically flouted the 'legally' stipulated nine-hour workday with an hour of rest in between. There were instances of work being carried on from 6 in the morning till 5 in the evening, especially in the busy manufacturing season. During this period, the working hours in the tea factories usually stretched well into the night, due to the increased pressures of meeting stipulated production targets.[27] Another peculiar 'invention' – garden time – in place in many tea gardens of Upper Assam, extended the *kamjari* by fixing the garden clock ahead of the normal clock.[28] The practices of prolonging the workday and intensifying the work process – integral to the plantation economy of the late nineteenth century – generated instances of interference and potential breakdown of 'customary' functions (e.g. meals) of everyday life.

Wages and remuneration on the *cha-bagaan* raised various other concerns pertaining to life and work. The common practice in the tea gardens of a combination of 'task-rate' assessment (daily tasks) and 'time-rate' payment (weekly/monthly) generated some degree of confusion and returnees felt that they had been 'duped'.[29] The task-rate work, in particular, open to different 'interpretations', was viewed with apprehension, and some colonial officials even realized its 'unpopularity' during famine work.[30] Many time-expired labourers related their experience of task-work in the *cha-bagaan*, describing the amount of work expected to earn a daily wage as 'excessive'.[31] A revision in tasks, as being much higher than in the past, was also felt by some with the result of a decline in their earnings.[32] Sometimes tasks were hiked as a mode of disciplining *coolies*.[33] The penalties for falling short (short-work) and even for minor delays in attendance (muster) led to many deductions.[34] Other apprehensions included being left with hardly any cash after the costs of 'rice-benefit' (5 *seers* of rice per week) were deducted from wages.[35] During times of absence due to illness the workers were completely deprived of any 'cash earnings' since they were given just a subsistence allowance or diet without any payment. But such periods of absence (*kuthia*) were added to the contract terms.[36] Also, the cost of recruitment was often recovered from the wages.

Isolated instances indicate various doubts and concerns about the 'legitimate' possibility of earning sufficient income, which the *cha-bagaan* claimed to offer. Not only was the mode of assessment and payment perceived as 'puzzling', but also the work demanded to earn that wage was deemed as 'excessive'. Again, such assessments were open to multiple interpretations and further enhancement. A general trend of increase in tasks with stagnating wages marked the intensifying Assam plantation economy in the late nineteenth century.[37] Such limitations in the possibilities to earn were further constrained by the standard practices of deductions in place. This only corroborates the perception that the conditions of life and ability to earn on the *cha-bagaan* were difficult.

The 'extraordinary' nature of life on the plantations as particularly induced by practices of policing/discipline formed the substance of 'experiences' in the *cha-bagaan*. Various instances of confinement and extreme disciplining, even for 'irrelevant' and 'unjust' transgressions, raised anxieties and fear about the exceptional workplace. There were concerns of life being circumscribed within a compound system from where no one was ever permitted to leave.[38] People were arrested and beaten for leaving the 'compound', even when they just wished to visit acquaintances and relatives on other gardens.[39] Flogging and corporal punishments meted out by the manager and his native subordinates were inflicted even for trivial offences.[40] The life and activities of the *coolies* were said to be at the complete disposal of the manager / tea garden. *Coolies* were compelled to labour even when unwell, and had to turn up for work even during heavy rains.[41] Female *coolies* were not permitted to stay longer than four to five days at home after childbirth.[42] During longer periods of illness *coolies* were encouraged to leave for the nearby *basti* to be tended by their own caste/tribe people, but on recovery the managers compelled them to return to their 'original' gardens.[43] Some expressed a sense of helplessness in their inability to leave the garden to which they had been contracted even when they disliked it.[44]

The practices of control and immobilization, which were critical to the production of cheap, disciplined labour, were registered as infringements in the conduct of everyday life. The life of a *coolie* as depicted in these experiences entailed a loss of control over personal mobility, choice and well-being, and a potential breakdown of relationships, interactions and social obligations. *Coolies* in effect were seen as not able to move as they wished, not able to rest if they were unwell, and unable to keep in contact with friends and relatives. This sense of loss was induced and heightened by the practices of physical disciplining (even for irrelevant/minor transgressions), making it 'exceptional', 'excessive' and generally 'illegitimate'.

Songs and Oral Traditions of Tea Workers

The perceptions and anxieties about Assam's tea gardens also became a part of wider constructions of the *cha-bagaan* as a site of 'oppression' (places of *dukh* and *taklif*), which were articulated in other narratives sketching life on the tea gardens.[45] *Jhumur* songs, an important element in the oral/cultural traditions of tea labourers in Assam, points to one of the imaginings of the tea garden. The nature of these songs can be illustrated through some extracts:[46]

1

Assam desher chah pat	Assam, the land of tea
Pani boli bar mitha	Where the water is supposed to be sweet
Chal sakhi, chal jabo	Friends, let's go
Bagane tulbor pata anand mane	We'll pluck leaves on the gardens with joy.

2

Chal Mini, Assam jabo	Come Mini, let's go to Assam
Deshe baro dukh re	Our land is full of sorrow
Assam deshe re Mini cha-bagaan horiyal	Assam, Mini, is a land of greenery and tea
Kodal mara jemon temon	We could somehow could hoe the fields
Pata tula kam go	Do plucking work
Hai Jaduram	Oh Jaduram
Phanki diye pathali Assam	You deceived me to Assam.

3

Paka khata lekhaeli naam	Putting my name down [in the contract]
Re lampatiya Shyam	Oh nasty Shyam
Phanki diye bandu chalali Assam	You deceived us to Assam
Depughare maritari	Depots were marked by commotion
Uttaiele terene kari	Had to swim to come to the shore
Hoogly sahare dekholi akash	Only in Hoogly [Calcutta] could I finally see the sky
Mane kari Assam jab	When I wished to go to Assam
Jora pankha tanab	I thought I would pull the fan
Sahab dil kodaleri kam	But Sahab gave me hoeing job
Dina Udaya bhane	So says poor Udaya [the poet]
Akale peter tane	For the sake of the stomach
Tipki tipki parhe gham	I sweat in this heat.

4

Sardar bole kam kam	Sardar says work work
Babu bole dhori an	Babu says nab the fool
Sahab bole libo pither chan	Sahab threatens to peel the skin off my back
Re Jaduram	Oh Jaduram
Phanki diye bandu pathali Assam	You deceived us to Assam.

The songs, in a sense, map the transition of the Assam tea garden from being imagined as a site of hope to becoming a site of despair and difficulties. During the course of the late nineteenth century, tea gardens had also become a major avenue and opportunity for work and survival during periods of acute scarcity and conditions of deprivation. Large-scale migration to tea gardens during famine years attests to that process.[47]

Song 1 captures this optimism regarding Assam, as a land of hope, opportunity and work. The positive mood is again recreated in the opening lines of song 2, where the narrator contrasts the greenery of Assam *cha-bagaan* to the miseries (*dukh*) at home (*desh*). These hopes are shattered when the 'reality' of life on the tea garden is found to be harsh and oppressive. A painful scene is recreated in song 3 which narrates in graphic details the tortuous journey of a fresh recruit from home through depots, steamers and Calcutta to the tea garden. Again, the individual's experience of life and work is at variance to what he or she was made to believe. Song 4 harps on the agony of the *coolie* who is entrapped in the regimented disciplinary regime of the tea garden.

Life on the tea garden as depicted in these songs hint at the *dukh* and *taklif* of the *coolie*. This often comprised the realization of the nature of the work being different from what was anticipated. In song 3, the person was under the impression that he would have to pull fans (*pankha tanab*), which was much easier than the hoeing work (*kodaleri kam*) he was actually put to by the manager (*sahab*) in Assam. A perception of the relative 'ease' of plantation work was often associated with the plucking of tea-leaves (*pata tulna*), the primary occupation of women workers on the plantations, as expressed by the narrator of song 1: '*Bagane tulbor pata anand mane*' ('We will pluck the leaves on the gardens with joy'). This alludes to a persistent notion that plucking was 'effortless' and 'natural' to women as they biologically possessed the ideal nimble fingers essential for it. This essentialization and feminization of plucking work devalued female labour, and legitimized the hierarchical/patriarchal authority and wage structure.

Contemporary visual representations of tea-plucking show the dominance of such perceptions in the colonial capitalist imagination. These images unabashedly celebrate the 'joy' of plucking tea-leaves by creating an illusion of it being as simple/pleasurable as picking flowers in a garden and therefore ideal for women. Apart from the romanticization/feminization of work, the sexualization of female labour in some of these images, i.e. constituting the work in terms of a gendered social identity, indicates the marginalization of the female labourer's position in the plantation work/life hierarchy.[48] Such images were particularly influential in conditioning the perceptions about life and work on the Indian plantations in the metropolitan imagination, and became recurrent themes in tea advertisements.[49]

In contrast to this romantic perception/construction of tea-plucking and women's work, the actual nature of the work becomes evident in practice (see song 2). The everyday grind of work in heat and sweat (*tipiki tipki parhe gham*) had to be endured because of the necessity to make a living (song 3). This intensity of work (*kam kam*) was driven by threats and systematic physical disciplining by the authorities, i.e. the manager–native assistant–overseer (*sahab–babu–sardar*, as in song 4).

Deception of Recruiters and Fear of Assam

The *dukh* and *taklif* in the tea gardens, evocatively pictured in these songs, are premised on a narrative strategy where the path to the sites of 'oppression' was induced at some stage due to the deception (*phanki*) of the recruiter (Shyam/Jaduram) who lured them to contract (*paka khata*) and facilitated their passage to Assam in the first place.[50] In the anecdotes, stories and experiences about Assam's tea-garden recruitment, deception (*phanki*) and the act of luring (*phuslao*) figure prominently when characterizing the practices of the recruiter.[51]

A strict distinction between the colonial and planter discourses within the practices of the recruiters, i.e. the professional (*arkatti*) indulging in corrupt practices and the non-professional (*sardar*) working through familial and kin networks, is not sustained in these narratives. While the *arkatti* had earned a 'historical' reputation of fear and hatred built on indiscriminate *phankis* and *phuslao*-ing compounded with physical threat, kidnapping and other abuses, the *sardar* too aroused hardly any real confidence and there was a persistent feeling that he always spoke with a 'purpose'.[52] The exaggerations of the *sardar*, as narrated by many returnees, only confirmed that perception. In effect, fixing the identity of Shyam and Jaduram with absolute certainty in these narratives, as being an *arkatti* or a *sardar*, could be a futile exercise.

Apart from the deceptions and exaggerations of the recruiters, the lurking threats of being kidnapped by them elicited extreme 'pre-emptive' measures. There were stories from the district of Sambalpur (Orissa) of families sleeping tied together with a rope to prevent the recruiters from 'carrying them off'.[53] Also, unwilling/kidnapped recruits were reported to have jumped off moving trains to liberate themselves from the clutches of their recruiter/abductor.[54] Such 'extraordinary' responses starkly underlined a deep sense of desperation in face of rampantly abusive recruitment practices, and further accentuated the aversion against Assam recruitment and the 'oppressive' *cha-bagaan*. The fear of the Assam recruiter, remarked a magistrate of Hazaribagh district (Chhota Nagpur), was so acute that people became apprehensive of even visiting their *haats* and *bazaars*. He compared the paranoia to the 'days of *thugee*' when there was such 'widespread fear of travelling'.[55] Late nineteenth-century India was gripped with this deepening concern over the threat/idea of being taken to the tea garden. The already cited instances of workers from the Duars tea gardens, the upcountry labourers working on railway extensions in Assam and the Gandas lodged in Sambalpur prison who articulated their deep reservations regarding going to the tea gardens, becomes intelligible in this light. Three other cases can be cited in this regard.

A 'widespread' fear raged in the tribal districts of Bengal in the 1880s, during the enumerative drives of the colonial census. The numbering of people, according to some rumours in circulation, was merely a 'preparatory stage' for wholesale deportation of women to work as tea pluckers on the Assam tea gardens.[56] The perceived threat of being taken to Assam in large numbers and the appreciation of the participation of the colonial state in that process were also informed by the 'gendered' nature of that demand. In very particular ways the 'rumour' grasped the grammar of Assam recruitment during the period, whereby the colonial state was 'organizing' and 'encouraging' large-scale emigration, and the tea planters were stepping up the demands for workers in general and women workers in particular to rectify the 'sexual imbalance' of the workforce.[57]

Again in the late 1890s, a district commissioner of Chhota Nagpur (Chaibassa) was unsuccessful in getting hold of anyone to draw his *pankha* (fan) during a stopover at a local railway station. An individual who finally offered his services after much persuasion refused to wait for payment. On being asked to explain his strange action, he said that 'the *sarkar* would *chalan* him to Assam'.[58]

Invocation of the 'Assam bogey' sometimes became part of a larger political strategy to 'mobilize' popular support, as evident during the *Swadeshi* activity in the early twentieth century. Addressing a peasant gathering in rural Bengal, some local politicians hinted at the ulterior motive of the British government in introducing 'Assam laws' to take over their lands and transport a large number of them to the tea gardens to serve as *coolies*.[59] Raising the latent concerns of a population extremely wary of being 'recruited' for Assam, the choice offered to them was clear: of either waiting to become *coolies* of colonial plantations or joining the struggle for becoming citizens of an emerging nation.[60]

The idea and practice of recruitment for the tea gardens registered in other complicated ways among the migrating sections of society. Selling came to be synonymously used for Assam recruitment is some regions. Recruiting was called 'selling' by the people; it was looked upon as being sold into slavery. Suppose that a young woman wishes to go to Assam and I produce her father and prove by two witnesses that he is her father and he gives his consent to emigrating, when he goes back to his village he will be reproached by everyone for having 'sold' his daughter.[61]

Many other accounts related this 'loss of respectability' and the general disapproval of the community.[62] In some regions it was seen as a prelude to bondage.[63] In the *Mundari* language, the word *chalan* came to simultaneously signify the act of being taken to a depot (to be recruited for Assam) and being imprisoned.[64] There was an unmistakeable connection between the contract and the condition of being bound (to Assam) in the Chhota Nagpur region; which was one of the oldest migrating regions for the Assam *cha-bagaan*. The refusal of the Chhota Nagpuri labourers of Duars tea garden was on the ground that it was a place of agreement/contract (*agreement ka jagah*). In the district of Ranchi (Chhota Nagpur), the local police cited 'popular' reluctance to be hired as constables because the obligatory three-year contract made the people 'suspicious', as it was strikingly reminiscent of the Assam contract.[65]

The 'Choice' of Assam[66]

The notions about migration to and work on the Assam *cha-bagaan* were not always conditioned in 'isolation', but also framed through changing and emerging possibilities for employment and earning available near 'home' and at a 'distance'.[67] Chhota Nagpur, the primary recruiting ground for the tea gardens, witnessed a particular trend of some migrant streams moving towards the tea plantations of Duars (Bengal) in the last decades of the nineteenth century.[68] This could be attributed to the nature of the labour demand in Duars, where people would leave after the harvest to return in the rainy season after earning some money.[69] The 'seasonal' nature of migration allowed some individuals to participate in agricultural activity and accommodate wage-work on the tea plantations in the non-agricultural season.[70] Such 'other' opportunities of work in tea gardens created a comparative impression of the two work-sites. A local labour agent from Chhota Nagpur said that when 'you mention "Assam" to a villager it conveys the idea of hardship (*dukh*) . . . the Duars have no such name'.[71] Such a 'favourable' idea about Duars was articulated by a missionary who said that there was a strong opinion that in Duars they could stay 'as long as they like' and, further, 'one can go to another garden if they wish to'.[72] Such a view was also narrated by another missionary who said that Assam was not as healthy as Duars and that they are 'better treated on the Duars garden'.[73]

The choice of Duars plantations, as apparently expressed by the people of the region, cannot be simply read through the dichotomy of freedom (Duars) and unfreedom (Assam), as the plantation labour regime of Duars was also characterized by various excesses, coercion and strategies of immobilization. Such dichotomies simplify the fluidity with which and complexities in which migrating decisions were made. The difficulties induced by the Assam labour regime of contract(s) and the abusive practices of recruitment to sustain it more seriously threatened the conduct of individual and social life, and generated a comparatively 'favourable' notion about the Duars plantations. The *dukh* of Assam was greater than the *dukh* of Duars. Such choices did not exclude Assam as a region. A labour agent in Calcutta summed up this sentiment:

> In a few cases I have offered *coolies* a choice between the Assam Railway and Trading Company's one-year contract for its coal mines with Rs 7 wage and a four year contract on Rs 5 on a teagarden. The *coolies* invariably chose the former, and I understood that the choice was determined as much by the shorter term as by the higher wage.[74]

Conclusions

The 'popular' construction of the *cha-bagaan* was premised on an 'awareness' of the plantation system in the recruiting regions, stemming from personal/familiar experiences and wider circulation of information through rumours, stories and anecdotes about Assam. This again alludes to the ways in which the *cha-bagaan* was comprehended and 'negotiated' in the recruiting regions – where the strategies and practices mobilized in the production of *coolies* (for the tea gardens) came to be perceived as disruptive, excessive and unreasonable, engendering various anxieties. Such negotiations did not necessarily imply that the exploitative practices and abuses integral to the 'free' labour system were collectively 'resisted' and eliminated, or that 'voluntary' migration to the Assam tea garden completely ceased over time. It rather underlines the ignorance and gullibility of the social groups migrating to Assam, emphasizing how 'knowledge' of recruitment practices, conditions of life and the nature of work in the plantations, were registered and articulated in the context of their lived realities.

Notes

1 H. Grant, Tea Manager, Cachar, in *Proceedings of Assam Labour Enquiry Committee in the Recruiting and Labour Districts* (1906), Calcutta: 148.

2 Ibid.

3 J.M. Casey, Tea District Labour Supply Association Agent, Sambalpur, ibid.: 37–38.

4 The 1906 Enquiry Committee found a widespread sentiment of unpopularity associated with Assam in the different recruiting districts. A construction engineer from Ranchi (Chhota Nagpur) opined that it was a way of frightening a person to say that he could be taken to a tea garden. This proverbial 'bad name' of Assam was noted by an English recruiting agent from Purulia. Another contractor from Kharagpur (Bengal) felt that any kind of emigration to Assam seemed unpopular, which was very similar to the opinion held by a missionary from Sambalpur (Orissa). The District Commissioner of Raipur (Central Provinces) mentioned that the idea of going to Assam was 'something like being transported'. Ibid.: 18, 24, 45, 48, 81.

5 In light of the impending famine of Bengal in the mid-1870s, in a lecture delivered before the Society of Arts, the speaker strongly recommended 'that the populous tracts visited or threatened by distress, unemployed labourers may emigrate to places where food is in comparative plenty . . . such as tea districts, the Doars, the provinces of Assam'. One of the main objectives of 'free recruiting' of the early 1870s was to tap into this famine-distressed population in regions of Bengal and Bihar. In November and December 1873, several attempts were made by the local government in the districts of Saran and Tirhoot to encourage distressed families to go to Assam. This did not yield very positive results. Writing in the late 1880s, the Secretary to

the Anglo-Indian Evangelization Society stressed that 'the overcrowded districts in Bengal and elsewhere . . . should be encouraged and helped to emigrate to Assam, where they might readily find lucrative and easy employment'. A 1901 issue of the journal *Empire Review* stated that the 'Assam system has been beneficial to the Central Provinces, from the most famine-stricken portions of which, and from the poorest parts of Bengal, the Assam tea gardens are chiefly recruited'. Frere (1874): 79; *Hansard's Parliamentary Debates*, 11 February–4 March 1890: 1635–36; *The Empire Review*, Vol. 2 (7), August 1901: 471. Also see Baildon (1882): 222–23.

[6] One of the earliest systematic attempts was a deputation of residents of Santhal Parganas (Chhota Nagpur region) being sent to Assam tea gardens under the supervision of colonial officials and local planters to get first-hand information of the conditions of work and life. The deputation interviewed around 200 *coolies* from twenty-seven gardens in Assam Valley. Some of the questions posed to the workers were: 1. How is the country; 2. How is the soil; 3. How is the water; 4. Scale of daily work, length and breadth; 5. Rate of monthly wages for daily labour; 6. Rate of wages for contract work excepting Sundays; 7. Gardens whose *coolies* are in good condition; 8. Gardens whose *coolies* are not in good condition. The visit did not leave a good impression on the observers and it was advised by some colonial officials and the chairman of the Indian Tea Association (James Buckhingham) that their report be kept confidential. See Letter from G. Toynbee, Commissioner Bhagalpur Division to Secretary of Bengal, General Department, dated 14 July 1894, *Report of the Deputation on the Conditions of Coolies in Assam Gardens*, Revenue and Agriculture, Emigration B, Nos. 1–4, National Archives of India (henceforth NAI).

[7] Between 1871 and 1901, around 1,180,000 individuals moved to Assam from the different districts. 'Special Causes of Mortality of Immigrant Coolies, 1891–1901', in *Proceedings of Assam Labour Enquiry Committee in the Recruiting and Labour Districts* (1906): 235; Tinker (1974): 50.

[8] S. Bhattacharya (1998); S. Bhattacharya (2007): 11.

[9] The idea and concern of non-return was very evident in the interviews conducted by the 1906 Committee in the recruiting districts. This was a process which started from the early phase of Assam migration. For instance, in the late 1860s, around ten thousand people left for Assam tea gardens from Midnapur district in Bengal and they as 'a rule did not return'. *Proceedings of Assam Labour Enquiry Committee in the Recruiting and Labour Districts* (1906): 29, 45, 48, 52, 57, 58, 60; Hunter (1876): 52.

[10] Saurabh Dube makes a distinction between seasonal migration and long-term migration in Chhattisgarh. Assam migration was perceived as if the individual has 'passed beyond their kin'. S. Dube (1998): 256.

[11] *Report on the Conditions of Teagarden Labour in the Duars of Bengal, in Madras and in Ceylon.* The position at the turn of century was stated by the Secretary of State for India (George Hamilton) when he categorically suggested that 'the contracts entered into by emigrants to Assam have never included any stipulation for repatriation, and none is considered necessary'. *House of Commons Debates*, 23 July 1903, Vol. 126, c. 56.

[12] *Proceedings of Assam Labour Enquiry Committee in the Recruiting and Labour Districts* (1906): 93.

[13] Ibid.: 81.

[14] The anxieties of large-scale migration from Orissa crystallized in a belief that the god of wind blew pieces of bones of those who died in Assam back to their villages. These pieces of bones took the form of whirlwinds which blew away house-tops and anyone encountering them would fall ill. V. Elwin, *The Religion of an Indian Tribe*, New York, 1955, as cited in B. Pati (2001): 9.

[15] In 1901, almost twelve thousand persons from Sambalpur were enumerated on

Assam tea gardens, a process greatly facilitated by the completion of the Bengal–Nagpur railway line. *Proceedings of Assam Labour Enquiry Committee in the Recruiting and Labour Districts* (1906): 37–38; O'Malley (2007): 54.

[16] A 'version' of this rumour can be traced during the plague panic in the late 1890s, among the mill workers of Bombay. Here it was believed that colonial officials were getting hold of men and boys, hanging them head downwards over a slow fire and preparing a medicine drawn from the head. Another version is found in the 'vampire stories' from East and Central Africa which narrate the capture of humans by the agents of colonialism to be hung upside down, their throats cut and the blood drained into buckets. See Arnold (1988): 407; White (2000).

[17] Two versions of this rumour were narrated. See *Proceedings of Assam Labour Enquiry Committee in the Recruiting and Labour Districts* (1906): 55 and 57.

[18] Ibid.: 58.

[19] The expressions *dukh* and *taklif* were apparently used by individuals who had spent time in Assam to narrate the circumstances of work and life there. Common cultural codes of pain and anxiety were invoked to communicate a common sense of despair. Ibid.: 32 and 74.

[20] The notion that Assam had bad water was the unanimous opinion of 200-odd workers interviewed by the Santhali deputation of 1894. One member of the deputation, Sidhanta Desmanjhi, gave a reason for this when he noted that in Assam people drank well-water whereas back home they preferred the water of river or streams. Ibid.: 32; translation of Deputation's Report, Revenue and Agriculture, Emigration B, nos. 1–4, NAI.

[21] *Proceedings of Assam Labour Enquiry Committee in the Recruiting and Labour Districts* (1906): 32, 34, 64–65.

[22] Ibid.: 64, 66.

[23] Marina Carter cites instances of high-caste emigrants refusing cooked food on board steamers to Mauritius. They were given 'dry rations' instead. Carter (1995): 102; Alavi (1995).

[24] Burrows (1915): 164.

[25] *Proceedings of Assam Labour Enquiry Committee in the Recruiting and Labour Districts* (1906): 64.

[26] Ibid.: 87.

[27] A planter's composition titled 'The Teahouse Bloke' is suggestive in this regard: 'The Factory starts at 4 a.m., Oh Lord! Why ever did I come to this wretched job in tea . . . I have just to carry on and work right up to 10, and start the morning after, at 3 a.m. again'. Fraser (1935); Hanley (1928): 95.

[28] An Assam planter from the early twentieth century referred to 'Deundi Time' – where he operated the clocks of the garden (Deundi) one hour ahead of the rest of the tea districts, 'so that the labour force could work their first hour in the cooler period of the day, before other garden's labour had roused themselves from bed'. Fraser (1935). Also see Jain and Reddock (eds.) (1998): 127; Behal (2006): 159.

[29] *Proceedings of Assam Labour Enquiry Committee in the Recruiting and Labour Districts* (1906): 22 and 64.

[30] Ibid.: 58.

[31] A contractor from Jubbulpore mentioned that some returnees reported that the hoeing tasks on the garden – 20 to 25 *nals* of 12 feet – are excessive. Ibid.: 57.

[32] Ibid.: 18.

[33] In Santhali language the origins of the word *dalil*, which connoted extra work as punishment, was traced to the tea gardens. Ibid.: 57; Campbell (1899): 117.

[34] The members of the deputation learnt that if the daily work was not done, a day's wage (25 *annas*) was deducted. *Proceedings of Assam Labour Enquiry Committee in the Recruiting and Labour Districts* (1906): 57, 87.

[35] Ibid.: 69.

[36] Ibid.: 64 and 68. Practices of prolonging the term of agreement (as reported by officers in recruiting districts) by addition of *kuthia* days, or periods of absence, was taken by Chhota Nagpuri and Santhali workers as a breach of faith.

[37] A Chief Commissioner of Province demonstrated that the average wages paid in 1900 (including benefits and overtime) were substantially less than what was prescribed by the inaugural Contract Act (1865). The statutory wage at that point (Rs 5) was in fact half of what the daily labourer earned in Assam. Again, between the 1870s and 1890s, wages for tasks on tea gardens generally increased from around 25 to 30 per cent. Cotton (1911): 261–62; Crole (1897): 49. Also see Behal (2003).

[38] *Proceedings of Assam Labour Enquiry Committee in the Recruiting and Labour Districts* (1906): 69.

[39] Ibid.: 76.

[40] The members of the Santhali deputation noticed a new woman worker being beaten by the assistant manager because she plucked four leaves instead of three. Ibid.: 87, 64, 17.

[41] Ibid.: 13, 87, 64.

[42] This was again brought up by the Santhal deputation where they were required to work within six days of birth. Ibid.: 64.

[43] The missionary Dowding observed that contracts were cancelled when it was 'more profitable to send them home than treat them and give subsistence allowance'. A transport fund which was instituted in the 1870s for such purposes was said to be very miniscule, and could repatriate only a very limited number of *coolies*. Dowding (1894): 32.

[44] *Proceedings of Assam Labour Enquiry Committee in the Recruiting and Labour Districts* (1906): 74, 29.

[45] Chattopadhyaya (1901); Bidyaratna (1888).

[46] The *Jhumur* songs represented here are compiled from varied sources, particularly drawn from Sengupta and Sharma (1990): 131–42; Mahato (1990): 214–26; and Mahato and Mahato (2007): 36–47. Some of these songs were collected by Kali Dasgupta (1926–2005) – a singer and folk song collector – and later released as an audio volume. See *Folk Songs of North-East India*, Calcutta, 2003.

[47] During a tour of famine-affected Bilaspur in the late 1890s, an 'invariable answer given in reply to the question "Where is your husband" was, "He has gone to Assam to the gardens".' On further enquiries he learnt that the civil doctor of the station was passing around 1,600 people per week (for Assam). Merewether (1898): 130–31; *Resolution on Surgeon-Major Campbell's Report on the Arrangements for Transit of Emigrants to Assam*, Revenue and Agriculture, Emigration A, June 1897, NAI.

[48] For a detailed discussion and criticism, see P. Chatterjee (2002): 112–13.

[49] Ramamurthy (2003), especially the section, 'The Orient as female and the representation of the Tamil woman tea picker' (pp. 119–25).

[50] Bandyopadhyaya (1897).

[51] The practices of deception were associated with recruiters for other destinations. The Surinam *arkattis* allegedly called it as *Sri Ram* (Lord Ram) or *srinam* ('sublime name'), thus suggesting that the trip was in honour of the almighty. Hoefte (1998): 36; Choenni (2009): 112.

[52] *Proceedings of Assam Labour Enquiry Committee in the Recruiting and Labour Districts* (1906): 54.

[53] Ibid.: 89 and 61.

[54] Ibid.: 61.

[55] Behal and Mohapatra (1992): 155.

[56] The men were believed to be sent to Afghanistan as camp-followers of the British

army. There were several census-induced fears expressed in north Bihar during the census operations of men being taken to foreign countries, often Afghanistan. See *New York Times*, 1 June 1890; Yang (1987.

57 The threat of the single woman being decoyed to the Assam *cha-bagaan* became a powerful social anxiety provoking various responses in the late nineteenth century. See S. Sen (2002); S. Sen (2004); S. Sen (1996).

58 Hoffman's Note, Emigration Department, Financial Branch, Nos. 62–128, April 1899, West Bengal State Archives (henceforth WBSA), cited in Das Gupta (2009).

59 S. Bandhopadhya (1997): 68.

60 Such a rhethoric becomes even more articulate in the case of Assam plantations in the 1920s.

61 *Proceedings of Assam Labour Enquiry Committee in the Recruiting and Labour Districts* (1906): 44.

62 Ibid.: 15, 17, 75, 44.

63 Ibid.: 70, 18.

64 *Mundari–English Dictionary*, p. 207. Depots are 'unpopular as being synonymous with Assam', as stated by European Labour Agent, No. 25, *Proceedings of Assam Labour Enquiry Committee in the Recruiting and Labour Districts* (1906): 21.

65 No. 15, *Proceedings of Assam Labour Enquiry Committee in the Recruiting and Labour Districts* (1906): 12; and No. 17, ibid.: 20.

66 Assistant Comissioner, Bilaspur, No. 65, ibid.: 54.

67 R. Das Gupta (1976).

68 Between 1880–1900, around 46 per cent of the recruits came from Chhota Nagpur. See Behal and Mohapatra (1992): 153.

69 *Proceedings of Assam Labour Enquiry Committee in the Recruiting and Labour Districts* (1906): 14.

70 *Dufferin Report*, No. 351R, Ranchi, 31 May 1888. Emigration to Assam was of a more permanent nature, but from the Duars about 10,000 people returned every year, bringing back a saving of approximately one lakh rupees.

71 *Proceedings of Assam Labour Enquiry Committee in the Recruiting and Labour Districts* (1906): 30.

72 Ibid.: 13.

73 Ibid.: 14.

74 Ibid.: 89.

References

Alavi, S. (1995), *The Sepoys and the Company*, New Delhi: Oxford University Press.

Arnold, David (1988), 'Touching the Body: Perspectives on the Indian Plague', in R. Guha and G. Spivak (eds.), *Selected Subaltern Studies*, New York: Oxford University Press, 1988.

Baildon, S. (1882), *Tea Industry in India,* London.

Bandhopadhyay, S. (1997), *Caste, Protest and Identity in Colonial India*, Richmond, Surrey: Curzon Press.

Bandyopadhyaya, Harilala (1897), *Arkati: A Drama on the Methods by which Coolies are Recruited for Work in Foreign Countries*, Calcutta.

Behal, R.P. (2003), *Wage Structure and Labour: Assam Valley Plantations, 1900–1947*, Noida: V.V. Giri National Labour Institute.

——— (2006), 'Power Structure, Discipline, and Labour in Assam Tea Plantations under Colonial Rule', in R. Behal and M. van der Linden (eds.), *Coolies, Capital and Colonialism: Studies in India Labour History*, New Delhi.

Behal, R.P. and P.P. Mohapatra (1992), 'Tea and Money versus Human Life: The Rise and Fall of the Indenture System in the Assam Tea Plantations, 1840–1908', in *Plantations, Proletarians and Peasants in Colonial Asia*, special issue, *Journal of Peasant Studies,* Vol. 19 (3 and 4).

Bhattacharya, S. (1998), 'The Labouring Poor and their Notion of Poverty: Late Nineteenth and Early Twentieth Century Bengal', Working Paper No. 1, Labour History Series, Noida: V. V. Giri National Labour Institute.

——— (2007), 'Introduction', in R.P. Behal and M. Linden (eds.), *India's Labouring Poor: Historical Studies, c. 1600–c. 2000,* New Delhi: Cambridge University Press India.

Bidyaratna, Ramakumara (1888), *Kuli Kahini* (*Sketches from Coolie Life*), Calcutta.

Burrows, Lionel (1915), *Ho grammar, With Vocabulary*, Calcutta.

Campbell, A. (1899), *A Santali-English Dictionary*, Manbhum.

Carter, Marina (1995), *Servants, Sirdars and Settlers: Indians in Mauritius, 1834–1874*, New Delhi: Oxford University Press.

Chatterjee, P. (2002), *Time for Tea: Women, Labour and Post/Colonial Politics on an Indian Plantation*, Durham: Duke University Press.

Chattopadhyaya, Yogendranatha (1901), *Cha-kulir atmakahini* (*The Experiences of a Coolie in a Teagarden in Assam: A Tale Founded on Fact*), Calcutta.

Cotton, Henry (1911), *India and Home Memories*, London.

Crole, D. (1897), *Tea: A text book of tea planting and manufacture*, London. Choenni, C.E.S. (2009), 'From Bharat to Sri Ram Desh: The Emigration of Indian Indentured Labourers to Surinam', in R. Rai and P. Reeves (eds.), *The South Asian Diaspora: Transnational Networks and Changing* Identities, London: Routledge.

Das Gupta, I.S. (2009), 'Agrarian Expansion under Colonial Rule and its Impact on a Tribal Economy', in E. Basile and I. Mukhopadhyaya (eds.) *The Changing Identity of Rural India,* New Delhi, London and New York: Anthem Press.

Das Gupta, Ranajit (1976), 'Factory Labour in Eastern India: Sources of Supply, 1855–1946: Some Preliminary Findings', *Indian Economic and Social History Review*, Vol. 13 (3).

Dasgupta, Kali (2003), *Folk Songs of North-East India*, Calcutta, 2003.

Dowding, C. (1894), *Tea Garden Coolies in Assam*, Calcutta.

Dube, S. (1998), *Untouchable Pasts: Religion, Identity, and Power among a Central Indian Community, 1780–1950*, Albany: State University of New York Press.

Elwin, V. (1955), *The Religion of an Indian Tribe*, New York.

Fraser, W.M. (1935), *The Recollections of a Tea Planter*, London.

Frere (1874), *On the Impending Bengal Famine: How it Will be Met and How to Prevent Future Famines in India*, London.

Hanley, M.P. (1928), *Tales and Songs on an Assam Teagarden*, Calcutta.

Hoefte, Rosemarijn (1998), *In Place of Slavery: A Social History of British Indian and Javanese Labourers in Suriname*, Gainsville: University Press of Florida.

House of Commons Debates (1903), Vol. 126, 23 July.

Hunter, W.W. (1876), *Statistical Account of Bengal, Districts of Midnapur and Hugli*, Vol. III, London.

Jain, S. and R. Reddock (eds.) (1998), *Women Plantation Workers: International Experiences,* Oxford: Berg.

Mahato, P.P. (1990), 'World View of the Assam Teagarden Labourers from Jharkhand', in S. Karotemprel and B.D. Roy (eds.), *Teagarden Labourers of North East India*, Shillong: Vendrame Institute, 1990: 214–26.

Mahato, P.P. and K.C. Mahato (2007), 'The Collective Wisdom and Excellences Related to World Views on Forest, Biodiversity and Nature–Man–Spirit Complex of the Indigenous People of Eastern India', in C.K. Paty (ed.), *Forest, Government and Tribe*, New Delhi: Concept Publishing Company: 36–47.

Merewether, F.H.S. (1898), *A Tour through the Famine District of India*, London.

O'Malley, L.S.S. (2007), *Bengal District Gazetteers: Sambalpur*, reprint, New Delhi: Concept Publishing Company.

Pati, B. (2001), *Situating Social History: Orissa, 1800–1997*, New Delhi: Orient Longman.

Proceedings of Assam Labour Enquiry Committee in the Recruiting and Labour Districts (1906), Calcutta.

Ramamurthy, A. (2003), *Imperial Persuaders: Images of Africa and Asia in British Advertising*, Manchester.

Report of the Deputation on the Conditions of Coolies in Assam Gardens (1894), Revenue and Agriculture, Emigration B, Nos. 1–4, National Archives of India (NAI).

Sen, S. (1996), 'Unsettling the Household: Act VI (of 1901) and the Regulation of Women Migrants in Colonial Bengal', *International Review of Social* History, Vol. 41, Supplement S4: 135–56.

——— (2002), 'Questions of Consent: Women's Recruitment for Assam Tea Gardens, 1859–1900', *Studies in History*, Vol. 18 (2).

——— (2004), '"Without his consent?": Marriage and Women's Migration in Colonial India', *International Labour and Working-Class History*, Vol. 65, Spring: 77–104.

Sengupta, S. and J.L. Sharma (1990), 'Jhumur Folksongs and Dances of Teagarden Labourers of Assam', in S. Karotemprel and B.D. Roy (eds.), *Teagarden Labourers of North East India*, Shillong: Vendrame Institute: 131–42.

Tinker, H. (1974), *A New System of Slavery: The Export of Indian Indentured Labour Overseas, 1830–1920*, London: Oxford University Press.

White, L. (2000), *Speaking with Vampires: Rumor and History in Colonial Africa*, Berkeley: University of California Press.

Yang, A. (1987), 'A Conservation of Rumours: The Language of Popular "Mentalities" in Late Nineteenth-Century Colonial India', *Journal of Social History*, Vol. 20 (3): 485–505.

Brazilian Working-Class Associations and the Perception of Work

1870–1920

Claudio H.M. Batalha

A French traveller to Brazil in the mid-nineteenth century, while pointing to the similarity between European and Brazilian high society when it came to the working classes, wrote:

> Nothing, on the other hand, differs as much from our working class as Brazilian workers, especially when they belong to the white race. Used to having blacks under their orders and leaving to them the execution of the most crude tasks, they are so self-conscious of the dignity of mastery, that if you send for a cabinetmaker to fix a piece of furniture or a lock-smith to open a lock, he will not carry his own tools, and will present himself at your home wearing a black tailcoat and sometimes a cocked hat. He will be followed by one or often two slaves, charged of carrying his tools and of accomplishing, under the supervision of the master, the task you sent for him to do.[1]

A very similar account can be found in John Luccock, many years earlier:

> It was necessary to open a lock, of which I had lost the key; and the skill requisite to pick it was so rare, that the Master and the Waiter of the Hotel, where I was lodged, were greatly perplexed with my inquiries, at what place it was to be found. At length they advised me to apply to an English carpenter, who had been settled in Rio about two years, and employed several men, one of whom he requested to go with me, – for the masters did not venture to command, – assuring that the man would execute what I wanted. He detained me a long time, but to compensate for the delay, made his appearance at last in full dress, with a cocked hat, shoe and knee buckles, and other corresponding paraphernalia. At the door of the house he still loitered, wishing to hire some black man to carry his hammer, chisel, and another small instrument. I suggested that they were light, and proposed to carry a part, or the whole, of them myself; but this would have been as great a practical solecism as using his own hands. The gentleman waited

> patiently, until a negro appeared; then made his bargain, and proceeded in due state, followed by his temporary servant. The task was soon finished, by breaking the lock, instead of picking it; when the man of importance, making me a profound bow, stalked off with his follower.[2]

Despite the obvious differences both accounts have much in common, and we cannot rule out that the French author was inspired by the preceding British anecdote. It is highly unlikely that by the second half of the 1850s (the first edition of the book is apparently from 1859 and the text contains references up to 1854) anybody would still be wearing a cocked hat. Furthermore, it is uncertain if a French traveller under the initials N.X. ever existed or laid foot in Brazil. From many aspects the book seems to be a collection of excerpts from various travellers' accounts covering a large period of time. In some cases authors and titles are quoted, especially those that are older or most likely to be known by the French public, such as Jean de Lery and Ferdinand Denis. Of course, this book could entail a methodological discussion on the need for greater caution by historians using travel narratives as sources, but that is not the issue here. The question is if the situation described in the passage I have quoted, of slaves working for a craftsman, was still plausible by the late 1850s.

Zephyr Frank's study of the barber José Antonio Dutra, a former slave who by the time of his death in 1849 owned thirteen slaves, shows that slave property was practically the only means of acquiring wealth for small entrepreneurs.[3] Hence slaves working for artisans or craftsmen as hired slaves on a daily basis, or as property, were a common scene in Rio de Janeiro during the first half of the nineteenth century. Skilled slaves represented the elite of slavery and a sure source of income to their masters. Protests of white free men against the acceptance of slaves in the apprenticeship of crafts had no effect. Besides the presence of slaves in skilled trades, they were also present in a wide range of urban occupations such as domestic service, workshops and factories, i.e. both private and state property.[4]

In 1850, the Atlantic slave trade was suppressed due to British pressure, and although illegal trade persisted, the offer of new hands was incapable of meeting the growing demand as coffee production expanded in southeastern Brazil. As prices rose in the following years, slave property became less accessible for artisans and small shop-owners. Urban slavery saw a sharp decline in the second half of the nineteenth century. This does not mean that the scenes described by the travel narratives above disappeared from one day to another, but that they became less common in the last decades of slavery (abolished in 1888).

> Whereas Dutra's world of the 1840s had seen the apogee of slavery in Rio de Janeiro, in terms of the value of slaves relative to other assets and in

> terms of the ratio of slaves to the free population, the 1870s saw the retreat and the 1880s saw the complete unravelling of the institution. In the early 1870s, slave wealth accounted for less than 10 per cent of net wealth, down from a high of 17 per cent in the late 1840s. By the late 1880s, slaves made up less than 10 per cent of the total wealth. The slaves that remained were likely to be owned by the wealthy, not the middle groups, and to labour in domestic service or reside outside of the city on a city dweller's rural estate.[5]

In the city of Rio de Janeiro the total number of slaves went down from an estimated 100,000 in 1864 to 7,488 in 1887, one year before abolition.[6] According to the official statistics, in the Census of 1849 slaves were 38 per cent of the population of Brazil's capital, while in the 1872 Census they represented 20 per cent.[7]

During most of the nineteenth century, free craftsmen – whether white or not – had to deal with the competition of skilled slaves, could not count on guilds (forbidden by the 1824 Constitution) to assure control over the market or over apprenticeship, and, furthermore, lived in a society in which manual labour was viewed with contempt. The perception that hard work was not intended for free men had been long before incorporated into the Portuguese language through expressions such as 'work as a moor', which signified working as hard as a black or as a slave. In both the aforementioned travellers' accounts craftsmen seemed to think it was incompatible with their status to be seen carrying their tools. If, at first, status and colour were closely associated, as with Dutra himself, many craftsmen and shop-owners had been former slaves, since skilled slaves were among those who could more easily obtain resources to buy their freedom. With a growing number among the free population being composed of blacks and mulattos, legal status prevailed over colour.

By the 1830s, in older urban centres such as Recife, Salvador and Rio de Janeiro where artisans' corporations previously existed, mutual aid societies uniting craftsmen began to be formed. The 1824 Constitution, although forbidding corporate organizations and strikes in the same spirit as the French 1791 Le Chapelier Law and various British measures which culminated in the 1799–1800 Combination Acts, did not ban the lay brotherhoods dedicated to patron saints of the crafts. These brotherhoods coexisted with the corporations, and thus, in some measure, craftsmen's organizations persisted. Nonetheless, lay brotherhoods were dedicated mostly to religious matters and to philanthropy, not being able to assume entirely the activities performed by corporations. In this way self-help societies seemed to be the only legal way to ensure in a disguised manner the persistence of craft organization, particularly seeking the control of craft apprenticeship.

Until very recently, the persistence of craft organization through mutual aid societies lacked substantial evidence. Historians like me who sustained this hypothesis have made use of certain aspects of the scarce written documents that survive to our day and were produced by these societies. It is particularly their statutes that have been used to try to demonstrate this theory.[8] According to this view, mutual aid societies, mostly composed of skilled manual workers, assured in some measure functions held previously by corporations, but also engaged in demands concerning pay and working hours which later on would be upheld by trade unions. Nevertheless the matter remained controversial, for a number of historians argued that rather than fronts for craft or class organization, mutual aid societies were no more than what they proclaimed to be, i.e. associations devoted to providing diverse modalities of help to their members.[9] This last group of historians also denied that craft-based mutual aid societies chronologically preceded the creation of labour unions, for according to them they were almost contemporaneous.

The main concern of this argument is to establish that mutual aid was clearly distinct from both craft corporations and labour unions. In fact, differently from cities with an older craft tradition, such as Recife, Salvador and Rio de Janeiro, mutual aid societies devoted to workers or based on craft began to be created in southern Brazil, in provinces such as São Paulo and Rio Grande do Sul, from the late 1870s onwards, while the first trade unions were created in the 1890s. In other words, mutual aid societies were created earlier than trade unions in those places, but with a shorter lapse of time as compared to places where the corporate tradition existed previously. In any case, the fact that certain types of mutual aid societies eventually accomplished tasks expected from trade unions did not imply that mutualism disappeared when trade unions were created.

A major contribution to this ongoing debate was Marcelo Mac Cord's Ph.D. thesis which uses as one of its main sources, the only known case of a mutual aid society whose records from the 1840s to the 1890s have survived. The society was composed mostly of craftsmen in the wood trades, such as carpenters and cabinetmakers, and was located in Recife (in the northeastern province of Pernambuco).[10] This study shows not only the close ties between a pre-existing lay brotherhood of Saint Joseph (patron saint of carpenters) and the mutual aid society founded in 1836, Sociedade das Artes Mecânicas e Liberais (Society of Mechanical and Liberal Arts), but also that under the cover of mutualism, the latter continued to perform the activities of a corporation, such as examining aspiring master craftsmen, forbidding journeymen to open shops, establishing fines for actions that did not comply with the norms established for the practice of the craftand exercising control over apprenticeship.[11] Of course, under Brazilian law, these activities were completely illegal and, for obvious reasons, did not appear in the public statutes of the society, yet it seems quite unlikely that for decades they could be kept secret. Therefore Marcelo Mac Cord concludes that for various reasons, i.e. the political ties the society developed and its weight in the construction market, local authorities chose to look the other way.

No society so openly sustained the re-establishment of a monopoly of the ancient craft corporations as did the Associação dos Artistas Brasileiros – Trabalho, União e Moralidade (Brazilian Craftsmen's Association – Labour, Union and Morality) based in Rio de Janeiro. Its statute of 1857 carried references that were vetoed when it was submitted to the Council of State for approval in 1861. To ensure that Brazilian free craftsmen had control of the labour market, it also proposed that slaves and foreigners should not be admitted to the crafts – proposals that the State Council ruled as illegal.[12] This association proved to be quite long-lived and was still in activity in 1920; again sustaining xenophobic proposals when it called for a meeting against the immigration of 'pernicious elements', referring to foreign anarchists.[13]

Another aspect that makes the case of the Recife Society of Mechanical and Liberal Arts especially interesting is that all its founders are described as being black or mulattos who were born in the province of Pernambuco. All these were free men at the time and it is not certain how many, if any, of them had been slaves in the past.[14] Many years later, in a photograph taken in 1880 in front of the School of Arts and Crafts that was created by the efforts of the society, its members, posing formally dressed for the occasion, were still composed of a vast majority of blacks and mulattos.[15] This was a demonstration that by then the society had earned the respectability and public recognition it had strived for.

In Salvador (province of Bahia), the first mutual aid society dedicated to craftsmen was the Sociedade dos Artífices da Bahia (Craftsmen's Society of Bahia) founded in 1832, having among its members mostly workers of the army and navy arsenals.[16] In Rio de Janeiro, the first society of the kind was probably Sociedade Auxiliadora das Artes Mecânicas e Liberais (Auxiliary Society for Mechanical and Liberal Arts) founded in 1835, followed by Sociedade Animadora da Corporação dos Ourives (Society for the Encouragement of the Goldsmiths' Corporation) in 1838. While the former was not dedicated to any particular trade and the only condition for membership was to practice a mechanical or liberal art, the latter established as a condition for membership to be in the craft or business of gold and silver handicrafts, or watch and clock-making.[17] Who should be admitted and who should not be admitted as a member of the associations became a crucial matter in the years to follow.

A typical example of the rules for admission can be found in the statute of a shipbuilders' mutual aid society created in 1856 in Rio de Janeiro:

Art. 1 – The Society is named Beneficente dos Artistas do Arsenal de Marinha da Corte and has an unlimited number of members.
Art. 2 – To become a member of the Society, it is necessary to.
§ 1 Be free and have a good reputation.
§ 2 Have an occupation in a Craft or Mechanical Art.
§ 3 Be no less than 16 years old, and no more than 50 years old
§ 4 Have perfect health.

Except for the age limits in this example, which could vary from one craft or industry to another, all the other conditions were very similar across various societies. Sometimes, being a freeman was considered a superfluous condition of admittance and thus would not figure in the statutes since only freemen had civil rights, among which the right to organize. Each time statutes that were ambiguous on this issue or openly admitted slave membership were presented to the authorities for approval, they were rejected. On the other hand, enjoying a good reputation, having a high moral reputation and so forth were conditions on which most, if not all, statutes insisted. This was an integral part of what in contemporary language was called the ennoblement of labour, part of the effort to rid manual labour of the stigmatization it suffered so as to present it as artistic, morally necessary and socially useful.

If no association could admit slaves, they could not legally adopt any condition of admittance containing restrictions of colour or race, although some of them tried to. In Rio de Janeiro, the Sociedade Protetora de Barbeiros e Cabelereiros (Barbers' and Hairdressers' Protective Society), founded in 1869, established in its statute that it was composed of an 'unlimited number of associates except those of black colour', which led the Council of State to suggest the suppression of the condition.[19] This condition of admittance seems particularly astonishing in a city where this craft was commonly practised by slaves and former slaves like Zephyr Frank's Dutra. However, this was not a unique case. In 1875, the Sociedade Beneficente dos Artistas de São Cristóvão (Beneficial Society of the Craftsmen of Saint Christopher), which organized workers most likely of Portuguese origin in a particular neighbourhood of Rio de Janeiro, submitted a statute to the Council of State which established in its fifth Article: 'Individuals of black colour, freed slaves of any colour, and those that are not included in the circumstances established by the paragraphs of Art. 3 cannot be admitted as members.'[20] The statute was approved by the Council of State without it being noticed that this membership restriction was clearly illegal. Only in 1878, when the society presented a new statute that still contained this restriction, did the Council of State issue a very harsh notice, establishing that if the society insisted on maintaining those 'impolitic and offensive' limitations, the statute could not be approved.[21]

Despite the continuation of corporate traditions in many mutual aid societies, and their efforts to control handicrafts, competition from skilled slaves and foreign goods, the lack of political and legal support for their claims, and, furthermore, the low prestige of manual labour in Brazilian society, led to the abandonment of corporative language in the public sphere. A process similar to what happened in France, according to William Sewell Jr., where corporate language gave way to a broader political language, can be observed in Brazil.[22] This can be noticed despite some major differences, for example, the absence of the experience of revolution, the existence of slavery (particularly of skilled slaves) and much less force of a corporative tradition that did not stretch back for centuries. In the last decades of the eighteenth century only some trades in Rio de Janeiro were organized in guilds or corporations, and even those which had their regulations and privileges assured by law usually did not manage to see those that challenged their trade monopoly punished.[23] In other words, even before their banning by the 1824 Constitution, craft corporations in Brazil never attained the prestige and power of their European counterparts.[24]

The policy of membership selection was one among other means by which skilled workers and their organizations publicized their conception of work. As we have seen, statutes could also contain conceptions about the control of the labour market and proposals against what they considered as unfair competition. Petitions, manifestos and leaflets, although more common after the establishment of the Republic in 1889, were some of the means used to raise the issue. In 1876, a hatters' association published a leaflet inviting 'national industrialists' to take a common stand with them for a protectionist industrial policy against foreign competition.[25] A much more ambitious proposal was contained in the 1885 manifesto of the Corpo Coletivo União Operária (Collective Corps Labour Union), which was addressed to the emperor Don Pedro II and was intended to stimulate national industry through prizes, no taxation on machinery imports, taxation of foreign goods, creation of a bank to supply industry with credit, establishment of occupational statistics, and so forth.[26] In many respects this labour union, created in March 1880, i.e. in the political turmoil that followed the Vintém Riot in Rio de Janeiro,[27] was very different from the other mutual aid associations of the time, in that it adopted a concept of class that was not restricted to the limits of trades, as well as a concept in which skilled and non-skilled workers were admitted. Its statute spoke of the 'interests of the working class'.[28] Furthermore, this union developed close ties with a number of outstanding middle-class abolitionists and republicans who composed a consultative council of the organization, which thus acquired a clear political feature.

Besides skilled workers' organizations and the change they sought to introduce in the knowledge of work, from the 1860s onwards an even more public means of raising this discussion appeared through the publication of periodicals which made this question their major subject. Beginning in 1862, Fernando Luiz Ferreira, a military engineer, published with the help of his three sons (all of them engineers), a paper under the title *O Artista* (*The Artist*),[29] dedicated to industry and especially to the arts. At first the paper was printed in Ferreira's home town, São Luiz (in the northern province of Maranhão), where it lasted for a year. In 1868–69 the publication was restarted, also in São Luiz. The following year it was moved to Rio de Janeiro where it lasted for yet another year. The editorial content of *O Artista* focused on two main issues: professional education for craftsmen as a means for their elevation as a class, and the need for political participation by craftsmen so they might be able to defend their interests.[30] Education – either professional or formal – was a major theme in the nineteenth-century discourse of workers, and was thought of as a sure way to obtain social recognition. In practically all workers' associations at least the intention of establishing libraries and courses can be found.

A number of other papers with similar intentions followed, but a mere look at their titles indicates that a broader conception of class began to prevail as we move to the end of the century: *O Proletario* (*The Proletarian*), 1877–1878; *O Trabalho* (*Labour*), 1879; *Gazeta dos Operarios* (*Workers' Gazette*), 1885. As craftsmen began to be replaced by working classes, proletarians, workers and finally the working class, it was less the public addressed by the discourse that changed, and more the concept of class that was transformed and widened. The world of organized labour was still, and would long remain, composed of skilled workers. Even when skill was no longer associated with independent artisans, it was still represented in pay, working and living conditions of the elite within the working class. The creation of labour unions did not bring great changes to this situation, and only the great strikes of 1917–19 would finally bring women and unskilled workers to organized labour. Thus, if the discourse by the end of the nineteenth century employed a widened concept of class, it would still take some time before this was really incorporated into practice.

In the beginning of the twentieth century, as trade unions became the dominant form of expression of working-class demands, the meaning of work had to be resignified. The understanding of who were the workers had been changing, but at the same time organized labour was mostly, as we have seen, composed of skilled workers. Thus, in 1907, a writer in a labour journal felt compelled to explain this to his readers:

> All comrades think that only craftsmen are workers, but not only shoemakers, tailors, stonemasons, carpenters, cabinetmakers, turners, blacksmiths, locksmiths, founders [are workers], therefore every person that says: I will

> work to eat, and eat to live (for his salary will not suffice for more), because all of those that say these words: I will work, is a worker.
>
> Not only the craftsman can be called a worker, but also the coachman, the wagon driver, the porter and even the street sweeper are workers and of the most exploited, as these that work day and night for a miserly salary below their needs.[31]

This definition of who are the workers, i.e. all those who are forced to work in order to survive, implied that non-work was reserved to the idle classes or those who lived off the work of others. Nonetheless, this very large definition of who are the workers was not implemented without contradictions. Although the nineteenth-century discourse of craftsmen, frequently marked by pride in workmanship, became less common, it still persisted among certain skilled trades, especially to deplore the loss of the artistic vein. Thus, in 1907, an article published in the paper of the marble workers' union of Rio de Janeiro lamented the degradation of the members of the trade from the condition of craftsmen to that of simple manual workers.[32] While the printers' union in 1918 decided to promote an exhibit of masterpieces of the trade and confer a prize to the best work,[33] this did not seem to the publishers of the union's paper to contradict an article published a few months later in which the whole working class was compared to the plebs.[34]

The main concern here was to deal with the changes in the perception of work and of who constituted the workers, between the second half of the nineteenth century and the first decades of the following century. Of course, this process was not due exclusively to a change in the conscience of labour leaders and organizers, but owed a lot to the transformation that work itself underwent with the expansion and consolidation of capitalism on the world level. Nevertheless, this dimension was left out because it had a marginal presence in the discourse of working-class associations, which is the main focus here.

Notes

1 N.X. ([1859] 1869): 119.

2 Luccock (1820): 107. Special thanks to Marcelo Mac Cord for the indication of Luccock's anecdote.

3 Frank (2004). Special thanks to Sidney Chalhoub for sharing with me his knowledge of Rio de Janeiro's urban slavery and suggesting Frank's book.

4 Karasch (1987): 194–98, 199.

5 Frank (2004): 87.

6 Reis (2000): 91.

7 Karasch (1987): 112; *Recenseamento em 1872 – Municipio Neutro* (1872 Census – Neutral Municipality): 60.

8 See Batalha (1999): 41–68.

[9] See da Silva Júnior (2005); Viscardi and de Jesus (2007).
[10] Mac Cord (2009).
[11] Ibid.: 34–35.
[12] Lacerda (2011): 122–25. This is one of the most comprehensive studies based on the statutes of mutual aid societies.
[13] 'Reação', *O Proletario*, Rio de Janeiro, Vol. 1 (1), 7 September 1920: 3.
[14] Mac Cord (2009): 18–19.
[15] Ibid.: 337.
[16] See Castellucci (2010): 44–46.
[17] Lacerda (2011): 109–11.
[18] AN Conselho de Estado, 526/2/20.
[19] Lacerda (2011): 126.
[20] AN Conselho de Estado, 553/2/19.
[21] Lacerda (2011): 128–29.
[22] Sewell Jr. (1980).
[23] See Lima (2008): 19–21, 229–36.
[24] Cf. Debes (1982): 198–99.
[25] *À Sociedade Auxiliadora da Industria Nacional offerecem os Artistas Chapeleiros* (1876).
[26] *Manifesto do Corpo Coletivo União Operaria, Em 7 de setembro de 1885, À Sua Majestade o Imperador, À nação, À Imprensa Fluminense* (*Manifesto of the Collective Corps Labour Union, on 7 September 1885, to His Majesty the Emperor, to the Nation, to the Fluminense Press*), reproduced in Carone (ed.) (1979): 204–10.
[27] The Vintém Riot broke out in the first days of January 1880 as a result of meetings called to protest the one *vintém* tax on city tramway tickets, which escalated to violence and open confrontation between the protesters and police forces. On the subject, see Graham (1980): 431–49.
[28] AN Conselho de Estado 559/2/14.
[29] In nineteenth-century Portuguese, anyone who practised either a mechanical (i.e. craftsman) or a liberal art could be called an artist.
[30] 'O Artista' (1870): 1–3.
[31] Ramos (1907): 3.
[32] de Andrade (1907): 2.
[33] 'A Exposição Graphica' (1918): 1.
[34] Ferreira (1918): 3.

References

'A Exposição Graphica' (1918), *O Graphico*, Rio de Janeiro, Vol. 3, 50, 16 January.

À Sociedade Auxiliadora da Industria Nacional offerecem os Artistas Chapeleiros (*To the Protective Society of National Industry offered by the Hatmakers*) (1876), Rio de Janeiro: Typ. Economica, de Machado & Co.

Batalha, Claudio H.M. (1999), '*Sociedades de trabalhadores no Rio de Janeiro do século XIX: algumas reflexões em torno da formação da classe operária*' ('Working-Class Societies in Nineteenth-Century Rio de Janeiro: Some Reflections on the Formation of the Working Class'), *Cadernos AEL*, Vol. 6, 10/11: 41–68.

Carone, Edgard (ed.) (1979), *Movimento Operário no Brasil, 1877–1914* (*Labour Movement in Brazil, 1877–1914*), São Paulo/Rio de Janeiro: Difel.

Castellucci, Aldrin A.S. (2010), '*A luta contra a adversidade: notas de pesquisa sobre o mutualismo na Bahia, 1832–1930*' ('Struggle Against Adversity: Research Notes on Mutual-Aid in Bahia, 1832–1930'), *Revista Mundo do Trabalho*, Vol. 2, 4, August–December.

da Silva Júnior, Adhemar Lourenço (2005), '*As sociedades de socorros mútuos: estratégias privadas e públicas. Estudo centrado sobre o Rio Grande do Sul – Brasil, 1854–*

1940' ('Mutual Benefit Societies: Private and Public Strategies: Study Centred in Rio Grande do Sul–Brazil, 1854–1940'), Ph.D. thesis, Porto Alegre, PUC-RS.

de Andrade, Mario (1907), 'Pobr' Arte', *O Marmorista*, Rio de Janeiro, Vol. 2, 6, 1 April.

Debes, Célio (1982), '*Relações de Trabalho no Brasil: Aspectos de sua evolução histórica, 1822–1917*' ('Labour Relations in Brazil: Aspects of their Historical Evolution, 1822–1917'), *Anais do Museu Paulista*, 31.

Ferreira, Eurico (1918), 'A Plebe', *O Graphico*, Rio de Janeiro, Vol. 3, 67, 1 October. Frank, Zephyr L. (2004), *Dutra's World: Wealth and Family in Nineteenth-Century Rio de Janeiro*, Albuquerque: University of New Mexico Press.

Graham, Sandra Lauderdale (1980), 'The Vintém Riot and Political Culture: Rio de Janeiro, 1880', *Hispanic American Historical Review*, Vol. 60, 3.

Karasch, Mary C. (1987), *Slave Life in Rio de Janeiro, 1808–1850*, Princeton, NJ: Princeton University Press.

Lacerda, David P. (2011), '*Solidariedade entre ofícios: a experiência mutualista no Rio de Janeiro imperial, 1860–1882*' ('Crafts Solidarities: The Mutualist Experience in the Imperial Rio de Janeiro, 1860–1882'), M.A. thesis, Campinas, UNICAMP.

Lima, Carlos A.M. (2008), *Artífices do Rio de Janeiro, 1790–1808* (*Craftsmen in Rio de Janeiro, 1790–1808*), Rio de Janeiro: Apicuri.

Luccock, John (1820), *Notes on Rio de Janeiro and the Southern Parts of Brazil; Taken During a Residence of Ten Years in that Country, from 1808 to 1818*, London.

Mac Cord, Marcelo (2009), '*Andaimes, casacas, tijolos e livros: Uma associação de artífices no Recife, 1836 –1880*' ('Scaffolds, Dress-Coats, Bricks and Books: An Artists' Association in Recife, 1836–1880'), Ph.D. thesis, Campinas, UNICAMP.

N.X. ([1859] 1869), *L'Empire du Brésil: Souvenirs de Voyage* (*The Empire of Brazil: Travel Souvenirs*), collected and edited by J.J.E. Roy, Tours: Alfred Mame et Fils.

'O Artista' (1870), *O Artista*, Rio de Janeiro, Vol. 3, 1, 27 November: 1–3.

Ramos, J.F. (1907), 'Operariado', *Semana Operaria*, Rio de Janeiro, Vol. 1, 4, 27 May.

'Reação' (1920), *O Proletario*, Rio de Janeiro, Vol. 1, 1, 7 September.

Recenseamento em 1872 – Municipio Neutro (1872 Census – Neutral Municipality); available at http://biblioteca.ibge.gov.br/visualizacao/monografias/GEBIS%20-%20RJ/Recenseamento_do_Brazil_1872/Municipio%20Neutro.pdf, accessed on 15 March 2012.

Reis, João José (2000), '*Presença negra: conflitos e encontros*' ('Black Presence: Conflicts and Encounters'), in *Brasil: 500 anos de povoamento*, Rio de Janeiro: IBGE.

Sewell Jr., William (1980), *Work and Revolution in France: The Language of Labour from the Old Regime to 1848*, Cambridge: Cambridge University Press.

Viscardi, Cláudia Maria Ribeiro and Ronaldo Pereira de Jesus (2007), '*A experiência mutualista e a formação da classe trabalhadora no Brasil*' ('Mutual Aid Experience and Formation of the Working Class in Brazil'), in Jorge Ferreira and Daniel Aarão Reis Filho (eds.), *As esquerdas no Brasil: A formação das tradições (1889–1945)* (*The Left in Brazil: The Making of Traditions, 1889–1945*), Vol. 1, Rio de Janeiro: Civilização Brasileira.

Labour History in a Comparative Perspective

Labour Historiographies in India and Brazil and Enlarged Visions about the Working Class

Marcelo Badaró Mattos

Nowadays, in Brazil, more than 50 per cent of the occupied members of the economically active population are not legally registered and/or do not contribute to social security. From this data we can have an idea of the degree of 'underemployment', 'informality' or 'precariousness' of labour in the contemporary context.[1]

In the most critical level of this situation, we can observe the 'unfreedom'. In thirteen years, more than 30,000 workers subjected to contemporary slave labour were released by a federal Special Mobile Force for Inspection. Although it is difficult to calculate the number of workers in these circumstances, the estimate is that 25,000 are working in conditions analogous to slavery in Brazil now. In 2008, out of 5,244 workers released, 49 per cent were working in plantations of sugarcane, mainly used to produce ethanol. Nowadays, it is the modern capitalist rural enterprise, or the agri-business, not the archaic traditional plantation, that is exploiting the workers in this way.

In India, during the 2000s, 93 per cent of the labour force was constituted by the so-called informal sector.[2] And the estimate is that 15 million people (two-thirds of them children) are performing bonded labour in the country nowadays.[3] Even in the developed countries, since the 1980s, we can observe breaches of labour laws, high unemployment and mounting informality. The situation caught the attention of social scientists and they are now trying to explain that capitalist 'development' is not simply synonymous with 'modern' labour relations (understood as 'free' wage labour, protected by welfare rules). Notions of 'accumulation by dispossession'[4] and the emphasis on a trinary process – expropriation–exploitation–expropriation – rather than a binary one – expropriation–exploitation[5] – are attempts to overcome the simplistic modernization approach. This context helps us to understand how historians are now more sensitive to a long history of relationship between capitalism and non-free-wage labour forms. This is especially the case in the periphery, where the history of capitalism has always been a history of both continuous expropriation and a large variety of forms of labour force exploitation.

This essay aims to analyse the recent trajectories (from the 1980s to the current decade) in the labour historiography of Brazil and India, focusing on the discussions about the coexistence and combination of 'free' and 'unfree' as 'formal' and 'informal' working relationships, and their roles in each process of formation of the working class. My purpose is not to add new empirical elements to this discussion, but to compare different traditions of research that have many issues in common.

In addition, the essay also proposes to identify the paths and major course of recent labour history in these countries, as well as to focus on the relevant conceptual discussions on the working class to which those recent researches and historiographical discussions point.

These purposes are connected with the assumption that these two traditions of labour history could actively contribute to enlarge the project of global labour history, as defined in an exploratory study by Marcel van der Linden. According to his study, concerned with the overcoming of eurocentrism and methodological nationalism, the project of a global labour history may be delimited:

> As regards methodology, an 'area of concern' is involved, rather than a well-defined theoretical paradigm to which everyone must closely adhere. . . . As regards themes, Global Labour History focuses on the transnational – and indeed the transcontinental – study of labour relations and workers' social movements in the broadest sense of the word. . . . The study of labour relations encompasses both free and unfree labour, both paid and unpaid. Workers' social movements involve both formal organizations and informal activities. The study of both labour relations and social movements further requires that equally serious attention is devoted to 'the other side' (employers, public authorities). Labour relations involve not only the individual worker, but also his or her family where applicable. Gender relations play an important part both within family, and in labour relations involving individual family members. As regards the historical period studied, Global Labour History places no limits on temporal perspective, although in practice the emphasis is usually on the study of the labour relations and workers' social movements that emerged with the expansion of the world market from the fourteenth century.[6]

In this essay, I will focus on a limited temporal dimension – mainly the nineteenth and twentieth centuries – but both historiographical traditions could contribute to reach this aim of an enlarged time frame. On the other side, global labour history is also concerned with reshaping traditional frames of analysis centred in North–South and North–North international perspectives, so as to include a South–South view. India and Brazil are rich cases to try this approach.

Historiographical Trajectories

Brazil

Academic studies about the Brazilian working class are relatively recent. Until the 1950s, the only books about working-class struggles and organizations were ones written by militants of leftist parties and trade unions, in the form of individual or collective memoirs. They were important, of course, because they recorded what academic historians were not taking into account, and were also part of the workers' public presence. But, as in other places,[7] the labour history produced by the militants was very traditional in its conception of history (centred on facts and heroes), and was also used as an instrument in the battle of ideas among different groups inside the labour movement.

During the 1950s and the 1960s, while urban workers' movements were increasing in number and also in terms of political impact, sociologists, especially from São Paulo (the biggest industrial city in Brazil since the 1920s), developed several studies about the industrial workforce, labour organizations, strikes and working-class consciousness. The dominant interpretation that emerges from these studies places the focus on what the Brazilian working class was not – that is to say, they presumed that working-class formation was a linear process based on the transition from an unorganized and unconscious stage to one characterized by trade union and political party organization that were seen as the main indicators of a developed class consciousness. And in Brazil, at that time, the real working class seemed to be for these social scientists very different from this model which they presumed was the historical trajectory of the Western European working class.[8]

To explain this anomaly or absence of a working class, this generation of academic work attributed important reasons to the nature of the political system in Brazil, which was generally defined as populism; the specificity of trade union regulations (that directly linked them to the state); or even to patterns of the political conception of the main left workers' leadership (especially the Communist Party). However, the most frequent answer to the question about the insufficiency of the working class was one that focused on the origins of the workers at the point of Brazil's industrialization take-off. According to this interpretation, the rural origins of the majority of the industrial workers acted as a great obstacle between the workers and the class consciousness that researchers supposed they should have had.

Historians have arrived late into this tradition of research. In the 1970s, when the labour movement returned to the centre of the political arena, giving power to the struggle against the military dictatorship (1964–85), they started to give attention to the working class as an academic subject.[9] Their studies started to investigate the first decades of the twentieth century, less studied initially by social scientists. However, the historians' perspectives about the working-class trajectory were almost the same. They revisited the past, searching for a period of absence of state regulation on trade unions, and what from their historical point of view was supposed to be a period of vigorous class consciousness. This was possible, according to these studies – almost all considering São Paulo's case – because in those early years, the urban workers were mostly European immigrants who carried the experience of trade unionism, socialist and anarchist ideas; that is to say, a formed class consciousness.

With the development of historical studies there was a questioning of some of these points of view, arguing, for example, that São Paulo could not be seen as the whole of Brazil. In other regions of the country, immigrants may not have been as many as in São Paulo, but the labour movement was as important as it was there. Another aspect demonstrated by the new research was that even where European immigrants were in the majority, like in São Paulo, their origins were not urban. Most of them came from rural areas of Italy, Spain and Portugal, and they brought to Brazil no experience of labour organization or movement. The new studies were very useful in explaining the national and regional contexts that help us to understand the emergence of an organized and strong urban labour movement in a country where 70 per cent of the labour force was concentrated in rural areas.

During the last twenty years, historians and social scientists in general have reviewed many other aspects of these first investigations. Historical researches have advanced in their time delimitation and reviewed the 1930–64 period, establishing new boundaries for concepts about relations between the state, capitalists and workers.[10]

Despite of these advances, until some years ago, there was one aspect of the working-class formation process that remained relatively less explored by labour historians in Brazil. Even when the studies questioned the vision of a dominance of the European immigrant presence in the early working-class composition, they paid little attention to the specificity of the national workers' trajectory. This was perhaps because they still worked within the European model of working-class formation, and looked for artisans and other 'free' workers undergoing the proletarianization process. As a result labour history in Brazil started typically only in 1888 (when slavery was legally abolished).

On the other hand, the historiography of slavery has been distant from labour history, and the racial question after 1888 was for a long time discussed in terms of 'the black people's place in class society'.[11] But in some cities like Salvador (the former capital in the northeast), Pelotas and Rio

Grande (cities in the south, characterized by meat production and ports to export it), and especially in Rio de Janeiro, the capital and the biggest city until the 1910s, slave workers constituted nearly 40 per cent of the urban population in the middle of the nineteenth century. They were engaged in many kinds of activities from domestic service to the first factories, including all kinds of services on the streets. In several of these activities they worked alongside freemen and other 'free' workers.

Drawing attention to this situation, in recent years, some slavery historians and other labour researchers have been more interested in a discussion on the repercussions of these shared experiences between enslaved and free workers in the process of formation of the working class.[12]

Both historical researches which studied recent forms of labour and labour movements, and the ones that returned to the nineteenth century in order to seek the links between free and unfree labour have now to deal with some questions in common. The urbanization and industrialization processes were not necessarily accompanied by the dominance of formal wage, organized workers; supposedly older forms of informal, non-wage or partial-wage labour and even unfree labour were still present, and as they are not simply remnants of old times, it is also necessary to look at the past without the traditional teleological view. Labour history, thus, must be concerned with crossing the boundaries of rural and urban, formal and informal, free and unfree.

India

In the colonial context, labour was a strategic matter for the colonial authorities and British economic interests in India since the nineteenth century. That is why for labour historians in India there are a lot of sources in the colonial archives that are still very important for studies in many fields. Of course, this kind of material cannot be called historiographical in a strict sense, but it can be seen that these sources have deeply impacted historians' views on labour.

Like in most of labour historiography, those engaged in militant political activity were the first to introduce labour as a matter of concern in India's public sphere. But, as Sabyasachi Bhattacharya argues, in India there was an 'absence of literate autodidact workers such as the British journeymen and skilled artisans one meets in the pages of E.P. Thompson or Eric Hobsbawm'.[13] This has been linked to the lack of a native (in terms of class) leadership in the first stages of the labour movement, which resulted, as Bhattacharya points out, in:

> the assumption of this surrogate role by members of the intelligentsia in relation to the working class in factories, mines, and plantations – and the intelligentsia were a numerically insignificant section of the total popula-

> tion, and, further, insufficiently definable in terms of categories of capitalism. 'Outsider' leadership, i.e. leadership of labour organizations by persons of non-working-class origin and social status, was a characteristic feature of colonial South Asia.[14]

That is one of the main reasons why the first attempts to rescue labour histories were dependent on a dominant European mode of understanding capitalist development and social categories in India. Militant writers from both nationalist and Marxist backgrounds were in general influenced by a dual view that distinguished very clearly between the old India – peasant, rural, caste, religion and community-based – and the modern India – proletarian, industrialized, urban, class-conscious, despite their differences (the class basis of analysis and compromise with an ideal of emancipation that went further than political independence). Capitalism development in Europe was assumed to be the path all countries would necessarily traverse.

In the 1950s, when economists, sociologists and, later, historians began to produce academic studies on labour, the picture was very similar, and two paradigms – modernization and Marxism – dominated the scene. But, as Prabhu Mohapatra points out, they had some important convergences: 'Despite important and fundamental differences between these two paradigms there was apparent similarity in the way in which they visualized the formation of the industrial factory labour and its action and behaviour through an optic of transition.'[15]

In the struggle for political independence and during the post-colonial period (from 1947 onwards), the nationalist leadership in India laid stress on industrialization as a way to modernize the economy, society and institutions. Economic growth was presented as the key to maintaining political freedom. The Marxists saw political independence as a result of social contradictions and struggles. Once they characterized India's development as weak, because of the predominantly feudal/semi-feudal relations in the rural areas caused by colonial constraints, they could not see a direct way ahead for socialism, without the first stage of capitalist growth, with the development of a strong industrial sector and, consequently, a class-conscious proletariat. Therefore, in 'both these frameworks, the newly industrializing countries were perceived as in a stage similar to the early stage of industrialization in advanced countries'.[16]

Labour studies emerging from these two main paradigms were concerned with the male, formal, organized and industrial worker as an agent of capitalist modernization or as the subject of the social transformation toward socialism. But in India, the persistence of identities related to caste, religion and community/region challenged the linear conceptions of development of modern or revolutionary consciousness among the working class. This persistence was explained as remnants of old forms, and the modern consciousness was always seen as incomplete – 'incipient', 'elementary', 'embryonic'.[17]

In the 1970s the deterministic frame of these approaches was deeply criticized. The critique of economism within British social history, especially by E.P. Thompson, 'had a powerful impact on historians, making them more sensitive to the need to study the power of cultural traditions in understanding crowd behavior'.[18]

Against the background of this critique, in the early 1980s, emerged a new historiographical movement, Subaltern Studies, which had some impact on Indian labour history but still remains important nowadays internationally.[19] It was inspired by the idea of *history from below* popularized by the British social historians, and by the idea of subaltern classes discussed by Gramsci so as to incorporate peasants into the historical analysis of labour. Ranajit Guha was the main founder of this movement and his work focused particularly on rural rebellions. He paid more attention to the cultural backgrounds and specific forms of 'peasant insurgency', the political consciousness of the peasantry, which stood in opposition to the 'elitism' of the former historiography that he identified as 'colonialist elitism' or 'bourgeois nationalist elitism'.[20]

Although Guha's perspective was, in the beginning of the movement, especially concerned with Marxist questions of the social subject of social change, and his analysis connected cultural aspects of social conflicts with those related to economic and political power, subsequent developments in Subaltern Studies, particularly in the 1990s, were more influenced by linguistics and the post-modern approach. In the field of labour history, this inflection was responsible for a critique of Marxism as economic determinism – and a new valorization of caste and community identities. But, as Behal, Joshi and Mohapatra have said about Dipesh Chakrabarty's work, which is a critique that could be extended to other studies, while he 'critiques frameworks which reduce culture to economic determinants, he tends to reify culture by seeing identities in terms of fixed cultural meanings'.[21] The recent years, the 2000s in particular, are evaluated as a time of re-emergence of labour history in India. In terms of themes, the recent studies are concerned with going beyond urban, formal, male wage workers, and paying more attention to migratory labour, mobile labour, artisans, women, peasants, plantation workers, informal workers and so on. We can summarize the issues raised by the new labour studies by quoting from three of the most recognized Indian labour historians involved in this re-emergence:

> The earlier Eurocentric labour history often processed an implicit comparison: development in the West was the model for the future of the periphery and the rest of the world was to be measured against the West. At the heart of classical labour history stood the figure of the free, male wage worker,

labouring in the modern factory and a member of a trade union. However, it is increasingly evident that this figure – if he ever existed – was a minority, even in the industrialized West. With the expansion of the process of informalization and the increasing feminization of the workforce, assumptions about the centrality of the male unionized worker are no longer tenable. The same processes have also thrown into question the privileging of formal employer–employee relationships. As the dualities of free–unfree labour, wage-work and non-wage work, formal and informal labour blur, labour historians have to take into account the multiplicity of relationships, locations and temporalities that underpin forms of labour and within which the individual worker is embedded.[22]

Central Issues

It would be impossible, in these few pages, to point to all the important contributions that recent labour history studies from each of the two countries could provide to one another. I will focus my discussion here on one theme or a group of issues which cross the two national historiographies in order to highlight some possibilities of dialogue.

The issue is related to the necessity to overcome the dichotomies of 'formal' and 'informal', or 'free' and 'unfree' labour. That is a major point of the debates in recent labour history in the two countries, and it is a key question to think through the labour relations and working-class movements of the past or even of present times in these nations.

Marcel van der Linden and Prabhu Mohapatra, in their 'Introduction' to a collection of essays, argue that historians are perceiving now with more acuity that it is really difficult to trace the boundaries between free/unfree and formal/informal labour, and are trying to build new approaches to surpass these binaries.

> As the binaries of free–unfree, wage work–non-wage work, formal–informal become more obscure, labour historians need to look for new nodes of comparison that take into account the multidimensionality of relationships, locations and temporalities that undergird the labour forms within which the individual worker is embedded.[23]

A very similar argument is also present in the reflections of Alessandro Stanziani. His research on serfdom in Russia and comparative studies about labour contract laws and practices in France and Britain lead him to argue that contract labour forms, like indenture and debt bondage, were thought to be 'free' labour in the dominant economic and political presumptions between the eighteenth and the major part of the nineteenth century. He argues:

> In fact, until the middle, if not the end, of nineteenth century, the notion

> of 'free' labour was not that to which we are now accustomed, it included indenture, debt bondage, and several other forms of unfree labour; conversely, the official abolition of slavery saw not the disappearance of forced labour but rather the emergence of new forms. In both cases, coerced labour was in legal terms 'free labour'.[24]

Stanziani also argues that these kinds of conceptions are not exclusive to the periphery of the world capitalistic market. A global view must be applied to this matter, according to his analysis, in a two-way perspective which attempts to perceive how, for example, in the case of colonial India under British rule, 'Not only did the British regulation of labour mould Indian practices; the evolution of British jurisprudence and legislation governing the relationship between master and servant were strongly influenced by Indian jurisprudence.'[25]

The key idea behind conceptions which were dominant until the second half of the nineteenth century was, according to Stanziani, the notion of labour as a service, which was spread around European countries and their colonies.

> Our first point is that global economic dynamics from the seventeenth to the end of the nineteenth century (a period which saw 'revolutions' in agriculture, trade and consumption, protoindustrial growth and the first industrial revolution) were anchored to a notion and practices of labour as a 'service', in which the boundary between freedom and unfreedom was flexible and the master/employer acquired ownership of all the labour time of the worker/servant over the engagement period. Labour as a service was at the root not only of serfdom and slavery, but also of the indentured, servants and wage earners (labour being rented out as a service under a contract).[26]

Stanziani's discussion is interesting because it introduces empirical data from Europe to show how our contemporary notions of free and unfree were historically constructed in a relatively recent moment – in the last decades of the nineteenth century and at the turn of the twentieth century, in parallel with the emergence of trade unionism, welfare policies and the effects of the second industrial revolution.

This kind of debate was the centre of Tom Brass's concern in a broader discussion about free/unfree labour.[27] Brass, taking into account his own research on peasants and rural workers in South Asia and Latin America, as well as the contributions to a large volume edited by him, gives great prominence to the connections and movements between free and unfree labour relations. Such an argument does not exclude, according to him, the significance of the differences between both forms of labour relations. As he points out, concerning the movement between labour situations, 'in the course of class struggle (workforce de-/re-composition) labour can experience a two-way transition, both from freedom to unfreedom and vice-versa'.[28] The differences remain important, and are especially perceived in the relations between workers and labour markets, particularly when one is confronted with the needs and possibilities of leaving his/her position in this market. As Brass argues in his theoretical contribution to the debate:

> Any definition of what constitutes an unfree production relation has to begin by focusing on the labour power of the subject as private property, and hence as an actual/potential commodity over which its owner has disposition. Unlike a free labourer, who is able to enter or withdraw from the labour market at will, due to operation of ideological constraints or extra-economic coercion, an unfree worker is unable personally to sell his or her own labour power (in other words, to commodify it), regardless of whether this applies to employment that is either of time-specific duration (e.g. contract work, convict labour, indentured labour) or of an indefinite duration (chattel slavery).[29]

In order to explain how unfree labour is useful to and managed by capitalists according to historical circumstances, as well as how workers can be brought to proletarianization but also to leave that condition, Brass introduces the concept of deproletarianization. The way in which these movements are established depends upon the dynamic of class struggle. Capital is always trying to contain labour power in collective bargain and also in the broader political arena.[30]

> Such actions and struggles on the part of capital (with their economic, political and ideological expressions) aim to bring about deproletarianization, in the sense of diminishing or eliminating all together the freedom of wage labour as defined above: the ability of owners of the commodity labour power to exchange it as they choose. . . . In other words, it is precisely by means of deproletarianization that capital is able to effect a double dispossession of its workforce: both from the means of labour, and also from the means of commodifying labour power itself.[31]

According to Brass's argument, capitalists do this both to improve profits in moments of crisis by reducing wages with the introduction or reintroduction of foreign unfree workers (or reducing local wage workers to being unfree), and to reduce the organizing power of labour and put constraints on the development of class consciousness (like in situations of segmentation and even racism which the presence of foreigners demonstrate).

Brass's arguments can be subjected to some criticism. For example, his emphasis on the possibility of withdrawing from the labour market is important, but to define a labour relation it is necessary to take into account the whole process, including the way someone comes to the labour market, the specific relation he is involved in and the possibilities of leaving it. Jairus Banaji has pointed to the limitations of a rigid distinction between free/unfree labour as ambiguous and to various forms of exploitation under the capitalist logic of accumulation. For him, the idea of proletarian/proletarianization in Brass is focused only in political consciousness and it underestimates Marx's definition centred in dispossession and the legal right to sign contracts in the labour market (which is quite different from the idea of absence of non-economic constraints).[32] Despite such criticism, Brass's assumption that capitalism is able to deal with both free/unfree labour and that it is a dynamic process which can have a double movement, is more historically sustainable than notions that operate solely with the pair capitalism/free labour.

A historical situation in which this dynamic of reducing workers to unfree labour, even under the ambiguous definition of freedom, and in which regulations of the state have had a strong role, is the Indian case in the nineteenth century as studied by Prabhu Mohapatra in his discussion of 'regulated informality'. Going against the commonsense notion of informal labour as defined in terms of absence of state intervention, Mohapatra declares his aim to:

> delineate the process by which labour relations were constructed by colonial State action, especially through legislative intervention in nineteenth century colonial India. I will argue that in the process of such construction, labour relations were deeply impressed by pervasive informality, which has shaped subsequent developments in the post-independence India.[33]

According to his argument, we should not look for the differences between 'natural' and spontaneous informal relations on the one hand, and capital and state-ruled formal relations on the other, but learn to distinguish between 'different modes of regulation implied in informal and formal relations'. In one case you have privatization of regulation and in the other greater public regulation. And this supposes that 'both formal and informal relations are no longer a self-sustained whole but imply a combination of different forms of regulations'. It is also essential to distinguish between the 'realm of juridical freedom and contract and the domain of production where despotism of capital reigns'. And a third important proposition is that we have 'to take into account the role of law, which ensures not just the appearance of equality in the public domain and domination in the private, but also creates the very division of public and private'.[34]

Mohapatra works with a large time-frame in his article, from 1814 to 1926, dividing it into three moments in order to locate the laws and rules imposed by the colonial state, always with the aim to guarantee private control of the labour force. The rote for this aim was the criminalization of breach of contract.

At the beginning of the nineteenth century, as Stanziani has stated in general, Mohapatra shows that in India the oppositional terms 'slavery' and 'freedom' were not used in the same sense as we do now. The 'contract' was a mark of freedom, even if it established new forms of servitude like indentured labour. He demonstrates, based on wide research of primary sources, that in the mid-nineteenth century, responding to masters' and employers' demands who argued that workers had the 'custom' of breaking contracts after receiving an advance, the colonial state created new rules that considered the breach of contract as a kind of embezzlement, and punished it with prison sentence. About these new rules Mohapatra wrote:

> Irrespective of the extent of its use as evidenced in its prosecution there is no doubt that the central presumptions of the criminal breach of contract agreements seem to have pervaded the general work culture which gave an absolute power to set the terms of employment to the employer, normalized State intervention on behalf of the employer to curb the mobility of labour.[35]

In the last part of the article he describes the special labour legislation in Assam, the region of tea plantations, known for the use of indentured labour of the coolies.[36] There the planters were successful in gaining the right to prosecute deserting workers and to arrest them (besides the 'informal' right to use physical punishment against them). Contracts of three to five years of work for these coolies brought from the central Indian uplands and Gangetic plains, were, after the rules approved in the 1860s, penal contracts with extensive powers granted to private players like the planters. Explaining the aims of this kind of legislation in terms very close to those used by Brass to explain the capitalist's intentions of economic and political control over labour power, Mohapatra argues:

> The primary function of the legislation was to restrict an increase in the wages, that a burgeoning demand consequent on expansion would normally have led to. A second function of the legislation was to immobilize the labourer, thereby regulating competition among the individual planters themselves. Operation of the penal labour contract was thus crucial in fuelling expansion of plantations. Further, long-term penal contracts of five years' duration, ensured predictability and control over labour costs during the period. The most important function of the penal legislation was however in ensuring 'labour discipline', that is to deter the ever-present possibility of workers withdrawing their labour power.[37]

The efficiency of this labour control system for the purpose of maintaining and increasing planters' profits for almost a century is proved by numbers. As Behal demonstrates, 'tea companies reaped profits over a long time despite fluctuating international prices and slumps'.[38]

Returning to Mohapatra, the key point of his argument is that many academicians tend wrongly to associate informality and some kinds of unfree labour with surveillance of traditional or customary labour relations, while in fact they are historical constructions, in most cases regulated by state rules, in order to ensure control of capital over labour power.

This argument related to free/unfree and formal/informal labour is very interesting from the point of view of Brazilian labour history. A classical debate that took place in the 1980s there focused on the strategies that some planters used – in general as a response to slaves' demands – by permitting their slaves to plant foodstuff in the margins of the plantations in order to release some of the social tensions in the rural areas. Ciro Flamarion Cardoso, inspired by Sidney Mintz's argument, has called that situation the 'peasant breach' in colonial slavery.[39]

Also, in Brazil, the transition from slavery to free wage labour was traditionally thought of as a simple, unidirectional and direct change motivated by the introduction of capitalism or economic modernization. However, since the 1970s, many research studies have complicated this model.

To focus first on the 'transition' in coffee plantations in the southeast, the most dynamic and externally linked area of agricultural production: here, especially in São Paulo, the demand for labour power after the 1850s could not be met by the internal slave traffic (the African slave trade was stopped in 1850), and planters began asking for solutions. Many private initiatives of bringing Chinese coolies were undertaken, and some governmental efforts were also made to provide plantations and mines (in Minas Gerais) with workers. The *Congresso Agrícola* (Agricultural Congress) organized by the planters in 1878 approved the idea of bringing coolies from China in large numbers to substitute for enslaved workers as a transitional solution.[40] However, all the efforts to establish a regular supply of coolies failed – in part because of the British and Chinese rules, and in part because the coolies, although brought to work under contracts (of two or more years), were perceived and treated as 'new slaves', resulting in revolts and escapes.

This failure impelled planters to try to bring more European migrants to their plantations. The first attempts in this direction were made in the 1840s and they were planned according to the same logic of contracts based on debts incurred by the immigrants for the costs of the transatlantic voyage, which the planters paid in advance. Even as these attempts picked up, frequent rebellions by the European migrant workers – called *parceiros* (partners) – against their unfreedom and the treatment meted out to them, which was like that of the slaves, moved the planters to explore another solution: subsidized migration of European workers. They proposed to transfer the costs of transportation to the state so that, without having to incur initial costs, the planters would have a large supply of 'free' labour power to replace the slaves.

The 'Labour Force Question' was a central political issue in Brazil in the 1880s. As the monarchical central state, dominated by planters of Rio de Janeiro Province who were interested in receiving monetary compensation for the slaves' emancipation, refused to subsidize the migration costs, the planters of São Paulo progressively started to support the federalist/republican solution. The Republic was proclaimed in 1889, one year after the abolition of slavery. With the costs of transportation granted first by the provincial government and then by the federal government, more than 1 million European migrants (most of them Italian, and also Portuguese and Spanish) arrived in the province/state of São Paulo between the 1870s and 1900.

Even with the subsidized migration, as José de Souza Martins has demonstrated in a classical study,[41] the new coffee-plantation workers were not typical wage earners. The *colonato*'s regime set up in coffee plantations towards the end of the nineteenth century was based on contracts with the families of migrant workers to plant coffee in parcels of land in large estates, in exchange for receiving some money as advance, a precarious habitation and the tools to work the land. Between the planting and the harvesting – an interval of some years – they were also expected to plant subsistence food-crops. Of the harvested coffee, one part was considered the landowner's and another part was assigned to the *colonos*, who were forced in turn, by the terms of their contracts, to sell their share to the planter (at a price set by him) in order to receive monetary payment.

New studies in recent years show that the 'transition' from slavery to freedom was thus much more complex. The manumission processes of many slaves were based on contracts legally registered by their masters, whereby they agreed to provide services to their former masters for many years after the manumission (or the manumission was conditional to such services), with or without monetary payment.[42]

Even in the cities, the 'transition' was not so simple. There are a large number of historical studies focusing on urban enslaved workers that demonstrate the importance for urban dynamics of forms like slaves for 'rent' or even *escravos de ganho* or *ganhadores* ('money-earning slaves'), who had the permission of their masters to walk around the town trying to sell their labour power for money – as carriers of craft skills – the major part of which was given to the master on a daily or weekly basis.[43] And there were some hybrid forms as exemplified by the situation of the *africanos livres* ('free Africans'), whereby Africans who were brought to Brazil after the enactment of laws that put an end to transatlantic slave trade were considered the state's responsibility for fourteen years, and were granted by the state to private employers who used their labour power for those (or even more) years.[44]

Thousands of people from the Portuguese islands of Madeira and Açores were also brought to Brazil under contracts based on debt bonds; they were called *engajados* (engaged workers). A certain number of them were employed in urban activities, especially in small shops. According to Luiz Felipe de Alencastro's estimate, the Portuguese represented about 10 per cent of the Court's inhabitants in 1849, and reached 20 per cent in 1872. Many of them were or had been *engajados*. Alencastro concludes that Rio de Janeiro's labour market passed through three phases during the nineteenth century: 'the first phase, African, extends until 1850; a Portuguese–African phase, that goes until 1870 and, eventually, a Portuguese–Brazilian phase',[45] taking into consideration the significance of the 'free' and 'freed' Brazilian workers whose presence increased during this last phase.

Therefore, the labour market in Brazil cannot be seen as an exclusively wage labour market even after the abolition of slavery in 1888. That is why in big cities like Rio de Janeiro – the former capital of the monarchical government and the capital of the Republic – in the first decades after the end of slavery, the absence of labour legislation (in the sense of work-time limits and welfare) should not be confused with a lack of state intervention to make workers conform to the rules of the labour market. The Penal Code of 1890 (enacted one year before the Constitution of the Republic) was a fundamental tool for criminalization of all kinds of people's behaviour that were considered as resistance to working, as it was understood by the ruling classes. In the first decades of the new Brazilian Republic, the police of Rio the Janeiro imprisoned and persecuted thousands of men and also women under charges of vagrancy.[46] In the countryside too the situation was not very different; the planters – concerned with ensuring that the migrant labour force would work according to their expectations and also in controlling the 'national' (former slaves and Brazilian 'free' workers) labour force – also took recourse to and used penal laws in order to 'educate the people for agricultural work', as they justified it.[47]

It is not necessary to say much more to show how discussions about the complexity of the free/unfree labour categories and the idea of regulating informality, i.e. state intervention in the labour market via criminalization of workers' behaviour, could be useful for Brazilian labour history.

The common interest shared by Indian and Brazilian historians creates better conditions for comparative studies. But comparisons and transnational perspectives are more fruitful when built on a conceptual common terrain. Narrow definitions of the working class are, hence, not very useful.

Final Considerations: On the Conceptual Debate of Class

The class question has been posed by many who are concerned with capitalist expansion in the periphery. For example, criticizing the typically western and narrow way of classifying labour propagated by the International Labour Organization (ILO), Cohen, Gutkind and Brazier suggested 'that it is not necessary to adopt a restrictive definition of "working class" in order to understand how surplus value is expropriated in Third-World societies'.[48] From an analytical point of view markedly different from a 'third world' approach, and determined to highlight the complexity of the 'transition' from peasantry to proletariat, they argue that:

> As soon as we pose the question in this way, we are drawn to examine the whole spectrum of underclasses drawn into relations of capitalist production, distribution and exchange. The peasantry is rarely solely engaged in subsistence production; more frequently the products of their labours are specialized and treated via a host of middlemen to local, regional and international world markets. Moreover, the land is deserted in favour of contract, seasonal or temporary wage labor. The collapse of subsistence economies in the face of capitalist penetration has led to the growth of a large group of workers who are ambiguously and simultaneously 'semiproletarians' and 'semipeasants'. Women in the rural areas are either engaged both in household and petty commodity production, thus lowering the cost of the reproduction of labor power . . . or enter directly into manufacturing production, at least for some periods of their lives. Large numbers of agricultural or rural proletarians, whose social characteristics have often escaped formalized definition . . . act as a concealed source of cheap labour power. The same is true of the so-called unemployed, marginalized segments of the labour force of burgeoning Third-World cities, whose economic role is better characterized in terms of Marx's 'latent', 'floating' and 'stagnant' sections of the relative surplus population.[49]

The attempts to rivisit labour history by historians as discussed in this essay are concerned with the same issues in different ways. That is why Bhattacharya, criticizing what he calls a wrong reading of Marx in labour studies with a 'myopic concentration on the industrial wage-worker', proposed the use of an alternative concept that is more inclusive in relation to non-wage and informal labour: the concept of 'labouring poor'.[50] Bhattacharya is conscious that he is defending the use of a 'fuzzy' concept, but he argues that,

> possibly a fuzzy concept like the 'labouring poor', without sharply defined boundaries, is more appropriate to transitional economies in less developed countries where class boundaries are porous, where gradations shade

> into each other, where individuals and families are simultaneously located in more than one of the conventional class categories which counterpoise wage labour and non-wage labour. Where the transition to capitalist/wage-labour relationship is incomplete or is not sufficiently generalized, we have what is almost a 'permanently transitional' situation, which calls for concepts other than the clear-cut ones of advanced metropolitan economies.[51]

This attempt to go beyond narrow definitions of the working class in order to include in our research the non-organized, non-formalized and even non-wage workers is the most important contribution of the discussions I have tried to summarize in this article. But I see some problems in the proposal to introduce the concept of 'labouring poor' as a key to understand the specificities of labour relations in the periphery.

The first problem with this concept is related to how it could be exclusionary in another way. That is certainly not Bhattacharya's aim, but by looking only for the 'labouring poor' one could restrict one's focus to the 'informal sector' as non-wage labour and thus ignore all contacts between wage and non-wage workers, which is not the case. After all, as Mohapatra argues, the Indian labour situation today is characterized by more than 90 per cent of informality, but 'this has occurred at a time when the numerical preponderance of wage earners in India is no longer a matter of debate'.[52]

In my view, a more inclusive notion of labour should not be one that focuses exclusively on informal/non-organized/non-wage labour. It must be a combined view that includes both sections of the working class. I think that this is the intention of Marcel van der Linden when he refers 'to the class as a whole as the *subaltern workers*', and within this he includes 'chattel slaves, share-croppers, small artisans and wage-earners'.[53]

This attempt to enlarge the labour history approach is constructed on the basis of a combination of two concepts with a long tradition and extensive debate, especially in the Marxist field: 'working class (or classes)' and 'subaltern classes'. The chief formulator of the idea of 'subaltern classes' was Antonio Gramsci, who used it in his attempts to understand the possibilities and to defend the necessity of a 'united front' between rural peasants and the urban working class.[54] In a more recent and more peripheral approach, the idea of subalterns was used 'to denote the entire people subordinate in terms of class, caste, age, gender and office, or in any other way'.[55]

Van der Linden is conscious of the differences within this enlarged definition of *subaltern workers*,[56] although he places emphasis on what these different subaltern workers have in common, in order to present his 'provisional definition':

> Every carrier of labour power whose labour is sold (or hired out) to another person under economic (or non-economic) compulsion belongs to the class

> of subaltern workers, regardless of whether the carrier of labour power is him- or herself selling or hiring it out and, regardless of whether the carrier him- or herself owns means of production.[57]

Returning to the questions posed by Bhattacharya, if the narrow definition of working class as industrial organized wage labour is a 'wrong reading' of Marx's writings on class, and I totally agree with that, it could be useful to rescue Marx's discussion of working class in an enlarged perspective. It is not possible, within the scope of this essay, to posit more than a brief comment on Marx and Engels' discussion about class, but I would like just to make just two points.

The first is that Marx's distinctions between productive and unproductive labour, or between formal and real subsumption of labour under capital, were never based on the presumption that the working class was restricted to industrial workers. A rich analysis of this issue that refers to the enlarged conception of class present in *Capital*, and aims to demonstrate that there is no sense in restricting the definition to productive labour, was further developed by Bensaid.

> We do not thus see in Marx any reductive, normative or classificatory definition of classes, but a dynamic conception of their structural antagonism, at the level of production, circulation and reproduction of capital: classes are never defined only at the level of the production process (the face off between workers and employers in the enterprise), but determined by the reproduction of the whole when the struggle for wages, the division of labour, relations with the state apparatuses and the world market enter into play. From this it is clear that the productive character of labour that appears notably in Volume 2 of *Capital*, with respect to the circulation process, does not define the proletariat.[58]

That is important because, from this point of view, even if we cannot include some labour situations (like that of 'self-employed' workers) – which the notion of 'labouring poor' tries to include – in the strict definition of working class, we can evaluate their subordination to capital in the dimension of its general reproduction.

In addition, the concept of class becomes even more complex if we note that, for Marx, it was not limited to an economic matter. According to Marx and Engels, it was within capitalism that for the first time it was possible for an oppressed class to be conscious of its situation of exploitation. Their theories were a result of this process. Michel Lowy shows how the foundation of historical materialism (1840s) is explained by their relation with labour movements of the period.[59] In other words, class-related issues had assumed a political dimension with possibilities of social and political transformation.

If all past class conflicts revealed class struggle as an essential dimension of the historical process, now class would acquire class consciousness, which cannot be defined only in economic terms but also in its political dimension, as Marx states in his correspondence with Bolte:

> The political movement of the working class has as its object, of course, the conquest of political power for the working class, and for this it is naturally necessary that a previous organization of the working class, itself arising from their economic struggles, should have been developed up to a certain point. On the other hand, however, every movement in which the working class comes out as a class against the ruling classes and attempts to force them by pressure from without is a political movement. For instance, the attempt in a particular factory or even a particular industry to force a shorter working day out of the capitalists by strikes, etc., is a purely economic movement. On the other hand the movement to force an eight-hour day, etc., *law* is a *political* movement. And in this way, out of the separate economic movements of the workers there grows up everywhere a *political* movement, that is to say a movement of the *class*, with the object of achieving its interests in a general form, in a form possessing a general social force of compulsion. If these movements presuppose a certain degree of previous organization, they are themselves equally a means of the development of this organization.[60]

Awareness of the complexity of the concept of class within historical materialism should lead us not to be content with a uniquely economic dimension as the economic dimensions do have a broad sense (production, commodity circulation, unequal division of work product, i.e. enlarged reproduction of capital). Moreover, Marx never restricted his definition of class to an economic dimension. On the contrary, he estimated its political role, which would only be defined in relation to a class consciousness, which is not developed alone but within class struggles.

It is interesting to note how, in combining these issues, one of Marx's best readers – at least in terms of the discussion on class – demonstrated, in the core of capitalism, the emergence of the new working class with its class consciousness during the late eighteenth century and the first decades of the nineteenth century, i.e. when formal subsumption still predominated. I refer to E.P. Thompson and his brilliant book on the making of the English working class.[61]

Before finishing this essay I would like to return to Bhattacharya's discussion on the 'labouring poor' in order to point to a second problem. In some readings, the idea of an 'incomplete' or not sufficiently generalized 'transition to capitalist/wage-labour relationship' could be understood as a reinforcement of a model that Bhattacharya is determined to criticize: one that configures western/developed societies as 'the' capitalist societies and the periphery as societies mid-way to capitalism. The main question in these societies cannot be why they are not still sufficiently capitalist in their labour relations. Instead it should be: how are they capitalist societies with such diverse and combined labour relations? I believe that Bhattacharya's notion of a 'permanently transitional' situation is closer to certain debates on the best critical traditions of historical materialism which have a long course of discussion.

Two classical theoretical traditions can be drawn upon to help me out here. The first is the 'law' of uneven and combined development. This perspective came from Lenin's consideration of 'uneven growth' in times of global expansion and monopolistic concentration of capital, i.e. imperialism; and Trotsky's analysis of how in Russia (and in other even more peripheral–backward areas) capitalist development was capable of skipping stages and combining production/labour relations from the past with the most advanced productive forces and social relations in a very complex way. At the same time, the imperialistic logic of capitalist development did not allow all countries to play the same role in the global concert, which explains the unevenness of the relationship of core and periphery.[62]

The idea of uneven and combined development was a matrix for many critics of the dualistic conception that was dominant in the Marxist/communist reflections about peripheral societies and the revolutionary strategies they experienced during the twentieth century. One of the most interesting positions taken, with a certain autonomy from the traditional Trotskyist approach, was the so-called 'theory of dependence'. Its first formulation was made in Brazil, in the early 1960s, in the documents of a political organization named POLOP,[63] and in the writings of the economist Ruy Mauro Maurini (and also Theotônio dos Santos). The main aim of the theory of dependence was to show that Brazil and other Latin American countries had not had their capitalist development hampered by feudal or semi-feudal social relations, and that they were plain capitalist economies and societies. However, in the specific form conditioned by imperialism, their capitalism and their capitalists were linked by dependence with the core capitalist economies.

Concerning labour, Marini's main suggestion, stated simply, was that since capitalist economies in the periphery are in a situation of an uneven exchange, they must generate an enlarged amount of surplus value, a large part of which is externally appropriated by transnational enterprises and core capitalism, and that therefore labour is necessarily submitted to 'super-exploitation'. That is not a situation that can be understood in terms of specific relations in one particular space or moment of labour relations, but should be evaluated in terms of the combined forms of exploitation in the whole society.

Marini was very concerned about specifying and explaining his use of the concepts. According to him, the problem for a dependent capitalist economy was not simply to counteract the value transfers, but to

> compensate a loss of surplus value, and [since] it is incapable of preventing it in the ground of the market relations, the reaction of dependent economy is to compensate it at the level of internal production. The increase of labour intensity appears . . . as a surplus value increase, done by a major worker's exploitation and not by the increase of his productive capacity. The same could be said about the labour journey's increased duration, i.e., about the increase of absolute surplus value in its classic form. . . . It should be marked, finely, a third procedure, that consists in reducing the worker's consumption beyond its normal limit.[64]

These ideas were very influential among a whole generation of Brazilian social scientists, from the 1960s until 1970s, that produced a vast number of books demonstrating how an industrial/financial, modern capitalist face of the Brazilian economy had been possible not *despite* but *because* of the maintenance of 'archaic' labour relations, especially in the countryside.[65] They were also important to understand the specific – not 'incomplete' – forms of the transition to capitalism and of the 'bourgeois revolution' in Brazil.[66]

At this point I introduce the second and last theoretical tradition, as well as the discussions inspired by it, which could throw some light on the issues I have been discussing so far. I refer to the historical and dynamic (not physiographic) view of western/eastern societies, and to the interpretation of the diverse forms of transition to capitalism presented by Antonio Gramsci's notion of 'passive revolution'.[67] Writing from the specific point of view of an Italian (defeated) revolutionary, Gramsci tried to understand how proletarian revolution could be successful in a country with uneven capitalist development (the industrial/urban civilization in the 'western' North, and the rural 'eastern' South) and a class of capitalists which avoided the French/Jacobin model of bourgeois revolution – mainly because of the fear of workers' mobilization – and instead led the transition by molecular changes, in alliance rather than in confrontation with the traditional ruling classes (the 'passive revolution' process).

It is important to note one methodological procedure in Gramsci's writings that is very useful here. He worked with dyads, not with dichotomies, and these conceptual pairs – like west/wast, coercion/consensus, civil society/political society, passive/active – should not 'be conceived as rigid schemes, but only as practical criteria of political and historical interpretation. In the concrete analysis of real events, the historical forms are determined and almost "unique".'[68]

This methodological perspective animated, for example, Ashok Sen's discussion of 'hybrid modes of exploitation' and the combined dynamics of passive and active elements in the Indian process of transition to capitalism and the bourgeoisie's role in modern India.[69] The article opens a wide range of issues, and here I would like just to point out the combined analysis of community and class, and the view of class struggle, that underline how the Indian dominant class was not capable of controlling the subaltern groups in their rupture with the colonial situation, and, concomitantly, how subaltern insurgency was not organized in a nationalist dimension in order to drive social transformation. Giving attention to Marx's assumption that the idea of community is 'immanent in [the] concept of classes and class struggle', his discussion tries to explain how 'subaltern rebels, though more akin historically to pre-capitalist labourers, often belong to intermediate situations between the peasantry and the proletariat, characterized as they are by complex alignments of capitalism and pre-capitalism.'[70]

For Brazilian historians, the idea of the passive revolution is extremely useful to explain the state forms in which the process of urban/industrial predominance took place after 1930, and also to discuss the specific forms of class struggle considering the modernization process 'from above' that took place in the country.[71]

The aim of this essay is not to present a new, substantial contribution to labour history in any way, but to suggest some possibilities of exchange between two historiographical traditions that deal with similar problems – concentrating on how they work with concepts of free/unfree, formal/informal labour. In conclusion, I also suggest some interesting conceptual debates opened up by these traditions of labour history. Emphasizing how readings from the 'global South' (re)interpreted classical analytical frames and formulated new frames to understand those issues, my intention is to show possibilities beyond Eurocentric approaches.[72] These are only a few examples of the wide possibilities which are in front of us and they deserve more exploration.

Acknowledgements: I would like to thank Marcel van der Linden for his comments on the first version of this article, and for the friendly reception at the International Institute of Social History in 2010, where I enjoyed the best conditions to study and write. I also thank Paula Nabuco and Mirna Aragão for reviewing the article. I am also grateful to CAPES for the fellowship in Amsterdam.

Notes

1 A broad analysis of the Brazilian working class today can be seen in Mattos (2009).
2 Mohapatra (2005): 66.
3 Enhuber (2008).
4 Harvey (2003).
5 Linebaugh (2008).
6 van der Linden (2008).
7 See Hobsbawm (1984).

[8] Rodrigues (1970); Weffort (1973).
[9] Fausto (1976); Lobo (1976).
[10] See, for example, among many recent works, Fortes *et al.* (1999); Mattos (1998).
[11] Fernandes (1965).
[12] Loner (2001); Cruz (2000); Reis (1997); Mattos (2008).
[13] Bhattacharya (2006).
[14] Ibid.: 8.
[15] Mohapatra (1998): 3.
[16] Behal, Joshi and Mohapatra (2010): 294.
[17] Ibid.: 296.
[18] Joshi (2005): 5.
[19] For a general idea of the movement, see the series under the title *Subaltern Studies* (1982 to 1999). Guha, Spivak and Chakravorty (eds.) (1988). Also see Guha (1998).
[20] Guha (1982): 1.
[21] Behal, Joshi and Mohapatra (2010): 297. For a broad critique of subaltern studies, see Bahl (2005).
[22] Ibid.: 290–91.
[23] van der Linden and Mohapatra (eds.) (2009): xii.
[24] Stanziani (2009): 352.
[25] Ibid.: 357.
[26] Ibid.: 357–58.
[27] Brass (1997a).
[28] Ibid.: p. 20.
[29] Brass (1997b).
[30] Ibid.: 60–61.
[31] Ibid.: 61.
[32] Banaji (2003). For a reply, see Brass (2003). Banaji's reading of Marx is very rich, and his discussions on capitalism and labour very provocative. Although I agree with his criticism, it is also noticeable that his definition of proletarian does not take into account Marx's discussion on class consciousness, which is a point I briefly address at the end of this essay.
[33] Mohapatra (2005): 67.
[34] Ibid.: 69.
[35] Ibid.: 83.
[36] On Assam tea plantations, see Behal and Mohapatra (1992); Varma (2009).
[37] Mohapatra (2005): 89.
[38] Behal (2006): 143.
[39] Cardoso (1987); Cardoso (1988).
[40] A reference book on this debate is da Costa (2008). Also see, da Costa (2000), especially Chapters 5 and 6. Recent research on the Chinese migration is presented in Dezem (2005).
[41] Martins (2010).
[42] Lima (2009). Also see, Aladrén (2010).
[43] Soares (1988).
[44] Mamigonian (2002).
[45] Alencastro (1988): 44.
[46] Mattos (1993).
[47] Mendonça (1997): 68–78.
[48] Cohen, Gutkind and Brazier (eds.) (1979): 12.
[49] Ibid.
[50] Bhattacharya (2006). The concept is also presented in the Introduction to Bhattacharya and Lucassen (eds.) (2005). Also see Breman (2003).
[51] Bhattacharya (2006): 11.
[52] Mohapatra (2005): 66.

[53] van der Linden (2008): 31.

[54] Gramsci (1992).

[55] Sen (1987): 203.

[56] I remember here the issue pointed out by Brass, who sees a two-way process by which capital can exploit labour in specific historical combinations of free and unfree labour, arguing that 'a connection between free and unfree labour does exist, but not one which eradicates difference'. See Brass (1997a): 20. Differences not only in the legal statutes, but also in social relations outside the workplace, and especially in workers' self-evaluation of their position in society and political consciousness could be pointed out here.

[57] van der Linden (2008): 32 (author's emphasis).

[58] Bensaid (2008): 35. Also see Bensaid (2002).

[59] Lowy (2005).

[60] 'Marx to Friedrich Bolte in New York (1871)'.

[61] Thompson (1963).

[62] Lenin (1982): 139. Also see Trotsky (2007) (in particular, Tomo I, cap. 1). In English Lenin's book is available at http://www.marxists.org/archive/lenin/works/1916/imp-hsc/index.htm and Trotsky's at http://www.marxists.org/archive/trotsky/1930/hrr/index.htm; last accessed on 18 February 2014. For a recent and comprehensive summary of the discussion, including Novak's and Mandel's contributions to the debate, see van de Linden (2007).

[63] For a brief history of POLOP – Organização Revolucionária Marxista-Leninista Política Operária (Marxist-Leninist Revolutionary Organization Workers Politics) – see Mattos (2002).

[64] Marini, *Dialética de la Dependencia* (*Dialetics of Dependency*), available at http://www.marini-escritos.unam.mx/ , last accessed on 18 February 2014.

[65] de Oliveira (2004).

[66] Fernandes (1977).

[67] Gramsci (2002).

[68] Gramsci (2001): 67.

[69] Sen (1987): 207–15.

[70] Ibid.: 238.

[71] For studies on twentieth-century Brazil inspired by Gramsci's notion of passive revolution, see Coutinho (2012).

[72] Following the advice of Linden (2008): 3.

References

Aladrén, Gabriel (2010), '*Ratoneiros, Atravessadores e Formigueiros: Trabalho e Experiências Sociais de Libertos em Porto Alegre nas Primeiras Décadas do Século XIX*' ('Work and Social Experiences of Freed Men in Porto Alegre in Early Nineteenth Century'), in Marcela Golmacher, Paulo e Mattos Terra and Marcelo Badaró (eds.), *Faces do Trabalho: Ecravizados e Livres* (*Faces of Work: Enslaved and Free Workers*), Niterói: Eduff.

Alencastro, Luiz Felipe (1988), '*Proletários e escravos: imigrantes portugueses e cativos africanos no Rio de Janeiro, 1850–1872*' ('Proletarians and Slaves: Portuguese Migrants and African Captives in Rio de Janeiro'), *Novos Estudos*, no. 21, São Paulo, Cebrap.

Bahl, Vinay (2005), *What Went Wrong with 'History from Below': Reinstating Human Agency as Human Creativity*, Kolkata: K.P. Bagchi.

Banaji, Jairus (2003), 'The Fictions of Free Labour', *Historical Materialism*, Vol. 11, 3.

Behal, Rana (2006), 'Power Structure, Discipline and Labour in Assam Tea Plantations under Colonial Rule', *International Review of Social History*, Vol. 51, Supplement.

Behal, Rana and Prabhu Mohapatra (1992), 'Tea and Money Versus Human Life: The Rise and Fall of the Indentured System in the Assam Tea Plantations, 1840–1908', *The Journal of Peasant Studies*, Vol. 19, 3–4.

Behal, Rana, Chitra Joshi and Prabhu Mohapatra (2010), 'India', in Joan Allen, Alan Campbell and John McIlroy (eds.), *Histories of Labour: National and International Perspectives*, London: Merlin Press.

Bensaid, D. (2002), *Marx for Our Times*, London: Verso.

——— (2008), *Os Irredutíveis*, São Paulo: Boitempo; English version available at http://www.marxists.org/archive/bensaid/2004/12/resist.htm, last accessed on 18 February 2014.

Bhattacharya, Sabyasachi (2006), 'Introduction', *International Review of Social History*, Vol. 51, Supplement.

Bhattacharya, Sabyasachi and Jan Lucassen (eds.) (2005), *Workers in the Informal Sector*, New Delhi, Macmillan.

Brass, Tom (1997a), 'Introduction', in Tom Brass and Marcel van der Linden (eds.), *Free and Unfree Labour: The Debate Continues*, Berne: Peter Lang.

——— (1997b), 'Some Observations on Unfree Labour, Capitalist Restructuring, and Deproletarianization', in Tom Brass and Marcel van der Linden (eds.), *Free and Unfree Labour: The Debate Continues*, Berne: Peter Lang.

——— (2003), 'Why Unfree Labour is Not "So-Called": The Fictions of Jairus Banaji', *The Journal of Peasant Studies*, Vol. 3, 1.

Breman, Jan (2003), *The Labouring Poor in India: Patterns of Exploitation, Subordination, and Exclusion*, New Delhi: Oxford University Press.

Cardoso, Ciro F.S. (1987), *Escravo ou Camponês? O Protocampesinato Negro nas Américas* (*Slave or Peasant? The Black Peasantry in Americas*), São Paulo: Brasiliense.

——— (1988), 'The Peasant Breach in the Slave System: New Developments in Brazil', *Luso-Brazilian Review*, Vol. 25, No. 1, Madison. Enhuber, Tamara (2008), 'From Karma to Agency: Identities and Economic Opportunity Structures in the Struggle against Bonded Labour in India', paper presented at the conference on 'Labour Crossing: World, Work and History', Johannesburg, September.

Cohen, Robin, Peter C.W. Gutkind and Phyllis Brazier (eds.) (1979), 'Introduction', in *Peasants and Proletarians: The Struggles of Third World Workers*, London: Hutchinson.

Coutinho, Carlos Nelson (2012), *Gramsci's Political Thought*, Leiden: Brill.

Cruz, Maria Cecília Velasco (2000), '*Tradições Negras na Formação de um Sindicato: Sociedade de Resistência dos Trabalhadores em Trapiche e Café, Rio de Janeiro, 1905–1930*' ('Black Traditions in the Formation of a Trade Union: The Resistance Society of Coffee Porters'), *Afro-Ásia*, No. 24, Salvador: 243–90.

da Costa, Emília Viotti (2008), *A Abolição* (*The Abolition*), eighth edition, São Paulo: Unesp.

——— (2000), *The Brazilian Empire: Myths and Histories,* revised edition, Chapel Hill/London: University of North Carolina Press.

de Oliveira, Francisco (2004), *Crítica da Razão Dualista (e O Ornitorrinco)* (*The Critique of the Dualistic Reason*), São Paulo: Boitempo.

Dezem, Rogério (2005), *Matizes do Amarelo: A Gênese dos Discursos Sobre os Orientais no Brasil, 1878–1908* (*Hues of the Yellow: The Origin of the Discourses about Eastern People in Brazil*), São Paulo: Humanitas.Harvey, David (2003), *The New Imperialism,* Oxford: Oxford University Press.

Fausto, Bóris (1976), *Trabalho Urbano e Conflito Social* (*Urban Labour and Social Conflict*), São Paulo: Difel.

Fernandes, Florestan (1965), *A Integração do Negro na Sociedade de Classes* (*Black Integration in Class Society*), São Paulo: Dominus.

——— (1977), *A Revolução Burguesa no Brasil* (*The Bourguois Revolution in Brazil*), Rio de Janeiro: Zahar.

Fortes, Alexandre *et al.* (1999), *Na Luta Por Direitos* (*In the Strugle for Rights*), Campinas: Unicamp.

Gramsci, A. (2001), *Cadernos do Cárcere* (*Prison Notebooks*), Vol. 3, Rio de Janeiro: Civilização Brasileira.

——— (2002), *Cadernos do Cárcere* (*Prison Notebooks*), Vol. 5, Rio de Janeiro: Civilização Brasileira.

Guha, R. (1982), 'On Some Aspects of the Historiography of Colonial India', in *Subaltern Studies*, Vol. I, New Delhi: Oxford University Press.

——— (1998), *Subaltern Studies Reader: 1986–1995*, New Delhi: Oxford University Press.

Guha, R., G. Spivak and D. Chakravorty (eds.) (1988), *Selected Subaltern Studies*, Oxford: Oxford University Press.

Hobsbawm, Eric (1984), 'Labour History and Ideology', in *Worlds of Labour: Further Studies in the History of Labour*, London: Weidenfeld and Nicolson.

Joshi, Chitra (2005), *Lost Worlds: Indian Labour and its Forgotten Histories*, London: Anthem.

Lenin, V.I. (1982), *El Imperialismo, Fase Superior Del Capitalismo*, Moscow: Editorial Progresso.

Lima, Henrique Espada (2009), 'Freedom, Precauriousness, and the Law: Freed Persons Contracting Out Their Labour in Nineteenth-Century Brazil', *International Review of Social History*, Vol. 54, Part 3, December.

Linebaugh, Peter (2008), *The Magna Carta Manifesto: Liberties and Commons for All*, Berkeley: University of California Press.

Lobo, Eulália M.L. (1976), *História do Rio de Janeiro: Do Capital Comercial ao Capital Industrial e Financeiro* (*History of Rio de Janeiro: From Comercial Capital to Industrial and Financial Capital*), Rio de Janeiro: IBMEC.

Loner, Beatriz Ana (2001), *Construção de Classe: Operários de Pelotas e Rio Grande, 1888-1930* (*Making of Class: Workers in Pelotas and Rio Grande, 1888–1930*), Pelotas: Unitrabalho/EdUFPel.

Lowy, Michel (2005), *The Theory of Revolution in the Young Marx*, Chicago: Haymarket.

Mamigonian, Beatriz (2002), '*Revisitando o Problema da "Transição Para o Trabalho Livre" no Brasil: A Experiência de Trabalho dos Africanos Livres*' ('Re-visiting the Issue of Transition to Free Labour in Brazil: The Experience of "Free Africans"'), Comunicação apresentada às Jornadas de História do Trabalho, Pelotas, mimeo.

Marini, Ruy Mauro, *Dialética de la Dependencia* (*Dialetics of Dependency*), available at http://www.marini-escritos.unam.mx/, last accessed on 18 February 2014.

Martins, José de Souza (2010), *O Cativeiro da Terra* (*Captivities of Land*), ninth edition, São Paulo: Contexto.

'Marx to Friedrich Bolte in New York (1871)', in *Marx and Engels: Collected Works*, Vol. 44: 257–58; available at www.marxists.org/archive/marx/works/cw/volume44/.

Mattos, Marcelo Badaró (1993), '*As Contravenções no Rio de Janeiro do Início do Século XX*' ('The Misdemeanours in Rio de Janeiro in Early Twentieth Century'), *Revista Rio de Janeiro*, 2ª. Fase, No. 1, Rio de Janeiro.

——— (1998), *Novos e Velhos Sindicalismos no Rio de Janeiro, 1955–1988* (*New and Old Unionisms in Rio de Janeiro, 1955–1988*), Rio de Janeiro: Vício de Leitura.

——— (2002), '*Em Busca da Revolução Socialista*' ('The Search for the Socialist Revolution'), in Reis Filho and Daniel Aarão (eds.), *História do Marxismo no Brasil* (*History of Marxism in Brazil*), Vol. 6, Campinas: Edunicamp.

——— (2008), *Escravizados e Livres: Experiências Comuns na Formação da Classe Trabalhadora Carioca* (*Enslaved and Free Workers: Experiences in Common in the Making of the Working Class in Rio de Janeiro*), Rio de Janeiro: Bom Texto.

——— (2009), *Reorganizando Em Meio Ao Refluxo: Ensaios de Intervenção Sobre a Classe Trabalhadora no Brasil Atual* (*Reorganizing amid the reflux: working class in contemporary Brazil*), Rio de Janeiro: Vício de Leitura.

Mendonça, Sonia Regina (1997), *O Ruralismo Brasileiro* (*Brazilian Ruralism*), São Paulo: Hucitec.

Mohapatra, Prabhu (1998), *Situating the Renewal: Reflections on Labour Studies in India*, Noida: V.V. Giri National Labour Institute.

——— (2005), 'Regulated Informality: Legal Constructions of Labour Relations in Colonial India, 1814–1926', in Sabyasachi Bhattacharya and Jan Lucassen (eds.), *Workers in the Informal Sector*, New Delhi: Macmillan.

Reis, João José (1997), 'The Revolution of the Ganhadores: Urban Labour, Ethnicity and the African Strike of 1857 in Bahia, Brazil', *Journal of Latin American Studies*, Vol. 29, 2: 355–93.

Rodrigues, Leôncio Martins (1970), *Industrialização e Atitudes Operárias: Estudo de um Grupo de Trabalhadores* (*Industrialization and Workers' Atitudes: A Study of a Group of Workers*), São Paulo: Brasiliense.

Sen, Ashok (1987), 'Subaltern Studies: Class, Capital and Community', in R. Guha (ed.), *Subaltern Studies: Writings on South Asian History and Society*, Vol. V., New Delhi: Oxford University Press.

Soares, Luiz Carlos (1988), 'Urban Slavery in Nineteenth-Century Rio de Janeiro', Ph.D. thesis, University College, London.

Stanziani, Alessandro (2009), 'Introduction: Labour Institutions in a Global perspective, from the Seventeenth to the Twentieth Century', *International Review of Social History*, Vol. 54, Part 3, December.

Thompson, E.P. (1963), *The Making of the English Working Class*, London: Gollancz.

Trotsky, Leon (2007), *História da Revolução Russa*, São Paulo: Sundermann.

van der Linden, Marcel (2007), 'The "Law" of Uneven and Combined Development: Some Underdeveloped Thoughts', *Historical Materialism*, Vol. 15: 145–65.

——— (2008), *Workers of the World: Essays Toward a Global Labour History*, Leiden/Boston: Brill.

van der Linden, Marcel and Prabhu Mohapatra (eds.) (2009), *Labour Matters: Towards Global Histories*, New Delhi, Tulika Books.

Varma, Nitin (2009), 'For the Drink of the Nation: Drink, Labour and Plantation Capitalism in the Colonial Tea Gardens of Assam in the Late Nineteenth and Early Twentieth Century', in Marcel van der Linden and Prabhu Mohapatra (eds.), *Labour Matters: Towards Global Histories*, New Delhi, Tulika Books.

Weffort, Francisco (1973), '*Origens do Sindicalismo Populista no Brasil*' ('Origins of Populist Trade Unionism in Brazil'), *Cadernos Cebrap*, No. 4, São Paulo, April/June.

Contributors

ERDEN ATTILA AYTEKIN is Assistant Professor, Faculty of Economic and Administrative Sciences, Middle East Technical University, Ankara. His doctoral dissertation at the State University of New York Binghamton was on 'Land, Rural Classes, and Law: Agrarian Conflict and State Regulation in the Ottoman Empire, 1830s–1860s'. His recent research has focused on the history of working-class community spaces and places undergoing economic restructuring.

CLAUDIO H.M. BATALHA is Associate Professor, State University of Campinas (UNICAMP), Brazil, and Member, Research Center on Social History of Culture (CECULT/UNICAMP). He is also a researcher with the National Council of Scientific and Technological Development (CNPq).

SABYASACHI BHATTACHARYA was formerly Professor of Economic History, Jawaharlal Nehru University, New Delhi; Vice Chancellor, Visva Bharati University, West Bengal; and Chairman, Indian Council of Historical Research. He is the founding president of the Association of Indian Labour Historians. His work has ranged widely from economic history to cultural and intellectual history of modern India. Among his many books are *Financial Foundations of the British Raj: Ideas and Interests in the Reconstruction of Indian Public Finance, 1858–1872* (2005); *Talking Back: Idea of Civilization in the Indian Nationalist Discourse* (2010); and *Rabindranath Tagore: An Interpretation* (2011).

SABYASACHI DASGUPTA is Assistant Professor, Visva Bharati University, West Bengal. His Ph.D. dissertation at Jawaharlal Nehru University, New Delhi is on 'Military History of the Indian Mutiny'. He is the author of the forthcoming book, *In Defence of Honour and Justice: Sepoy Rebellions in the Nineteenth Century*.

SURAIYA FAROQHI is Professor of History, Bilgi University, Istanbul. A leading authority on Ottoman history, she was formerly Professor of History, Ludwig

Maximillan University of Munich and Middle East Technical University, Ankara. Among her numerous books are *Subjects of the Sultans, Culture and Daily Life in the Ottoman Empire* (2000) and *Artisans of Empire: Crafts and Craftspeople under the Ottomans* (2009). She is the editor of *The Cambridge History of Turkey, Vol. 3* (2006).

JAN LUCASSEN is currently Honorary Fellow, International Institute of Social History (IISG), Amsterdam; he was formerly Professor, Free University Amsterdam and Senior Research Fellow, IISG. An eminent scholar of labour migration in early modern Europe, he has been one of the pioneers in extending the frontiers of Global Labour History. Among his many books are *Migrant Labour in Europe 1600–1900: The Drift to the North Sea* (1987, co-edited with Leo Lucassen); *Migration, Migration History, History: Old Paradigms and New Perspectives* (2005); and *Global Labour History: A State of the Art* (editor, 2006).

D.W. KARUNA MIRYAM completed her Ph.D. from the Department of History, University of Delhi on the 'Handloom Industry and Weavers of South India in the Nineteenth and Twentieth Century'. Her research interest is the social history of artisan communities, and the historical development of cottage industries and small-scale industries in post-independent India.

SANTOSH KUMAR RAI is Associate Professor, Department of History, University of Delhi. His doctoral dissertation at Delhi Univesrity was on 'Handloom Industry and the Muslim Weaving Community of Eastern Uttar Pradesh in the Twentieth Century'. His research interest is in the historical development of artisan communities and politics in post-independent India.

VIJAYA RAMASWAMY is Professor of History, Jawaharlal Nehru University, New Delhi and currently Senior Fellow at the Nehru Memorial Museum and Library, New Delhi. She is the author of *Textiles and Weavers in Medieval South India* (1985 and 2006); *Divinity and Deviance: Women in Virasaivism,* (1996); and *Walking Naked: Women, Society and Spirituality in South India* (2007). She is the editor of *Devotion and Dissent in Indian History* (2014).

H. TARIK SENGUL is Associate Professor, Department of Political Science and Public Affairs, Middle East Technical University, Ankara. His research interest is in Urban Social and Political Theory, Local Government, Urban Survival Strategies and Political Geography.

ALESSANDRO STANZIANI is Professor at the EHESS (Ecole des Hautes Etudes en Sciences Sociales) and Senior Researcher at the CNRS (Centre National des Recherches Scientifiques), Paris. He is the author of *Bondage: Labour and Rights in Eurasia from the Sixteenth to the Early Twentieth Centuries*

(2014) and *Rules of Exchange: French Capitalism in Comparative Perspective, Eighteenth–Twentieth Centuries* (2012).

MATTHIAS VAN ROSSUM is a Researcher at the International Institute of Social History (IISG) and Lecturer in Social and Economic History at Leiden University. He received his Ph.D. in History at the VU University Amsterdam (2013) for a study of intercultural relations among Asian and European sailors working for the Dutch East India Company. He is currently involved in a research project on the history of labour camps in the Netherlands-Indies (1730–1942).

NITIN VARMA is Research Fellow at the International Research Centre, Work and Human Lifecycle in Global History, Humboldt University, Berlin. His Ph.D. dissertation at Humboldt University was on 'Tea Garden Labour in Assam in the Nineteenth and Twentieth Century'.